ADVANCE PRAISE FOR *THE PLATFORM DELUSION*

"Jonathan Knee delivers a precise, irreverent, and informative diagnosis of Big Tech. *The Platform Delusion* explains why the largest companies succeed, including why we consumers let them run amuck. Required reading."

> —Sudhir Venkatesh, author of *Gang Leader for a Day* and William B. Ransford Professor of Sociology at Columbia University

"Knee's book is an invaluable guide for anyone trying to understand how the platform economy works. His critical lens uncovers often overlooked aspects of platforms. Definitely a must-read."

> —Bradley Tusk, cofounder and managing partner, Tusk Ventures

"The CEOs of the tech giants know where their competitive advantages *really* come from—but they're not telling. Jonathan Knee debunks the conventional wisdom and explains how these companies dominate."

> —Geoff Colvin, bestselling author of *Talent Is Overrated* and senior editor, *Fortune*

"Jonathan Knee has created the essential framework to analyze digital platforms. Indispensable, entertaining reading for anyone interested in how these businesses work and create value." —Jeremy G. Philips, general partner, Spark Capital

"Thought-provoking and counterintuitive, Jonathan Knee's *The Platform Delusion* is a must-read for anyone interested in the secrets of successful technology businesses." —Alex Kantrowitz, author of *Always Day One* and founder of Big Technology

"As usual, Jonathan Knee has written with unique insight and clarity on network effects and platform economics. Anyone interested in separating myths from reality in these areas whether for business or investment purposes will find this book essential."

> —Bruce Greenwald, Heilbrunn Professor of Finance, Columbia Business School, and author of *Value Investing: From Graham to Buffet and Beyond*

"Knee is a talented and engaging writer. Agree with him or not on digital business models, he doesn't just accept commonly held assumptions but encourages the type of critical thinking that is so important for both policy makers and investors." —Justin Muzinich, former Deputy Secretary of the U.S. Treasury

"Anyone competing in or investing in the digital economy should read Jonathan Knee's *The Platform Delusion*. Knee looks insightfully into the business models of such tech stars as Facebook, Netflix, Google, Amazon, Apple and Airbnb, overturning conventional wisdom and delivering valuable lessons for big companies as well as start-ups."
                                                    —Steve Swartz, president and CEO, Hearst

"If you invest in a digital platform, work for one of them, or compete with the platforms (so that's everybody) you need to read this book. You will understand how the platforms got where they are and where they're going, which new digital darlings will succeed or fail, and why. A brilliant, indispensable bible not only for those in 'platform' businesses, but also for those in all businesses."
                            —Jeff Bewkes, former chairman and CEO, Time Warner

"The term 'platform' has become one of the most overused terms in the tech world. This book is a brilliant and practical examination of what a platform really is and why it matters for success in tech."
                            —Deven Parekh, managing director, Insight Partners

"Knee outlines what truly sets digital winners apart by returning to the fundamentals. A powerful reminder that the principles of competitive advantage endure even in digital environments."   —Bill Ford, chairman and CEO, General Atlantic

"An impressive book that digs under conventional wisdom about the digital economy and addresses its unprecedented complexity, with essential insights for business leaders and policy makers. *The Platform Delusion* is timely, important, and illuminating."
                            —Julius Genachowski, managing director, Carlyle, and
                            former chair, Federal Communications Commission

"Jonathan Knee has done a great service to managers, investors, regulators, and students by cutting away all the fanciful thinking about platform companies and by showing how the standard tools of competitive analysis apply effectively to let us understand these businesses."
                    —John Roberts, John. H. Scully Professor of Economics and Strategic Management
                    Emeritus, Stanford Graduate School of Business and author of *The Modern Firm*

ALSO BY JONATHAN A. KNEE

The Accidental Investment Banker: Inside the Decade
That Transformed Wall Street

The Curse of the Mogul: What's Wrong with the
World's Leading Media Companies
(with Bruce Greenwald and Ava Seave)

Class Clowns: How the Smartest Investors
Lost Billions in Education

THE
PLATFORM
DELUSION

Who Wins and Who Loses in
the Age of Tech Titans

JONATHAN A. KNEE

PORTFOLIO / PENGUIN

Portfolio / Penguin
An imprint of Penguin Random House LLC
penguinrandomhouse.com

Most Portfolio books are available at a discount when purchased in quantity for sales
promotions or corporate use. Special editions, which include personalized covers, excerpts,
and corporate imprints, can be created when purchased in large quantities. For more
information, please call (212) 572-2232 or e-mail specialmarkets@penguinrandomhouse.com.
Your local bookstore can also assist with discounted bulk purchases using the Penguin
Random House corporate Business-to-Business program. For assistance in locating
a participating retailer, e-mail B2B@penguinrandomhouse.com.

Library of Congress Cataloging-in-Publication Data

Names: Knee, Jonathan A., author.
Title: The platform delusion : who wins and who loses in the
age of tech titans / Jonathan A. Knee.
Description: 1st Edition. | New York : Portfolio / Penguin, 2021. | Includes index.
Identifiers: LCCN 2021005704 (print) | LCCN 2021005705 (ebook) |
ISBN 9780593189436 (hardcover) | ISBN 9780593189443 (ebook)
Subjects: LCSH: Success in business. | Entrepreneurship. | Electronic commerce. |
Internet marketing—Management. | Industrial management. | Competition.
Classification: LCC HF5386 .K64 2021 (print) |
LCC HF5386 (ebook) | DDC 658—dc23
LC record available at https://lccn.loc.gov/2021005704
LC ebook record available at https://lccn.loc.gov/2021005705

Printed in the United States of America
1st Printing

BOOK DESIGN BY ELLEN CIPRIANO

In memory of my beloved mother,

Rokki Knee Carr,

a force of nature

CONTENTS

Introduction   xi

PART I: DIGITAL ADVANTAGE AND DISADVANTAGE

1. The Four Pillars of the Platform Delusion   3

2. Network Defects: Scale in the Digital Era   23

3. It Takes a Village: The Sources of Digital
   Competitive Advantage   33

PART II: IN THE LAND OF THE GIANTS

4. Facebook: The Ultimate Network   68

5. Amazon: Can You Have Too Much of a Good Thing?   85

6. Apple: What's at the Core?   108

7. Netflix: Content Was Never King and Still Isn't   131

8. Google: Letter-perfect Alphabet   161

PART III: IN THE SHADOW OF THE GIANTS

9. E-commerce: If Amazon Is the Everything Store,
   What's Left to Sell?   179

10. Fly Me to the Moon: Who Makes Money
    When Air Travel Goes Digital?   200

11. "To Travel Is to Live!": How Priceline Became
    Worth $100 Billion   217

12. It's Nice to Share, Sometimes: Why Airbnb Will
    Always Be a Better Business Than Uber   238

13. Mad Men, Sad Men: Advertising and Adtech Meet
    the Internet   252

14. Big Data and Artificial Intelligence: When They
    Matter and When They Don't   268

    Epilogue: Start-up Fever: Is It a Cure or a Disease?   287

    Acknowledgments   295
    Notes   299
    Index   347

INTRODUCTION

THE PLATFORMS ARE TAKING OVER the world. Hide the children. Take only what you can carry with you.

Their dominance is inevitable. Resistance is futile. Those who do not capitulate will be relegated to the bottom rung of our increasingly stratified economy.

The rulers of this new global order are the early platform investors and the visionary entrepreneurs they back. Those who join them have a chance of survival. All the rest are collateral damage.

There is much to commend this narrative.

In industry after industry, this new breed of so-called platform companies are sucking all the value, returns, and growth out of the companies that actually do things.

A slide presented at an IBM for Entrepreneurs event in 2015 perfectly captured this zeitgeist and immediately went viral. Under the heading "The Digital Disruption Has Already Happened," IBM's leading executive for start-ups shared a list of eight massive sectors of the economy that have come to be dominated by platforms.[1] A photo of the slide continues to circulate widely online today, and slightly modified versions have been extensively appropriated by technology bankers and consultants trying to shock potential clients into engagement.

The Digital Disruption Has Already Happened

- World's largest taxi company owns no taxis (Uber)
- Largest accommodation provider owns no real estate (Airbnb)
- Largest phone companies own no telco infra (Skype, WeChat)
- World's most valuable retailer has no inventory (Alibaba)
- Most popular media owner creates no content (Facebook)
- Fastest growing banks have no actual money (SocietyOne)
- World's largest movie house owns no cinemas (Netflix)
- Largest software vendors don't write the apps (Apple & Google)

Figure Intro.1

Source: http://vrworld.com/2015/11/09/ibm-disruption-has-already-happened

These succubus enterprises often lull growth-starved incumbent competitors into collaboration that accelerates their demise. Lured by the promise of sharing in a digital bounty and recapturing their corporate mojo, they reveal too much, forget who they are, and are reduced to an unrecognizable shadow of their former selves.

Around 2000, Circuit City, Borders, and Toys 'R' Us all thought it was a good idea to outsource digital orders to the Amazon platform. Circuit City and Borders filed for bankruptcy in 2008 and 2011, respectively.[2] In 2004, Toys 'R' Us sought to take back its operating control. Too little, too late. Litigation and a 2005 buyout by the deepest-pocketed private equity firms followed.[3] After five years in the courts, Amazon ultimately agreed to pay Toys 'R' Us all of $51 million in a "confidential" settlement.[4] Toys 'R' Us filed for bankruptcy in 2017.[5]

When Netflix launched a streaming service in 2007, the entertainment conglomerates eagerly sold it the digital rights to the content produced by their film and television studios, viewing it as found money. The 2008 recession further incentivized these companies to ignore the longer-term implications of satisfying short-term profit needs through the sale of streaming rights.

In 2010, Jeff Bewkes, the last CEO of an independent Time Warner, was still dismissive of Netflix's aspirations to become more than a source of extra high-margin revenues for the established studios. He scoffed, "It's a little bit like, is the Albanian army going to take over the world? I don't think so."[6]

A few years later, in 2014, in part to justify its rejection of a hostile takeover bid by Rupert Murdoch's 21st Century Fox, Time Warner unveiled plans for its own HBO streaming service to compete with Netflix.[7] After spending hundreds of millions in an unsuccessful effort to build the online capability internally, the company hastily outsourced the effort to Major League Baseball's digital business in order to achieve its publicly announced launch date.

By the time Time Warner subsequently completed a sale of the company to AT&T in 2018, the value secured was less than half the public market value of Netflix.[8] AT&T gave up on the asset less than three years later.[9] In 2019, even Rupert Murdoch sold out 21st Century Fox in the face of the traditional entertainment industry's increasingly gloomy prospects.

An accepted narrative has emerged to explain the triumph of digital platforms over the hapless analog businesses trampled by the tech titans' apparently relentless march. In this worldview, digital platforms are a kind of unstoppable virus. Indeed, the 2020 pandemic seemed to accelerate its spread. Nasdaq—the natural home of these platforms—thrived while the NYSE stagnated.[10] This storyline, however, despite the compelling anecdotes that appear to support it, does not hold up to close scrutiny. But close scrutiny is precisely what those with clear financial incentives to maintain the fiction have sought to avoid. And the promise of a digital bonanza has discouraged the rest of us from looking too closely.

The siren song of easy money is hard to resist. Its seductive strains lead us to replace what we know to be true with what we want to be true. In the age of digital disruption, it is not just the proliferation of unicorns—onetime start-ups that seemingly overnight, and sometimes with little or no revenues, achieve billion-dollar valuations—or the inexorable climb into trillion-dollar territory of the largest technology leviathans that captures our attention. It is the apparent simplicity with which it seems that anyone can outperform the market by placing exclusively digital bets.[11]

The truth that is often forgotten in the pursuit of internet-inspired riches is that the same basic investing disciplines apply to digital as to analog opportunities. An understanding of the structural competitive advantages present or absent in a business is essential to assessing whether it is worth financing and at what price. The current crop of tech-enabled promoters are not the first who have sought to direct attention away from fundamentals in favor of magical thinking. The media moguls of yore reveled in convincing investors for a generation of their mystical skills in managing talent and picking hits even as their shares consistently underperformed.

The goal of this book is to turn off the hypnotic digital music for a moment, take a deep breath, and return to first principles that provide tools to distinguish the resilient from the fragile, the franchise from the fraud. Although the economic concepts underlying competitive advantage are immutable, the ways in which such advantages are likely to present in digital environments are strikingly different. These are the book's focus.

What I call "the Platform Delusion" has a dual meaning, one very specific and another more general. In the first chapter, I define quite precisely the elements of a particular fallacy that underpins the systematic tendency to overestimate the potential and the resiliency of a wide range of digital businesses. But more broadly, the Platform Delusion signifies an entire class of loosely connected words and phrases used to imply supernatural powers on the part of the business described. Not just "platform" but also "artificial intelligence," "winner-take-all," "network effects," "big data," and other buzzwords are routinely invoked as a kind of "trigger" to inspire the belief that you clearly have a winner on your hands and that no further close examination is required.[12] The use of these terms is designed to render superfluous the more pedestrian considerations of competitive advantage.

Like all good delusions, these beliefs have more than just a grain of truth. Plenty of people have gotten plenty rich by backing a business associated with one or more of the attributes referenced. The problem is that these concepts are inconsistently defined and applied. And when an effort is made to examine these characteristics systematically, there is usually little correlation with success.[13]

What's more, the underlying ideas are often misleadingly presented as if they were entirely new, imbued with transcendental powers derived from the internet. Yet the core concepts and technologies involved, whether platforms or artificial intelligence or the others, in most cases predate the internet. And although the digital ecosystem has changed their nature and availability, this has not always been in a good way. Unfortunately for investors, entrepreneurs, and corporations alike, the structural changes wrought by the internet, more often than not, have hindered rather than helped businesses' ability to secure and maintain strong barriers to entry.

The *Wall Street Journal* has said that *platform* is "the word that most defines the [tech] industry's boom over the past decade" and explains how the internet "became a springboard for enormous growth and wealth."[14] Although platform businesses make money in a wide variety of different ways, the defining characteristic of a platform is that its core value proposition flows from the connections it facilitates. Many of the most iconic and valuable digital businesses fit this definition: the operating systems that connect software developers and users (Microsoft and Apple), the marketplaces that connect buyers and sellers (Amazon), the social networks that connect communities (Facebook), the search engines that connect advertisers and digital publishers with searchers (Google).

But although the term *platform* has only relatively recently entered the vernacular, businesses with precisely this defining characteristic were around for decades before the invention of the internet. What's more, as we shall see, many of these were actually better businesses than the internet-infused versions of the same enterprises. By lowering fixed-cost requirements and making switching easier, the internet has amped up the ferocity of competition among platforms to the detriment of their owners. No one called a local monopoly newspaper a platform, but it was: it connected advertisers to readers as well as buyers to sellers through the classifieds. The inability to support more than one such enterprise in most midsize cities is why it was a winner-take-all business that managed to generate 40 percent-plus margins long after readership and circulation began their inexorable declines. On the internet, the proliferation of competing news content and classified sites has ensured that such levels of profitability are largely unheard of in these digital platforms.

The long history of charismatic, iconic CEOs associated with the most notable platform businesses—Steve Jobs, Jeff Bezos, Reed Hastings—has also indirectly supported the prevalence of the Platform Delusion. These figures became so intertwined with the identity of their respective companies that it complicated the ability to distinguish the results of exceptional management from the impact and nature of the structural advantages involved. Leadership, execution, and culture all contribute to the success of any business, but they are fundamentally different from competitive advantage. A company's long-term prospects, and the durability of its competitive edge, can only be properly assessed through a close examination of the specific sources of its structural advantages.

In short, the fact that many of the best digital businesses are "platforms" does not imply either that most platform businesses deliver superior returns or that it is the platform status of the demonstrably superior businesses that is responsible for their superior results. In fact, consistent superior returns are only achievable through structural competitive advantage, and the resilience of the best platform businesses are the result of multiple mutually reinforcing advantages that are notable more for the differences than the commonalities in each specific case. To suggest otherwise—that is, to proffer a simple unitary all-encompassing platform-driven basis for their success—is reminiscent of a particular sleight of hand favored by media moguls: if you only count the hits, inherently risky businesses suddenly seem invincible.

Not all delusions are necessarily bad. Professor Harold Hill was a con artist who didn't actually provide music lessons, but he did manage to instill in those children a confidence that allowed them to play a little. There are plenty of empirically validated examples of where the belief in the possibility of superior performance actually facilitates its achievement. Students who are told they can do well on an exam are more likely to do so than those told the reverse.[15]

The problem with the Platform Delusion is that it does not generate systematically superior performance. Rather, it actively undermines the ability to distinguish robust business models from weak ones. By glossing over the dispositive attributes providing the structural advantages that have allowed the best platform businesses to thrive—and failing to draw appropriate lessons from the fate of the much longer list of unsuccessful platform businesses—this particular delusion has proven very costly.

The tenacity with which the Platform Delusion has taken hold, not just in the public imagination but among institutional investors, reflects in part the sustained efforts of those who have a vested interest in its continued vitality. Technology executives, venture capitalists, private equity partners, and portfolio managers all have many millions of reasons to want the high and growing valuations of the platform businesses to which they have committed to persist. While publicly reaffirming a belief in the inherent indomitability of these companies, private communications have come to light suggesting a much more nuanced view of their actual strengths and weaknesses.

There are echoes of the dynamics underlying the first internet boom in this unholy alliance of self-interested constituencies. In that era I was a senior investment banker, first at Goldman Sachs and then at Morgan

Stanley, where I was co-head of the media group. I saw up close the financial pressures these once venerable private banking partnerships faced after becoming public companies with shareholders demanding constant growth and market share gains. As for the businesses they underwrote—many had no realistic prospect of profit and in some cases no meaningful revenues but were routinely sponsored by these banks in the public markets in clear violation of what had been the firms' long-established institutional standards. Research analysts cheered on acquisitions by more established companies that were simultaneously strategically incoherent and financially destructive.

This time around, the stakes are far higher and so are the economic incentives toward dissembling or even outright deceit. In the twenty years since the collapse of that bubble, the explosion in mobility, computing power, and bandwidth have allowed the establishment of entirely new or radically enhanced businesses and business models of real size and substance. The largest handful of these companies now represents an unprecedented proportion of overall stock market value. The venture capital and private equity sectors that rely on these lofty valuations now manage almost ten times as much capital as they did back in 2000.[16] And although regulation has moderated the worst excesses of the full-service investment banks of that era, the fees currently at stake dwarf those previously in play.

After the collapse of the original tech bubble, I wrote *The Accidental Investment Banker: Inside the Decade That Transformed Wall Street*, documenting how these investment banks fueled it and by doing so damaged their own cultures.[17] In the aftermath, I remained in the industry and continued to advise companies on strategic transactions but have moved increasingly into academia. As the codirector of the Media and Technology program at Columbia Business School and the Michael T. Fries Professor of Professional Practice of Media and Technology, my focus has shifted from the decision-making of the banks to the industry structures and optimal strategies of the businesses they advise and finance. My subsequent books, *The Curse of the Mogul: What's Wrong with the World's Leading Media Companies* and *Class Clowns: How the Smartest Investors Lost Billions in Education*, examined where investors have gone badly wrong by ignoring the essential connections between business strategy, industry structure, and valuation. This book applies the same lens to some of the most significant and valuable companies of our era, the so-called FAANG companies of Facebook, Apple, Amazon, Netflix, and Google/Alphabet.

The point of this book is not to undermine confidence in the resilience of the handful of massive franchises that have materialized in the digital era. My goal instead is to explain the very different sources of advantage underlying each. To do so, however, necessarily challenges conventional wisdom with respect to not just the nature of platforms but also of digital competitive advantage generally. The specific advantages attributed to some of the best-known companies of the digital era are called into question.

If I am successful, by the time you have finished the book you will have adopted the following counterintuitive propositions:

- Network effects have been touted as the dominant source of competitive advantage in the digital age. This phenomenon makes a product inherently better with the addition of every new user. But most businesses that exhibit network effects, either because of the structure of the particular industry or the absence of any reinforcing advantages, do not deliver exceptional results. What's more, strong network effects are not, as commonly supposed, exhibited in all platform businesses. Of the group of digital goliaths that have come to be referred to as FAANG, only Facebook is a predominantly network effects driven franchise.
- Many of the new growth vectors spurring the unprecedented valuations of the FAANG companies receive limited support from

the competitive advantages upon which their core franchises rely. Notably, in the case of Apple's entertainment initiatives in music and television and Amazon's accelerating investments in international markets and grocery, it can be argued both that the firms operate at a competitive disadvantage in these areas and that the sectors in any case are inherently unattractive.

· Netflix does not enjoy meaningful network effects and its decision to enter the original content arena is not justified or supported by the imagined ability of artificial intelligence to systematically deliver "hits." The abandonment of the previously articulated strategy of avoiding creative risk, while justified by the dramatically increased competition in the sector, has made Netflix a worse, not a better, business.

· The acquisition sprees by many FAANG companies reveal vulnerabilities in their armor and the limits of their advantages. The ability of independent e-commerce players to establish durable leads over Amazon in diapers, footwear, fabric, pet supplies, and furniture and the ability of Instagram, WhatsApp, and TikTok to establish global online communities independent of Facebook reflect these structural constraints. Most of the specific companies noted have been acquired, but the regulatory environment will restrict future acquisitions (or even undo previous ones) and intensify future competitive challenges to FAANG.

· The power of network effects in the context of any given sector is significantly influenced by the complexity of the product or service being provided and the break-even economics for a given market. This explains why Airbnb will always be a far better business than Uber and why Booking and Expedia make most of their money from selling hotel rooms and almost nothing from flights. Many of the most resilient network effects driven platforms, in sectors like travel and payments, predate the internet by decades.

- Artificial intelligence has been promoted almost as vigorously as network effects as driving the unassailability and inevitable global domination of digital platforms. The proliferation of new vertically focused multibillion-dollar software companies undermines the predictions that AI will lead to "the gradual demise of traditional specialization"[18] and an increasingly winner-take-all world.

The FAANG businesses collectively represented over $6 trillion of market capitalization at the end of 2020. In 2015, these companies were worth under $2 trillion; their subsequent appreciation was more than three times greater than the overall growth in value of the S&P 500. Their collective dramatic outperformance during the pandemic has reinforced the perception of their unitary and inherent invulnerability. Understanding the strengths and weaknesses of these remarkable companies is essential to making intelligent decisions not only related directly to them but to any company facing actual or potential competition from them—which is most companies.

The inadequacy of the conventional wisdom regarding digital platforms generally is best demonstrated by its inability to explain radically different outcomes from apparently similar business models. Legions of online and off-line retailers have famously fallen in the face of Amazon's might. Yet Amazon has been powerless to vanquish dozens of specialized marketplaces where independent operators like Wayfair and Etsy are established leaders. In contrast to the success of the hundreds of new vertical software platforms, hundreds of ad-supported and adtech platforms have collapsed despite frequently attracting widespread adoption. *The Platform Delusion* attempts to explain these and many other apparent anomalies through a narrative organized into three parts.

Part I provides the context required for thinking clearly about competitive advantage in digital environments. Chapter 1 closely examines the tenets holding up the Platform Delusion. Each of these has attracted remarkably broad acceptance, which explains the durability of the overarching delusion, but is demonstrably false. Chapter 2 explores the concept of scale as it often manifests in digital environments—through network effects. The benefits of network effects are very different from the benefits of traditional scale, which derive primarily from spreading fixed costs. I also identify the key industry characteristics that determine the potential strength of network effects and the continuing relevance of traditional scale benefits to network effects businesses. Chapter 3 sets out a broad framework within which to think about competitive advantage in digital environments. Scale of any kind without additional reinforcing competitive advantages is vulnerable to competitive incursion. The existence (or absence) of platforms and network effects can be relevant to this analysis, but it is never dispositive in itself.

Part II (chapters 4–8) applies this framework to the five FAANG companies, giving an overview of the history and performance of each. I examine in detail the various sources and levels of intensity of their respective competitive advantages. I also consider the companies' specific vulnerabilities and likely paths forward.

Part III (chapters 9–14) looks at a range of sectors and business models, many operating in the shadow of the FAANG giants, specifically in travel, adtech, big data, e-commerce, software-as-a-service (SaaS), and the sharing economy. In each case, I explore the history of how the domain emerged or has been transformed in the digital ecosystem. The structural features that explain the most notable successful and failed investments are highlighted.

Finally, an epilogue provides observations about some dangers of the Platform Delusion outside of simply losing boatloads of money. In the areas of public policy and our culture more broadly, simplistic assumptions about the structure of digital industries and the path to riches have led to shortsighted and often self-defeating decision-making.

This book is meant as both a reminder of the fundamental importance of competitive advantage and a field guide to how competitive advantage manifests itself in digital environments differently from analog ones. Over two decades of experience working with one foot in invest-ment banking and the other in academia has confirmed for me the ur-gency of this enterprise for a broad audience. Too often, even sophisticated boards, seasoned executives, and professional investors have allowed them-selves to be drawn into misguided digital transactions based on faulty extrapolations of near-term results. The same misunderstandings about industry structure that underpin these bad deals and failed investments have also led too many graduating business students to pursue careers at young ambitious technology companies that are destined to evaporate, leaving them and society poorer for the squandering of their potential.

As the global economy regroups following the massive retrenchment wrought by the coronavirus pandemic, and as every branch of government appears poised to scrutinize its relationships with technology companies generally, there has never been a better time to examine the structural strengths and weaknesses of the so-called platform economy. Only by identifying the true sources of today's competitive advantage can inves-tors, managers, and entrepreneurs consistently create value during this period of unprecedented technological and market change. But business and investing strategies aside, citizens and policy makers also need an un-derstanding of these structural attributes if they are to make a positive con-tribution to the ongoing national debate. Our collective ability to realize the promise while avoiding the dangers of our contemporary economy hinges on our willingness to embrace a clear-eyed view of market and in-dustry structure and overcome the Platform Delusion.

PART I

DIGITAL ADVANTAGE AND DISADVANTAGE

THE FOUR PILLARS OF
THE PLATFORM DELUSION

THE PLATFORM DELUSION MOST OFTEN manifests itself subtly, as an unspoken assumption underlying confident assertions regarding the direction of the economy or the imagined invincibility of a particular enterprise. Regardless of exact terminology—"the platform economy," "the platform revolution," and "the platform effect" have emerged as common terms—the central fallacy relies on a consistent mythology and the confident expectation of world domination by a select few megaplatforms. This conventional wisdom rests overwhelmingly on four core pillars of belief.

Each of these is demonstrably false.

THE CORE TENETS OF THE PLATFORM DELUSION
1. Platforms Are a Revolutionary New Business Model.
2. Digital Platforms Are Structurally Superior to Analog Platforms.
3. All Platforms Exhibit Powerful Network Effects.
4. Network Effects Lead Inexorably to Winner-Take-All Markets.

PLATFORMS ARE A REVOLUTIONARY
NEW BUSINESS MODEL

It is true that business school professors only started writing in earnest about platform business models after 2000. But it is a terrible mistake to date a social or economic phenomenon only from the moment that academics decided to take note. Well before the internet was even conceived, much less commercialized, the average consumer interacted with platform businesses on a daily basis.

The definition of a "platform" business is straightforward. Although they take many forms, what platforms have in common is that their core value proposition lies in the connections they enable and enhance. "They bring together individuals and organizations," a recent review of platform businesses and research summarized, "so they can innovate or interact in ways not otherwise possible."[1]

The persistent confusion regarding what constitutes a platform business, despite the relatively simple definition, is mostly due to unhelpful market incentives. As is often the case, when a moniker emerges that affords a premium valuation, all manner of enterprises twist themselves in knots to claim a credible association with the term. So, for instance, it should not be surprising that a fast-food salad chain would promote itself as a "food platform." The company, Sweetgreen, has even attracted a distinguished Harvard Business School professor to the board to lend legitimacy to the pitch.[2]

That said, the diversity of connections made possible by the internet has spawned a mind-boggling array of legitimate platform businesses, often with very different business models. Sometimes the platform's source of value comes from a financial transaction by matching a buyer and a seller in a marketplace, sometimes it comes from facilitating innovation through the addition of functionality and content to a shared environment like a gaming platform, and sometimes it comes just from the interaction itself, as in the case of a social network. This explosion of new platforms has led to a strange amnesia regarding the ubiquity of platform businesses long before the dawn of the digital age.

Some of the platform businesses that predated the internet were primarily electronic, like credit cards. Introduced by Diners Club in 1950 and pervasive by the 1970s after the establishment of American Express,

Visa, and Mastercard, credit cards serve as a platform on which merchants and customers can transact.[3] By the end of 2020, Visa was worth almost half a trillion dollars, with Mastercard not far behind.

Other long-established platform businesses are physical, like the iconic malls that connect retailers with shoppers throughout the country. The Southdale Center in Edina, Minnesota, generally identified as the first modern shopping mall, opened in 1956[4] and still operates today. Movie theaters similarly are platform businesses. Exhibitors negotiate with studios to get the best films on the best terms and market the experience to local moviegoers. The ability to get the best films is in part a function of the credibility of their claim to be able to attract the biggest possible audience, and their ability to fill the theater will be in part a function of the films they secure.

This chicken-and-egg dynamic inherent in platform businesses has not fundamentally changed with the internet. Operators face the same basic business issues—who and how to charge, encouraging platform loyalty, and "traffic" monetization strategies, for instance—in seeking to build and maintain successful multisided platforms.

What is surprising is that it took so long for it to occur to anyone to study the structure and economics of platform businesses. Nobel Prize–winning economist Jean Tirole is the coauthor of an article from 2003 which, if not the absolute first to examine the phenomenon, is most widely cited and appears to have launched the avalanche of research and publications that have followed.[5] Interestingly, given the supposed connection between the "discovery" of platforms and the availability of the internet, the seminal article was not published in a US journal despite that the most notable digital platforms of scale were developed here.

The authors of this groundbreaking article seem slightly bemused that the topic had previously attracted such "scant attention" despite decades of research focused on network economics and chicken-and-egg problems.[6] What's more, although some internet businesses are discussed, most of the examples used in their analysis (including video games, credit cards, and operating systems) substantially predate the internet and in many cases (like discount coupon books, shopping malls, and real estate brokers) are decidedly low-tech.[7] This has not dissuaded the media or other academics from characterizing Tirole's intellectual contribution as somehow applying uniquely or differently to "Internet-era companies."[8]

The conviction that platforms are something new and different seems only to have intensified in recent years. The term "platform" has entered the vernacular with a vengeance, as a review of search terms over the past decade reveals. Whether this coincides with a corresponding increase in understanding of the distinguishing characteristics of platform businesses seems questionable at best.

Google Trends: "Platform" Interest Over Time

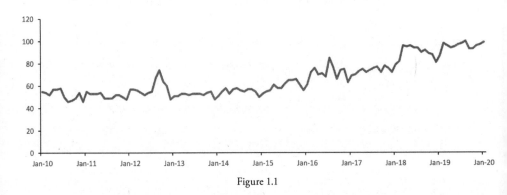

Figure 1.1

DIGITAL PLATFORMS ARE STRUCTURALLY SUPERIOR TO ANALOG PLATFORMS

Even if platforms are not a new concept, the internet has vastly expanded the range, scope, and size of potential platform businesses. In many cases, these new digital models have proved devastating to long-established franchises. But bigger is not always better, and the ability to upend does not always signal a capability of creating lasting value.

The undeniable, sometimes shocking strength of the handful of the largest digital platforms established in recent decades—Google and Facebook in particular—has led to a broader assumption that digital platforms are consistently better businesses than the analog equivalents. This is an assumption that does not bear up to scrutiny. It has also proven costly to many investors.

A comparison of the key business characteristics of one familiar analog platform and its digital equivalent demonstrates the depth of this fallacy. Shopping malls and their digital counterpart, e-commerce websites, represent the simplest of two-sided platforms connecting sellers and buyers.

Traditional malls had two major benefits: their vendors were committed to long-term leases and their shoppers' next best option was many miles away. Before committing to construction, a mall developer will typically secure a handful of anchor tenants and often obtain not only an extended commitment, but a promise not to open any other stores within a certain distance of the mall. The original site-selection process incorporates considerations of demographics, shopping alternatives, and land cost and availability. A key analysis here is to confirm that the subsequent establishment of a competing nearby mall is impractical. These features ensure that the mall operator is able to secure superior returns for its investors.

On the internet, the platform's relationships with both buyer and seller typically exhibit none of this durability. Alternatives for buyers are only a click away, and sophisticated sellers dynamically optimize their ability to reach customers across competing platforms or directly. There are few levers a digital commerce platform can pull to combat this structural reality. Estimates of e-commerce failure rates are as high as 97 percent.[9]

The case of Amazon is complex and the subject of its own chapter. It is worth noting, however, that the most successful operators in the shopping-center sector are wildly more profitable than Amazon's e-commerce operations.[10] The point isn't that you would rather invest in a mall operator than Amazon during a pandemic but simply that off-line business models have surprising relative resilience. It is not a coincidence that, despite the secular trends, right up until the COVID-19 crisis hit, struggling online retailers were increasingly looking to solve their structural woes by opening up mall outlets![11]

A disproportionate number of the earliest dot-com flameouts—names like Pets.com, Kozmo, Boo.com, and Webvan—were e-commerce companies. These elicit some nostalgia for those of us who lived through the first internet boom but likely cause recurring nightmares for some of the biggest names in venture capital who actually backed them.

The more recent entries into the category have hardly proven much more resilient, although remarkably this has not seemed to significantly dampen the willingness of public and private investors to aggressively finance the category. The "flash sale" craze lasted a few years and briefly produced its own signature unicorn, Gilt Groupe.[12] Online deal marketplace Groupon's 2011 IPO was the largest since Google's in 2004, valuing the company at well over $10 billion.[13] Today, it is a largely forgotten microcap.[14] In 2019, the highest profile crop of e-commerce IPOs, Jumia, Revolve, and Chewy—targeting commerce in Africa, clothing, and pet products, respectively—all soared on their first day of trading but ended the year at a small fraction of the value reflected by that initial euphoria.

Although COVID-19 initially interrupted the IPO dreams of many in the planned e-commerce class of 2020—for instance Poshmark, another fashion retailer, which had previously delayed its IPO[15]—the sector dramatically recovered as investors came to believe in a permanent shift to online buying. Casper, in bedding, tapped the public markets just before the full force of the pandemic was felt and lost 75 percent of its value in the first month—but managed to regain at least some of its IPO price by year end.[16] More dramatically, the once unloved Chewy, described as the Pets.com of the current era,[17] exploded to a market capitalization of over $40 billion. And in September, Poshmark went ahead and filed its IPO paperwork, ultimately becoming one of the earliest hot offerings of 2021.[18] Shifting market sentiment, however, can only mask the fundamental economics of e-commerce for so long.

Digital retail environments provide consumers with bountiful information with respect to both price and product options. But the friend of the buyer is typically the enemy of the seller—as power shifts to consumers and away from producers, exceptional profit opportunities become rare. Online commerce may have been correctly identified as one of the first "killer apps" of the World Wide Web, but overwhelmingly who gets killed are the investors in these businesses.

Of course, all digital commerce businesses are not the same, and these important distinctions are examined more closely later. Some are pure platforms that simply connect buyer and seller, such as eBay. Others, like Casper, actually are the sellers themselves and sometimes even the manufacturers. And still others, like Amazon, operate a hybrid model of some sort. And there are large e-commerce sectors, like online travel businesses, that sell services rather than things. Despite their diversity of business models and products, as a group they are surprisingly consistent in at least one regard: disappointing financial performance over time.

During the quarter century since the birth of the commercial internet, dozens of companies in some form of e-commerce have gone public. Almost a quarter have gone bankrupt or delisted. Of those that managed to get acquired before facing that unpleasant prospect, over two thirds sold out for less than their original public offering price. Of the third that remain public companies, over 60 percent have lagged the overall market since their respective IPOs.[19]

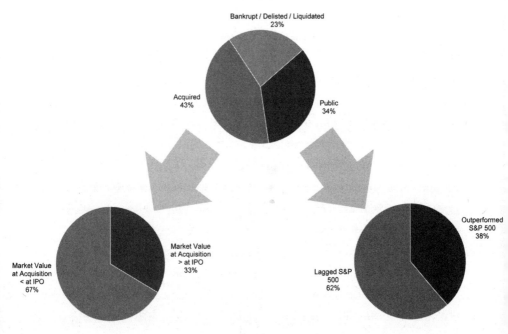

US E-commerce IPOs

Figure 1.2

Source: S&P Capital IQ. Company filings, press releases.

Note: Displays US Internet and Direct Marketing Retail

Companies with IPOs from 1995–2020

ALL PLATFORMS EXHIBIT POWERFUL NETWORK EFFECTS

The imagined talismanic qualities of platform business models are often attributed to the inherent availability of an important economic phenomenon known as "network effects." Sometimes also referred to as the "flywheel effect," it means that every new user increases the value of the network to existing users.

What is so irresistible about network effects is their potential to feed off themselves. There is something compelling about the virtuous circle of steadily increasing advantage reflected in the most successful businesses built on network effects. In theory, every new user increases the relative attractiveness of the business, simultaneously attracting still more new users and making the prospect of successful competitive attack ever more remote.

The logical association between platform businesses and network effects is understandable. Platforms, after all, are generally in the business of managing and facilitating the interaction among network participants. But it is a mistake to conclude that all platforms are powered by strong network effects.[20] In fact, plenty of platform businesses receive little assistance from network effects.

For instance, all ad-supported media businesses, from television broadcasters to internet content providers, serve as platforms to connect advertisers and consumers. The "water cooler" effect may generate some psychic benefit from knowing that others share your interests and advertisers are undoubtedly attracted to a larger audience, but the economics of these businesses are primarily driven by traditional fixed-cost scale. It is the production of hit shows and compelling web content that power these businesses, not network effects either between or among viewers and advertisers. When the content succeeds, the significant fixed infrastructure costs can be spread across the heightened revenue base generated by attracting more viewers and better advertising rates.

Similarly, movie theaters, as noted earlier, represent platforms connecting moviegoers and studios. Their economics, however, have little to do with network effects. Rather, relative profitability has historically been predominantly a function of whether the theaters are regionally clustered in small markets that support few theaters or spread nationally across highly competitive big cities.[21]

Even Zoom, the video communications platform that is perhaps the most iconic success of the pandemic era, is not really a strong network effects business. By the end of 2020, the company was worth over $100 billion and its stock traded at around ten times its 2019 offering price. Zoom is a fabulous product, but its very success in eliminating any friction or complexity in adoption has severely limited how powerful its network effects can be. At this point, multiple competitive products also permit participation by simply clicking on a browser link, so obtaining access to the broadest possible pool of potential network participants is not a differentiator. Without any meaningful costs of switching or real challenges in coordinating among users, the value of any network effects is limited.[22]

It is true that most platform businesses do exhibit network effects. Nonetheless, even where they exist, the nature, extent, and impact of the effects on the attractiveness of the enterprises vary widely. Finally, when, as in the case of Facebook, strong network effects are a crucial feature of a powerful digital platform, there is invariably more to the story. Understanding whether and why to invest in a platform business requires an examination of multiple factors well beyond the presence of network effects.

NETWORK EFFECTS LEAD INEXORABLY TO WINNER-TAKE-ALL MODELS

The perceived power of network effects business models and the unique ability of digital platforms to weaponize these on a previously unimaginable scale lie at the heart of the Platform Delusion. Network effects, like platforms, existed in the analog world. In an example close to home, the resilience of the rankings of the world's top research universities over many decades in the face of well-funded global new entrants is a function of the entrenched network of students, faculty, funders, and alumni.

But the internet is a network of networks. Its emergence as the indispensable instrumentality of commerce and communication is perhaps the defining characteristic of the modern economy. Its very fluidity and ubiquity would seem to enable an intensification of network effects where they previously applied and a vast expansion of potential new applications.

The imagined result is of an economy dominated by behemoths benefiting from the winner-take-all (or, more modestly, winner-take-most) dynamics of digitally enhanced network effects in a growing number of domains.

The problem with this story line is that it is not supported by even a cursory survey of the landscape. For every Facebook and Microsoft there are literally hundreds of network effects businesses operating in crowded sectors or ones in which it is not clear that anyone will ever turn a profit. There is simply no actual evidence for the oft-repeated assertion that network effects are "likely to strengthen a market's winner-take-all tendency."[23]

To see that winner-take-all outcomes do not follow necessarily or even usually from the mere existence of network effects, let's look at a subset of e-commerce businesses in which the presence of network effects is most intuitive. So-called marketplace businesses serve as matchmakers to buyers and sellers. They don't produce their own products and do not typically hold inventory. Rather, their success is based on the ability to create an appealing forum within which to transact. This is the classic indirect network effects business model—more buyers attract more sellers and vice versa. Founded a quarter century ago, eBay was one of the first successful digital marketplace businesses, but hundreds of others have followed using different approaches and targeting different markets.

Even in this well-established sector, the range of industry structures and outcomes varies wildly based on a number of factors, such as what is being sold and the geography being served. In the US, for instance, the automotive market supports well-established general marketplaces like eBay, Amazon, and Craigslist; multiple large specialized services such as Autotrader, Cars.com, CarsDirect, and Edmunds.com; and captive sites of a variety of dealer groups and associations as well as dozens of smaller players and a continuing stream of relatively new entrants like CarGurus, TrueCar, and Carvana. Amid this diversity of resulting industry structures, however, "winner-take-all" or even "winner-take-most" as an equilibrium outcome is only rarely observed.

More broadly, the authors of *The Business of Platforms*[24] looked at two decades of performance, from 1995 to 2015, of platform businesses and noted that relatively few had survived. Specifically, "only 17 percent (43 out of 252) remained in 2015 as independent public companies."[25] Much of the book is preoccupied with drawing lessons from the wide variety of factors that led to the 209 platform business failures catalogued. For our purposes, the most interesting finding is what was the *least* likely source of failure: "In a relatively small number of platform spaces, failure was a function of a genuine winner-take-all or winner-take-most outcome for a competitor."[26]

The rich tapestry of business models and wide variety of ultimate financial results suggests that the identification of network effects should represent the beginning, not the end, of the analysis. Time and again, apparently promising network effects businesses have attracted capital from venture and private equity investors based primarily on a business plan or early traction in building a network. Sometimes these early capital sources have been rewarded as the networks have continued to grow, and the businesses have been sold either to larger companies or the public through an IPO. Too often, however, the ultimate owners have been disappointed as the financial results over time reflect that all network effects businesses are not created equal and that the simple existence of network effects does not ensure world domination or even a promising future.

IN AUGUST 2018, Apple became the first trillion-dollar tech company.[27] Amazon and Microsoft soon followed,[28] and Google's parent, Alphabet, more recently attained this once unimaginable valuation threshold.[29] Just the appreciation of the FAANG stocks alone during the first six months of 2020 exceeded $1 trillion. In August 2020, Apple became the first $2 trillion tech company![30] Taking a longer view, however, what may be more startling is how few durable independent internet businesses of scale and substance have actually managed to establish themselves in the quarter-plus century since the broad consumer availability of the World Wide Web.

Although something north of two hundred internet IPOs occurred during the first twenty years following Netscape becoming a public company in 1995,[31] outside of FAANG not much more than a handful have grown into proven large-cap public companies.[32] Far more have gone out of business, been subsumed at a fraction of their previous public valuation by someone else, or muddled along as marginal enterprises.

Since 2015, the number of new large-cap internet companies has accelerated. Many of these described themselves as a "platform" of one kind or another but to date have generally failed to achieve consistent profitability. At the same time, an increasing number of private platform companies have achieved "unicorn" status—attracting private investors at a valuation of over $1 billion—only to be forced to return to the private market at lower valuations in order to secure additional capital to survive. WeWork is the highest-profile company in this category, which includes many others. Sometimes the IPO itself serves as a down round, with the initial market value—as was the case for Square and Pinterest—sometimes billions of dollars less than the final private round.[33]

The acceleration in the number of new large-cap internet companies in recent years stems in part from the structural incentives to wait longer before tapping the IPO market.[34] With unprecedented levels of private capital willing to deliver liquidity and steadily increasing headline valuations—sometimes using questionable structural and accounting tools[35]—outside the glare of public scrutiny, former Uber CEO Travis Kalanick spoke for many peers when he said his company would go public "as late as humanly possible."[36]

The companies born in the original dot-com boom around the turn of the century had been in existence for three years on average when they went public. The more recent crop stayed private for a decade or more on average before looking to public investors.[37] These same tendencies to continue to take additional private money for longer before going public are reflected in the accelerating growth in the number of unicorns as well. But as the cumulative number of active unicorns has swelled, the number of successful exits as a percentage of the total has experienced a correspondingly rapid decline.

As of late 2013, there were only 32 active unicorns, and with consistency each year investors in about a quarter of the outstanding companies were able to find an exit, whether through an IPO or otherwise.[38] From 2015, however, when unicorns numbered over 100 for the first time, until the end of the decade, by which time there were 222, the percentage of exits has remained stubbornly at around 10 percent.[39] This remained true even in 2020, with unprecedented opportunities—well beyond the previous record set during the 1999 dot-com boom—to tap the public markets.[40]

Looking at this data, one is reminded of the Aesop's fable of the fox who declines to visit the supposedly sick lion in his cave because "he can only see tracks going in, but none coming out." Horace relied on this tale to attack the get-rich-quick culture that characterized Roman bankers.[41] If anything, these outcomes suggest that it is harder rather than easier to make a buck in digital environments.

Of course, starting a successful new company or outperforming the overall market has always been a devilishly difficult undertaking. That the losers significantly outnumber the winners should not be surprising or concerning in itself. What is alarming, however, is the extent to which the euphoria triggered by the Platform Delusion has led investors to forget that, ultimately, the existence of competitive advantage is what drives the ability of any business, digital or analog, to produce consistently superior returns.

The basic concept of competitive advantage has been the subject of much needless confusion. This is partially the result of the sheer volume of scholarship that has been produced on the subject. But it is also a function of the practical difficulties encountered in applying the classic "five forces" framework for assessing competition developed by Harvard Business School professor Michael Porter over forty years ago.[42] What I mean here by competitive advantage is disarmingly simple: the structural characteristics that allow a company to do what its rivals cannot.[43] This simplicity does not detract, however, from its central importance.

WHY UNDERSTANDING COMPETITIVE ADVANTAGE MATTERS

Understanding competitive advantage is indispensable to pursuing successful long-term business or investing strategies in both the analog and digital worlds. A company can expect to deliver exceptional results in two ways. It can be a better operator or it can benefit from structural attributes that impede effective competitive attack. Such structural attributes are called competitive advantage. Identifying which of the two routes is the basis for any particular instance of outperformance is critical for leaders and investors looking to repeat the feat.

The fundamental difference between value creation deriving from operational and from structural sources is their respective durability. And it is during periods of market euphoria—when financial success is available indiscriminately without the need for deep understanding of the true value of individual assets—that an appreciation of durability is especially important. When the music stops, as it always does, only those who were able to make these critical distinctions will survive. Efficient operations can eventually be copied; great leaders can be poached. Process and culture do not have the resilience of a structural advantage. A natural monopoly, a patented critical proprietary technology, and an exclusive long-term government franchise are extreme examples of structural advantages that support persistent success.

Think for a moment about the interchangeability of the terms "competitive advantage" and "barrier to entry." If a business exhibits characteristics that give it a defensible advantage over any competitors, this will inhibit new entrants and drive superior returns. When superior returns are being achieved, in the absence of impediments, entrepreneurs and opportunistic existing businesses enter. And they continue entering until that so-called advantage is no longer an advantage at all but simply table stakes in a competitive business. Competitive advantages are precisely those features of incumbency that shut down the process of relentless entry because potential new entrants know they will suffer from a relative structural handicap.

Now consider the most efficient operator with a fabulous culture and extraordinary internal processes. This might set a high bar for a would-be competitor in terms of getting its act together before entering, but if the playing field were otherwise level, do you doubt that many would take a shot? And although there are plenty of cases of the same company consistently performing as best in class in highly competitive sectors without meaningful structural advantages, it can only do so by relentlessly upping its game. Changes in management, ownership, or the competitive set inevitably bring these impressive runs to an end.

For managers, knowing to what extent a company owes its success to efficiency and competitive advantage should fundamentally drive resource allocation. Strategy is all about actions that will allow a business to perform better than its peers over the long term. The focus must accordingly be on establishing or reinforcing competitive advantage and will involve interrelated considerations of how to invest internally and how to interact with other constituents in the broader ecosystem. Efficiency, by contrast, has a relatively shorter-term horizon and is overwhelmingly focused internally on optimizing operating performance.

Effective strategy requires an appreciation of the precise sources of competitive advantage in order to better protect and exploit the barrier. Some advantages manifest on the supply side, facilitating the delivery of an otherwise largely identical product at a lower cost than that of a competitor (or sometimes a better product at the same cost). Other entry barriers enjoyed by lucky incumbents are demand-side phenomena. These keep customers captive in the face of apparently equally attractive, or even somewhat better or cheaper, alternatives.

Each particular variety of demand and supply advantage calls for different forms of reinforcement. For example, habit, a demand advantage, is strengthened by encouraging repeated use, whereas proprietary technology, a supply advantage, is protected by continual investment. The strongest franchises usually manage to benefit from a combination of supply and demand advantages, which often buttress each other.

In the absence of barriers to entry, however, managers should focus exclusively on operating efficiency. But a culture of efficiency is still important for businesses with competitive advantages for two reasons. First, relative efficiency makes a huge difference in returns to investors. In technology as in other domains, the delta in key performance indicators between the best and worst operators is substantial. Second, even "sustainable" competitive advantage is not forever. Changes in technology, consumer demand, government policies, and any number of other factors can change the extent or even the existence of advantage. The lack of strong operating capabilities will significantly undermine the ability to effectively manage shifts in industry structure.

Unfortunately, strong competitive advantage has a tendency to dull the senses when it comes to operating efficiency. If great results can be achieved without sweating, why sweat? Furthermore, it is convenient to imagine that solid results are the outcome of one's own strategic brilliance or operating prowess rather than simply industry structure. The newspaper industry suffered from notoriously weak management yet outperformed the market and delivered operating margins as high as 40 percent or more for decades. The failure to cultivate operating skills or understand the true sources of the sector's outsize performance made the seismic changes to newspaper economics wrought by the internet far more wrenching than they needed to be. This was bad for shareholders, employees, readers, and democratic society, which relies on a vibrant independent news sector.

For investors, all profit is not created equally. Valuing a company correctly involves determining how high a multiple to apply to the profit in calculating the worth of the overall business.[44] But to do this correctly requires an understanding of whether and to what extent there are competitive advantages. This is true for two reasons, one obvious and one less so.

On the obvious front, if the level of profitability is exclusively due to the superior execution by a stellar management team rather than structural entry barriers, an investor will likely have some skepticism regarding the longevity of these results. A valuation multiple represents a mathematical calculation of the current value of anticipated future cash flows generated by a business discounted back to the present. As a practical matter, this involves making predictions regarding future results for the upcoming years—with each successive year becoming increasingly speculative—and an assumption regarding the growth rate into perpetuity applied to the final year of projections. Presumably, the forecast for that final year and any perpetuity growth rate would be lower where entry barriers are absent— resulting in a lower multiple.

On the less obvious front, the existence of competitive advantage is a critical factor in deciding whether to place any value at all on growth. To achieve growth, a business must make investments. Those investments create value only to the extent that they yield returns greater than what you were charged for the money used to invest. Said another way, there is an opportunity cost to using capital to generate growth—what economists call the "weighted average cost of capital," or WACC. If the business has no barriers to entry, those proposed growth investments will attract competitors until the returns are reduced to the WACC. As a result, growth in the absence of competitive advantage is worthless.[45]

For those who have succumbed to the Platform Delusion or are simply immersed in the culture of internet investing, the notion that growth could ever lack value will likely come as a bit of a shock. It has become something of an article of faith in digital investing circles that a little disruption and a lot of growth necessarily translates into a big opportunity.

A reflection of the intensity of this belief is the prevalence of digital business models in which the gross margin is actually negative. In other words, even ignoring indirect overhead costs, the business loses more money every time it makes another sale. On the one hand, it is certainly disruptive to sell product below cost and likely to spark plenty of consumer interest and thus growth. On the other hand, when you have unprofitable unit economics, it is simply not possible to make it up on volume.

At some level, this criticism may seem unfair. The entire concept of "competitive advantage" applies definitionally only to incumbents, not new entrants. How can a new entrant benefit from a barrier to entry? Indeed, many of these negative-gross-margin businesses are start-ups. And maybe their plan is to grow into sustainable competitive advantage: once they get big enough, unit costs could go down based on greater purchasing clout and they may be able to raise prices so that gross margins will become positive. The losses incurred along the way could be justified by the quality of the scale franchise ultimately established.

That sounds reasonable enough, but in practice, not so much. In a widely read 2015 blog post by the uncommonly thoughtful venture capitalist Fred Wilson of Union Square Ventures, he complained bitterly of the "tremendous number of high growth companies raising money this year with negative gross margins."[46] Wilson is highly skeptical of plans based on an ability to flip the economics once you scale up. Notably, "if there are other start-ups competing with you and offering a similar service, you aren't going to be able to take prices up without losing customers to a similar competitor, unless your service truly has 'lock in.'" That is highly unlikely, Wilson argues, "given the massive amount of start-up capital that is out there and the endless number of entrepreneurs starting businesses similar to each other these days."

At the heart of the problem lies a question that has perplexed mankind for ages: When does size matter? Scale is the single competitive advantage that is almost always present in every robust business franchise. Importantly, it is different from mere size. The internet has altered its availability, its usefulness, and how it is likely to manifest, meaning that successful management of the Platform Delusion requires a nuanced understanding of digital scale.

KEY CHAPTER TAKEAWAYS

1. The defining characteristic of a platform business is that its core value proposition lies in enabling and enhancing connections between individuals and organizations. Although frequently presented as peculiar to the internet, platform business models have long been ubiquitous. What's more, in many instances, the digital versions of these models have proven less resilient than the analog counterparts that they displace.

2. Although many platform businesses exhibit significant network effects, many do not. Even where network effects are present, the nature, extent, and impact of the effects on the attractiveness of the enterprises vary widely.

3. The emergence of the internet has enabled an intensification of network effects where they previously applied and a significant expansion of potential new applications. But even digitally enhanced network effects do not lead inexorably or even usually to either winner-take-all or winner-take-most markets. Being digital, in fact, often lowers barriers to entry, not the opposite.

4. Durable digital business franchises, like their analog counterparts, owe their success to the establishment of sustainable competitive advantage, not the existence of platforms or network effects alone. Without such structural barriers to entry, or a credible prospect of achieving them, investors cannot expect sustainable superior returns. Great management and efficient operations yield enormous benefits, but valuing these must reflect their inherently transitory nature. Growth in the absence of competitive advantage generally does not create shareholder value.

NETWORK DEFECTS:
SCALE IN THE DIGITAL ERA

WHEN BIG REALLY IS BETTER:
AN INTRODUCTION TO SCALE

Scale is a highly intuitive concept, but it is an intuition that has an unfortunate tendency to lead investors astray. The intuition of scale most often is associated with the idea of absolute size. But the advantages of scale are always relative. Very large companies in very large markets that can support many similarly sized giants have no scale advantage vis-à-vis each other, whereas much smaller businesses in smaller markets that can only support a single profitable operator do.

The intuitive value of scale is that it offers an opportunity to spread costs across a larger user base. This results in a lower average cost and a higher profit potential per unit than smaller competitors can achieve. And this intuition is precisely correct.

The subtlety, however, is that the observation only applies to a certain kind of cost—namely, fixed costs. Fixed costs are those that do not vary with sales—a Super Bowl ad, R&D, and facilities all cost the same regardless of the size of the company paying for them. In contrast, variable costs go up and down based on how much is sold—for example, commissions and raw materials. By definition, fixed costs get spread, but variable costs don't. Scale can also offer benefits at the variable cost level, potentially expanding gross margins from greater purchasing clout, as noted in the previous chapter, but on the supply side, scale makes the biggest difference to fixed costs.

The intrinsic value of scale in any particular sector is accordingly related to how much of that industry's cost structure is fixed and how much is variable. The relative predominance of fixed costs drives the most important advantages associated with scale. Where costs are mostly variable, being the biggest simply doesn't provide nearly as much of a leg up, and it can sometimes prove a hindrance as communication, management, and coordination become more complex.[1] And, of course, the less significant the fixed-cost requirements, the easier it is for a new competitor to enter in the first place.

The benefits of spreading fixed costs derived from scale underpin many well-known long-established franchises. Notable sectors that benefit from such advantages are consumer products with massive fixed marketing and distribution infrastructures (think Coke and P&G) and technology businesses with massive fixed R&D costs (think Intel and Oracle).

THE INTERNET AND SCALE ADVANTAGES: THE BAD NEWS AND THE GOOD NEWS

The immediate financial impact of the internet was to lower many of the fixed costs of operations, particularly around marketing and distribution. Everybody likes a discount, so even many incumbents who had long relied on scale advantages to drive shareholder returns appeared to relish the chance to reduce fixed costs. This was particularly the case in media and information businesses where entirely electronic distribution of product would be possible. Arthur Sulzberger, the publisher of the *New York Times*, was hardly alone when he exulted, "it's wonderful,"[2] at the prospect of a future without printing presses, newsstands, and delivery trucks.

The trouble is that it is those very fixed costs that had served as a key barrier to entry against subscale players unable to afford them. Once the excitement over getting a bargain on their fixed-cost obligations subsided, these incumbents looked around and noticed some unexpected guests: new competitors. The resulting revenue pressures from competition invariably overwhelm the benefits of fixed-cost reductions. To add insult to injury, while certain fixed costs decline, many other fixed and variable costs are likely to escalate as the new entrants bid up industry salaries and prices for key supplies. To be fair, these tendencies can be mitigated by other favorable trends. In the case of the SaaS software sector profiled in chapter 14, although absolute fixed costs are lower than for traditional software, they now represent a greater proportion of total costs.

The good news is that the internet facilitates the establishment of an entirely different breed of scale advantage that does not owe its existence to high fixed costs. As discussed, network effects have been repeatedly identified as the defining structural competitive advantage of the digital age and lie at the core of the Platform Delusion.

Although digital platforms do not always generate network effects, the internet has clearly expanded the range of potential commercial environments within which they could manifest. Rather than representing a supply advantage, network effects yield a benefit on the demand side of the equation: the bigger you are, the easier it is to attract new customers and incremental revenue.

So, if the internet makes it harder to secure supply-side scale but easier to develop demand-side scale, the obvious question is, What is the net impact on the availability of scale advantages? Sometimes this question is posed as a competition between "traditional" fixed-cost-driven scale and the emerging category of digital network effects: Which one is better?

Recent conventional wisdom regarding platform businesses has suggested that their intrinsic superiority is their foundation built on demand-side rather than supply-side scale. There is actually a venture firm, called NfX, that was established based on this belief, claiming to have demonstrated that network effects "are responsible for 70 percent of the value created by tech companies since the Internet became a thing."[3]

Harvard strategy professor Bharat Anand's perspective on the funda-

The Strategic Importance of Relative Fixed Costs

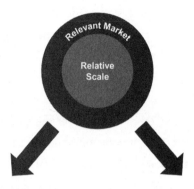

Source	Supply	Demand
Benefit	Cost	Revenue
Primary Driver	Predominance of Fixed Costs	Intensity of Network Effects

Figure 2.1

mental difference between the network effects associated with digital businesses and the fixed-cost-driven scale economies associated with traditional ones is typical in this regard. In his book *The Content Trap*, Professor Anand argues that "chances are you win everything" in network effects markets in contrast to supply-side scale that he believes is more easily copied.[4] Ironically, in the very market Professor Anand leads with—newspapers—the opposite was true. Local newspaper franchises were a winner-take-all market precisely because the fixed costs required made only a single paper economically feasible, whereas most online classified marketplaces, while benefiting from network effects, appear to support multiple competitors.

The critical issue, however, is not whether supply-side or demand-side scale is "better" in the abstract. The more interesting issue is how the two forms of scale interact with each other. In practice, the resiliency of network effects businesses is strengthened by the presence of significant fixed costs in their operating model.

It is true that in digital business models, the absolute fixed-cost requirements can be significantly lower and flow from entirely different categories of fixed expenses. But this does not reduce the continuing importance of supply-side economics in successful demand-side scale business models. This is evident from simple economics. The minimum fixed-costs needs and gross margin profile of a business in a given industry determine break-even volume and the corresponding required minimum market share to achieve profitability.

Knowing the required market share to achieve commercial viability yields two significant insights with profound implications for the intensity of actual and potential competition to be anticipated in any domain.

First, it is possible to identify the maximum number of profitable competitors. If a particular sector opportunity can sustain a competitor at a 5 percent market share, twenty market participants can thrive indefinitely. If high fixed costs dictate a 35 percent break-even market share by contrast, monopoly or duopoly are the only sustainable market structures.

This dynamic explains why truly global markets often are significantly less lucrative for operators than the purely local ones that had previously prevailed—with the dramatic increase in total market opportunity typically comes a decrease in the newly relevant global (as opposed to local) market share at which viability is achieved. When two or three manufacturers dominated their respective national markets, whether automotive or electronics, shareholder returns were significantly higher than in international markets where a single-digit market share is usually all that is required to eke out a profit.

Second, it is possible to estimate how long it would take for a new entrant to achieve breakeven. The stronger the barriers to entry in a given sector, the less movement there is in market shares in a given year. A good sign of high barriers is a normalized share shift within a sector of under 5 percent over a two-to-three-year period. A new entrant to a market that requires a 15 percent share to break even and in which shares never move more than 3 percent annually could not hope to achieve profitability in under five years.

While valuable in theory, it could be argued that such data is simply not available for explosive new disruptive markets and digital business models. Who could have anticipated the size and characteristics of the markets for search and social networking in advance? Venture capital pitches for even the most trivial "innovation" invariably include a description of the multibillion dollar "total addressable market" (TAM) potential.[5] If nothing else, these demonstrate how arbitrary such market definitions are and how challenging it is to identify a meaningful break-even market share.

Nonetheless, the focus on steady-state industry break-even market share highlights the strategic importance of supply-side scale and economics in establishing enduring network effects businesses. While TAM is hard to put one's finger on, gross margins and fixed-cost requirements are not. Viable industries without meaningful fixed-cost requirements often allow competitors to operate at very low break-even market shares. And even industries where costs are predominantly fixed, but extremely low relative to the overall addressable market opportunity, can support many competitors. Either circumstance implies a relatively short time to achieve a sustainable level of turnover and makes market entry relatively attractive. It also makes the establishment of relative scale in the first place less likely and amplifies the vulnerability of an early mover who managed to secure it nonetheless.

The concept of break-even economics defines the maximum potential number of scale players in an industry. This is relevant for assessing either the demand- or supply-side advantages that could be available in a given business line. There are, however, other characteristics specific to network effects that constrain their potential value in particular contexts.

The Strategic Importance of Relative Fixed Costs

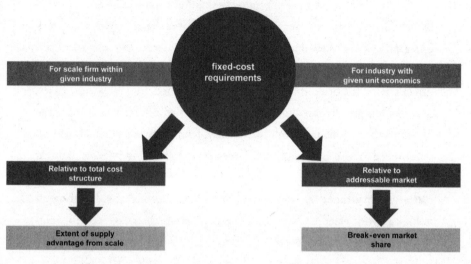

For scale firm within given industry

fixed-cost requirements

For industry with given unit economics

Relative to total cost structure

Relative to addressable market

Extent of supply advantage from scale

Break-even market share

Figure 2.2

Two are worth highlighting—one related to the nature of the network's value proposition and one related to the structure of its participants.

First, how big a network needs to be to achieve product viability—and the extent and duration of incremental product enhancement from additional size—depends primarily on how complex the product or service being offered is.[6] In marketplace businesses, in which the importance of broad selection is negligible and the relevant product characteristics are few, the value of network size tends to have a cap. So, in ride sharing, where the ability to deliver a car within three to five minutes dominates all other customer considerations, adding drivers to the network beyond this point is of little value. Even in a domain like restaurant reviews, where the number of salient considerations is broader, the incremental value of recent reviews beyond a certain number tails off quickly. By contrast, in dating applications, where the breadth and variety of relevant human attributes is endless, the continuing value of additional network participants is more durable.

Second, where a single or relatively small group of users are responsible for disproportionate activity on the network, the ability of a network operator to retain the value created by scale is hindered. In these instances, the users will have leverage to capture value whether through pricing, direct payments, or establishing their own network. In any of these cases, it is challenging for an independent operator to establish a compelling platform that is able to secure the benefits from network effects for itself.

Indeed, there are many examples where large users have banded together to establish their own highly successful platforms. For instance, the largest insurance companies and banks have both created highly profitable network effects driven businesses built on their collective ownership of a critical mass of valuable categories of risk data. The insurance industry created a nonprofit called Insurance Services Office (ISO) fifty years ago to pool data from their property/casualty insurance members to improve their collective risk assessments. The business became a for-profit in 1996 and today represents the core asset of Verisk Analytics, a $30 billion public company.[7] Similarly, in the 1990s, large banks realized they could mitigate deposit losses if they shared data. They turned this into a wholly owned business called Early Warning, which today provides broader fraud protection to over twenty-five hundred financial institutions.[8] This ability of large users to capture value or establish their own platforms is also why smart private investors who look at "marketplace" businesses usually limit their search to so-called many-to-many markets, where the risk of disintermediation by customers is limited.[9]

The potential demand and supply advantages that may flow from relative industry scale should not be viewed as in competition but potentially mutually reinforcing. Take a business like Ancestry.com, the world's largest genealogical service.[10] In addition to the fixed costs associated with developing and maintaining the platform, the company has built up a database of 27 billion family history records across eighty countries,

Potential Impact of Network Effects by Industry Use Case

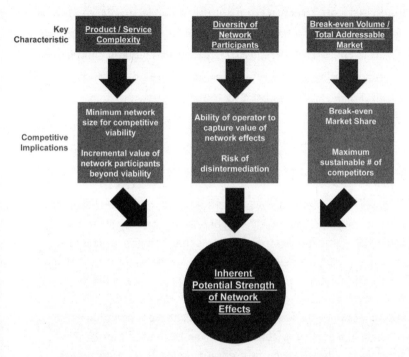

Figure 2.3

much of it purchased or licensed. The original data assets may have attracted subscribers initially, but it is the network effects that come from the unique user-generated content and the increasing likelihood of connecting with a long-lost family member that makes any effort to just license the same records where possible or outbid Ancestry.com for new data sets seem futile. And the more network effects drive subscriber growth, the more Ancestry.com is able to invest further in content and technology enhancements that make the prospects for a potential new entrant even more bleak. If the business relied either only on fixed-cost supply advantages or only on the network effects from users, it would be much more vulnerable to competitive attack from alternative platforms.

Debating which flavor of scale advantage is preferable in the abstract is not meaningful. Different sectors exhibit stronger or weaker demand- or supply-side advantages from scale. Nor are network effects or a fixed-cost-dominated cost structure strategically valuable in the absence of relative scale. And although it is not impossible for a network effects business of scale to consistently produce superior returns without complementary advantages either on the supply side or otherwise, as we discuss in more detail shortly, it is a whole lot harder.

KEY CHAPTER TAKEAWAYS

1. The advantages of scale are central to most strong franchises. The internet-facilitated reduction of fixed-cost requirements undermines the extent of supply-side scale benefits available to incumbents. Conversely, the internet has enhanced the potential availability of demand-side benefits of scale through the power of network effects.

2. All network effects are not equal. Their inherent potential value at scale in a particular context is driven by the complexity of the product or service being offered, the diversity of network participants, and the break-even market share required given the market size and industry cost structure.

3. Demand-side and supply-side scale advantages are not in competition but, in many of the strongest digital franchises, mutually reinforcing. The importance of break-even market share in determining the likely intensity of competitive pressure in a sector highlights the continuing relevance of supply-side considerations even in assessing the attractiveness of network effects businesses.

3

IT TAKES A VILLAGE: THE SOURCES OF DIGITAL COMPETITIVE ADVANTAGE

ONE IS THE LONELIEST NUMBER

One fundamental thing that demand-side and supply-side scale advantages have in common is that neither is terribly durable on their own.

Relatively few markets can really only support a single competitor—a so-called natural monopoly. A single scale incumbent that dominates a sector that can sustain multiple participants will certainly enjoy superior returns for a time. But if its only advantage is scale on the supply side, it is vulnerable to anyone with deep pockets and an interest in sharing the spoils. If there is nothing that otherwise impedes customers from easily moving, a compelling business plan could be developed to invest—either by rolling up smaller competitors or building a new scale one organically—in establishing a comparably sized competitor. And depending on the market characteristics, even after these two scale players split the market, they could be susceptible to attack from a third and so on.

This fate can be avoided, however, where a supply-side scale advantage is complemented by other competitive advantages that impede the ability of others with ready cash to easily copy and divide the market. Historically, the strongest analog supply-side-driven scale franchises have been paired with a variety of demand-side advantages. What all these fortifying advantages have in common is that they encourage existing customers to stay put in the face of an identical, or even somewhat better, offer by a new entrant. The combined impact of fixed-cost-supported scale and a captive customer base is that an incumbent can avoid splitting the market by aggressively matching any offer made by a well-financed insurgent. By making this match strategy clear up front, financing is likely to dry up for potential competitors and the threatened insurgency may never materialize in the first place.

Network effects—the key demand-side advantage potentially enabled by relative scale—by themselves can be similarly fragile. What's more, in digital environments, the ability to secure complimentary "customer captivity" advantages is often compromised. Beyond simple habit, the most typical forms of customer captivity are switching costs and search costs. What makes the internet such a revolutionary medium for consumers is the ease with which it allows switching and searching. These advantages for the consumer are usually not so good for the producer.

A simple historic example demonstrates the point. In the 1990s, the SEC introduced rules that allowed alternative trading systems to emerge, enabling market participants to inexpensively trade equities outside of the established exchanges. The resulting Electronic Communications Networks (ECNs) were classic network effects businesses: buyers attracted sellers and market liquidity attracted more market liquidity. And the sector experienced huge growth as new technology platforms emerged to wrest trading volume away from the high-cost incumbent platforms where most activity had previously occurred.

But the hedge funds and professional traders who participated in these networks had no more loyalty to one ECN over another than they had had for the predecessor exchanges that they had quickly abandoned. Each new ECN would invariably offer lower transaction fees. The impact of even a fraction of a cent reduction in the rate charged often resulted in immediate and massive shifts in liquidity pools among ECNs. Traders cared only about "best execution"—the net price available for a given security after commissions—resulting in wild shifts in market share among new low-cost competitors and a race to the bottom in commissions. As far as network effects are concerned, a virtuous circle can quickly become a vicious one.

THAT'S WHAT FRIENDS ARE FOR

But the news is not uniformly bad for demand-side scale. There are some unique benefits available to producers operating in digital environments relative to analog ones. Specifically, businesses interacting with their users digitally are able to learn more about and develop a direct relationship with their customers in ways that their analog counterparts cannot. This closer digital customer connection can translate into a number of other competitive advantages. Continuous interactions facilitate continuous product improvement and could accentuate the slope of the learning curve. Existing digital customers can more easily be a source of new customer referrals, potentially reducing customer acquisition costs.

More generally, depending on the use case, the availability of "big data" collected over time from these digital customers could have any number of beneficial applications, including those leveraging predictive analytics or even artificial intelligence. Although truly foundational proprietary technology that alone creates a sustainable competitive advantage—think of Qualcomm's wireless technology patents—remains exceedingly rare, the combination of cutting-edge technology with unique data sets can yield distinctive insights that provide real operational advantages. Google Search's greatest advantage over Bing derives not from how much better its secret search algorithm is but how many previous searches by the same user it has already undertaken.

So, if strong analog fixed-cost-scale businesses are most often paired with customer captivity, digital network effects businesses seem to lend themselves to reinforcing advantages on the supply side, whether from learning, data and artificial intelligence, fixed-cost scale itself, or a combination of cost advantages. This is not to suggest that such network effects can only be buttressed in this way. For instance, the ability to personalize the product experience can mitigate the tendency of internet applications to undermine customer captivity. The point is simply that the structural commonalities of the underlying industrial organization of each of these categories of advantage supports a directional shift in likely sources of competitive advantage.

Likely Sources of Competitive Advantage in Strong Digital and Analog Franchises

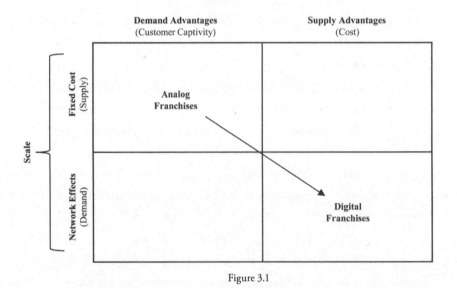

Figure 3.1

The more fundamental point is that the core narrative that underpins the Platform Delusion is misguided. Even when platforms do generate network effects, this by itself should not be convincing to investors and they should certainly not be counting on dominating a winner-take-all, or even winner-take-most, market. The existence of network effects should represent the beginning rather than the end of the analysis.[1]

Resilient franchises must rest on multiple sources of competitive advantage, which typically reinforce each other. For example, although I have described big data as primarily a supply advantage, the data may be generated by a network effects flywheel and manifest its benefits primarily through enhanced customer captivity on the demand side. And as the case of Ancestry.com from chapter 2 demonstrates, data can support supply-side scale advantages as well. But the very structure of digital environments makes it harder, not easier, for network effects businesses to secure many of these potential complementary advantages like customer captivity or scale advantages that flow from high fixed costs. This would partly explain the skewed tally of failed internet businesses versus those that have not just survived but sustainably thrived.

Some combination of high break-even market share, an ability to establish entrenched customer relationships, and a use case that can take advantage of the availability of large quantities of transactional data when paired with network effects can indeed result in remarkably powerful business franchises. What is most notable, though, is not only how unusual such businesses are but also the fact that most of the largest internet businesses do not rest primarily on network effects at all.

It is popular among adherents to the Platform Delusion to assert that the digital revolution necessitates a fundamentally new approach to business strategy.[2] Nothing could be further from the truth. Strategy has always been and always will be about establishing and reinforcing barriers to entry. Even the core categories of competitive advantage have not changed: scale, demand, and supply. There are other supposed categories of advantage—most frequently proffered are a first-mover advantage and branding—that we address elsewhere. Suffice it to say for now that although these can sometimes help establish or reinforce some of the competitive advantages identified, it is the industry structure that determines whether this will be the case—and more often than not, it is simply not the case.

Digital environments have changed the precise form these entry barriers usually take, what combination of them is achievable, and how difficult it is to establish great companies—and generally not for the better as far as investors are concerned. Investors should not look for fundamentally new strategic paradigms or fall prey to the Platform Delusion but rather remember fundamental principles when looking for opportunities in the internet era. This requires a clear-eyed perspective on the disadvantages as well as the advantages of operating in digital environments.

SOURCES OF DIGITAL COMPETITIVE ADVANTAGE								
Scale		Customer Captivity / Demand			Cost / Supply			
Fixed Cost / Supply	Network Effects / Demand	Search	Switching	Habit	Learning Curve	"Big Data"	Propri- etary Tech	
The Bad News	Fixed- cost require- ments system- atically lowered	Profitable scale often achiev- able at very low market shares	Searching is easier	Switching is less costly	Habit less likely to be developed when technology is changing	Often others can quickly catch up	Applica- tions that move the needle are few	Speed of the super- ceding inventions increasing
The Good News	Even low fixed cost can be mean- ingful barrier when coupled with network effects	Digital plat- forms facilitate network effects	Personal- ization may make finding identical alterna- tives more difficult	Personal- ization lowers willing- ness to switch	Digital application may increase frequency of use	Slope of learning curve is magni- fied	Digital exponen- tially increases quantum of data	Truly propri- etary technology is equally rare in analog world and data may strengthen in digital

Figure 3.2

ALL THE NEWS THAT'S FIT TO DIGITIZE

Earlier, I poked fun at *New York Times* publisher Arthur Sulzberger's jubilation over the prospects of a digital future. The case of the *New York Times* is an interesting one in assessing the net impact of the availability of digital distribution and technologies. The *Times* is rightly viewed as a rare internet success story in the news business. But success, like scale, is a relative concept.

To be sure, unlike local newspapers whose content is of little value outside of its home turf and for whom the internet was an unmitigated financial disaster, the *New York Times* has been able to substantially expand its subscriber base from a print peak of not much more than 1 million in daily circulation. Although print subscribers are now closer to half that, total subscribers exceed 7 million. As of 2020, almost 5 million took the core digital news product and another million-plus subscribe to either the crosswords or cooking products. The booming podcast business, which attracts 2 million daily listeners, relies exclusively on advertising, but its younger-skewing audience could become future digital subscribers. Over a half million of the digital subscribers come from outside the US. The *Times* has set a goal of 10 million paying readers by 2025, including 2 million internationally.[3]

But over twenty years after Sulzberger's euphoric predictions, the *New York Times* stock price had still not reached its highs from that era again.[4] And although the number of subscribers has multiplied, the average subscription price has fallen dramatically; advertising, once a majority of revenues, has collapsed entirely. Despite the success of podcasting and other new initiatives like the Wirecutter product review site, "efforts to diversify its ad products beyond display advertising are still in nascent monetization stages."[5] Its total annual digital revenues of $800.8 million, a slight majority of which comes from subscribers, is far less than the revenues generated by print advertising alone in the pre-paywall era. And the company's total 2019 revenue of $1.8 billion, a majority of which on both the advertising and subscription sides still came from the legacy print business, is far below what the print franchise produced alone in 2000.[6]

Let's consider the impact of the emergence of digital on each of the core *New York Times* competitive advantages by category, starting with scale. The *New York Times* long operated in local, national, and international markets, each of which has its own structure and dynamic.

In the local market, the *New York Times* historically was one of several competing local papers of scale. Although not the largest by local circulation, the vast size of the New York market and the *Times*'s leading position in the high-end demographic made this a very profitable segment. Despite the dramatic collapse in total revenue available from that market from both subscriptions and advertising, the number of local competitors has increased in both the print and digital realms. The main traditional competitors, the *New York Post* and *Daily News*, have been joined by multiple free ad-supported papers, with the result that none of the legacy leaders makes money. Although the *New York Times*'s scale relative to its two main historic competitors has improved slightly, its overall share of this fast-shrinking market has actually fallen. The circulation of the largest free paper is double that of any of the paid ones.[7]

Internationally, in the English-language newspaper market, the *Times* for many years operated through the *International Herald Tribune*, which competed primarily with the international editions of the *Wall Street Journal*, the *Financial Times*, and *USA Today*. A descendant of a Paris-based paper founded in 1887, it had operated through a 50-50 joint venture with the *Washington Post* since the 1960s.

This was never a large market—the *Herald Tribune* was the largest player in most countries but attracted scant advertising and at its peak had a circulation of little more than 250,000 spread across the globe—and the fixed costs associated with supporting it made the business unprofitable for everyone. Despite these dire economics, in 2003, the *New York Times* threatened its thirty-five-year partner with introducing a new competing *New York Times* product into the market.[8] The *Washington Post* happily agreed to accept $70 million for 50 percent of the perennial money-loser. A decade after making the acquisition, the *Times* finally rebranded the paper as the *International New York Times* as part of its new digital strategy.[9] In 2020, international subscriptions represent barely 10 percent of digital subscriptions but are anticipated to reach 20 percent by 2025. Although the original reasons for buying out their partner, likely a mixture of vanity and pride, made little economic sense, it may be that the decision was a fortuitous one. The internet's ability to ultimately facilitate over $100 million in incremental subscription revenue in 2025 with relatively little incremental cost against it demonstrates the value of a wholly owned unitary brand in this narrow market.

The main event is in the national news market. The *Times* had primarily been in competition with the *Wall Street Journal* and secondarily with *USA Today*, which had national circulation but no meaningful paid individual subscriber base, and the US edition of the *Financial Times*. In a digital environment, which eliminated prohibitively high fixed distribution costs, the list of competitors for news has multiplied. The top online news sources include not only these traditional print competitors but other primarily local newspapers like the *Washington Post*, which had largely exited the national market because of the economics but reentered it with renewed zeal under the ownership of Jeff Bezos.[10] In addition, existing news producers from other media (broadcast, cable, magazines, and even radio) that have been able to add a digital manifestation relatively inexpensively and a wide range of digital-only players using a combination of original and aggregated content round out the top sites. Even some UK-based news business (notably, the BBC, the Mail Online, and the *Guardian*) that otherwise would not have had any shot of participating in the US market are among the top US news sites.

2000 National Newspaper Circulation (Millions)		2020 Most Popular News Sites (Monthly Unique Visitors in Millions)	
Wall Street Journal	1.8	Yahoo! News	175
USA Today	1.7	Google News	150
New York Times	1.1	HuffPost	110
Other	<0.2	CNN	95
		New York Times	70
		Fox News	65
		NBC News	63
		Mail Online	53
		Washington Post	47
		Guardian	42
		Wall Street Journal	40
		ABC News	36
		BBC News	35
		USA Today	34
		Los Angeles Times	33

Figure 3.3

Source: Newspaper Association of America, eBizMBA rank derived from Quantcast, Alexa, and SimilarWeb

Among actual news subscribers, the *New York Times*'s relative scale has actually improved somewhat. Although Apple News Service's 100 million monthly active users[11] dwarfs that of the *New York Times*, all evidence is that growth in its subscription News+ service has stalled after attracting 200,000 users in the first forty-eight hours after its March 2019 launch.[12] Nonetheless, it is hard to argue that the *New York Times*'s overall relative scale has not declined as it has moved from the distinct national newspaper market in which it was one of a few clear leaders to a much more crowded global English-language news market where lines across media and geography have blurred.

2020 Digital National/International News Subscribers

New York Times	4,896,000
Wall Street Journal	2,000,000
Washington Post	1,700,000
Financial Times	1,000,000
Barron's	615,000
Apple	200,000
Business Insider	200,000
Guardian	190,000
Los Angeles Times	170,000
Chicago Tribune	100,000

Figure 3.4

Source: Public filings and statements, news reports

But how do these benefits of reduced but still significant scale manifest themselves in an increasingly digital environment? Interestingly, not at all on the demand side. As we explore more deeply in chapter 6 on Netflix, content creation businesses, whether digital or analog, do not typically lend themselves to network effects. Indeed, the print *Times* once had a modest but highly profitable classified advertising segment, which did benefit from network effects. The digital *Times*, by contrast, has no significant classified business, so arguably it exhibits fewer network effects.

On the supply side, the benefits of scale at the *Times* are enhanced in its digital form because of the increase in the percentage of its cost structure that is fixed. Because of the elimination of raw materials and other variable elements that underpin the cost of producing a newspaper, a digital news product is overwhelmingly a fixed-cost affair. On the other hand, as is evident from Figure 3.2, the radical reduction in the total costs required has dramatically expanded the number of competitors, which in turn explains the reduction in relative scale upon which this relatively greater benefit applies. To assess the net impact, however, the impact of the digital model on the other sources of competitive advantage must also be considered.

As far as customer captivity is concerned, the impact on advertisers and readers is quite different, but directionally similar. Advertisers have many more opportunities to reach a desired demographic than ever before, and the *New York Times*'s former ability to claim a singular ability to deliver its audience is no longer credible. More disturbing, as discussed in greater detail in chapter 13, is the fact that programmatic advertising allows marketers to reach *New York Times* readers on other websites. This reality is reflected in the dramatic reduction in absolute advertising revenue in both print and digital products and the continuous declines in advertising rates (CPMs or cost per mille, or a thousand impressions).

For subscribers, the unique value proposition is potentially more compelling, but the availability of so many free alternatives has resulted in a reduction in the average subscription price from the print environment, although not as precipitous as the reduction in CPMs. What's more, the potential for customer churn has increased dramatically in the digital realm as both signing up and signing off have never been so easy. Customers now demand that they be able to cancel online without confronting endless hold music and a not-so-friendly customer service agent. The *New York Times* only began enabling online cancellations in 2020.

For years, the *New York Times* mostly lost subscribers because they moved (hopefully temporarily) or died (usually permanently). This is quite similar to the *Wall Street Journal*, whose most frequent cause of cancellation at one point was the deceased's estate discovering that the credit card was still paying the subscription. As recently as 2015, the *New York Times* had fewer than ten employees focused on customer retention.[13] This number is now vastly expanded, and the entire corporate ethos has shifted toward attracting and keeping readers. This is a testament to the *New York Times* management's appreciation for the shifting potential sources of competitive advantage as subscriptions came to represent the vast majority of revenues. Remarkably, the company reports having been able to achieve digital churn rates not much different from its analog ones.

But even best-in-class consumer subscription services like the *New York Times* will always experience significant online churn, and managing this becomes increasingly challenging as the customer base moves beyond the most loyal early adopters. Netflix, widely viewed as a leader in customer engagement and retention, still has churn of around 3 percent each month or 36 percent annually. The *New York Times* may do this well or even better, but there is a structural limit.[14] As impressive a job as the company has done in this area, subscribers are simply not as captive as the advertisers who previously could only reach the rarefied *Times* readership through its print edition.

In the context of platform businesses, this ability to easily shift among or support the simultaneous use of multiple platforms is often given a fancy digital moniker: multi-homing. There is nothing objectionable in this term, but it is sometimes treated as an entirely novel category of phenomenon rather than simply a manifestation of weaker demand-side barriers to entry.[15] Digital environments often create heightened challenges to effectively maintaining customer captivity—in this instance both among advertisers and readers—but in assessing the overall strength of a business, this must be analyzed in the context of the full portfolio of available entry barriers.

This structural reduction in demand-side advantages must be considered alongside new supply-side advantages. The *New York Times* now learns not only about what its subscribers spend time reading but when they exhibit behavior that suggests a heightened risk of churn. This allows timely interventions, but more broadly provides the tools to present and recommend the product to individual readers in ways that are likely to be more satisfying. Although journalists often rebel at the idea that editorial choices might actually relate to what interests readers, it would be strategic malpractice not to at least take this into account in designing the most compelling possible product for a given cost.[16] Yet while these digital attributes give the *Times* more ammunition to combat churn than those with a smaller subscriber base, the absolute numbers suggest that this mitigates rather than eliminates the challenges to customer captivity in a digital environment.

The value of user data might intuitively seem more valuable in the context of keeping advertisers rather than readers. Following readers' behavior on the site presumably allows the *Times* to provide a new level of precision to advertisers looking to target their message. It also facilitates continuous improvement of response rates for specific sales leads in the more attractive pay-for-performance advertising categories where publishers deliver quantifiable engagement rather than just consumer impressions. But unlike in the context of managing subscriptions, where the *Times* enjoys a scale advantage because of its paywall, the *Times* has meaningfully less relevant personal data than some other free news sites—not to mention the advertising giants Google, Facebook, and Amazon.

A final potential upside from data is that by observing engagement, it may finally be theoretically possible to fill in the demand curve—some subscribers will pay a lot for access, some will pay a little, and better data means that it's increasingly possible to identify the clearing price for each subscriber. Publishers have been slow to pursue such data-driven revenue-maximization strategies, although it is not clear whether this is because of a lack of sophistication or a nervousness about irritating customers who realize they are paying more than their friends. It is not obvious how much value such optimization strategies can add in digital environments with such radical price transparency.

It is increasingly certain, given the subscriber boost from the pandemic and the Trump presidency, that the *New York Times* will deliver or exceed its lofty goal of 10 million subscribers in 2025. In so doing, it may finally exceed the revenue the print paper achieved a quarter century earlier in 2000. But its shareholders will likely still see a more modest bottom line. While the *New York Times* will undoubtedly remain one of the largest scale English-language news providers in the world, and may also boast the highest paid subscription base, the structural limits on the degree of competitive advantage available to a news content producer in a digital world impose constraints on potential size and returns.

Some have argued that these results are artificially skewed by the burden of the legacy print operations. On this view, a purely digital *Times*, liberated from the shackles of its ink-and-paper heritage, would fly far

New York Times Results (2000–2025E)

($ in millions)	2000A	2020E	2025E
Revenue			
Digital	$ -	$589	$1,223
Print	477	597	524
Total Subscription	$477	$1,186	$1,747
Digital	$ -	$216	$292
Print	1,306	165	117
Total Advertising	$1,306	$381	$410
Other	$145	$193	$206
Total Revenue	**$1,927**	**$1,761**	**$2,363**
Expenses and Profitability			
Raw Materials		($73)	($63)
Other Production		(675)	(848)
Total Production Costs		($747)	($912)
Fulfillment & Distribution		($145)	($127)
Other SG&A		(671)	(832)
Total SG&A		($817)	($958)
D&A		($62)	($72)
Total Operating Expenses		**($1,626)**	**($1,942)**
Add-backs (D&A, Pension, Other)		$75	$75
Adj. EBITDA	**$514**	**$210**	**$495**

Figure 3.5

Sources: Company filings, Evercore ISI author estimates

Note: 2000A financials exclude *NY Times* Digital, which had ~$67m of revenue and ~($37m) of EBITDA in 2000 faster and far higher. But modeling what an entirely online operation would look like in 2025 reveals something far more pedestrian. A digital *New York Times* in 2025 would be a smaller and less profitable business, even ignoring the cost of eliminating the printing and distribution operations. Even with the generous assumption that all 80 percent of print subscribers who have ever gone online take a digital subscription, the price is so much lower and the advertising losses so great that the overall profit margin stays the same despite the elimination of hundreds of millions of dollars in print-related costs. New digital subscribers do have higher gross margins, so that the overall profit margin will increase in time with growth, but it is starting from a much lower base.[17]

New York Times Digital Economics

($ in millions)	2025E	Adjustment	Comment	2025E Digital
Revenue				
Digital	$1,223	$67	80% of print	$1,290
Print	524	(524)	subscribers take	-
Total Subscription	$1,747		digital	$1,290
Digital	$292	$23	20% of print ad	$316
Print	117	(117)	revenue shifts to	-
Total Advertising	$410		digital	$316
Other	$206	($20)	Lose commercial	$186
			printing	
Total Revenue	**$2,363**			**$1,791**
Expenses and Profitability				
Raw Materials	($63)	$63	Lose materials	$ -
Other Production	(848)	100	costs and printing	(748)
Total Production Costs	($912)		operations	($748)
Fulfillment & Distribution	($127)	$127	Lose distribution	$ -
Other SG&A	(832)	166	cost and 20% of	(665)
Total SG&A	($958)		overhead	($665)
D&A	($72)			($72)
Total Operating Expenses	**($1,942)**			**($1,486)**
Add-backs (D&A, Pension, Other)	$75			$75
Adj. EBITDA	**$495**			**$381**
% Margin	21.0%			21.2%

Figure 3.6

Sources: Company filings, Evercore ISI, author estimates

The *New York Times* case highlights the incongruity between how one particular digital market works in practice and the underlying conceits of the Platform Delusion. More broadly, it should encourage a certain amount of humility about generalizing too readily from legitimate structural tendencies of digital ecosystems. It is true both that network effects are more prevalent in digital businesses and that these are often paired with supply-side advantages not available to analog counterparts. But sometimes scale digital businesses display no network effects, and the extent and nature of their advantages—and the ways in which they work together—always requires a careful consideration of the market and industry structure.

BIG BROTHER IS WATCHING AND SOMETIMES HELPING: GOVERNMENT AS A SOURCE OF COMPETITIVE ADVANTAGE

The availability of one other significant form of competitive advantage has not changed in any basic way by virtue of the internet: the government. Structural benefits bestowed or reinforced by the government are rarely highlighted by companies, which instead tend to cast the government more usefully as an obstacle to the unfettered functioning of capitalism in the service of shareholders.[18] Better to position the inherent strengths of management or the business as responsible for consistent superior performance—and maybe, for good measure, claim extra credit for actually overcoming misguided government meddling. The steadily increasing investment in lobbying by the internet giants, however, implicitly reflects the importance of government munificence to their respective franchises.[19]

The range of government-conferred structural advantages is broad and includes both the obvious and the subtle. This is particularly true on the internet, itself famously the result of the work of taxpayer dollars and government agencies rather than competitively fueled innovation from the private sector.[20]

In the obvious category are government-awarded monopolies or oligopolies, which can take many forms. Individual US airlines receive the right to fly to specific international destinations—sometimes exclusively except for a single foreign carrier, with strict restrictions on capacity—secured through bilateral government negotiations at absolutely no charge. Television and radio broadcasters receive free perpetual leases to use the limited spectrum available for that purpose, subject only to perfunctory renewals every few years. Similarly at the local level, officials offer exclusive franchises for everything from cable systems to public signage.

In the less obvious category, government regulation—often, with no small irony, directives supposedly developed to encourage "fair" competition and new entrants—imposes significant fixed costs that benefit the largest incumbents. When Congress punished the ratings agencies for their lapses in the lead up to the 2008 market meltdown, the result was actually a benefit to these firms. By imposing new burdensome requirements on any ratings provider, Congress ensured that only the largest existing players could afford to comply. After having a brief negative impact on profitability as legions of new compliance officers were hired, the agencies soon surpassed their previous high-water marks of profitability. The leadership of the agencies sleep well, secure in the knowledge that almost regardless of how aggressively they raise prices, no new entrant could ever bear the massive cost of adherence to the newly reinforced regulatory regime.

Warren Buffett made a rare error in financial judgment when he significantly lightened his position in Moody's in the face of the regulatory turmoil.[21] At the height of the financial crisis, Berkshire Hathaway owned as much as 20 percent of Moody's. After a series of sales in 2009 and 2010, its stake fell below 15 percent and approached 10 percent after further selling in 2013. Moody's shares have dramatically outperformed both the market and Berkshire since 2009.

In the digital realm, there is evidence of a very similar dynamic at play in the case of the European Union's imposition of strict General Data Protection Regulation, or GDPR. These rules went into effect in

2018. The ability of Google and Facebook to quickly and effectively comply with regulations appears to have given the companies an additional advantage in the battle for advertisers. GDPR has "entrenched the interests of the incumbent," according to the CEO of the world's largest advertising agency, WPP, by handing "power to the big platforms because they have the ability to collect and process the data."[22]

Government-bestowed advantages can be on the supply/cost side, as in the case of regulatory regimes imposing significant fixed costs, or on the demand/revenue side, as where a public entity provides an exclusive long-term contract or designated "approved" vendors. In the example of the emergence of the ECN market described earlier, the incumbent exchanges being disrupted had benefited from both demand and supply advantages. Traders were previously required to use their facilities (demand) and the new open regime lowered fixed operating costs and volumes required to break even (supply).

What almost all of these benefits have in common—and as the example of the elimination of onetime protections that spawned the proliferation of ECNs demonstrates—is that they can be fleeting. Relying exclusively on structural protections that are subject to changes in the political winds is a dangerous game. Better to use the inevitably limited time behind these fragile barriers to build multiple alternative competitive fortifications.

The risks of failing to do so are well documented. The vast for-profit higher education industry emerged almost entirely out of a lax regulatory regime that entitled applicants to government loans regardless of the appropriateness of the course of study for the student or whether the education being sought was likely to lead to the employment opportunities needed to pay the loan off. The result was an extended period of market outperformance in the sector, during which only a handful of players used the time to build scale and captivity within targeted disciplines, demographics, and geographies. The rest simply grabbed as much government-fueled money as possible while the going was good, using increasingly aggressive direct marketing strategies to often unsuitable students. When the Obama administration cracked down on these practices, many players lost as much as 90 percent of their value or went bankrupt.[23] The Trump administration reinstated the laissez-faire approach, but it is not clear how many investors or operators learned lasting lessons from the last ride down—or how the Biden administration will change the rules yet again.

Amazon is an example of a company that worked to protect its regulatory advantage even as it prepared for its eventual loss. For the first twenty-plus years of Amazon's rise, it benefited from not having to charge the same sales taxes that its analog competitors did.[24] The loophole the company exploited was a requirement that in-state operations were required to impose state taxes on sales. Amazon limited operations to a handful of states with few sales to maximize the benefits of this advantage. Even as it fought to preserve this anachronistic benefit while it gained scale in key categories, Amazon prepared to radically expand its sales and distribution infrastructure so that the cost savings from optimizing its logistics networks would mitigate the need to charge sales tax.

The government's overall attitude toward the technology industry has undergone something of a sea change. Until recently, the global dominance of US tech—at least outside of China—has been a source of pride and a symbol of our innovative spirit. Until very recently, the result has been, with few exceptions, a surprisingly hands-off approach to the entire sector. Indeed, the 1996 Telecommunications Act explicitly exempted the internet from most regulation and included the now controversial Section 230 protection from lawsuits. This perspective had been particularly stark in the area of antitrust enforcement.

Even as the Justice Department had closely scrutinized or even blocked deals in secularly challenged analog industries seeking to rationalize operations to survive, hundreds of acquisitions by the digital giants have been consummated largely unperturbed. According to Columbia

Law Professor Tim Wu, Facebook, Amazon, and Google "managed to string together" a breathtaking record of consecutive unchallenged acquisitions: 67, 91, and 214 deals respectively have sailed through mostly without a regulatory peep.[25]

Part of this oversight was structural, not merely cultural. As many significant technology businesses have few assets and little revenues, a number of competitively questionable transactions have slipped under the financial thresholds for the required government antitrust notification of the Hart-Scott-Rodino (HSR) Antitrust Improvements Act.[26] Google had even found a loophole to avoid giving regulators a heads-up on its billion-dollar acquisition of Waze.[27] Although there is no restriction on the government reviewing a transaction after the fact, in practice they rarely do and even more rarely act given the inherent complexities in undoing already integrated acquisitions. The FTC belatedly requested data on a full decade of transactions to correct these omissions in connection with the sweeping government probe of big tech announced in 2019.[28]

Regulators waking up to the potential dangers of big tech is welcome news. But there is a difference between identifying a problem and locating the most problematic issue and the most effective remedy. The fact that the antitrust authorities chose blocking AT&T buying Time Warner—a deal so incoherent that AT&T reversed it in less than three years—as most worthy of extensive (and failed) litigation to protect the public suggests that the chances that the government will get it right in big tech are low.

The shift in perspective from big tech being given a pass on principle to now being subject to heightened scrutiny on principle reflects one consistency: the misguided notion that these businesses have so much in common that they deserve a singular approach to enforcement.[29] This conceit is a regulatory manifestation of the Platform Delusion. In both instances, the assumption is that their size and strength are not only comparable, but flow from the same sources. A deep dive into the elements of advantage enjoyed by each of the largest digital leaders is the best route to disabusing investors and regulators of this deeply flawed supposition.

THE EMERGENCE OF THE INTERNET has not fundamentally changed the primary categories of competitive advantage or the necessity of multiple reinforcing advantages to build resilient franchises. Scale supplemented by some combination of demand and supply advantages have always been found in the strongest business models. Yes, there are structural tendencies that shift the most likely mix of digital advantages as opposed to analog advantages. But there continue to be a wide variety of combinations exhibited in different successful digital businesses, including many in which network effects play no meaningful role at all. Moreover, though the digital environment creates opportunities for new advantages where none could have existed before, the overarching impact of lower break-even market shares and weaker customer captivity suggests that digital franchises are generally not as strong as the analog ones they replace.

And yet the emergence of the internet seems to have corresponded with an entirely new category of company that is at once larger and more impervious to competitive attack than any that have come before. This observation seems more consistent with the Platform Delusion than the suggestion that every franchise derives its strength from a diverse collection of competitive advantages. And the sheer size of these digital giants undercuts the suggestion that digital franchises are generally not as strong as the analog ones they replace.

The only way to assess which perspective comes closer to capturing the truth is to look closely at the sources of advantage that support each of these vast enterprises. Regardless of what we conclude, the very existence of these enormous companies in itself impacts the structure of the markets in which everyone else operates, in ways that must be examined.

Summary of Demand- and Supply-Side Competitive Advantages

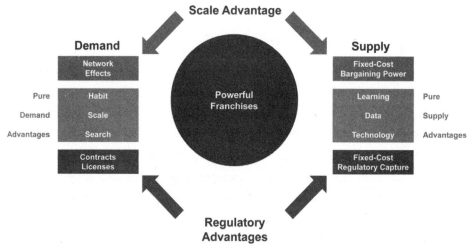

Figure 3.7

The balance of this book concerns itself with this twin enterprise. We begin in part 2 by examining the basis and nature of the stunning success of the largest technology companies themselves and then, in part 3, explore the fate of those who have sought to build successful businesses in their shadow. In cataloging the successes and failures, the strengths and weaknesses, the focus is on the same web of potential competitive advantages that underpin every durable franchise, whether analog or digital.

KEY CHAPTER TAKEAWAYS

1. Scale advantages by themselves, whether manifested through demand- or supply-side benefits, are fragile without reinforcing entry barriers. The most powerful business franchises in digital environments, as in analog ones, typically benefit from a portfolio of demand and supply advantages.

2. Although the key categories of competitive advantage have not changed, the structure of digital operating environments has shifted where and how competitive advantage is most likely to manifest. Digital models undermine the ability to sustain certain entry barriers but potentially facilitate the establishment of others. Overall, however, the level of competitive intensity faced has generally increased because of these structural changes.

3. In digital environments, strong network effects businesses often exhibit supply advantages from some combination of data, technology, and learning but frequently from significant fixed costs as well. The particular combination of advantages that underpin resilient digital businesses vary widely. In many cases, notably in content businesses such as the *New York Times*, the advantages are unlikely to be network effects driven.

4. Government regulation can often itself be a source of competitive advantage on either the demand or supply side or both. Relying exclusively on such advantages is a dangerous strategy given the inherent volatility of local and national political regimes. A wiser strategy is to assume that they are temporary and to use the time to build a collection of more structurally durable entry barriers.

PART II

IN THE LAND OF THE GIANTS

The five enormous companies that constitute FAANG—Facebook, Amazon, Apple, Netflix, and Google—owe their inclusion in this ubiquitous acronym to television personality James Cramer. Back in February 2013, Cramer introduced the concept on his CNBC television show *Mad Money* when a colleague, Bob Lang, came up with the nickname for a handful of digital "companies that represent the future" and offer "the potential to really take a bite out of the bears."[1]

The phrase—originally just FANG, but before too long expanded to accommodate a second A for Apple—has proven remarkably resilient as a shorthand to describe the core platforms poised to suck a disproportionate share of value out of the economy. In the years since its introduction, the acronym has spawned multiple alternative formulations by various investors and analysts—my personal favorite was BAGEL, adding Alibaba, Expedia, and LinkedIn and dropping Apple, Facebook, and Netflix[2]—as new platforms have emerged and markets have gyrated.

Goldman Sachs attempted to tweak the group's composition by substituting Microsoft (which we discuss separately in chapter 14) for Netflix on the grounds that the latter's market capitalization, a mere $70 billion or so at the time, "was not large enough to have a significant impact on" the S&P index.[3] The influential Goldman's efforts since establishing FAAMG as its preferred alternative in 2017 have seemed only to increase the relative interest in the original.

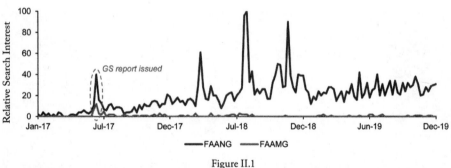

Figure II.1

Source: Google Trends

Even Cramer himself unsuccessfully tried to change the acronym in 2016 to FAAA, reflecting his frustration with inconsistent Netflix performance and Alphabet becoming the publicly traded moniker for the various Google entities in 2015.[4]

Notwithstanding efforts to critique the concept, holders of a FAANG portfolio for the five years after its official naming were well rewarded. Even the worst-performing stock among them during this period—Apple, which only joined the acronym in 2017—did 70 percent better than the overall market.

FAANG Performance vs. S&P 500 (2013–2018)

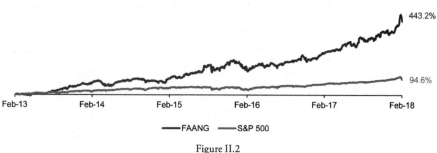

Figure II.2

After a brief pause in 2018, these companies soon regained their momentum, and only accelerated with the 2020 pandemic. More broadly, "growth" stocks have outperformed for over a decade, driven largely by FAANG and its tech brethren, and corresponding to resounding underperformance by value stocks over the same extended period. Along with regular pronouncements of the "death" of value investing, a variety of theories have been put forth to explain this phenomenon, from the persistence of low interest rates to increased market efficiency.[5]

FAANG Performance vs. S&P 500 (2019–2020)

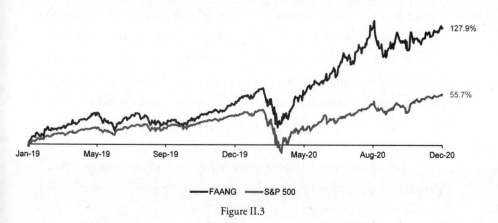

Figure II.3

There is a close connection between the value investing ethos and the overall enterprise of this book—the "economic moats" popularized by value investing icon Warren Buffett[6] are just another term for "competitive advantage" and "barriers to entry." If value investing has been truly dealt a death blow by recent market performance, one might legitimately question the wisdom of applying principles of competitive advantage to drive investing decisions in digital environments. Yet even if one remains skeptical of the relevance of book value—the indispensable financial metric relied on by value investors—for valuing high-flying stocks or asset-light business models, it still may be prudent to distinguish among growth-oriented digital businesses based on their respective vulnerability to competitive attack.

Obsessing over either the precise composition or the ups and downs of FAANG distracts from a much more fundamental question: What do these businesses really have in common that investors should care about?

Across a wide range of operating and financial metrics that matter to investors, the FAANG Five do diverge from the norm—but in much different ways. Take a benchmark as basic as profitability, for instance. A company's profit margin reveals how much of the top line (revenue) translates to the bottom line (profit). Businesses within the same industry usually display similar margins and industries with comparable operating and competitive structures should have comparable profitability. The ability of a business or an entire sector to demonstrate consistently superior profit margins is an indicator of structural competitive advantage.

Of the original four FANG stocks touted by Cramer, all are outliers from the average profitability of other members of the S&P 500. But two are on the high side and two are on the low side. Apple, the late joiner to FAANG, has results that hew closer to the group that distinguishes itself on the high side.

There are a number of different measures of profitability. In Figure II.4, we use the overly generous metric favored by the companies themselves—

EBITDAS, which adds back to operating profit a number of non-cash items like stock-based compensation, which represent real economic costs to shareholders—to make the relevant margin comparison. Even using the more hard-nosed financial yardsticks of actual operating profit or operating cash flow, however, FAANG's operating performance relative to the rest of the market displays the same two-sided divergence.

Another dimension on which the FAANG companies differ dramatically is the extent and success of their efforts to diversify beyond their

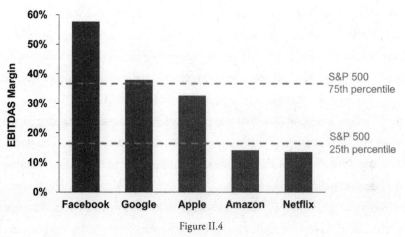

FAANG Profitability Benchmarking vs. S&P 500 (2017–2019)

Figure II.4

Source: S&P Capital IQ, company filings

core franchises. At the extremes are Netflix, which remains almost entirely a subscription-based streaming service, and Amazon, whose far-flung initiatives include the Amazon Web Services (AWS) division that now contributes more profit to the bottom line than the still much bigger e-commerce operations. In the case of Facebook, although two of its three largest acquisitions—Instagram and WhatsApp—are broadly in the same "social" arena as the original platform, these have continued to operate largely independently. With the establishment of Alphabet as a holding company to allow the separation of the search-related activity from other endeavors and investments, most of these companies are now valued on a sum-of-the-parts basis—that is, by calculating and then adding the worth of each distinct business line.[7] Although we examine these companies in their entirety, and touch on their diversification efforts, our primary focus remains the respective central engines of their historic achievements.

More fundamentally, the underlying sources of success for each of these businesses are quite diverse. Only one of the five platforms—Facebook—exhibits characteristics broadly consistent with the narrative of the Platform Delusion. And even Facebook's primary reliance on network effects and its commanding global market share does not tell the full story—either about the complementary competitive advantages that have been central to reinforcing the company's position or its continuing vulnerabilities. The subsequent five chapters are a closer examination of the sources and extent of advantage enjoyed by FAANG.

Taking a deeper dive into the foundation for the remarkable accomplishments of these five businesses serves two purposes. First, the diversity and complexity of the various combinations of structural advantages and operational approaches upon which each of these franchises rests demonstrates the disconnect between the assumptions of the Platform Delusion and how value has actually been created in the digital era. Second, highlighting the true sources of strength and weakness of these digital giants will facilitate a clear-eyed view of the prospects of each and of those that compete in their shadows. The chart on the next page summarizes the conclusions drawn from the analyses of chapters 4–8.

If the core tenets of the Platform Delusion do not hold for FAANG, they are unlikely to prevail elsewhere. Indeed, the Platform Delusion is a symptom of FAANG envy. It reflects the desire for a simple road map to getting in on the ground floor of the next company that might get added to the acronym. If you're going to dream, you might as well dream big. Continued widespread adherence to the Platform Delusion in the face of

Diversity of FAANG Competitive Advantage

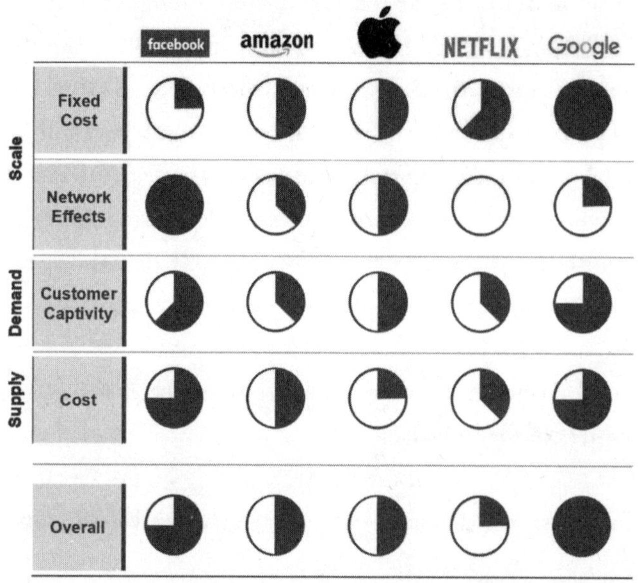

Figure II.5

overwhelming evidence to the contrary reflects the intensity of this de-sire. "The secret of their strength," as Freud said in his classic work on the subject of beliefs based on wish fulfillments, "is the strength of these wishes."[8]

One cannot help but feel that FAANG envy is fed in large part by the leadership of FAANG itself. The fallacy of each of the underlying as-sumptions of the Platform Delusion is well known to each leader, but they all still find value in conveying the overarching impression of in-domitability. To both the audience of investors who ensure a lofty valua-tion and potential insurgents who could threaten the core business, the inevitability of global supremacy is a useful assumption to instill. Just as the media moguls of yore worked tirelessly to convince the outside world of their magical abilities to create hits and manage talent, the tech elite—not just the executives, but the private and public investors who back them—want us to believe that they have the gift of creating unassailable franchises.[9]

Of course, it would be far too crass—and a dangerous red flag to antitrust regulators—to directly make these claims publicly. But there are subtler means to express these sentiments, whether by informal communications to gullible research analysts, journalists, and "thought leaders" or simply by not contradicting statements of others that reaffirm the delusion. And what statements corporate officers do make publicly are still a far cry from the frantic and fearful admissions of vulnerability revealed in their private communications. The trove of private emails recently obtained from top FAANG executives by Congress read more like the pleas of scared children hanging on for dear life than the brave pronouncements of masters of the universe:

> "The businesses are nascent but . . . they could be very disruptive to us."
> "They apparently have lower fulfillment costs than we have."
> "They are our largest and fastest-growing competitor."
> "How do we deal with the problem of 'proliferating verticals'?"
> "We should've owned this space but we are already losing quite badly," and so on.[10]

A solution to this parade of horribles is proposed by one FAANG CFO: "We need a simpler 'platform' story."

Even before we turn to a more detailed analysis of each of the FAANG companies, it's worth making some general observations about the group. Based on the strength and breadth of their respective competitive advantages, the two strongest franchises among them are Facebook and Google. It is notable that both of these, unlike the other three, operate in essentially new business sectors made possible by the internet. Neither was a "first mover," but social networking and search had not been consumer business lines for very many years before they were established.

And although each of these businesses displaced an "incumbent" for leadership, the nascence of the industry meant that the earlier players enjoyed only modest scale and limited customer captivity.

By contrast, the retail, smartphone, and pay television sectors attacked by Amazon, Apple, and Netflix, respectively, were and continue to be massive established multibillion-dollar industries. It is also notable that R&D represents a surprisingly small portion of the overall cost structure of these three FAANG members. Prodigious R&D investment is rightly viewed as central to the success of the great historic technology franchises from IBM to Intel to Microsoft and is still the single fixed expense category most associated with the technology sector generally. Yet all three direct a surprisingly similar and modest share of their spending— under 10 percent—toward R&D. Among all S&P 500 companies that separately disclose R&D spending, not just those in the technology sector, R&D comprises 10 percent of expenses.

Although in Figure II.6 Amazon appears to dedicate slightly more than 10 percent of expenses, a disproportionate amount of its R&D spending is directed toward its newer (founded in 2006) and entirely separate Amazon Web Services division providing technology solutions to enterprises.[11] Adjusting for this factor and focusing on its core consumer businesses places Amazon exactly in line with the other two. Much is made in the press of Amazon spending more on R&D than any other company in the world.[12] But as a percentage of overall costs, this still represents a surprisingly low number. And none of this takes into account that by reporting "Technology and Content" costs, rather than R&D like its peers, both the absolute and relative levels of spending are undoubtedly overstated when making comparisons.[13]

Facebook spends far less in absolute terms on R&D than any of the FAANG companies other than Netflix. But Facebook and Google are the clear outliers when it comes to relative R&D spending. Both consistently dedicate north of 20 percent—and in the case of Facebook, approaching and in some years north of 30 percent—of its total costs to

R&D. If you are ultimately convinced that these are indeed the two strongest FAANG franchises, this additional distinguishing characteristic is strongly suggestive of the continuing central strategic importance of supply-side scale in digital environments, regardless of the existence of complementary network effects.

FAANG R&D Spend

	Facebook	Amazon	Apple	Netflix	Google (Alphabet)
R&D as % Costs	29.1%	13.5%	8.3%	9.5%	20.4%
Absolute R&D ($Bn)	$13.6	$35.9	$16.2	$1.7	$26.0

Figure II.6

Source: Company filings

Note: Reflects FY 2019 financials

Notably, all five of these businesses are global, but none appears to have any chance of achieving a genuinely winner-take-all result. For instance, even Google is not only far behind Baidu in China (where Google is a distant fourth or fifth) but also behind Yandex in Russia, and it has meaningful competitors in South Korea (Naver) and Japan (Yahoo). Broad-based global domination is generally not possible because of important differences in market structures, whether on the demand or supply side and whether imposed by organic economic or government imperative.

The power of specialization is that it is easier to achieve and maintain relative scale within a narrower region of expertise. The smaller size of the targeted market and fixed costs associated with serving it drive a higher break-even market share and correspondingly less competition. Specialization can be geographic but even when geographic distinctions are less relevant, product market specialization can be equally or more powerful. Google does indeed dominate search in the US and most other countries, but Amazon now has a majority of product searches. Although product search is a small part of overall search, given the psychic proximity of this subset of searches to spending money, it is among the most valuable.

The story with Facebook is the same. There are many countries in which Facebook is not the leading social network, and often not a close second. That includes not only countries like China, where it is blocked, but countries like Russia and Japan, where it is far behind both home-grown and other international competitors.[14] And across geographies, there are many specialized social applications with which Facebook has not been able to effectively compete. LinkedIn dominates professional networks and Facebook's belated job application feature is unlikely to change that.[15] Even on the consumer side, a number of emerging social networks have quickly attracted usage built on specific audiences, topics, and ways of interacting—Pinterest, Twitter, and most recently TikTok are just a few. If you count YouTube as a social network, which based on a number of popular use cases many do, it is actually comparable in size to Facebook.[16] Indeed, the core charge of those seeking to break up Facebook is that it has used serial acquisitions of just such competitors—notably Instagram and WhatsApp—to illegally maintain its monopoly position.[17] Notwithstanding those acquisitions, the net impact of these emerging networks has been to steadily chip away at Facebook's still impressive overall market share.[18]

The haphazard birth of FAANG, and how little the businesses have in common beyond their size and success, makes the continuing relevance of the acronym almost a decade later all the more surprising. Examining the varied paths to their respective remarkable achievements reinforces how far from reality the Platform Delusion lies and can provide more systematic and rational tools to search out value in the age of digital disruption.

FACEBOOK:
THE ULTIMATE NETWORK

THE POWER AMASSED BY FACEBOOK, the world's largest social network, is Exhibit A in support of the Platform Delusion—Facebook is the ultimate network effects driven platform that quickly took over the global market. Facebook is a purely digital creature, something for which the analog world offers no real counterpart. Sure, as Professor Niall Ferguson details in his history, *The Square and the Tower: Networks and Power from the Freemasons to Facebook,*[1] social networks have been around for quite some time. But until now, no vehicle has been able to serve as a ubiquitous all-encompassing platform on which to share, communicate, and transact, much less one that could proffer with a straight face an overarching corporate mission of bringing the world closer together.[2] At some point, differences in degree become differences in kind.

And no one could seriously claim that this platform does not feed network effects. Every new user is a potential new connection for existing users, instantly improving the product with no incremental effort by the company. Facebook has over 2 billion users globally, including seven in ten adults in America, which is precisely what makes attracting those new additions so seemingly effortless and networking there so compelling.[3]

This all leads to the inevitable result predicted by the Platform Delusion that Facebook is the beneficiary of an inherently winner-take-most market. Facebook is the ultimate flywheel. And the data would generally support this perspective. Depending on how you define the "online social network" market and which metric is employed in calculating share, Facebook clearly represents a majority—and maybe even close to 90 percent.[4] This has been achieved in the face of aggressive attack by the world's biggest companies—direct competitor Google+, launched with much fanfare in 2011, was finally officially discontinued in 2019[5]—and, more recently, challenges from government regulators.[6]

NOT THE FIRST, BUT WILL IT BE THE LAST?

A closer examination reveals that the Platform Delusion delivers scant insight into either the source of Facebook's original success or its stunning resilience. To start with, Facebook displaced what had been a series of

LAUNCH DATE & PEAK USAGE FOR SELECTED SOCIAL MEDIA			
Name	Launch Year	Peak Usage (MAU)	Peak Year
SixDegrees	1996	3.5M	1999
Friendster	2002	24.9M	2008
Myspace	2003	74M	2006
LinkedIn	2003	260M	2020
hi5	2004	50M	2006
Orkut	2004	~100M	2011
Facebook	2004	2.7B	2020
Bebo	2005	15M	2008
Qzone	2005	650M	2014
Twitter	2006	336M	2018

Figure 4.1

Source: Nick Routley, "The Rise and Fall of Social Media," Visual Capitalist, October 9, 2019; https://www.visualcapitalist.com/rise-and-fall-of-social-media-platforms/; Matthew Jones, "The Complete History of Social Media: A Timeline of the Invention of Online Networking," *History Cooperative*, June 16, 2015.

earlier social networks, each of which for a time was assumed destined for world dominance. The rise and fall of MySpace—which briefly in 2006 overtook Google as the most visited site in the United States[7]—has been well documented, but years before that there was SixDegrees.com. And who remembers Google's Orkut, which predated both MySpace and Facebook and owned the Brazilian social market—until it didn't. All of these businesses displayed the same network effects as Facebook—the hollowness of the Platform Delusion is its inability to distinguish between those that died, those that took over the world, and those that ended somewhere in between.

Monthly Active Users on Selected Social Media (2003–2009)

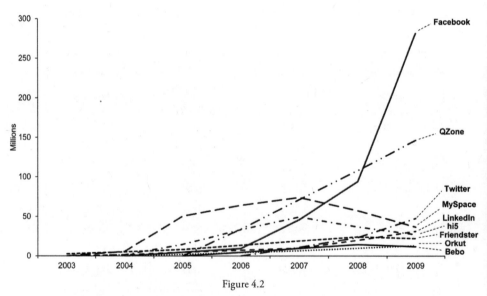

Figure 4.2

Source: Nick Routley, "The Rise and Fall of Social Media," Visual Capitalist, October 9, 2019;
https://www.visualcapitalist.com/rise-and-fall-of-social-media-platforms/

What then enabled Facebook to succeed on such a massive scale, where others collapsed or were relegated to a narrower use case? One answer that may seem flip but actually has profound relevance, not only for Facebook but for all successful technology products, is timing.

No matter how often debunked, the imaginary first-mover advantage continues to be regularly invoked by entrepreneurs seeking funding and executives touting their indomitability. The problem is that where the consumer use case or basic technology are still in flux, it is simply not possible to secure the real advantage sought by going first: scale. It typically requires a succession of first-movers before both of these factors settle down enough to allow a significant investment to pay. It is simply not possible to secure meaningful scale in a market still being defined by fundamentally evolving consumer preferences. And where the technology is viewed as still changing, consumers will be reticent to become too attached to any product or platform, particularly any one that requires a significant financial or emotional investment.

And there is a good argument that Facebook was the beneficiary of propitious timing. With respect to the identification of a scalable social networking use case, Facebook learned from the successes and failures of those who came before as well as from its own test kitchen, first at Harvard and then more broadly within the .edu domain community. The systematic growth of the network by adding successive authorized communities— some colleges, all colleges, high schools, corporates—requiring verified email addresses avoided the Wild West atmosphere that exposed the fragile foundation of earlier competitors. Indeed, it is more than a little ironic given Facebook's more recent challenges[8] that this early trust was such an important differentiator in establishing the franchise in the first place.

The fact that the network was built on deep established networks of existing connections rather than finding new friends with shared interests also created a more resilient platform in the event that inevitable challenges arose.[9] When Facebook launched Chat in 2008, it drew on the lessons of the "chat wars"[10] that preceded it, realizing that a chat function would have particular resonance in the context of a social network. Integrating this feature to allow users to only chat with those in their networks allowed Facebook to resolve previous security concerns with other messaging tools, while also driving existing retention with this added functionality.

Although social networking platforms are not a terribly high-tech affair, a number of developments aided both the functionality and scalability of Facebook vis-à-vis earlier initiatives. Improvements in internet connectivity and platform scalability, both of which proved Achilles' heels for predecessor networks, provided significant benefits. And Facebook's 2007 launch of its application developer platform[11] laid the groundwork for the FarmVille craze that drove its growth and captured more than 20 percent of Facebook's users.[12] Rather than driving out third-party developers on the platform as MySpace had done, Facebook found a way to not only coexist with these applications but also leverage them to attract new users. Importantly, this reinforced Facebook's direct network effects with indirect effects and turned what was a simple social network into a broader conduit for sharing and experiencing third-party software and content.

Timing is critical to achieving scale but cannot alone explain Facebook's remarkable staying power. We have seen in the case of financial exchanges, for instance, that network scale by itself is singularly fragile when not coupled with some customer stickiness. Nothing stops a new entrant from using the exact same timing advantages enjoyed by Facebook for its own purposes. In the case of financial exchanges, the new entrants just lowered commissions and watched the buyers and sellers shift networks overnight. To be sure, anonymous buyers and sellers concerned only with best execution might be easier structurally to move than real relationships with identified individuals. But if someone were offering a demonstrably better deal—free move tickets or iTunes, anyone?—how hard would it be to convince your most important user groups to join you on a new platform?

From day one, founder Mark Zuckerberg was maniacally driven by the need to invest in reinforcing customer captivity in all its forms— switching, habit, and search. "I think the strategy of Facebook," Zuckerberg said, synthesizing the company's primary focus, "is to learn as quickly as possible what our community wants us to do."[13] That ranged from the obvious, like building exhaustive user profiles chock-full of details and photos that would be a total drag to re-create elsewhere, to the subtle, like instituting addictive notifications related to friends' changes in status that made regular interactions with the platform a habit of daily life. One can

SELECTED FACEBOOK FUNCTIONALITY ADDITIONS			
Feature	Year Added	Related Acquisitions	Notes
Facebook Photos	2005	DivvyShot (2010)	
Facebook Groups	2005	ShareGrove (2010)	
Facebook NewsFeed	2006	FriendFeed (2009)	
Facebook Platform	2007		3rd Party Developer API
Facebook Games	2007		
Facebook Chat	2008		
Like Button	2009		
Facebook Community Pages	2010		Wikipedia Integration
Facebook Messenger	2011	Zenbe (2010), Beluga (2011)	Replaced Facebook Chat
Facebook Emoticons	2013		
Facebook Instant Articles	2015		Streamlined Display for Published Articles
Facebook Marketplace	2016		
Facebook Live	2016	Fayteq AG (2017)	
Facebook Workplace	2016	Redkix (2018)	Slack Competitor
Facebook Pay	2019		Payments through Messenger
Calibra (rebranded Novi)	Announced 2019	ServiceFriend (2019)	Bitcoin Wallet Service
Facebook Gaming	2020		Gaming Livestreaming

Figure 4.3

look at the rollout of the Facebook product road map as a relentless digging of the customer captivity moat around the citadel of scale.

When it comes to customer captivity, Facebook is the ultimate Hotel California. In addition to making it a lovely place, Zuckerberg and his minions make it really hard to leave. A number of years ago, a happily married investment banking colleague of mine, having been friended by one too many exes, decided that exiting the platform was a prudent move. Although he ultimately succeeded, his painful description of the process made it evident that such a move would be likely abandoned by anyone less persistent.[14]

Since my colleague's experience, Facebook has made deleting an account far more seamless. But removing all trace of oneself from Facebook—not to be confused with deactivating an account, which allows a later change of heart and the service to continue to follow your every online move in the interim—still involves a number of steps and is likely to be far more painful than anticipated.[15] First you will probably want to let all the people you normally communicate with either through Facebook or Messenger know your new preferred mode of contact. Then you need to delete the app from any devices on which it sits and, most important, download a copy of all of your Facebook data. Most problematic is the web of third-party apps you currently sign into with your Facebook account. This will require you to log into each of these to disconnect that feature, but some of these, like Spotify, may require you to set up an entirely new account.[16] Other apps actually insist on an active Facebook account. And, of course, you will need to delete Instagram and WhatsApp separately. Facebook helpfully provides thirty days for you to change your mind, and if you log in during that time, even accidentally through an app you forgot to disconnect, you will have to start the process all over again.[17]

In addition to these deep demand advantages that buttress Facebook's network effects, the company is also blessed with prodigious supply advantages. The ability to aggressively roll out new, valuable product features is enhanced by Facebook's unmatched ongoing learning regarding how its users interact with the platform. Yes, the most successful new features can be copied. But Facebook can always stay one step ahead.

What's more, Facebook doesn't just have bigger data, the data it has is extraordinarily useful in predicting purchasing behavior.[18] As a result, Facebook can be smarter about how to target specific ads to generate higher click-throughs and more relevant impressions. Facebook works hard to leverage its data advantage with both members and advertisers. Its massive user base is an ideal petri dish through which to examine the attractiveness of features and the effectiveness of ads.

Facebook then enjoys hefty advantages on both the demand and supply side flanking the core network effects upon which the franchise rests. What's more, the sheer size of Facebook has endowed it with supply-side scale derived from large fixed costs as well as the demand-side scale of network effects. Although Facebook's R&D spend is a fraction of Amazon's, Google's, and Apple's, at more than $10 billion annually, it still represents a formidable barrier to a new entrant, and its investments have actually been growing faster than these peers in recent years.[19] R&D also represents a higher percentage of its overall cost base than for any of the other FAANG members.

In addition to this impressive collection of structural advantages, Facebook exhibits two valuable characteristics that are related but distinct: focus and a culture of operating efficiency. Most of the other FAANG companies have become conglomerates of sorts, entering a variety of entirely new lines of business quite different from where they began. With few exceptions—we can forgive Zuckerberg the Oculus VR acquisition— every major organic and inorganic investment has been directed toward enhancing or protecting the core social network franchise. As we discuss shortly, that protection has sometimes come in the form of simply taking out an emerging competing network that relies on an entirely different basis of interaction among members.

Focus facilitates but does not ensure effective operations. It is easier to attract top talent committed to the core activity, and sometimes even to entice acquisition targets to take less than top dollar, when there is no question as to business priorities. And a key corporate asset—the time and attention of top management—can be directed toward optimizing a singular mission rather than managing warring internal factions that inevitably vie for attention and resources. Facebook's emphasis on efficiency as well as focus, however, has proven an additional tool to both protect and fully leverage the demand and supply advantages that are needed to buttress scale.

The key risk to customer captivity (the demand advantage) is to disappoint or just surprise an otherwise loyal customer. There are many ways to lose a customer, and operating disciplines are an important protection against most of them. Product flaws or inconsistencies can break a habit or provide an excuse to switch. Failure to deliver on any promised benefits or improvements can have similar results. Finally, the relentless addition of new product enhancements—and Facebook has long been famous for an aggressive culture of continuous improvement[20]—increases satisfaction and ingrains habit while making it more difficult to successfully search out a comparable alternative.

Proprietary technology or data (the supply advantage) on the other hand, is only as valuable as an effective operator makes it. It is de rigueur today, when a company puts itself up for sale, to tout the "untapped potential" of the data amassed over time. In truth, often the data is of little value. But sometimes information can actually be useful, and the failure to exploit it is simply a reflection of ineffective management (an odd quality for management to tout). The speed with which a company barrels down the learning curve is a function of how good a management team is at learning from experience by leveraging its informational and technological resources. And this too is an area in which Facebook has consistently excelled.

So it seems that Facebook enjoys almost every conceivable structural competitive advantage, each of which reinforces the other and all of which are reinforced by its maniacal focus and operating disciplines. What could go wrong?

NETWORK VULNERABILITY

Every competitive advantage has its own Achilles' heel. For successful network effects businesses, there are two primary threats.

First, it is well established that there are diminishing returns to scale. Although the observation is usually made in the context of fixed-cost-scale businesses, it is often as true, if not more, in the context of network effects businesses. There comes a time when a network is plenty big for its purposes and incremental participants don't add much incremental value.[21] A review of the demise of Friendster shows that after a certain point in social networks, incremental participants—particularly if they are trolls, pedophiles, catfishers, scam artists, or hostile governments—can actually detract meaningfully from value.

Because scale is relative, the big guys in a sense always become a victim of their own success. Even without diminishing returns, the law of large numbers ensures that the most nimble insurgents are always able to gain relative scale off an initially small base. Doubling every year is harder when you have over $50 billion in revenues, as Facebook does, as opposed to $50 million or even $500 million. What's more, dominant mass scale usually hides relative scale vulnerabilities within particular geographies, demographics, or interest groups.

Such niches are fertile ground for new entrants, as effective customization through innovative specialized product functionality and creative marketing can quickly establish relative scale within the target market. Often scale in the niche is more relevant to endemic advertisers and targeted users than sheer absolute size. And, as many once dominant off-line and online media giants have learned from bitter experience, the presence of enough niche players with scale in their segment can really make a dent or even kill a mass business. Comdex, once the wildly profitable broad-based technology trade show, was niched to death by competing specialized shows focusing on increasingly narrow subsectors. Yahoo and AOL were for a time the indispensable on-ramps to the internet writ large but are now a shadow of their former selves as users increasingly turn to services dedicated to their particular needs and interests.

Facebook has always been well aware of this inherent risk and has aggressively tried to stay ahead of it both by continuous product development and by quickly copying the functionality of new entrants who seem to gain traction. Despite the prodigious structural advantages described, even these efforts alone have not been fully successful as a number of differentiated social networks have gained traction. Until recently at least, Facebook had one additional critical tool in its kit to push back against ongoing threats to its relative position: mergers and acquisitions.

A company's acquisitions serve as an important "tell" with respect to its leadership's own perception of potential vulnerabilities. The list of disastrous deals is far longer than the list of the wildly successful. There are many ways for a deal to be perceived as a failure, from bad strategy to bad execution to just overpaying. Often it is some combination of these factors. Given the apparent risks, particularly of large, high-profile M&A, it is safe to assume that the perceived dangers of not doing the deal were even greater. Hence the potential insight into a company's self-assessment of the risks to its standalone organic business plan and the limitations of its internal development capabilities.

Facebook's acquisition of Instagram in 2012 for $1 billion and WhatsApp in 2014 for $19 billion—as of December 2020 both are now subject to retroactive attack by the newly aggressive state and federal antitrust authorities[22]—are only its most notable acquisitions of competing social media and communication tools that managed to establish meaningful scale notwithstanding its own prodigious advantages. Instagram was strongest in the teen demographic and mobile, where Facebook was weakest, and WhatsApp had been acquiring users faster than any company in history.[23] Zuckerberg's emails highlight his belief that there are "a finite number of different social mechanics to invent" but that these alternative "social products" would have their own network effects. Buying as many of these potential threats that operated completely outside of the orbit of Facebook was a key strategy, as there are no easy or obvious ways to directly compete with one social mechanic from within the framework of another. But at the end of the day, finite can still be a big number, and you can only buy so many—eventually regulators will catch on. As Zuckerberg conceded in an email to his CFO, "what we are really buying is time."[24]

My Columbia colleague Professor Tim Wu has ruefully noted that "Facebook managed to string together sixty-seven unchallenged acquisitions."[25] But time does appear to have run out on the strategy of using acquisitions to preserve its relative scale. Even before the Justice Department announced its broad review of Facebook and other tech giants in 2019,[26] the company had decided to abandon a potential acquisition of the video-focused social network Houseparty "for fear of inciting antitrust concerns," according to a *New York Times* report.[27] Zuckerberg's apparent aggressive efforts in 2020 to hobble TikTok using political influence may have simply reflected a sense of civic responsibility, or it may have just been the realization that the government would have blocked any attempt to buy the latest competing "social mechanic."[28]

That the government has actually filed its long-anticipated suit seeking to break up Facebook is unlikely to have a meaningful impact on the company. Most obviously, the complaint will take years to resolve and is difficult to prove[29] and even harder to implement.[30] But the supposedly damning communications by Zuckerberg that lie at the heart of the case actually reveal an even more fundamental problem.[31] Competing social networks based on different social mechanics compete for users' time and attention, but there is little evidence that a leadership position in one mechanic would provide a clear gateway to dominating another.[32] It seems fanciful, for instance, that an independent WhatsApp would have been inclined or able to launch a successful traditional social network that competes directly with Facebook. Indeed, given that WhatsApp has generated almost no revenues in the seven years since Zuckerberg parted with $19 billion to own it—even as Facebook invested generously to build the messaging service's functionality and user base—the alternative narrative that consumers are far better off as a result of Facebook's improvements seems pretty credible. The emails reveal a frantic and frightened Facebook CEO scrambling to own and optimize as many alternative social mechanics as possible to ensure his company's continued relevance in a changing landscape, far more than an effort to suffocate an emerging competitor in the cradle.

An empire-building CEO ranting to subordinates online may not be attractive, but it is not clear that it calls for government intervention. Even if one day Facebook is forced to divest the two acquired companies, it may be an "existential threat"[33] to Zuckerberg's social standing in Silicon Valley, but the shareholders will do just fine. This is most evident in the case of WhatsApp, the far more expensive acquisition being targeted by regulators, as it detracts meaningfully from Facebook's bottom line, doesn't sell advertising, and still runs on an independent encrypted platform.[34] If it were to be spun off, Facebook's profits would go up and shareholders would separately own an independent WhatsApp whose public value would be rooted in some nonprofit-based metric or speculation regarding an alternative deep-pocketed purchaser.[35]

The second primary threat to network effects businesses stems from the inherent challenges to securing customer captivity in the digital realm. Yes, the internet provides new opportunities to augment switching costs by integrating historical usage data, personalizing products to increase search costs, and facilitating the regular use that builds habit. But at the end of the day, good enough alternatives are generally only a click away. For a business, the problem with all the remarkable attributes of the internet is that they are available to every other business. The speed with which competitors can replicate your best new feature or collect enough data to be able to entice your customers can be startling.

Inadvertently giving a customer an excuse to try something else is a truly bad idea. Holding on to regular users requires relentless vigilance on product, on technology, and on customer service for starters. And when the business you are in is social networking, it requires trust. And a series of corporate scandals at Facebook have shaken the trust of the user base—not just members, millions of whom have figured out how to drop the service despite the obstacles noted,[36] but also advertisers.[37]

Cambridge Analytica; Russian (and Iranian and other) influence campaigns; privacy violations; the use of the platform to spread hate, fake news, and even facilitate genocide; secret data-sharing agreements; security bugs; shady opposition research operations; inflated user metrics: and that was just 2018.[38] Shockingly, this catalogue of unfortunate events actually *followed* Zuckerberg's New Year's pledge to make it his "personal challenge" to focus on "fixing" the issues related to misuse of the platform that had already emerged before that time.[39] Since then, at least according to a blog post by a group of anonymous Facebook employees, "things have gotten worse" on a number of existing and new fronts, from increasingly vocal charges of institutional racism[40] to an employee "virtual walkout" protesting the company's continued refusal to police political speech, no matter how inflammatory, to intermittent advertiser boycotts.[41]

When the experts weighed in on what went wrong at Facebook, they overwhelmingly pointed to its culture. Specifically, the story goes that its "cult-like" culture "has contributed to the company's well-publicized wave of scandals"[42] by discouraging dissent, using the "stack-ranking" performance pioneered by Jack Welch at General Electric in the 1990s, and using peer reviews to artificially encourage collaboration.

Earlier we highlighted the importance of a culture of operating excellence in protecting customer captivity and suggested that Facebook had long had such a culture. Ironically, until recently, the strong culture had been frequently cited—even by those who now saw it as the source of the trouble[43]—as a key element of what made Facebook "the best run company in technology."[44] What's more, the intense mission-driven performance culture was typically given as a key driver of why it was ranked for the third year in 2018 as the single best place to work in America.[45] After the scandals of 2018, the company fell to number seven (marking the ninth consecutive year on the list) and was still higher ranked than any of the other FAANG companies.[46] The following year it fell another sixteen slots to twenty-third, falling behind Google and even Microsoft.[47]

There is obviously a problem at Facebook. It is not clear, however, that its maniacal commitment to continuous improvement is the problem. Rather, the problem would seem to be the narrowness of the objectives upon which those improvements were applied and their relative priority. The structural fragility of even the largest social networks demands that protecting trust requires a vastly broader and more nuanced set of corporate aims than optimizing customer engagement and short-term monetization.

The range of issues that have threatened Facebook actually highlight the need for greater, not relaxed, operating discipline. As a user or an advertiser, I love the idea of a cult committed to protecting the integrity of the network in the face of everything from hostile governments, scam ads, and fake profiles. The problem has not been that Facebook is a cult. The problem is the end to which that cult has been dedicated.

Trust, once broken, is not easily regained. Whether the current leadership at Facebook is up to the task remains an open question. Earlier we noted the irony of the fact that it was trust that allowed Facebook to permanently overtake the many social networks that preceded it. Another irony, not widely appreciated, is that there is strong evidence that Facebook's enormous scale has enabled it to combat "fake news" and other subversive forces on the internet far more effectively than its smaller peers. After the 2016 election, Facebook hired thousands of engineers and content moderators to great effect. A recent study demonstrates that this reduced the problem on Facebook by more than half, even while it continued to grow on other networks like Twitter.[48] The fact that the overall problem of misinformation on social media has increased during the last election cycle[49] highlights the inherent challenges to effectively combatting this scourge. But although the public and regulators see Facebook with some justification as the biggest part of the problem, it also has the potential to be the biggest part of the solution.

This is not to imply that anyone should feel sorry for Facebook or that they are without fault. To borrow from a superhero movie,[50] with great power comes great responsibility, and the bar for Facebook *should* be significantly higher. But in designing optimal regulatory solutions, both the advantages and dangers of scale must be considered. And in the meantime, users and advertisers do not seem inclined to give Facebook credit for making an important but necessarily imperfect contribution to the problem of malicious use of the internet regardless of how much the company invests in the effort. But the fact that this will represent a continuing and potentially intractable PR problem for Facebook does not diminish the importance of Zuckerberg devoting his cult to doing everything it can to solve the issue nonetheless.

The good news for Facebook, or whatever alternative "social mechanic" succeeds them, is that contrary to the simplistic conceit of the Platform Delusion, the business does not rely simply on the flywheel of network effects. If it did, recent events would have ensured a swift exodus of users to any number of competing social platforms. Instead, the complex web of mutually reinforcing competitive advantages that bolster the network effects have bought Facebook something priceless in the otherwise mercilessly competitive digital jungle: time to get it right.

KEY CHAPTER TAKEAWAYS

1. Facebook, the leading social platform, is a network effects driven franchise that appears to represent a winner-take-much if not winner-take-most (depending on market definitions) market, broadly consistent with the assumptions of the Platform Delusion.
2. The ultimate failure of predecessor social platforms that temporarily achieved apparent market dominance suggests, however, that other factors beyond network effects underpin Facebook's resilience.

3. Timing of Facebook's growth was propitious based on the establishment of widely accepted social media use cases and the availability of technologies and connectivity that supported a satisfying user experience. The success of Facebook's developer platform also reinforced its direct network effects with indirect effects. In addition, Facebook's initial focus on serving already established networks and continuously investing in tools to demonstrate the value of the platform ensured a significantly stronger level of customer captivity once scale was reached.

4. On the supply side, those R&D investments, which represent a higher percentage of overall costs than any of its FAANG brethren, provide another important entry barrier. This scale advantage is reinforced by the learning advantages that allow Facebook to deliver uniquely effective advertising opportunities. It is this powerful combination of supply and demand advantages that make the barrier formed by Facebook's core network effects so solid.

5. Solid is not impenetrable, network effects notwithstanding, as the emergence of new significant players in its core markets and its failure to displace incumbents in other markets reveals. Just as the early trust bestowed by its methodical growth around established networks built important early customer captivity, the failure to reestablish Facebook as a safe place to undertake deeply personal social interactions poses real long-term risk to the franchise.

AMAZON: CAN YOU HAVE
TOO MUCH OF A GOOD THING?

ONE COMPANY HAS COME TO most represent the fears, hopes, and assumptions associated with the Platform Delusion in the public imagination: Amazon. This is in part because Amazon is the only company that has made broad global domination its explicit corporate objective. Nothing, in theory, is beyond the reach of "the everything store," and it seems that a month rarely goes by without Amazon announcing a new domain that it plans to conquer. And based on its spectacular stock price performance, it seems like the hubris of these pronouncements must be fully justified. Between the end of 2015 and the end of 2020, Amazon stock appreciation was nothing short of breathtaking, multiplying its value almost five times in five years.

IN THE BEGINNING: A SHORT HISTORY OF AMAZON

It is easy to forget Amazon's humble beginnings given its current iconic status. If Facebook is the FAANG company whose path comes closest to the narrative of the Platform Delusion—network effects fueled growth leading to winner-take-all outcomes—then Amazon is the polar opposite. Amazon started out as an online book seller whose value proposition was to offer superior selection, service, and price. Its strategy and its motto as formulated by founder and longtime CEO Jeff Bezos was to "Get Big Fast" in this domain in order to improve terms with key wholesale book distributors on which it relied for product.[1] The next growth vector of its early years was to offer other media products, music and videos, that had the virtue of being logically connected (off-line book stores sold these as well) and simple to ship together with books.

Even as it went public in 1997 and continued to branch out into other, farther-flung product categories, Amazon remained very much a digital version of a traditional retailer. Already a notoriously thin-margined, competitive sector, retail seemed only more so online. Not a network effect in sight.

It would be almost a decade after Amazon's founding in 1994 before it launched the "marketplace" business that does indeed benefit from network effects. Amazon Marketplace serves as a platform connecting independent vendors with buyers in these transactions rather than as the actual retailer. Since then, that business has steadily grown far faster than direct sales of their own product.[2] Today Amazon transacts more so-called third-party sales on its platform—around double the volume—than direct sales. But because the revenues resulting from third-party sales are simply a 15 percent commission[3]—unlike direct sales for which the full purchase price counts as revenues—as an accounting matter this still represents a tiny portion of the company's overall business.

There were other advantages to the Marketplace beyond the network effects and faster growth—most notably that, unlike Amazon's original business model, it was strongly profitable. What's more, Amazon has been able to build a broader third-party services business providing fulfillment and other support off the back of its marketplace vendor relationships. This has allowed Amazon to leverage the expensive infrastructure of its almost certainly—even today—money-losing direct sales business. But the integration of Marketplace product into the Amazon digital storefront had a downside as well: a loss of control over the customer experience. For a business whose success hinged on delivering client satisfaction seamlessly and consistently, leaving that experience in the hands of independent sellers—some of questionable provenance—posed serious and unavoidable risks.[4] At the end of the day, given how central the Marketplace business is to the economic viability of the entire e-commerce operation, those hazards would just need to be managed.

Shortly after the initial launch of Amazon Marketplace, a vice president in finance suggested free shipping for customers willing to wait a few extra days as a way to price discriminate between different customer segments, as airlines do with flyers who stay over Saturday night.[5] The resulting "Super Saver Shipping" laid the groundwork for a more revolutionary innovation in 2005: the subscription membership program called Amazon Prime.

Like the frequent-flyer "membership" programs airlines introduced in the 1970s, the aim of Amazon Prime was to introduce some customer captivity into a highly price-competitive retail sector. "It was really about changing people's mentality so they wouldn't shop anywhere else," according to the executive in charge of Amazon's ordering system at the time.[6] Unlike frequent-flyer programs, however, Amazon charged for membership—initially $79/year. In return, Amazon provided a more immediate and more valuable benefit: free expedited shipping on orders of any size.

Amazon has cultivated a certain mythology around the birth of Prime, given its importance to the company's subsequent growth. According to former executives Colin Bryar and Bill Carr—who wrote *Working Backwards: Insights, Stories, and Secrets from Inside Amazon,* a kind of quasi-official treatise on the secrets of being "Amazonian"—the establishment of Prime was a radically original idea that flowed naturally from "the most basic Amazonian drive: customer obsession."[7] This narrative reinforces the spirit of Amazon's first (of fourteen currently, originally just ten) leadership principles: "Although leaders pay attention to competitors, they obsess about customers."[8]

But the idea of a membership model in retail had been pioneered long before in the off-line world by warehouse operator Costco.[9] And, more directly relevant, smaller online competitor Overstock.com had launched a membership program with shipping benefits seven months before.[10] CEO Jeff Bezos sent a surprise email to his team in October 2004 directing them to establish a new shipping membership program within weeks.[11] In 2004, Amazon's stock was stagnating as Overstock's exploded. The retailer was being lauded in the press as "the New Amazon."[12]

During the fifteen years since the launch of Amazon Prime, the company has entered a number of new businesses, overwhelmingly ones in which one or more focused incumbents already had established leadership positions. These ranged from consumer electronics, with the Kindle, Kindle Fire, Fire TV, Fire Phone, Ring Video Doorbell, and Echo, and physical stores, with Amazon Books, Amazon 4-Star, Presented by Amazon, Amazon Go, and the acquisition of Whole Foods, to a wide range of entertainment content businesses, including streaming video with Prime Instant Video, video games through the billion-dollar acquisition of Twitch and Amazon Game Studios, and music through Prime and the independent Amazon Music Unlimited service. None of these products or businesses has meaningfully moved the needle for Amazon's almost $400 billion in 2020 revenues. (Possible exceptions are Echo, which was a first-mover leader in the smart speaker space but has been subsequently losing share to Google and Apple,[13] and the Kindle, which while not first did become the largest player in what evolved into a modest product category.[14]) All, however, are arguably connected to Amazon's core commerce business by either facilitating sales or enhancing the Prime offering.

The one new business that has unambiguously moved the needle at Amazon since the 2005 Prime launch has essentially nothing to do with its core business. Amazon Web Services (AWS), the B2B cloud computing infrastructure business that launched in 2006,[15] has represented a majority of Amazon's profits since 2014 and is anticipated to continue to do so for the indefinite future.[16]

Another mythology has built up around Amazon Web Services' history to the effect that the business grew out of an effort to monetize unused cloud computing capacity at Amazon.[17] This would make the business analogous to the various third-party services aimed at marketplace sellers that Amazon has aggressively launched to amortize the costs of its direct sales logistics infrastructure.[18] But that is not what happened. The idea for what would become AWS emerged from brainstorming sessions around potential services that developers could use. When the head of the company's IT infrastructure, Chris Pinkham, announced he was leaving to move back home to South Africa, he was assigned this project to keep him connected to the company. Pinkham developed the AWS capability that became the core product engine largely in isolation in South Africa.[19]

The fact that AWS has little to do with the rest of Amazon does not diminish Bezos's visionary daring in financing and supporting the project. Microsoft, Google, IBM, Oracle, Alibaba, and others wouldn't enter the market for years after AWS launched.[20] This more recent competitive onslaught has resulted in significant pricing pressure. But the combination of fixed-cost scale and customer stickiness—rather than primarily network effects—that characterizes the industry allows Amazon to remain well positioned and well ahead. What's more, the increasing adoption by large corporations and governments of both basic cloud infrastructure outsourcing and higher value-added services "up the stack" suggests an opportunity to create significant incremental shareholder value here for some time to come.

But what about the rest of Amazon, the disruption machine that aims to sell everything to everybody everywhere? What are its sources of competitive advantage and how deep are they?

THE AMAZON ADVANTAGE

We have already noted the presence of network effects scale in the Marketplace business that constitutes a majority of its transactions but a small part of Amazon's recognized revenue. All one needs to do, however, is look at the company's cash-flow statements to see what competitive advantage it has placed its bets on: old-fashioned fixed-cost scale. As noted earlier in Figure II.6, Amazon frequently spends more on R&D in absolute dollars than any other company in the US,[21] and its largesse extends to capital expenditures more generally. Although much of this spending is directed toward the largely unrelated AWS buildout, Amazon has continuously invested in raising the table stakes in fulfillment and distribution.

The ability to leverage this ubiquitous and mysterious network of futuristic high-tech warehouses connected by a fleet of trucks, aircraft, and now drones makes Amazon the Borg of retail: Resistance is futile. In some ways, Amazon has been the most aggressive FAANG company in publicly promoting its own special version of the Platform Delusion—that when it comes to selling just about anything, it can do it better than anyone else.

But how insurmountable is this scale advantage really? If the cheapest way to sell everything everywhere was with one humongous Death Star technology–enabled distribution center that shipped throughout the galaxy, fixed-cost scale would be a formidable barrier. But the most efficient warehouses are actually regionally located and limit the number of different product SKUs that are shipped from that location. And although scale absolutely matters for the efficiency of these local facilities, there is a point at which the value of size tops out—and that point can be reached by multiple competitors.

Yes, the central technology investment is spread across the regional centers, but these remain a decidedly low-tech affair even for Amazon.[22] Using Amazon as the poster child, as many do, for the case of a company for which "almost every human interaction is removed from the actual critical path in service delivery"[23] is a stretch in light of the company's one-million-plus employees.[24] Conceding that "the only exceptions might be a worker helping pick the item from a largely automated warehouse" only makes matters worse given that hundreds of thousands of these employees work in warehouses and Amazon has admitted full automation is at least a decade away.[25] It is the local density, not the overall size of operation, that overwhelmingly drives the economics.

Offering free two-day shipping required a huge investment by Amazon. The company spent almost $40 billion on shipping in 2019.[26] Fast, free shipping drove usage and market share as it took time for competitors to realize the magnitude of the threat. But today, although it took many over a decade to catch up,[27] free two-day shipping is available from dozens of online retailers, from broad-based off-line players like Walmart, Target, and Costco to specialty retailers and manufacturers like Apple, Best Buy, and Home Depot.[28]

Amazon announced in 2019 that it will move to one-day delivery for Prime members at a cost of $800 million just in a single quarter.[29] Walmart and Target both announced their own next-day programs within weeks. Amazon's continuous upping of the fixed-cost table stakes in online retail is a sensible strategy to protect scale advantage. But it must do so continually, and the period of competitive differentiation that results appears to be getting shorter and shorter, which suggests that the underlying scale advantage is not that strong to begin with.

The very concept of scale is relative within a specific market. "Everything, everywhere" is not a relevant market on either the demand or supply side. Although within a few product categories and geographies—notably books in English-language countries—Amazon is the clear dominant player, in most products and geographies it is one of several scale retailers, and in many it is distinctly subscale or nonexistent. The fact that Amazon profit margins fell in its core North American market in 2020 (as they had as well in 2019) even as the pandemic boosted sales by almost 40 percent is suggestive of the modest nature of Amazon's scale benefits in retail.

We have described why scale by itself is a fragile advantage. Weak scale is obviously even more fragile. Scale begs for customer captivity as reinforcement. In retail, many methods have been tried to instill captivity, with varying degrees of success: loyalty programs, personal shoppers, ancillary services, referral programs, contests and challenges, and creating a sense of community. In e-commerce, Amazon drove increasing consumer acceptance of online shopping through not just low prices but also constant innovations to improve the experience, from its easy return policy to 1-click ordering. These improvements certainly helped Amazon, but alone they seemed to drive limited loyalty as they quickly became the price of entry for all serious e-commerce competitors.[30]

In this context, the establishment of Prime was strategically sensible notwithstanding the fact that, as one Amazon executive conceded, "every single financial analysis said we were completely crazy to give two-day shipping for free."[31] If anything, the company underestimated the psychic power of free shipping; evidence suggests that Prime members spend double the amount as nonmembers. Nonetheless, it's possible that these incremental orders are unprofitable. For example, Amazon could be paying extra to ship lots of new small orders. The net economics of Prime are impossible to assess from the outside as a result—and they have only become more complex.

But there are two problems with customer captivity initiatives in highly price-competitive largely commodity retail sectors. They are very expensive and your competitors, both online and off-line, soon copy them.[32] That is, they become little more than a fancy discount program. This makes them a boon for consumers, but not so much for the enterprises offering them. Like buying a kitten for your adorable child, it is satisfying to all involved at the start but difficult to extricate yourself when it becomes inconvenient later on. Getting rid of the cat can be tricky. More likely, you will be convinced to buy a second one to keep the first company.

So even before upping the ante with next-day shipping, Amazon had spent the previous decade larding the Prime goodie basket up with new and increasingly expensive trinkets.[33] These trinkets were necessary to grow Prime in the face of increasingly aggressive competitive responses but do not appear to have had a corresponding incremental impact on the relative buying proclivity of Prime members.[34] Although Prime has been able to successfully implement membership fee increases along the way, these reflect little more than inflation rather than the full extent of incremental value the service provides.[35]

CEO Jeff Bezos has famously said in his shareholder letter following the 2015 fiscal year that he wants "Prime to be such a good value, you'd be irresponsible not to be a member."[36] But if it is irresponsible for consumers not to join, one wonders how much value is in the proposition for shareholders?

The single most confounding and increasingly expensive Prime benefit is Prime Video, a poor-man's version of Netflix that is free for Prime subscribers but costs Amazon an escalating king's ransom. Amazon disclosed that it had increased 2020 spending on entertainment content for Prime members by 41 percent to $11 billion.[37] And that was before paying 40 percent more than anyone else was willing—$8.5 billion—for MGM in 2021.[38] Costco probably loses money on the $4.99 rotisserie chickens it offers to keep its members happy, but not to this scale.[39] One of the authors of *Working Backwards* led the launch of Amazon Prime Video and Studios and judges its success by the fact that Amazon is now "on the map as a producer of high-quality, distinctive content."[40] No financial justification is proffered, however. In chapter 7, we examine the challenging nature of streaming content businesses even when they are charged for separately. The fact that Amazon feels a need to give away a service that is not only costly to provide but also exhibits notoriously high customer churn reflects how thin Amazon's customer captivity is even after all the hard work.

Amazon's maniacal focus on customer satisfaction, regardless of its cost-effectiveness, makes somewhat anomalous the inclusion of the company's commerce operations in the recently launched federal big tech antitrust probe.[41] For decades, the enforcement of the antitrust laws have been exclusively focused on protecting consumers from higher prices. Amazon's slim margins—a tiny fraction of the profitability achieved by the others included in the probe—and relentless drive to deliver customers more for less, make it an odd target for such a proceeding. Amazon's use of customer data and treatment of business partners are proper subjects of regulatory oversight, but it is hard to see these as antitrust issues, at least as antitrust is currently conceived.[42] An obscure antitrust law designed originally to protect small retailers from chain stores using their clout to impose restrictions or secure preferential terms with suppliers and manufacturers would appear to have the greatest potential application to Amazon. But that law, the Robinson-Patman Act of 1936, has been gutted by the courts and fallen into disuse by the regulators.[43]

The last potential source of advantage comes on the supply side from a combination of Amazon's investment in proprietary technology, unmatched learning from operating e-commerce distribution at massive scale, and valuable consumer data from deep purchasing history. Each of these are real, but the incremental benefits appear increasingly short lived, as the cycle time required for fast followers diminishes. The most recent manifestation of the value of "big data" is the explosion of Amazon's advertising business, representing one of its highest-margin revenue streams and becoming the third-largest advertising platform, although it is still a small fraction of the size of Facebook or Google.[44] Even here, however, it is unclear how sustainable the relative advantage will be vis-à-vis its online retail competitors who have now turned to capture their own piece of the advertising opportunity.[45]

In an unusually candid moment, the limited availability of competitive advantages in retail, whether online or off-line, has been acknowledged by Bezos himself. "We don't have a single big advantage," he admitted, "so we have to weave a rope of many small advantages."[46] Once again, a look at historic acquisitions provides clues to the company's fears and weaknesses. Why would Amazon need to buy Diapers.com—only to shut it down six years later[47]—if the advantages of its broad platform were as deep as suggested? And how could the founder of Diapers then go on to build an alternative "platform" in just a year that was compelling enough to attract a $3 billion bid from Walmart to use as the engine of its competing e-commerce business?[48]

When you are in a business that is obliged to either buy out every Diapers and Zappos that manages to establish a leadership position or invest internally at such levels that it would be "irresponsible" for a customer to choose an alternative, life becomes an endless game of Whac-A-Mole. The good news for Amazon shareholders is that there is no better suited executive for such an enterprise than Jeff Bezos. His initial preferred name for the company was Relentless.com, which perfectly reflects both his character and the needs of the enterprise he established. One wonders whether the only thing that is stopping him from now buying Wayfair or Chewy—the online retail leaders in furniture and pet products, respectively—is the same thing that stopped Mark Zuckerberg from buying Houseparty or TikTok: fear of government intervention.

Brad Stone, the author of the definitive history of the first twenty years of Amazon, has cited "relentless and ruthless" as the key defining characteristics of the company's culture. "Getting the lethal combination precisely right," Stone concluded in a 2018 preface to his 2013 bestseller, "has been Bezos's prodigious talent and perhaps Amazon's greatest asset."[49] Stone expresses the view that these are "familiar values at most successful companies."

A more generous interpretation, and more unusual aspect, of the culture that Bezos instilled was the simultaneous fostering of creativity and innovation on the one hand and thrift and efficiency on the other. How many tech companies include frugality as one of their five core values?[50] Given the inherent competitiveness of the retail sectors that Amazon seeks to dominate, there is little chance it could have gotten this far without applying the same relentlessness to both.

Regardless of whether one considers Amazon's culture ominous or fabulous, it seems obvious that it is a critical aspect of the company's success and inseparable from the personality of its unusual leader. This matters because neither a person nor a culture represents a structural competitive advantage—and because Bezos announced in February 2021 his intention to step down as CEO that summer. Indeed, while *Working Backwards* claims that Amazon's culture constitutes a "huge competitive advantage," by defining it as a collection of "teachable operating practices" the authors unintentionally make clear it is nothing of the sort.[51] And while repeatedly insisting that "you don't need a Jeff"[52] to apply the Amazonian principles effectively, *Working Backwards* leaves the strong impression that the effectiveness of the practices touted stems precisely from the fact that they perfectly reflect the ethos of Amazon's leader. The authors sometimes use the terms "Jeff-ian" and "Amazonian" interchangeably.[53]

Even before announcing that he would be moving to an executive chairman role, Bezos appeared to have had more distractions—turning around a newspaper, space exploration, a new relationship—just as the competitive threats became more intense.[54] His chosen successor, Andy Jassy, has proven himself as the long-time leader of the hugely successful AWS business. As noted, however, that enterprise has almost nothing in common with the much larger consumer-facing and more competitively challenged commerce business.[55] How likely is it that Amazon, a company with multiple but modest competitive advantages in its core business and heavily reliant on extraordinary execution and leadership, should have become one of the handful of most valuable companies in the world?

The answer is not very, although this is a decidedly minority viewpoint. In recent years, Amazon has largely eradicated the opposition, at least with respect to the investing skeptics. And the acceleration of sales and market value driven by the 2020 pandemic has marginalized that minority even further. Success, as they say, is the best revenge. The company has significantly outperformed the market over the last decade, including during all but three of the individual years, and in 2020 the stock appreciated 76 percent. It has built the profitable AWS and advertising businesses even as it has continued to gain share of global online commerce.

As recently as 2005, barely 10 percent of sell-side research analysts had a buy on the stock, which remained stubbornly under $50/share. By

2010, with the stock through $100/share, more than half the analysts had been converted to bulls, although a significant minority maintained a hold or even a sell rating. As shares broke $2,000 in 2018, literally 100 percent of the almost fifty research analysts covering the company had a buy on the stock. And that was before COVID-19 forced everyone to rely on their home computers for almost all forms of commerce. What could go wrong?

The source of the research analysts' collective enthusiasm is the potential for continued growth. While pointing to the share of online sales to demonstrate Amazon's invincibility, they also focus on the relatively small portion of *all* sales represented by the company: less than 5 percent in the US and less than 1 percent globally. This demonstrates significant "white space" on which Amazon can apply its disruptive magic. No reason, they argue, notwithstanding the law of large numbers, that Amazon can't continue to grow as it has in the past—only now fully leveraging the formidable fixed-cost infrastructure and technology investments it has already made.

Although a variety of methodologies are used to derive price targets of 50 percent or more above current levels, some point to the average revenue multiple at which the company has traded in the past and argue that this is a sensible benchmark for the future. Mathematically, this implies that the stock price should grow roughly in line with revenues. And since analysts anticipate Amazon revenue growth approaching 20 percent for the next three years—far above expected increases in equity market appreciation—they unsurprisingly conclude that Amazon is poised for continued outperformance.

All platforms are not equal, and neither is all growth. As we explained in chapter 1, not all growth creates value. The relevant question is not whether there is growth but how it is generated. In *The Curse of the Mogul,* my coauthors and I demonstrated that there was indeed a significant correlation between revenue growth and value creation among the largest media conglomerates over almost a quarter century.[56] Unfortunately, that correlation was decidedly negative. The conglomerates had achieved growth largely through overpriced acquisitions and foolish internal projects.

To assess the validity of research analysts' optimism accordingly requires an understanding of where precisely they see this growth coming from. That is, we need to consider what part of the "white space" Amazon plans to fill in and analyze whether this justifies an expectation of superior returns. In the online commerce business, the analysts point to two primary areas of growth—new product categories and new international geographies.

Before turning to an examination of each of these in turn, let's start with an obvious but highly pertinent observation. Over its history of growth, Amazon, like every other company, added the products and geographies with the greatest opportunity first, moving down the list to less-obvious opportunities. So, in product, after books, movies and music were added as the next logical adjacencies. Consumers were used to buying books, DVDs, and CDs together in an off-line environment and they were logistically easiest to jointly package and ship. Internationally, it began by buying the leading incumbent online bookstores in the two largest European markets closest to the US linguistically, structurally, or economically.[57]

Twenty-five years of relentless expansion later, not surprisingly the "white space" pickings, although still plentiful in absolute terms, are considerably less attractive in relative terms. This is demonstrated both by Amazon's most recent initiatives and the specific potential new categories highlighted by the analysts.

The product category that has attracted the most attention in recent years is grocery.[58] For those in search of growth, the good news is that grocery is the biggest category in which Amazon does not have a meaningful historic share and represents the largest retail category overall after motor vehicles and parts dealers.[59] For those in search of value, the bad news is that it has the thinnest margins and boasts the carcasses of an unusual number of high-profile online failures. Webvan raised almost $1 billion before crashing. Other has-beens include Kozmo, HomeGrocer, and ShopLink.

The online grocer that has attracted the most capital and attention is the UK's Ocado, which is both the leading online purveyor in that country (a 14 percent share in 2019) and a software and hardware solution provider to grocery partners around the world.[60] In the US, Ocado has partnered with Kroger. Many other US grocery chains have simply partnered with Instacart to provide online delivery; incidentally, Instacart has used the pandemic-related surge in business to accelerate its IPO plans.[61] As the pandemic has convinced investors that "grocery shopping is forever changed,"[62] Ocado is not anticipated to break even for many years despite its attractive hybrid business model and sky-high valuation.[63]

Online grocers from the 1990s that have survived, like thirty-year old Peapod, are few and have mostly done so because they were purchased by a deep-pocketed parent with off-line presence, not because they actually make money.[64] In 2020, Peapod stopped making deliveries in many of its markets, dwindling to the role of technology provider to its parent's off-line stores, which include Stop & Shop and Food Lion.[65] Even FreshDirect, which has raised hundreds of millions of dollars and been touted internationally as a "home delivery success story,"[66] has struggled to grow much beyond the New York market and is facing increasing operational challenges and competition there.[67]

What's more, in the US, the grocery business has already been disrupted—by Walmart. Today Walmart is by far the largest grocer, selling almost as much as the next four competitors combined.[68] Given Walmart's physical ubiquity, the fact that "click-and-collect" represents an increasing portion—today almost half—of online grocery shopping provides a built-in advantage over pure digital grocers. About 90 percent of Americans live within ten miles of a Walmart store.

Amazon had been testing Amazon Fresh since at least 2007, but by the time it announced the acquisition of Whole Foods a decade later, it had made little headway in the category. With a US share of under 3 percent, Whole Foods is a fraction of the size of many other off-line chains and focused primarily on "upscale suburban or metropolitan areas."[69] After the purchase of Whole Foods, Amazon announced it would suspend its Amazon Fresh grocery delivery service in many suburban zones across the country that were remote from any of the acquired stores. This move, along with the recent launch of Amazon Fresh stores, suggests a realization that an off-line presence is required to make an online grocery business viable.[70] Given, however, that off-line grocery businesses (even with online offerings) trade at less than a tenth of Amazon's lofty three to four times revenue multiple, the idea that this avenue of growth will be value accretive seems fanciful. Even Amazon's record-setting Whole Foods deal was at well under one times revenue.

What many of the other large product categories that Amazon neglected to attack over the last quarter century have in common is that, well, they really aren't worth attacking. This could be because they don't lend themselves to digital commerce (e.g., services like medical), they are already so digitally disrupted by others that the incremental value creation opportunity is limited (e.g., event or movie ticket sales), that the nature of the product is ill-suited to Amazon's distribution infrastructure or business model (e.g., cars or homes), or some combination of these. Such inherent limitations have not diminished the eagerness of analysts to promote these as promising vectors of future growth.

Take the two largest purchases a family makes: a house and a car. Before the internet, marketing for both was dominated by local newspaper classifieds and advertising, with real live realtors and dealers executing the actual transactions outside of some direct used-car sales.

The online home category leader Zillow took a hit to its stock a few years ago when Amazon added a web page hinting at expansion into real estate referrals.[71] The page soon disappeared,[72] Zillow has continued to soar, and Amazon is mostly limited to selling small prefabricated homes—with free shipping—online.[73] Zillow does also leverage its proprietary data to actually buy and sell homes for its own account as well as provide financing, areas in which Amazon is not well positioned to compete.

In autos, although it launched Amazon Vehicles in 2016 to provide reviews and specs for car buyers, it remains far behind over a dozen advertising-based lead generation businesses in the space. These include long established leaders like Autotrader and Cars.com and newer entrants like TrueCar and CarGurus, many of which have proprietary data and functionality well beyond Amazon's offering. Although strict state dealership laws limit new car buying online, in addition to advertising a number of these businesses have thriving peer-to-peer marketplaces for buying and selling used cars. But the very number of players in these markets, and continuing ability of more to enter, demonstrates the difficult economics of the space even as it has grown. The hugely disappointing performance of Cars.com since it spun off as an independent company several years ago is reflective of this structural sectoral infirmity—as is the inability of the company to find a willing buyer even after it put itself up for sale.[74]

More recently, purely digital used car retailers have emerged with the successful IPOs of Carvana (2017) and Vroom (2020). Others appear poised to follow. Amazon's warehouse infrastructure, however, cannot practically accommodate car retailing and it has no apparent plans to enter this part of the market.

Turning to the sources of potential international growth, it is worth remembering that for the most successful truly global companies, what is captured under the generic label "international" is really a series of tailored approaches to very different markets. The necessity of a multi-local rather than international strategy is driven by the often stark differences in market structure, consumer demand, and regulation across geographies.[75] This is particularly true in sectors, like retail, where the costs incurred in providing the product or service are predominantly local. These dramatic market-to-market distinctions are reflected in the fact that even among businesses with truly international operations, it is typical that a majority of profits are found in a very small number of countries or regions and may even require the adoption of distinct local branding to succeed.

Amazon has obviously come a long way from its first 1998 acquisitions of online booksellers in the UK and Germany. Today the company operates in around fifty-eight countries and reaches over a billion consumers. Many companies accept lower profitability from their international operations in return for a higher growth rate once the domestic market starts to become saturated. What has distinguished Amazon's international operations in recent years, however, is that they have grown significantly slower than the US business even while hemorrhaging money. For the entire decade between 2010 and 2020, international retail grew slower than its US counterpart and, until the pandemic hit in 2020, did not show a profit in any year since 2013.[76] When the international division posted its first quarterly profit in years during the height of a pandemic-fueled boom in online sales, even Bezos warned that it was a "highly unusual quarter" rather than a reliable trend.[77] The overall margin eked out in the division for the overall watershed year was well under 1 percent.[78]

This broadly tracks Walmart's experience growing its international operations a decade earlier, starting with its first store outside of the US in Mexico City in 1991. Although at least profitable, Walmart outside the US has never come close to achieving the results of its US operations. The reasons for this distinction are not that different from the reasons that Amazon outside the US is so much less profitable. Cultural and structural differences aside, Walmart generally entered after a local competitor had built up a brand and an efficiently clustered network of stores analogous to what Walmart had in the US. Walmart retreated entirely from Germany for similar reasons that Aldi is unlikely to make a return on its $5 billion, five-year US growth initiative begun in 2017.[79]

If every number one player in a market could easily become the number one player in every other market, all the markets would have a lot of number one players! The clear leader in the UK, Tesco, learned this the hard way only after it poured 1 billion pounds into its efforts to dominate the US before retreating entirely.[80] Walmart did somewhat better than that in the UK for a time but only because it bought up the number three player and operated under that local brand as it does generally abroad.[81] After its attempt to merge the struggling operation with the number two player was blocked, Walmart sold a majority stake to a private equity firm in 2020 after over a decade of trying to succeed in the UK.[82] Although today Walmart operates in twenty-seven countries, its international revenues and profits now come overwhelmingly from Mexico and Canada.

For Amazon, the situation is much the same.[83] In the US it has taken considerable share from off-line retailers. Internationally, it faces not just these corresponding off-line retailers, but scale online players as well. For instance, Alibaba dominates not just China but much of Asia, notably—unlike Amazon's approach—with a series of local brands while MercadoLibre is far ahead not just in Mexico but in most of South America.

Amazon's most aggressive international initiative in recent years has been in India. The story of its experience there so far should dampen the euphoria over the extent of the share price upside from the international opportunity.

It is not hard to see why Amazon was attracted to the Indian marketplace after its failure in China, where it launched in 2004. Amazon entered China through the purchase of a local online bookstore, and invested billions in warehouses and education programs to teach locals the Amazon way, but still had less than a 1 percent e-commerce market share even after launching Prime in 2016.[84] The company shut down its marketplace business in China in 2019.[85] Amazon rarely gives up— remember, it's relentless—and it has often demonstrated an ability to quickly learn from its mistakes. With India poised to become the third-largest consumer market behind the US and China,[86] it was the logical spot to place a big bet on taking a more nuanced locally tailored approach to international growth, adapting lessons learned in China.

Launching in 2013, Amazon followed a fundamentally different business model, driven not just by local market structure but local regulation. Amazon supported local manufacturers, distributors, and retailers to help build their online capabilities to allow them to work with Amazon. But at the end of 2016, the country put in place a series of rules that effectively barred foreign-owned sellers from operating e-commerce business except through a pure marketplace model.[87] By that point Amazon had already committed to investing $5 billion in the venture.[88] When Amazon designed a workaround by buying a number of large marketplace participants, new regulations were implemented to shut this down as well.[89]

The competitive landscape as well as the constraints on the permissible business opportunity are daunting in India. Not only does Amazon face its home country nemesis Walmart, which had spent $16 billion for a controlling stake in the leading local e-commerce player Flipkart,[90] the same giant online retailers that had trounced Amazon in neighboring China (Alibaba and JD.com) both had long been active there. Most intimidating, however, is India's own massive Reliance Group conglomerate, which already provided a broad range of financial and infrastructure services to a huge swath of India's business and consumer sectors, stunting Amazon's services business.

Undeterred, in early 2020, just before the pandemic halted international travel, Jeff Bezos arrived in India to announce an additional billion-dollar investment in the country.[91] Shortly thereafter it was revealed that the company has plans to launch a food delivery business.[92] Ominously, just before his arrival, which sparked local protests, the government decided to launch an antitrust investigation of the company.[93] On his departure, India's trade minister gave his ungracious take on the fresh billion-dollar investment: "It's not as if they are doing a great favor to India."[94]

A few months later, Reliance announced that it had raised $20 billion for its digital division, Jio Platforms, from the likes of Google and Facebook along with sovereign wealth and private equity funds. Chairman Mukesh Ambani announced that the money would in part be used to expand the platform, which already allowed small retailers to provide consumers with groceries and other local items, to offer electronics and fashion. If India is Amazon's most promising international opportunity—it certainly will be its most costly—investors can be forgiven if they don't place much stock on the odds of the company achieving a higher return on investment than it did in China.

Digital investors often obsess more about the total size of the potentially addressable market—to plug in corresponding potential growth rates—rather than how much of it is worth addressing. In chapter 9, we examine a number of e-commerce businesses that have managed to dig far deeper moats than Amazon by targeting narrower markets that lend themselves to stronger entry barriers. Although their franchises may represent untapped "white space" for Amazon's future growth, they are unlikely to represent upside for Amazon shareholders.

CEOs have an odd tendency to assert competitive advantage where none exists. The oddity is that achieving consistently superior results in the absence of competitive advantage is a much more impressive task than doing so with their structural assistance.

The extraordinary progress of Amazon on the back of "a rope of many small advantages" in its core markets is a testament to the remarkable skills of its leadership. Yes, Amazon is relentless and ruthless. But it has also earned—in contrast to its FAANG peers—an impressive track record of finding entirely new opportunities (AWS most astoundingly) and then applying fierce operating discipline to the nuances of those markets. Even if Amazon lacks strong entry barriers in its original core commerce markets, it is still a great company. Whether it is worth its current valuation, however, is another question.

KEY CHAPTER TAKEAWAYS

1. In its early years of growth, Amazon was a pure retail model, with no network effects and little customer captivity. It would be almost a decade before the Amazon Marketplace, which is a classic indirect network effects model, would be made broadly available.

2. Today, although more goods are sold through the Marketplace than directly by Amazon, it still represents only a tiny portion of overall revenues because rather than the full price of the products sold, the company only receives a commission. The vast majority of Amazon profits now come from the unrelated Amazon Web Services (AWS) segment, a B2B software business that benefits from traditional scale and customer captivity rather than network effects.

3. Amazon has secured some measure of customer captivity through Amazon Prime, whose members exhibit significantly higher buying proclivity. Without knowing the size or nature of these incremental orders, however, the economics of Prime are impossible to assess. On its face, the financial wisdom of many of the additional benefits subsequently provided to Prime members, notably Prime Video, is highly questionable. Similarly, the return on investment of the move to same-day delivery, quickly mimicked by multiple competitors, seems unacceptably low.

4. In addition to the continued success of AWS, Amazon's massive valuation is supported by the anticipated continued robust growth of its e-commerce business. Much of this expansion is predicted to come from new product categories and geographies. A closer look at these suggests that unattractive structural attributes of these markets are a significant reason that these areas were not pursued earlier. This raises the question of what value if any investors should place on this portion of Amazon's projected growth.

5. Amazon's formidable franchise has emerged from a combination of "relentlessness and ruthlessness" on the one hand and "a rope

of many small advantages" on the other. Its aura of invincibility, however, is not justified and the potency of this mixture of attributes varies widely across markets. The overall return on investment of its future e-commerce growth trajectory is likely to remain modest.

APPLE: WHAT'S AT THE CORE?

AT FIRST GLANCE, APPLE SEEMS quite different from any of the other
FAANG companies. In the first instance, the rest are children of the internet. Their basic business models were born of the distributive and com-
municative possibilities created by that ultimate network of networks.
Famously founded in 1976, decades before the first web browser, by the
two Steves,[1] Jobs and Wozniak, Apple primarily makes and sells physical
consumer products.

Of course, much has changed since that time about the business,
only some of it reflecting the emergence of the internet. In 2007, the
company dropped the word "Computer" from its name to reflect its push
into consumer electronics writ large.[2] But most of Apple's revenues still
come from selling physical consumer products. And in each year since the
death of Jobs almost a decade ago, a majority of sales have actually come
from a single product: the iPhone.[3]

In thinking about the sources of Apple's competitive advantage, however, another distinction between Apple and not only the rest of FAANG
but the rest of the technology sector looms large. Lawrence Ellison, the
multibillionaire cofounder of Oracle, was a longtime Jobs friend who
tried to back him in a hostile bid for the company after Jobs had been
pushed out. After Jobs's triumphant 1997 return to the company, Ellison
was the first new board member selected once the old guard was shown

the door. Ellison has no doubt about what distinguishes Apple: "Steve created the only lifestyle brand in the tech industry."[4]

When Apple became the first US company to exceed a trillion-dollar market capitalization in 2017, a flurry of articles appeared purporting to explain the phoenix-like rise of Apple from the brink of bankruptcy to these lofty heights. While these commentators offered a variety of theories as to the core source of the franchise's underlying strength, the one constant is the belief in the indispensable role of the Apple brand. In our earlier discussion of the key sources of competitive advantage, "brand" was not included. Yet brand is central to the accepted narrative of the Apple success story.

BRAND AND COMPETITIVE ADVANTAGE

The idea that brand is a sustainable competitive advantage in itself results from the observation that the brands of many of the seemingly most resilient franchises—not just Apple, but also Coke, McDonald's, and Nike—are inseparable from the success of these businesses. But that does not mean that the brand is the sole or even primary source of advantage. Nor does it mean that having a strong brand guarantees superior business performance. It is worth examining more closely the complicated relationship between brand and competitive advantage generally and the role of brand in supporting Apple's commercial success specifically.

The high-profile examples of strong businesses having strong brands are certainly worth noting. But a single counterexample is all it takes to disprove a misguided universal theory. Just such a counterexample lurks in Ellison's observations following his comment about the Apple brand: "There are cars people are proud to have—Porsche, Ferrari, Prius—because what I drive says something about me," Ellison continued. "People feel the same way about an Apple product."

Ellison's comment about the importance of brand in the automotive sector is well placed. Not just those he mentioned, but BMW, Mercedes, and other auto marques rank consistently high on the lists of the most "valuable" brands. But does a brand's value imply that it represents an inherent competitive advantage?

The fact that every few years brings the introduction of new luxury car brands suggests that strong incumbent brands do not represent a significant barrier to entry. Digging into the numbers confirms that the two indicia of sustainable advantage—consistently superior return on investment and market share stability—are notably absent from the sector. If the industry that boasts among the greatest number of valuable brands has not managed to produce a single company that exhibits the characteristics associated with strong competitive advantages, how can we conclude that brand is a competitive advantage?

Indeed, looking at Apple itself, even when its economics were disastrous, its brand was strong. The ranking of global brand value is a distinctly modern phenomenon that first emerged around 2000. But there is plenty of evidence that at least since the famous 1984 Super Bowl commercial introducing the Macintosh—routinely cited as one of the most effective advertisements of all time—Apple has been a leading global brand.[5] The very resilience of the brand in a company that only very recently in its history has begun to demonstrate consistent superior financial performance suggests that the brand itself is not the defining advantage.

IT'S THE INDUSTRY STRUCTURE, STUPID

If these brands are not competitive advantages, one might ask, how is it that so many of them are worth billions of dollars according to multiple brand surveys? The question of whether an asset is valuable is completely distinct from the question of whether the investment required to build the asset is likely to yield superior returns. As we will examine in detail in our discussion of content businesses in the next chapter, just because a hit movie is a valuable asset doesn't mean going into the business of trying to make a hit movie is a wise investment decision.

The analogy between making a hit movie and building a brand breaks down soon after this initial observation. Making a movie is typically a one-shot affair. Its success or failure will not typically influence how likely it is that subsequent films (sequels aside) will make money and has no structural impact on the overall business. By contrast, even after being established, a brand requires ongoing maintenance investment. What's more, brand building does have a structural impact on the business in at least two ways that are not relevant to the overall film business.

First, and most obviously, strong brands can drive some level of customer captivity, whether by facilitating buying habits, reinforcing a psychic switching cost, or communicating trust or product characteristics for which search costs would be incurred in identifying a comparable alternative. By contrast, if Universal has a hit movie, it has no particular impact on my inclination to go to the next Universal release. While brands can instill captivity of one sort or another, in the case of cars, less than 20 percent of car buyers stick with the brand of their trade-in. Although there is a significant level of variability among brands, makes, and models, loyalty typically tops out at around 30 percent.[6] The increasing infrequency of automotive purchasing decisions—ownership periods now approach seven years[7]—and the amount of time and research typically involved[8] undermine the potential intensity of brand captivity.

Second, the marketing costs associated with building and maintaining a brand constitute a fixed cost that accentuates the financial significance of relative scale. Making a movie, even a very expensive movie, involves few fixed costs as studio capacity is readily available for lease. Yet despite the importance of fixed marketing and R&D costs in the automotive industry, the overall cost structure is still dominated by variable raw materials and labor. What's more, as the industry has moved from a series of domestically focused oligopolies to an intensely competitive global marketplace, dozens of manufacturers are able to operate at a scale that supports the fixed-cost requirements, including brand building.

The point is not that brand doesn't matter. It is that industry structure will determine whether brand can serve as a sustainable competitive differentiator. Customer captivity and scale are the relevant structural barriers to entry. Brand can powerfully reinforce these barriers in sectors where the key supply and demand attributes lend themselves to such support. So, for instance, in consumer packaged goods categories where there is high usage frequency and marketing and distribution dominate the cost structure, brand really matters.

Apple is consistently ranked as the single most valuable brand in the world. At over $200 billion, some estimated valuations would rank the brand alone as a top 20 US corporation if it traded as an independent company. It is impossible to assess the strength and source of Apple's competitive advantages without coming to terms with both the nature of the Apple brand and how it interacts with other structural aspects of the businesses it is in and those it plans to enter.

APPLE ECONOMICS: A PRIMER

During the three decades that Apple Inc. was Apple Computer, the company rarely exceeded a 10 percent operating margin.[9] The exceptions are the few early years before IBM introduced the PC.

The story of Apple is often told as a story of continuous technological innovation leading to consistent superior financial results. Indeed, Jobs himself posited a romanticized version of Hewlett Packard, where he once had a high school summer job, as the model to which he aspired. His goal, according to biographer Walter Isaacson, was to "create a company that was so imbued with innovative creativity that it would outlive them."[10]

One can't argue with the innovations, but the best of these—like the Macintosh's graphical user interfaces—were quickly copied, leading for most of its history to anemic financial results.[11] And Apple's insistence on tightly integrating its software and hardware in a largely closed system ensured that the copycats would be able to scale Apple's best ideas faster than Apple itself. By the time Jobs was pushed out of Apple in 1985, its PC market share was dwarfed not just by IBM clones but by Commodore (remember them?). When he returned over a decade later in 1997, Commodore would be long gone, but Apple's own share had drifted further downward. Jobs succeeded in quickly stanching the bleeding by instituting significant layoffs and radically simplifying the product line. It would be five years, however, before the company would begin to experience sustained revenue growth and a full decade before margins would reach the teens.

The next big innovation that moved the needle in Apple's financial results was the iPod. Introduced in 2001, just nine months after launching iTunes (the iTunes Store would follow in 2003), Apple offered a product satisfying enough to be a compelling alternative to the free services that had disrupted the music industry. There is no question that Apple's original approach revolutionized the music business and reaccelerated growth in their own business. But the secret to what revolutionized the profitability of Apple lies less in the expansion of the internal Apple ecosystem beyond computers to music than the fundamental shift in its approach to the external ecosystem.

The iPod itself was a significantly lower-margin product than Apple computers, and the iTunes Store was never meant to be much more than a break-even exercise to drive iPod sales. The real engines of profitability growth at Apple were the decisions related to how the company managed its relationships with other tech giants. Specifically, in 2006 Apple decided to support Microsoft Windows on its devices,[12] which was made possible by its decision the previous year to abandon its PowerPC chips for the more powerful Intel technology. While iPod sales would outstrip Mac sales that year (for the first and only time), computers delivered the lion's share of profits.

Much has been made of the supposed "halo effect" of the explosion in iPod sales and the renaissance in Mac products, both desktop and portable. But by 2006, iPod sales had already plateaued. Between 2006 and 2011, computer sales would triple while iPod sales would decrease. Of course, one could claim that the halo effect has transferred to the iPhone, introduced in 2007, and the iPad, introduced in 2010. Although there is no question that the common software ecosystems[13] and the introduction of the Apple retail stores in 2001 provided a comarketing benefit, the data suggests a fairly weak correlation. Since 2012, computer sales have remained stable and iPad sales have declined precipitously while iPhone sales have more than doubled.

The introduction of the iPhone and iPad transformed the economics of Apple not simply because they were both wildly successful products. Rather, for the first time, the rapid adoption in both instances allowed Apple to benefit from deep network effects, which had previously eluded the company.

Operating systems are classic network effect businesses. The more users, the more developers develop software applications, which in turn attract more users. The Apple II's early success was attributable in part to the exclusive availability of VisiCalc—a predecessor to Lotus and Excel— just as Microsoft's development of Excel, Word, and BASIC programs compatible with the operating system were critical for the launch of the Macintosh.

Apple's long-standing refusal to license its operating systems to third-party manufacturers, in contrast to the ubiquitous Microsoft system that powered IBM and its clone army, ensured that it would be at a significant competitive disadvantage in attracting developers. Further exacerbating its scale disadvantage was the incompatibility of the different operating systems of Apple's earliest product lines, the Apple, Lisa, and Macintosh.

The iPod, Apple's first noncomputing product, had such a narrow use case that it didn't really benefit from network effects.[14] The only application that really mattered on the iPod was the iTunes software and store. The device achieved and maintained very high market share for a full decade until its basic functionality was subsumed by smartphones.[15] But because Apple played hardball with the desperate major music companies on terms, these partners insisted on nonexclusivity and aggressively made their content available to many others, often with less restrictive terms to encourage competition.

The iPhone finally allowed Apple to benefit from network effects. Announced in January 2007 and launched that June at an astounding $600 price point, the iPhone was a magnificent product that was "an iPod, a phone, an internet mobile communicator," all in one that could be operated through a touch screen.[16]

The real revolution began the next July when Apple introduced the much faster iPhone 3G at a $200 price point—and the App Store. At launch, the App Store carried around 500 applications, many from approved outside developers who had happily agreed to a 70-30 revenue split. Despite being "widely hailed for its beauty and functionality,"[17] the original phone had sold barely 6 million units in its first year. The device only included a few preloaded homegrown apps, and Apple had actively discouraged "hackers" from developing their own applications. The new model doubled the previous year's sales in just the last five months of 2008, and unit sales would continue to almost double every year through 2012, when annual unit sales reached 125 million. Annual iPhone unit sales plateaued at a bit over 200 million starting in 2015.

A year after the App Store appeared, it would have 50,000 apps, which had been collectively downloaded more than 1 billion times.[18] Ten years later the store would have over 2 million apps and 20 million registered developers. The store generated more than $100 billion of very high margin revenues over that first decade.[19]

By the time Jobs stepped onstage to introduce the iPad, his slightly less revolutionary notebook, in 2010, the central role of the App Store to Apple's value proposition was already clear. In addition to the dozen preloaded apps along with over 140,000 apps already available in the App Store, Apple highlighted the software-development kit it was making available to independent developers.[20] Indeed, much of the launch presentation was taken up with demonstrations by MLB.com, the *New York*

Times, Electronic Arts, and Gameloft of customized iPad apps they had already built. Each of these companies had embedded development teams at Apple headquarters for weeks in advance of the unveiling.

In addition to the core indirect network effects of the two-sided iOS marketplace connecting developers and users, Apple established a layer of direct network effects among users through communication tools available only through Apple products. Video chat software FaceTime, launched in 2010, and messaging service iMessage, launched in 2011, have both become ubiquitous tools for Apple users and are only accessible to other owners of Apple products.[21]

It is with the iPod, iPhone, and iPad that Apple first built and maintained strong relative market share with its products. The launch of the first commercial Android phone in 2008 came a few months after the introduction of the iPhone 3G. The launch of Android Market by Google quickly followed, creating an open-source alternative to the closed Apple ecosystem. Although Apple had come to embrace hosting third-party apps—once they had undergone their controversial approval process[22]—it continued to reject licensing its operating system to any third-party manufacturers.[23]

This led many to anticipate a replay of the earlier war between closed and open systems that had led to the resounding defeat of Apple by Microsoft and the IBM clones in the 1980s. And sure enough, smartphones powered by Android overtook iPhones in the US by 2010.[24] And a few years later, the number of apps available on the renamed Google Play exceeded those on the App Store.[25] But the similarities to the early PC wars are more apparent than real. The flawed analogy reflects defects in the conventional wisdom regarding the early years of both the personal computing and smartphone industries.

Walter Isaacson described the 1977 Apple II as "the first personal computer that was not just for hobbyists."[26] In fact, it was one of three launched that year (and not the first of these). By the time IBM introduced the PC in 1981, Apple was already in third place, selling fewer units than both Atari and RadioShack's Tandy. What's more, on its own, IBM surpassed Apple sales by 1983, even before taking into account the clones that were first introduced in 1982.

Although the outcome might ultimately have been the same, the seven-year gap between the introduction of Apple II and the Macintosh in 1984 was at least as fateful as the insistence on a closed hardware/software system. Confident of the inherent superiority of Apple's product and with no one fully in charge at the company to drive strategy, warring factions spent this strategically critical time period pursuing a variety of independent and inconsistent product strategies—with each product boasting its own incompatible operating system. If the time, money, and focus spent on the ill-fated Apple III and Lisa had been directed toward making the Apple II a more effective competitor to IBM and coordinating that product strategy (and operating system) with the Mac, it is hard to believe that it wouldn't have had an impact on the competitive landscape.[27]

By contrast, Apple's extraordinary success in the smartphone market was often attributed to its first-mover advantage over Android in building the App Store ecosystem. "Since Android came nearly six months later," *BusinessWeek* reported, "many [developers] will likely take a 'wait-and-see' approach to Android."[28] There are two problems with this theory. Apple wasn't first and, as noted, Google Play has boasted more apps than the Apple App Store for many years. At the time that Apple made available the 500 or so software applications with the opening of the online App Store, there were deeper more established pools of developers and applications available. Microsoft's Windows Mobile operating system, used by 160 carriers globally at the time, had more than 18,000 applications available.[29] Beginning in 2006, Nokia, then the global leader in smartphones, had launched a series of products under the names Catalogs, Download!, and Content Discoverer that provided access to a slew of apps, ringtones, and videos.[30]

The fallacy of the first-mover advantage is that the real advantage—scale—is only achievable once the profile of consumer demand and core technology has stabilized enough to allow an aggressive entrant to quickly secure significant share. During the year that the original iPhone was on the market, Apple was able to learn enough about both to place a huge bet on the integrated iPhone 3G and App Store. The company had upgraded its operating system and speed, improved compatibility with Microsoft Outlook, developed a core catalog of powerful apps that highlighted the unique utility of the iPhone, and, most important, dramatically dropped the price. The result was a sustained acceleration of iPhone adoption, third-party app development, and user downloads.

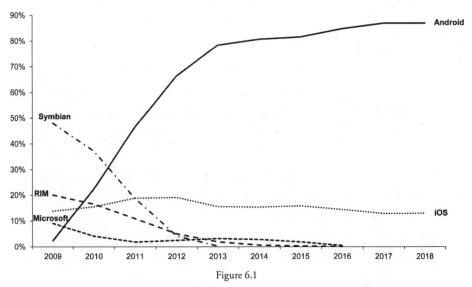

Global Mobile Operating System Market Share

Figure 6.1

Source: "Global Smartphone Sales to End Users from 1st Quarter 2009 to 2018, By Operating System," Gartner, August 2018

By 2010, it was clear that precipitous declines in mobile OS share of Symbian, RIM, and Microsoft would be mostly taken up by Android, establishing a duopoly in which iOS powered the iPhone and Android increasingly powered everyone else. The speed and magnitude of the Android march to victory came with some real costs, however. One does not need to buy into Steve Jobs's maniacal belief in the necessity of hardware and software to be tightly integrated to appreciate the challenges posed by the wide diversity of hardware environments within which the Android system operates. The success of Android in establishing itself as the independent alternative to Apple's mobile operating system only tells part of the story.

Although Android Market did follow fast on the heels of the App Store, even after Android surpassed iOS's global market share, Android Market faced a variety of structural challenges. "Because Google makes its software available free to a range of phone manufacturers, there are dozens of different Android-compatible devices on the market, each with different screen sizes, memory capacities, processor speeds and graphics capabilities," the *New York Times* noted in 2010. "An app that works beautifully on, say, a Motorola Droid might suffer glitches on a phone made by HTC."[31]

Some of what the *Times* described as Android's "clunky features" were smoothed out eventually. It would be 2012, though, before Google would consolidate Android Markets and its various content stores into Google Play,[32] and another two years after that before it would catch up and exceed the number of apps on the Apple App Store.[33] But all market share and all apps are not equal, and many of the structural distinctions between the Apple and Google ecosystems spawned persistent economic differences. So, for instance, in the early days of Android Market, the failure to have seamless payment mechanisms reinforced the tendency for apps to be free. But even after the technical issues were resolved, Google Play continued to host apps that were overwhelmingly free.

Even the paid apps on Google Play generate less revenue than those in the Apple App Store, despite the increasing divergence in respective global market shares. This primarily reflects the disparity in demographics between owners of more expensive iPhones and the rest. From a developer's perspective, the global mobile OS duopoly has made the decision to create apps for both platforms a relatively easy one: only around 3 percent of the top apps are now exclusive to either Android or iOS.[34] The more complicated question is which to develop for first. Not surprisingly,

2018 Worldwide Gross Revenue in $Bn

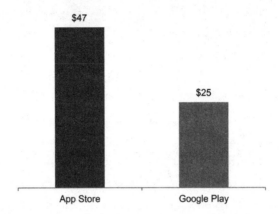

2018 App Downloads (Bn)

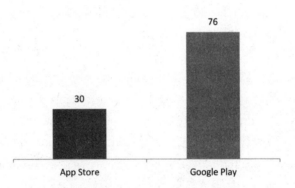

% Paid Apps (as of August 2019)

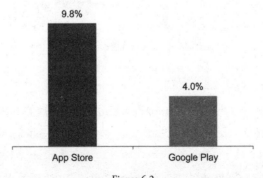

Figure 6.2

Source: Sensor Tower, 42matters

developers answer this overwhelmingly based on what demographic and geographic market they are targeting.

Despite being dwarfed by Android globally—and selling fewer total smartphones than either Samsung or Huawei—Apple has consistently commanded at least double the market share of the premium smartphone market of its next competitor, which in turn is more than twice as large as the next. There remain, however, significant differences among geographic markets, with Apple in second place even at the high end of the market in Latin America and Asia. In the US, by contrast, Apple maintains a slight lead in overall market share, given its historic strength and the relative importance of the premium segment.

Global Market Share of Premium Smartphone Vendors (2015–2019)

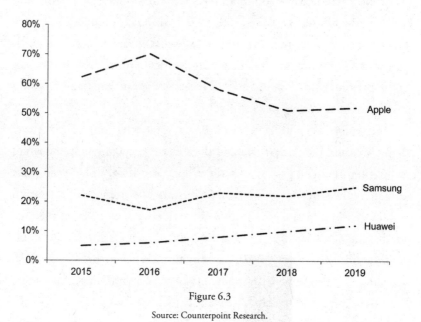

Figure 6.3

Source: Counterpoint Research.

The tenacity of Apple's share at the high end of the market explains the disproportionate share of industry profit extracted by the company. The intense loyalty of Apple users is well established. And Apple has constructed a complex web of addictive features and services, not to mention the seductive trade-in program started in 2013,[35] to reinforce customer captivity. What has changed in recent years, however, is the extent to which loyalty to the Android OS has come to match or exceed this. Both operating systems retain around 90 percent of users within their respective ecosystems when they buy a new phone.[36]

APPLE AND THE CURSE OF THE TOASTER

Professor Bruce Greenwald has crisply articulated the fundamental truism that keeps both grizzled technology executives and bright-eyed technology entrepreneurs up at night, "In the long run, everything is a toaster."[37] No matter how original or even revolutionary a new product is, over time it will become commoditized as cheap imitators get better and core functionality is integrated into entirely different product categories. There is no evidence that the iPhone is yet becoming subject to significant pricing pressure, but its sources of historical growth have dissipated, as the premium smartphone market has become saturated and Android has engendered comparable loyalty.

Innovators must keep innovating. At Apple, the Apple II gave way to the Mac and the PowerBook and then, as the company moved beyond computing, the iPod gave way to the iPhone and iPad. In between there were many incremental versions and features. The strength of the brand and, more recently, the power of its network effects, can extend the productive life of a franchise showing its age and facing more nimble competitors, until the next innovation provides a needed shot of financial adrenaline. But these benefits represent only a temporary reprieve—there is no known method to actually break the Curse of the Toaster.

There are organizational structures and cultures that encourage more innovation than others.[38] But Steve Jobs's aspiration to establish a company so imbued with creative innovation that it would establish a structural competitive advantage that outlived him was not an achievable goal. Toward the end of his life, Jobs seemed to acknowledge this at least implicitly. As Jobs fought the disease that would ultimately take his life, Hewlett Packard, the company whose legacy he had explicitly aspired to match, was mired in a seemingly endless cycle of scandal and decline. "It's being dismembered and destroyed," a somber Jobs told the Apple Board at his final lunch with them, as he stepped down as CEO just a few months before his death. "It's tragic."[39]

Jobs expressed the hope that he had "left a stronger legacy so that will never happen at Apple," although he conceded that the founders of Hewlett Packard "thought they had left it in good hands." In selecting Tim Cook, a former Compaq procurement and supply chain manager, as his successor, Jobs appointed a brilliant executive who had been remarkably effective at operationalizing Jobs's lofty vision. Yet ultimately Jobs knew it was all about the product. So, when he confided in Walter Isaacson that "Tim's not a product person per se,"[40] one wonders what Jobs really thought about the company's long-term prospects.

Jobs's partner on the product-design side of the business, Jony Ive, formally left the company after thirty years in 2019. It had been widely reported that he had been largely disengaged for some time, having withdrawn from the "routine management of Apple's elite design team" out of frustration with "a more operations-focused company."[41] That operational focus has ensured that Apple has continued to improve the functionality and performance of its core products, most notably through the recent introduction of the powerful new homegrown M1 chip to replace the Intel processors.[42] And since Jobs's death, Apple has introduced new product categories that integrate with the iOS ecosystem. But these have involved either already well-developed product categories that have underperformed (e.g., Apple Watch, HomePod)[43] or relatively narrow niches where even great success would make a modest contribution (e.g., AirPods). Nothing, in short, is anticipated to move the needle.

Nor has any such revolutionary new product launch been foreshadowed by management or anticipated by analysts[44]—unless they are counting on Apple's rumored plans to begin producing cars in 2024.[45]

Apple's prior 2019 target shipping date for an electric car had evaporated after a series of publicized strategy changes and layoffs.[46] Tim Cook's 2019 assurance that the company's greatest contribution will ultimately be "about health" should not instill any more confidence than their automotive ambitions.[47]

Yet the public valuation of Apple and its dramatic market outperformance both before and during the 2020 pandemic clearly implies something more than the continued extraordinary financial performance of its existing core product franchises. The company is banking on—and investors are betting on—dramatic growth in an entirely different kind of business. And given that the share price has outperformed even all of its FAANG brethren since sales of the iPhone (and iPad) leveled off in 2015—the stock appreciated by more than 400 percent in the five years leading to the start of 2021— the consensus seems to be that these new businesses will benefit from the very same competitive advantages or, if different, equally compelling new ones.

THE APPLE BRAND REVISITED: AT YOUR SERVICE

Apple began to make it clear where it wanted investors to focus—and where not—in 2018. To the anger of research analysts who had long tracked the company, Apple announced in November 2018 that it would no longer report iPhone unit sales.[48] The following quarter, Apple for the first time began reporting the relative profitability of the product and services businesses, which highlighted both how much more inherently profitable the services business was and how much faster it was growing.

Services always had been a part of Apple's revenue mix, but it didn't rate its own financial reporting segment until 2013. Over the years, a diverse collection of services—including iCloud, iBooks (now Apple Books), iTunes, the AppleCare Protection Plan, and a rotating selection of internet services had usually been bundled with whatever catch-all segment encompassed "Other" at the time. This changed in 2004 when iTunes was separated out and put first into "Other Music Products" before graduating to "Other Music-Related Products and Services." All the services were reunited as a distinct reporting category without any extraneous "other" revenues in 2013 under "iTunes, Software and Services" prior to being turned into the more economically titled "Services" category in 2015. As defined broadly by Apple, "Services" encompasses not just traditional services but also sales from its digital content stores and licensing revenues.[49]

Given the relative growth and profitability of services, they could account for a majority of Apple's revenues by 2030 if current trends persist. This shift should in theory strengthen the overall Apple franchise. But as the company stakes its future on services, investors should pause before going all in for at least three reasons.

First is the company's historic performance in services. Part of Apple's apparent ambivalence about how to report services related to what a small part of the overall business they represented until recently. But it also reflected the highly uneven performance of Apple's various initiatives in this arena, suggesting that skills and processes essential to designing remarkable gadgets are different from the requirements of developing addictive services. As recently as 2015, an article on how Apple became the world's most valuable company included a section titled "Why is Apple so bad at making online services?"[50]

The list of high-profile embarrassments is not short. Although the overwhelming success of iTunes in 2001 is what most remember, Apple unsuccessfully launched online services iTools and .Mac in 2000 and 2002, respectively. The former was a collection of free internet-based services and the latter was a subscription product touted as a "suite of Internet services and software that provides Mac users with powerful tools for their life on the Internet."[51] Both were widely panned. The relaunch of these in 2008 as MobileMe led to a classic Steve Jobs anecdote. "Can anyone tell me what MobileMe is supposed to do?" Jobs apparently demanded of the team after the service's disastrous debut. According to Adam Lashinsky's account in *Fortune*, once an engineer came up with an explanation, Jobs retorted, "So why the fuck doesn't it do that?" before summarily dismissing the team leader in front of the assembled auditorium.[52]

It would be four years before MobileMe was finally retired and key functionality ported over to the iCloud platform.[53] Although the iCloud service, launched in 2011, today is viewed as a success, it was plagued with reliability and performance problems for years.[54] Some of those reliability issues have persisted; the service is also hugely dependent on AWS.[55] Other high-profile service launches that have performed poorly and either required many years to stabilize or were simply discontinued include Apple Maps in 2012, which elicited a public apology from CEO Tim Cook and was completely rebuilt in 2018,[56] and Ping, its mercifully short-lived 2010 music social network.[57]

Second, although Apple services do indeed maintain a higher margin overall than their physical products, under the hood of what the company hopes will be a $50 billion business category in 2020 is a wide range of very different services with very different financial profiles. So, for instance, Google's multibillion-dollar annual license payment for being the default search engine on the platform must approach a margin of 100 percent profit and has been estimated to be as much as $10 billion.[58] Unfortunately, this prodigious and singularly valuable revenue stream, representing as much as 20 percent of the company's overall profit, is the precise target of the Justice Department's antitrust complaint against Google.[59] By contrast, many of the service categories that are anticipated to drive a disproportionate share of Apple's growth in services are much lower-margin businesses.

Since its launch in 2015, one of the fastest-growing services segments has been Apple Music subscriptions.[60] Although Apple does not reveal profitability by segment, direct competitor Spotify is now public and its gross margin is a mere 25 percent—the vast majority of the 75 percent that represents Spotify's direct costs are artist royalties, and the music labels reportedly extract even more from Apple. With a global subscriber base about double Apple Music's, Spotify only broke even for the first time in 2019. The business is unlikely to be profitable for Apple.

The most significant recent addition to projected services growth is from the Apple TV+ video subscription business launched in 2019. Unlike its music service, Apple is now in the business of creating original content as well as licensing from established rights holders. Like its music service, Apple is entering a market where a much larger incumbent is public, providing insight into the economics of the venture. We discuss the economics of Netflix and streaming entertainment in the next chapter and highlighted the cost to Amazon of Prime Video in the previous chapter, but suffice it to say that Apple is even less likely to achieve profitability in this service than in music.

Third and finally, we return to the nature and value of the Apple brand. Apple is not just any kind of brand. Yes, as Larry Ellison pointed out, it is a lifestyle brand. But it is also a global luxury brand, and the only one on this scale in the technology industry. This has reinforced the other structural advantages highlighted and helps explain how the company has been able to consistently extract a disproportionate share of industry profits. While the high-end segment represents a small minority of overall smartphone units sold, by dominating this market, Apple has been able to consistently command an average phone price more than triple that of Android phones.[61]

But a key characteristic of luxury brands is that they are notoriously difficult to extend beyond their core product categories and, potentially, very close adjacencies.[62] The brilliantly managed transition from Apple Computers to Apple facilitated the brand to successfully move from PCs and laptops to iPods and iPhones while reinforcing the underlying messaging. But even within the expanded potential electronics footprint, the track record of exporting the Apple halo to new product categories has been mixed. Although it is not possible to identify precisely the extent to which the problem was the product itself or the limitations of the brand, over the years Apple has disappointed in watches, televisions, video game consoles, and more.

The counterexample of iTunes is not really a counterexample given how tightly integrated with the experience of the wildly successful iPod equipment the service was. Although Apple Music benefits from the installed base of iOS users, within which it maintains a leading share, as a general-purpose consumer music service competing with many others it must attract significant numbers of Android users to attain competitive scale overall.[63] As a result, the service must be made as compelling as possible for users outside its ecosystem, particularly given the importance of being able to listen to the service through all their smart devices.

As we move to the realm of ubiquitous low-priced streaming video services, the value of the Apple luxury brand is even more tenuous. Here the core value proposition is not technological or design pizzazz but rather the provision of compelling proprietary entertainment content. Completely distinct from the fact that Apple has no experience or track record developing such original content—and its main competitors do—the brands of the content producers historically have had little to do with the success of the product. With the possible exception of Disney or Pixar within the narrow children's niche, neither the brand of the movie studio nor the overarching holding company that it may be a part of has been predictive of box office success.

Similarly, viewers have little loyalty to particular cable channels but rather particular shows. Within streaming services, the same is basically true—I subscribe to HBO to get *Game of Thrones*, not the other way around. If a service has a track record of regularly providing satisfying content, its brand may earn it some benefit of the doubt for a short time between hits, but as we will explore more deeply in the next chapter, the levels of customer churn at even the most successful services suggest the limits of brand value in this domain.

To be sure, Apple has demonstrated a remarkable ability to develop compelling services that increase the perceived value of its core products, whether iTunes for iPods or the App Store and iCloud for iPhones. But as the general consumer services Apple has launched highlight, no brand is strong enough to overwhelm the structural economics of the industries in which the new services compete. That said, it is clearly the power of that brand that has moved investor perceptions of Apple from an innovative product company to an unstoppable platform whose future expansion into as yet unseen applications supports an over $2 trillion market capitalization today.

Whether that valuation is a reflection of the Platform Delusion or the true potential of services will in part be a function of the extent to which the company can develop more services that meaningfully enhance the value of the Apple hardware/software ecosystem. The more recent focus on services that need to penetrate well beyond that ecosystem to be economically viable suggests the difficulty in developing new addictive use cases for the same machinery. That may mean that Apple's future will depend on whether the company still has the mojo to create compelling new physical products upon which to base such new applications.

KEY CHAPTER TAKEAWAYS

1. Operating systems are a classic network effects business, connecting users and software developers. Throughout most of its history, Apple remained subscale in operating systems, stemming from its maniacal insistence on the interdependence of its proprietary hardware and software products. Although this philosophy often resulted in innovative tools and products, it undermined Apple's ability to profit from them.

2. By softening the religious ardor with which this belief was enforced, while maintaining its design disciplines, Steve Jobs first saved the company—by abandoning its PowerPC chips for the more powerful Intel technology and supporting Microsoft Windows on its devices—and then turned it into what may now be the most valuable company in the world.

3. The 2008 launch of the App Store, embracing a curated model for outside developers, in connection with the $200 iPhone 3G marked a critical turning point in the company's fortunes. Android's need for compatibility with dozens of manufacturers' products provided Apple with a multiyear head start in the profitable high end of the market where it continues to dominate.

4. Unlike any of the other FAANG companies, for its entire history Apple has primarily made physical products. Since the death of cofounder Steve Jobs a majority of sales have come from a single product: the iPhone.

5. With no new "move-the-needle" products anticipated, Apple has bet its growth on services. Apple's historic track record in services, however, is highly mixed, and many of the particular services upon which projected growth is predicated have inherently low margins, face strong competition from specialized incumbents, and gain questionable assistance from Apple's strong brand in consumer electronics. Time will tell whether Apple can break the Curse of the Toaster by betting the company on services without another revolutionary new product.

NETFLIX: CONTENT WAS
NEVER KING AND STILL ISN'T

WE NOTED EARLIER THAT A number of commentators have argued for the expulsion of Netflix from FAANG based on a range of different justifications. The strongest argument against following this advice for current purposes is the simple fact that so many of the other FAANG members seem to want to *be* Netflix. Prime Video and Apple TV+ are direct assaults on the Netflix citadel. And although Google and Facebook have mostly avoided sponsoring competing subscription services, both have identified video content as core to their respective corporate strategies.[1]

"Content is king" is generally treated as a self-evident notion, universally embraced by professionals and the public alike. The origins of the phrase are alternatively attributed to media mogul Sumner Redstone and tech icon Bill Gates (neither actually coined it).[2] More substantively, the meanings variously attributed to the slogan range from the merely tautological to the demonstrably false. Most harmlessly, it is used to emphasize the inarguable point that popular and valuable entertainment content is indeed popular and valuable. Less benign is the interpretation that within the media and, increasingly, the technology industry value chain, the business of creating compelling content is responsible for a disproportionate share of value. This could not be further from the truth.

In his autobiography, Sumner Redstone, who had controlled ViacomCBS and consequently the TV network CBS and film studio Para-mount Pictures, traces his epiphany about the supreme importance of content to his early days in the movie exhibition business. "You can have the most beautiful theater in the world," Redstone realized, "but if you don't have a hot picture, forget it."[3] This led Redstone to the broader point regarding entertainment viewing: *They watch what's on it, not what it's on!*" (emphasis in original). His conclusion became his catchphrase: "Content was and is indeed king."[4]

A closer look at the simple movie theater example Redstone relies on reveals the flaw in this reasoning. The source of success of his National Amusements theater chain was its dominance of northeastern regional markets outside of the major cities. Redstone was right that you need a "hot" movie to get butts in seats. But his ability to get the most anticipated films, and the terms on which he was able to secure those for his theaters, was a function of his leverage with the studios. And like his leverage with local concession distributors, commercial realtors, and even employees, that came from being the only game in town. In the era before the industry was consolidated into three massive, largely undifferentiated chains,[5] the locally dominant regional theater chains boasted double the profitability of the higher-profile, more competitive, big-city-focused national chains.[6]

There are many different businesses of varying quality dedicated to the development of creative content. Enterprises, however, whose success relies on the regular production of fresh hits—"hot" blockbusters that draw the lion's share of attention in any given season—share a common characteristic: they generate anemic financial returns over time. The fundamental problem is a lack of entry barriers to financing the prospect of the next runaway success. Even when talent can deliver surefire success, if a star actor, writer, or director is well represented by managers and agents, the return on such investments remains pedestrian. What modest profit the largest content players do eke out has typically come from the ability to monetize ancillary businesses in marketing and distribution that do scale.

THE HISTORIC NETFLIX ADVANTAGE

But what does all this talk of content have to do with Netflix? The short answer is, until relatively recently in its almost twenty-five-year history, very little. Indeed, the initial angry emotional reactions from traditional-media executives to Netflix's continual share price appreciation and accelerating subscriber growth seemed to stem precisely from the fact that Netflix was *not* a content company. When former Time Warner CEO Jeff Bewkes compared Netflix to the Albanian army's trying to "take over the world" and Comcast CEO Brian Roberts dismissed the company as "rerun" TV, it was still years before Netflix would debut its first original production in 2013.[7] Even as CEO Reed Hastings announced his intention to finance a few original series in 2011, he confirmed that this would always represent a relatively small aspect of the tapestry of the overall Netflix experience.

"Generally, I am a believer in circle of competence," Hastings explained to investors at the time. "Reading a script and guessing who might be good to cast in it—it's not something that fundamentally as a tech company . . . we're likely to build a distinctive organizational competence in." His conclusion could not have been clearer: "We think that we're better off letting other people take creative risks."[8]

Over the years, there have been plenty of arguments—with expensive consequences for a long list of short sellers from Whitney Tilson in 2010[9] to Andrew Left in 2019[10]—that Netflix should not be as successful and as highly valued as it is. But the animating force of the original Netflix Paradox was a disbelief that a media company like Netflix that produced no original content could thrive while the media content giants, on whose output Netflix feeds, faced a secular tailspin. Remember that the company already effectively had as many US subscribers as HBO before *House of Cards* aired, ending 2012 with close to 30 million subscribers.[11]

Netflix was for most of its history primarily in the business of aggregating entertainment content created by other companies and selling access to it as a subscription service to consumers—first as a DVD-by-mail service and then increasingly, starting in 2007, as a streaming service (the first major SVOD, or subscription video on demand, service). In a media culture committed to the proposition that "content is king," the robust success of a mere redistributor is something incomprehensible and, frankly, a little unnerving, especially while those responsible for the creative life-blood that flows through its veins struggle for profitability.

In fact, the dirty little secret of the media industry is that content aggregators, not content creators, are the overwhelming source of value creation. Well before Netflix was founded in 1997, cable channels that did little more than aggregate old movies, cartoons, or television shows boasted profit margins many times greater than those of the movie studios that had produced the creative content. It had long been the case that the cash flows generated by the aggregation and distribution businesses of the media conglomerates dwarfed those of their content creation activities, despite the film and television studios' outsized place in the public imagination.

At the time CBS and Viacom announced their $30 billion merger in August 2019, the subsidiary Paramount studio had not turned a profit since 2015. Although much of the public discourse surrounding Disney's $71 billion purchase of 21st Century Fox earlier in 2019 involved the excitement over the uniting of Fox studio's X-Men and Fantastic Four franchises with the rest of Disney's Marvel multiverse, most of the profit of the business being purchased came from elsewhere—both the regional sports networks that Disney would be forced to divest as well as the collection of domestic and international cable networks that were kept contributed far more than the filmed entertainment division. Similarly, although reporting on Comcast's acquisition of NBCUniversal a decade earlier focused on Conan O'Brien's career prospects and the shifting fortunes of Universal Pictures, in reality, 82 percent of the new company's profits resulted from the cable channels.[12]

The structural superiority of the content aggregation business to the content creation business should not come as a surprise. The economic structure of the media business is not fundamentally different from that of business in general. The most prevalent sources of industrial strength have been the mutually reinforcing competitive advantages of supply-side scale and customer captivity. Content creation simply does not lend itself to either, while aggregation is amenable to both.

Take scale. Because making a blockbuster movie is expensive, people assume that it is a scale business. But the benefits of relative bigness flow from the ability of the largest players to spread high fixed costs most efficiently. Moviemaking is not this kind of business. The cost of a blockbuster does not vary based on the size of the studio producing it. Creating hit-driven content in any medium does not typically require significant fixed costs. Series-based, subscription, or other kinds of continuously produced content do have a larger fixed-cost component, but they are the exception and not the rule when it comes to the genesis of most megahits.

Aggregation, on the other hand, by its nature requires a large fixed-cost infrastructure to collect, manage, market, and redistribute content. This is why a cable channel with 20 million subscribers loses money but an identical one with 100 million subscribers might generate 50 percent margins.

Customer captivity—the "stickiness" of the company-to-consumer relationship—is similar. If Universal had a successful slate of movies last year, customers aren't more likely to seek out Universal films this year. Again, series or franchise films may be different, but as a result the talent is often able to reap much of the benefits of captivity. Just ask the studio executives in charge of enticing not just the stars, but also the writers and directors to return for film sequels. Or the producers with the unenviable task of discussing new contract terms with the casts of hit shows from *Friends* to *The Big Bang Theory*. Contrast the lack of customer captivity among pure content companies with the leverage cable channels and TV networks still enjoy to a surprising extent when they threaten to pull their signal from a distributor.

Time was when the content giants in the movie, music, and book industries could earn superior returns. But their ability to do so had nothing to do with content being king. It was a function of the scale and captivity inherent in their aggregation business: the massive marketing and distribution networks that they rented out to smaller, independent content producers, often at usurious rates. The decline of these enterprises does not reflect any change in the nature of content generation—it was as unattractive a business then as it is now. Instead, their decline reflects the loss of their advantages in aggregation—a loss resulting from a combination of external forces and self-inflicted wounds.

The obvious external force has been advances in technology. One reason that major book publishers had to deal with huge, half-empty warehouse and distribution facilities is that more books were being delivered electronically. The impact of technology on the music industry is the stuff of legend at this point, but now that the companies have discovered a sustainable piracy-free pricing model for digital distribution, the business has enjoyed a resurgence. It is still smaller and less profitable, however, than at its peak in 1999.[13] Without the fixed-cost requirements associated with producing and distributing CDs and managing racks at Tower Records, the barriers to entry into music are not what they used to be. The detriment of increased competition simply outweighs the benefit to established businesses of lower fixed costs.

It would be a mistake to give media managers a pass based on technological developments beyond their control. In industries like media, where a few large players share the same advantages of scale, the key to long-term success is avoiding destructive competition in pricing, costs, and capacity. In the mostly forgotten era of the MCA/Universal chief Lew Wasserman, being a media mogul meant enforcing a culture of informal cooperation, where the bottom line mattered more than one-upping your peers. Wasserman was not literally "the Last Mogul," as multiple biographers have dubbed him, but he may have been the last one who didn't think the defining genius of moguldom was outbidding all the other moguls for the hottest talent, technology, or property of the moment. Similarly, a culture that rewards "stealing" established authors or musicians from competitors the old-fashioned way—by overpaying—will never earn its shareholders a decent return, regardless of the technological environment. As we discuss shortly, the industry culture that seems to be emerging in connection with the new streaming wars looks much more like this than that enforced by Lew Wasserman. Interestingly, in the book industry, the culture appears to have moved in a more shareholder-friendly direction.

Netflix's early success in streaming video was therefore hardly paradoxical. The company sits squarely in the tradition of the most-successful media businesses: aggregators with economies of scale and customer captivity. Netflix used its leading position in its legacy DVD subscription business to quickly develop scale in the streaming business. The company had fewer than 9 million subscribers in 2008, when it began offering video streaming directly to the TV for its existing customers. That move accelerated subscriber growth and supported the introduction of a streaming-only service in 2010. Netflix's ability to spread the fixed costs of content, marketing, and technology across a subscriber base vastly larger than any other competitor's is continually reinforced by superior customer service, a powerful recommendation engine, and a great, habit-forming product.

Even if the Netflix business model is not original, some cultural and structural aspects do distinguish it from most media companies. Culturally, it is a remarkably well-run company that has always taken pride in both its operating efficiency and its customer focus. CEO Reed Hastings's 128-slide PowerPoint presentation from 2009 on Netflix corporate culture had been viewed by well over 15 million people, presumably not all employees, by the time it was updated and transformed into ten pages of prose in 2017.[14] Hastings collaborated with a well-regarded business school professor of organizational behavior to turn these ideas into a popular book in 2020.[15]

By contrast, media-content companies historically seemed to feel that efficiency either necessarily suggested a lack of commitment to artistic integrity or was somehow beneath them. Media-distribution companies, particularly in the cable and phone markets, have among the worst customer relations of any industry: cable companies' core services, internet service provision, and subscription television were the absolute worst of forty-six industries surveyed by the American Customer Satisfaction Index.[16] And most media aggregators, such as cable channels, structurally act as wholesalers, whose customers are not the individual consumers but the distributors who manage the physical pipe (or satellite feed) to the home. Netflix is the rare aggregator that manages the direct customer relationship itself, which allows it both to excel in customer service and to perfect the product by harnessing customer feedback.

These company characteristics are unusual, and yet they hardly constitute a puzzle. The media analyst Craig Moffett coined the term "Dumb Pipe Paradox" over a decade ago to describe the fact that a shift of consumer habits from cable television to online video streaming could actually help the economics of the cable operators.[17] Moffett correctly pointed out that cable companies would be far better off if they could charge customers based on direct bandwidth usage from video streaming without having to invest in cable boxes. Only in the media industry, however, would it seem a paradox that owning the exclusive broadband pipe into the home at a time of exploding usage makes for a good business. Relying on dumb pipes instead of expensive content or talent is always the smart bet.

IS CONTENT KING OR A HOUSE OF CARDS?

In the years since *House of Cards* debuted on Netflix, the company has continued to experience explosive growth. Between 2013 and 2019, the company's revenues grew from under $5 billion to over $20 billion, and its global subscriber count grew from 32 million to almost 200 million, with international subscribers now representing a significant majority of its users. During the first year of the COVID-19 pandemic, the company added another 36.6 million subscribers, easily blowing through the 200 million mark.[18] The biggest change during this period has been Netflix's reliance on original content. In 2016, the company formally announced "a multiyear transition and evolution" toward having half of the content on the service be original productions.[19] In 2018, for the first time a majority of Netflix new releases were originals, and that number was double what it had been in 2016.[20]

These developments have led some observers to conclude that Reed Hastings had a fundamental change of heart about the relative attractiveness of the business of taking "creative risks" on the one hand and the core source of the company's competitive advantage on the other. Neither inference is justified.

There is only one reason for a successful content aggregator of scale to go into the content production business: heightened competition leaves it no choice. Cable channel owners' collective recognition of the need to amp up investment in original content reflected a commercial necessity in the face of growing over-the-top (OTT) streaming alternatives and diminishing clout with distributors. Corresponding declines in profitability and, more precipitously, valuation multiples have been the predictable result. Taking on creative risk may be the right strategic choice compared to the alternative. But it doesn't make Netflix a better business than it was before. Rather, it highlights that it has become a worse one.

Apple TV+, Disney+, NBCUniversal's Peacock, ViacomCBS's Paramount+, and Quibi, the high-profile original content "start-up" SVOD service, all financed high-profile launches with expensive celebrity-driven original content and extensive marketing campaigns in 2019–21. AT&T-owned WarnerMedia started an SVOD version of HBO called HBO Now in 2015, but it also launched a souped-up version called HBOMax in 2020, which doubled the available content but kept the price flat. By then, the number of original scripted series produced annually had already exceeded 500—well more than double the 210 produced a decade earlier.[21] Various streaming services, including Netflix as well as Amazon Prime Video, Hulu, and CBS All Access were responsible for more of this explosion of content production than broadcast television, basic cable, or premium cable. Among the growing list of streamers, only Quibi, the sole player without a deep-pocketed parent, has thrown in the towel—but not before burning through almost $2 billion in a matter of months.[22] All the rest continue to compete aggressively for the most promising content and the most creative executives and artists with no end in sight.

The winners from this rapid expansion in creative output have been the viewers and the talent, but not the shareholders. This is definitively the golden age of television.[23] As noted, however, the genteel era when media conglomerates eschewed stealing talent from each other had ended long ago. The intensity of that competition had taken a particularly dark turn in the early 1990s, unleashed by Rupert Murdoch's brash push for respect for his fledgling Fox Broadcasting Company. Murdoch launched unprecedented bidding wars for sports and other content rights, talent, and local station affiliations.[24] But the scope and scale of the competition was now unlike anything seen before. These developments explain in no small part why Murdoch, the wiliest of his generation of moguls, decided to largely exit the sector—letting those who remain bid up the price of the assets he had accumulated over the prior thirty-five years.

Where bidding wars for a hot show or the services of a top star, writer, or director was a long-established if financially destructive practice (although one that has been taken to unprecedented extremes during the streaming wars),[25] the real bottleneck has become producers and show-runners who can effectively manage the volume of production. Guaranteed deals in the hundreds of millions of dollars for proven mass-production executives with names like Ryan Murphy, Greg Berlanti, J. J. Abrams, and Shonda Rhimes reflects the changing—and expanding—nature of the "talent" upon which the modern industry relies.[26]

It is hard to envision a happy ending for shareholders given these continuing trends, notwithstanding the stock outperformance of not just Netflix but Disney in 2020. A look at the bleak economics of Netflix's established streaming competitors is suggestive both of why, despite Netflix's structural advantages, the accelerating need to compete aggressively in content creation is bad news and what a hard slog the newer services piling into the market face. Hulu—originally a joint venture of News Corp and NBCUniversal but later joined by Disney and then Time Warner[27]—launched in 2008, added a subscription service in 2010, and began developing original content beyond what was licensed from its investors in 2012.[28] Amazon's Prime delivery service added a free streaming video product in 2011[29] and began producing original series in 2013,[30] making Prime Video available globally as a standalone service in 2016.[31]

In 2018, Hulu had 25 million domestic subscribers, a little under half of Netflix's 58 million US subscribers at the time.[32] Just a couple of years earlier, a respected Wall Street research analyst argued that Hulu's value was $25 billion based on a much more modest subscriber prediction for 2018.[33] But the analyst assumed 2018 profitability. In fact, losses had accelerated along with the subscriber count, far exceeding $1 billion.

Disney took operational control of Hulu in 2019 in a deal that assured Comcast (NBCUniversal's owner) a valuation for its stake of at least $27.5 billion.[34] In addition to the breathtaking price tag, the transaction allowed Comcast to use NBCUniversal's content for its 2020 launch of Peacock, its own proprietary streaming service. In addition, the content can be pulled entirely from Hulu starting in 2022. Notably, a variety of earlier efforts by shareholders to unload the money-losing Hulu (at a small fraction of the price secured by Comcast) had come to naught precisely because of its owners' unwillingness to continue to make their homegrown content exclusively available on the service.[35]

The economics of Prime Video are much more difficult to discern, given that the economics of Prime overall are somewhat opaque. But based on what is known about both, it is hard to believe that its financials aren't even more dire than Hulu's. Prime, when originally introduced in 2005, offered free two-day shipping for an annual fee of $79. As we saw, the impact of Prime membership on purchasing behavior was dramatic, but without knowing precisely how this spending is undertaken—many small low-margin orders or large higher-margin purchases—it is impossible to assess Prime profitability. The financial impact of Prime Video is even harder to assess. The jump in purchasing proclivity of Prime members was evident well before the introduction of free video.[36] So for Prime Video to make economic sense, it needs to be justified based on incremental profitable purchases and members along with the incremental impact on retention of existing members.

Prime membership has grown from about 5 million in 2011 to over 100 million today. How to determine how much of this is attributable to video as opposed to the core free shipping or any of the other perks, like free music streaming, that have been subsequently added? What is known is that, based on some internal Amazon documents obtained by Reuters in 2018,[37] the number of Prime members that actually watched any video was less than a third—today, not much more than the 28 million who actually pay for a Hulu subscription. Yet at around $5 billion,[38] Amazon's content spending in 2018 was about double that of Hulu.[39] And, given the $8.5 billion MGM acquisition, Amazon seems committed to chasing its current and future SVOD competitors by continuously expanding content budgets.

Netflix's need to develop its own original content and the cost of developing it will increase further thanks to the five surviving major new SVOD services that came online from 2019 to 2021. With the exception of Apple TV+, these new competitors are owned by important historical sources of exclusive material for Netflix, meaning that the service's need to develop its own original content and the cost of developing it will increase further.[40] What's more, the company has now committed to becoming a major force in a different and even riskier form of creative content: film production.

Netflix's decision to begin financing original films in 2015[41] made sense given the disproportionate share of viewing that films had always represented in Pay TV. That said, film production is a very different undertaking than producing television series. These important financial and operational distinctions are reflected in the fact that all the major studios historically maintained largely separate operations for each. What's more, to move in just a few years from making a modest slate of films targeting the interests of its subscribers to becoming potentially the largest single film studio, producing everything from art films to blockbusters across genres, is a major undertaking. And one rife with cautionary historic lessons.

Much has been written about the turnaround of Disney under the leadership of Michael Eisner and Frank Wells. Poorly appreciated, however, is that although Wells died tragically a decade into his tenure and Eisner remained for over twenty years, most of the stock outperformance happened in their first five years. This preceded the new generation of animated films launched with *The Little Mermaid* and *Beauty and the Beast* that many assume were the primary source of the studio's resurgence. When Wells and Eisner arrived in 1984, the studio lost money and made few films. By 1988, it was the number one studio with around 20 percent market share. It achieved this by making a very particular kind of film, using a very particular playbook that had been brought over with the team from Paramount—tightly managed story-driven fare that used inexpensive on-screen talent that was either undiscovered or in need of "rediscovering." After buying Capital Cities/ABC in 1995—along with the supposedly synergistic TV studio—Disney maintained its number one share for the next five years. But it required three times as many films to achieve roughly the same share. And by 2000, studio profitability was well below what had been achieved in 1988 on more than three times the revenues—much of it star-driven or special-effects laden.[42]

The moral here is not that Netflix shouldn't invest hugely in original production. Indeed, in the face of the competitive onslaught it makes absolute sense to press its relative scale to heighten the fixed-cost price of entry. And original rather than licensed product has advantages beyond being able to retain rights for their own competitive services. Notwithstanding high-profile global rights deals like the one Netflix recently secured for *Seinfeld*,[43] most content rights are licensed locally. As Netflix has gone global, the increasing number of international competitors looking to lock up local streaming rights for themselves[44] also justifies the shift toward fully-owned content.[45]

But, once again, just because something makes strategic sense compared to the alternative doesn't mean it is good news. What's more, as Disney's early forays into blockbuster territory showed, the film business does not scale naturally. How Netflix manages that unprecedented growth in output envisioned will determine just how bad the news is. In an interview in late 2016, Reed Hastings contrasted the "highest-end TV" at around $10 million an hour with high-end films where "budgets are one hundred million dollars of production cost an hour."[46] He anticipated that "we'll be able to figure out in the next couple of years what twenty-million-dollar-an-hour television will look like" but insisted that they do not have the distribution to support $100-million-an-hour productions. Yet, starting in 2019, Netflix has released or announced multiple projects at or very near that level.[47]

The ascension of longtime content chief Ted Sarandos to co-CEO in 2020 leaves little question as to where Netflix's future lies.[48] It is still unclear whether Netflix's organization is prepared for the range of operational challenges their ambitions will inevitably unleash. To date, Netflix has been remarkably adept at rising to whatever new challenges it faces. In content production, however, efficiency has historically been optimized through specialization within genre and audience, not total absolute production volume.

THE NEW NETFLIX ADVANTAGE?

But what does all this mean for the sources and strength of competitive advantages? The short answer is not much. But what has changed has, for the most part, not been for the better.

You wouldn't know that from the number of commentators who have fallen under the spell of the Platform Delusion. They are now attributing to Netflix significant competitive powers well beyond the same combination of scale (of the traditional cost–based supply-side variety) and customer captivity that it has long enjoyed. The two additional competitive advantages most often cited are the network effects and technology-driven learning benefits typically ascribed to platform businesses.

In 2019, Deutsche Bank upgraded Netflix shares to a "buy" explicitly based on its view that the company had now achieved platform status.[49] "Platform status," the lead analyst Bryan Kraft argued, "brings network effects not available to peers and competitors." He is not alone in the belief that Netflix benefits from substantial network effects. Indeed, this notion appears to have become conventional wisdom in both popular and academic settings. In *Platform Revolution: How Networked Markets Are Transforming the Economy and How to Make Them Work for You*, three consultants and academics similarly argued that Netflix has strong network effects.[50] The theories under which Netflix displays powerful network effects suggest that these are alternatively of the indirect and direct variety.

The indirect arguments portray Netflix as a marketplace business in which the ability to attract talent and content is driven by the increased numbers of viewers and vice versa. "Talent is attracted to Netflix's growing global audience" and corresponding growing "role in pop culture," argues Deutsche Bank's Kraft.[51] But except as a strained metaphor, Netflix is no more a "marketplace" than any other business that invests in product to attract more customers.

Kraft also suggests that the company has become so successful that it now qualifies as a "cultural necessity for people around the world." This argument for direct network effects—that the product is actually more satisfying to viewers simply by virtue of how many other viewers there are—has the benefit of being supported by some modest empirical evidence.[52] The existence of a water cooler effect has been shown to apply at the margin to movie consumption in theaters, and there is no reason to think it wouldn't have some application to Netflix viewership.[53] But there is also no reason to think the effect is significant or that it would be persistent without the need to continually produce new popular fare.

The other direct network effect sometimes cited is from the incremental user data every new subscriber brings to the service. This, it is argued, allows Netflix to improve the service for everyone, further spinning the flywheel of success beyond the reach of other competitors. This may seem a semantic distinction, but the new users do not improve Netflix. How Netflix mines their data improves the service. What precise learning benefits Netflix is able to derive from applying machine learning and artificial intelligence to its unparalleled user base is an important question to which we now turn. It is not, however, a network effect.

It is worth noting that Netflix itself has largely eschewed claims of network effects. Reed Hastings contrasts companies like Netflix that have "normal scale economies" with "those rare businesses like LinkedIn and Facebook where there are network effects."[54] It was not for want of trying. Digital content businesses typically try to create some kind of social element to create network effects and enhance customer captivity—few, however, succeed. "Over the years," Netflix conceded in frustration, "we have tried various ways to make Netflix more social."[55]

Even going back to the days of DVD by mail, Netflix tried to create "its own form of social networking" by establishing Netflix Friends in 2004. The program allowed members to invite other members to their networks, where they shared ratings and comments on films.[56] Despite never gaining traction, the company held on to the service until 2010 before shutting it down. As an alternative, Netflix established an initiative to integrate with Facebook Friends Connect. This was shut down in 2011 as a result of "user disinterest."[57] A new program called Netflix Social, which Mark Zuckerberg personally had a hand in designing, was introduced in 2013.[58] According to Netflix, that integration also "was never that popular so we shut the feature down in 2015."[59] Netflix even quietly eliminated user reviews altogether in 2018.[60] Hastings ultimately described his futile quest for network effects as a "competitive fantasy."[61]

Network effects aside, the competitive advantages Netflix is supposed to generate from its unique repository of "big data" fall into two broad buckets. The first relates to how it manages the customer experience, primarily based on how and what it recommends that subscribers should view. The second relates to the company's ability to consistently produce hit shows. The first of these is very real, although not new. The second is largely nonsense.

Well before Netflix was a streaming service, the company actively and effectively used customer data to develop a powerful recommendation engine. The benefits of these algorithms were two. First and most obviously, it enhanced customer satisfaction and reduced churn by constantly offering DVD selections most likely to be of interest. Second, because new releases are much more expensive to provide, the company could keep users happy and costs down by recommending older fare consistent with their interests.

In the streaming era, Netflix has much more data to work with. It knows not just what titles you hover on but whether and how you watch them. The service can track the movement of your cursor to divine which offerings you considered but decided against as well as every pause, fast forward, and show you never bothered to finish. It even knows what device you use to watch. Through relentless A/B testing across its user base, Netflix is uniquely positioned not only to perfect its recommendations but even to optimize which trailer to show which user on which device. As Netflix only somewhat hyperbolically likes to describe it, there are as many customized "different versions of Netflix" as there are subscribers.[62]

There is little reason to doubt that the increased level of data and sophistication facilitated by the rapid expansion of the streaming platform has genuinely improved the stickiness of the service, both relative to others and relative to what it would otherwise be. What one would want to be able to measure is the precise incremental proclivity of users to remain with the service by virtue of the positive attributes enabled by "big data." But the number of other moving variables—pricing, content available on the service, and competitive alternatives available in the market, to name a few—makes isolating these factors quite challenging, particularly from the outside. This is especially true in light of the company's decision in 2010 to stop reporting customer churn, even in the face of SEC resistance, based on the obviously specious justification that it is inadequate as a "reliable measure of business performance."[63]

Looking at the range of churn rates experienced by other subscription products reminds one just how fickle consumers (as compared to businesses) are in particular, with OTT/SVOD products manifesting some of the highest rates.[64] Estimates of Netflix annual churn mostly have ranged from 20 percent to over 35 percent.[65] Some research suggests that even with churn toward the higher end of this range, it is meaningfully lower than rates for many other SVOD services.[66] But this still means that, even using an assumption of 25 percent, with a global membership base of over 200 million by 2021, just to keep flat Netflix needs to attract more than 50 million new subscribers annually—well more than the total subscribers to Hulu. If we focus just on the approximately 75 million US subscribers, they would need close to 20 million new subscribers to keep flat—more subscribers than ViacomCBS reported that CBS All Access plus Showtime garnered together in their first six years of operation.[67] ViacomCBS has since folded CBS All Access into its 2021 entry into the SVOD streaming wars, Paramount+.[68]

None of this is to suggest that it is not worth wasting time on fully realizing the value of customer data to optimize customer relationship management. Indeed, in difficult markets like these, every little bit matters more and can sometimes mean the difference between life and death for a business. But because we don't know what churn would have been in the absence of big data, firm conclusions are difficult to draw. Although there is little doubt that Netflix customer retention is enhanced by using insights gleaned from customer data, it is hard to feel confident that for this use case big data is a strategic game changer. After all, a content subscription is mostly about the content, and no amount of big data is going to change that.

So how does big data change the ability of Netflix to deliver more compelling content at a lower cost, particularly in an environment where Netflix needs to produce an increasing proportion of that content itself? Contrary to conventional wisdom, the answer is almost not at all.[69]

Let's start with original production and the big lie at the heart of the narrative touting Netflix's apparent ability to algorithmically generate hits. It all begins with the origin story behind Netflix's first big hit, *House of Cards*. As the venerated David Carr of the *New York Times* described it, Netflix was able to prudently outbid all other comers for two seasons of the series—twenty-six episodes in total for a reported $100 million[70]—without so much as a pilot because of structural advantages bestowed by big data and artificial intelligence. In this telling, competitors were not privy to three key bits of data that together made *House of Cards* a sure-fire hit: the popularity of David Fincher–directed films, Kevin Spacey–starring films, and the original BBC *House of Cards* series with Netflix viewers. "With those three circles of interest," according to Carr, "Netflix was able to find a Venn diagram intersection that suggested buying the series would be a very good bet."[71]

This narrative is so ridiculous on its face that one would not feel a need to rebut it were various versions of this story not repeated so relentlessly. Such ex-post explanations for the selection of successful creative projects are designed to suggest a false level of predictability. They inevitably follow hits just as deafening silence follows flops.

Soon after the triumph of *House of Cards*, Netflix committed to a series more than twice as expensive—*Marco Polo*. Dropped by the original buyer, Starz, because of the prohibitive expense and complications of filming in China, *each* of the first two ten-episode seasons reportedly cost $100 million. When the show was canceled, no suggestion of an algorithmic glitch was provided. Indeed, the explanations originally proffered for the heavy financial commitment had a very old-school Hollywood sound to them.[72] Though it didn't feature any established stars, the series did share an executive producer with the popular HBO series *Game of Thrones*, and content chief Ted Saranos explained that "it is the kind of gripping action-adventure that Netflix members love."[73]

Marco Polo was one of the first Netflix series to be canceled.[74] The relative reluctance of Netflix to cancel shows, at least in the early years, is often cited as evidence of Netflix's talismanic abilities to identify hits. The service has claimed that it renews series it produces 93 percent of the time as compared to traditional networks' mere 33 percent of the time.[75] This difference, at least historically, is real, but it reflects that Netflix is a different business, solving for different economic outcomes.

Television networks need a certain level of national ratings to generate adequate advertising revenue for themselves and their broadcast affiliates. Some free streaming services do also rely on advertising—so-called AVOD services—and others, like Hulu, pursue a hybrid model. And the Nielsen ratings service claims that by 2024 it will have developed an entirely new ratings metric that incorporates digital and traditional viewing.[76] But none of this impacts Netflix, which is a pure SVOD business.

Netflix is managing subscribers that it has organized into no less than thirteen hundred different "taste communities" and looking to give them all enough options to feel satisfied.[77] It does not sell advertising and does not need to report usage, but the point is that it is playing a multi-flank long game to provide enough for a wide range of narrow interests along with some broader reach fare. What big data certainly does help with is knowing how much of each of these is needed to keep a subscriber engaged.

The use of data to help entertainment executives more systematically select projects has been around for almost half a century.[78] The use of traditional statistical techniques to find historic relationships between identified variables has given way to "neural networking" in which relatively indiscriminate masses of raw data can be fed into a computer to identify relevant relationships.[79] A wide range of AI start-ups have attracted both funding and studio customers for well over a decade,[80] and new ones continue to do so.[81]

All, however, face two fundamental limitations. First, they cannot account for changes in taste. Second, the number of potentially relevant variables (hundreds of thousands of possibilities) dwarfs the number of historic data points (merely thousands of films or series), inevitably leading to spurious correlations. It may be that some of these are helpful in optimizing marketing and distribution decisions, the primary reason for which these various "black box" approaches have been used for years.

There is, however, little evidence of the existence of an algorithmic hit-factory in any creative domain of substance. Jeff Bezos imagined he could leverage big data and crowd sourcing to dramatically increase the hit rate of original content from 10 percent to 40 percent. He ultimately abandoned his vision of the scientific studio and replaced it, in part, with his own extemporaneous articulation of the twelve elements he thinks all successful shows have in common. Bezos came to resemble an old world studio executive berating employees to "Bring me hits!" His modern version of this ancient refrain: "I want my *Game of Thrones*."[82]

Interestingly, as Netflix has started to report some selective data on the "ratings" of its most watched programs, the fundamental difference in the business Netflix is in has become more apparent. Its most watched programs of the last years—the films *Birdbox* with Sandra Bullock in 2018 and *Murder Mystery* with Adam Sandler and Jennifer Aniston in 2019—are not "popular" either with critics or viewers, at least if the lukewarm reviews on Metacritic and Rotten Tomatoes are any indication.[83] It is far from clear whether either of these films would have been successful had they been released into theaters.[84] Conversely, it is possible that if the high-profile big-budget flops of recent years, like *Cats* or *Dolittle*, instead had been released on Netflix, they would have attracted enough curiosity to be touted as resounding successes. OK, maybe not *Cats*.

Birdbox and *Murder Mystery* are in a class of mid-budget films that are neither sequel nor spinoff that have stopped being economic for theatrical distribution—even when topped off with a big-name star (or two).[85] Netflix has demonstrated that there is still a demand for some of these at least at home. What big data has not done, and will not do, is provide a template for how to make them well.[86]

Hastings's 2020 book with Professor Erin Meyer on the company's culture and management philosophy, *No Rules Rules: Netflix and the Culture of Reinvention*, contains a number of anecdotes about programming decisions at the company. What is most notable about these descriptions is just how small a role data appears to play in practice. Take children's programming. Hastings had long been of the view that such content neither attracted new subscribers nor played much of a role in keeping existing ones.[87] What changed his mind, apparently, was not big data, but an employee meeting in which parents shared the importance of access to trusted advertising-free content in their own subscription decision-making. The resulting decision to develop a global franchise based on a modest Indian animation series, *Mighty Little Bheem*, was the outcome of broad strategic imperatives, not artificial intelligence. In fact, the ultimate decision maker noted "a lack of historical data on preschool shows—even within India."[88]

As of 2020, although most of Netflix's new content is original production, the vast majority of what is watched remains licensed.[89] For obvious reasons, people only license content that has already proven popular. And between data and research services like Nielsen and Comscore, the popularity of films and television shows is widely known, along with the demographic profile of their viewers. Netflix may know more about the preferences of its own subscribers and what to recommend to a particular subscriber. But, at least in the US, the Netflix subscriber base looks increasingly like the overall market that it is close to saturating, so it is hard to argue that it has much greater insight on what programs to license.

The good news for Netflix—even if it still doesn't benefit from meaningful network effects, and the incremental benefits of big data are probably limited—is that it remains a supremely well-run company with real scale and customer captivity. What's more, Netflix is the poster child of a business that has been a beneficiary of the pandemic as binge-watching shut-ins all around the globe subscribed in unprecedented numbers.[90] And although some of this was simply pulling forward subscribers they would have gotten later, the acceleration of permanent cord-cutting provided long-term structural support to the SVOD sector.[91]

The bad news is that all the other SVOD services benefited from the pandemic as well, chipping away at Netflix's relative scale as it fell from almost half of all US SVOD subscribers to barely a quarter in under two years. That many of the best-funded competitors are entirely new exacerbates this challenge, despite Netflix upping the ante on the fixed cost required to play this expensive game competitively. The fact that this has been financially disastrous for the onslaught of newer SVOD entrants does not make it less bad news for Netflix, particularly given that those challenging results do not appear to have limited availability of competitor funding for the foreseeable future. And although data assets allow Netflix to enhance customer captivity, the emergence of these competitors suggests this dimension of advantage has been weakened as well.

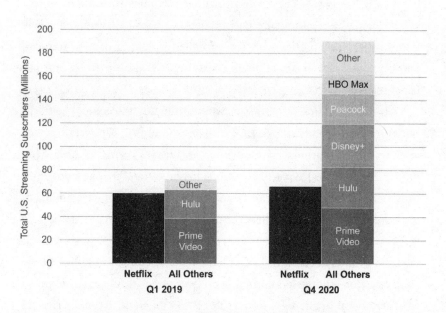

**Total US SVOD Subscribers
Netflix vs. All Others (Q1 2019–Q4 2020)**

Figure 7.1

Source: HarrisX, MoffettNathanson

Note: "Other" includes CBS All Access, Showtime, and Apple TV+

THE CONTENT CONUNDRUM

Within the media business, the business of content persistently attracts outsized interest and generates undersized returns. Over time, the lion's share of value (at least the value that is left over after the talent takes its cut) has always been retained by the aggregators and the distributors. This is simply because the industrial structure of these businesses lends itself to competitive advantages—notably scale and customer captivity— that content creation does not. Content that is produced continuously, as opposed to that created by the pure hit-driven studios and publishers that are the subject of particular public fascination, afford greater opportunity for scale and captivity. But even this form of content rarely attained the attractiveness of the best aggregation and distribution businesses.

Digital technologies have in general had the impact of lowering entry barriers in content creation by reducing the fixed costs required and making it easier to switch. For newly vulnerable incumbents, this has led to a variety of efforts seeking alternative potential barriers leveraging newly found digital capabilities—by, for example, exploiting data to improve performance or establishing direct consumer relationships and personalizing product.

This story has played out somewhat differently in each of the traditional media content sectors. But, to date, the impact on overall profitability of these various countervailing influences seems to have been mostly negligible on most of these hit-driven sectors. Music, book, and film margins have jumped around more over the years but have tended to settle in a similar range—where they remain.[92] At one level, this is hardly surprising. Given that the hit content creation racket was never a great business in the first place, it didn't have anywhere much to fall. And the ability of well-represented and proven talent to ensure that "the man"— whether digital or analog—doesn't retain too much of the spoils ensures that the upside is capped.

The bigger they are, however, the harder they fall. When digital intrusion threatens the profitable content aggregators, the downside is signifi-cant. And when your best defense is to move more aggressively into a less attractive business—content creation—margin pressure is the inevitable result. This is what the biggest and most successful content aggregation businesses—cable channels—have experienced as they face the choice to double down on content spending to retain as much distribution as possi-ble or simply give up the goat and milk the residual cash flows.

In the case of Netflix, the initial decision to go digital had the benefit of dramatically expanding the potential addressable market. But, even before introducing content into the mix, it also ensured that its busi-ness would become more competitive. Once Blockbuster missed the op-portunity to kill Netflix in its cradle or buy it,[93] the regional distribution hubs Netflix had built along with the customer loyalty it had earned made any serious effort to dislodge its commanding position in the DVD-by-mail business impractical. Netflix appreciated that if it stood still, other streaming competitors would eventually emerge that would eat away at its dominant DVD distribution service. And by virtue of its large in-stalled base and unique combination of skills in online customer manage-ment and marketing and negotiating with content owners, Netflix benefited from a much-invoked but rarely experienced phenomenon: a first-mover advantage.

The advantage is not in going first but in gaining scale. And the abil-ity to quickly gain scale by going first requires relatively stable product/market fit and technology. If either is in significant flux, customers are likely to hedge their bets before signing up, making gaining critical mass challenging for the brave first mover. That is why the winner in most mar-kets is someone who let others undertake what is effectively free R&D for them and only invests big once greater visibility emerges as to the shape of demand and technology requirements.

Netflix already had significant insight into all these critical matters. Its experience selling entertainment content subscriptions to consumers was absolutely unique, and Google's purchase of YouTube the year before it launched streaming provided comfort that the digital infrastructure would support an industrial-strength video service. And although the fixed-cost barrier that the physical distribution hubs once provided were eliminated in the streaming sphere, the fixed marketing costs required to launch a national subscription service were substantial, as was the technological infrastructure required to effectively support and manage a digital streaming customer base. Indeed, while there were no longer regional distribution hubs needed, Netflix had to establish major content storage hubs around the country in order to minimize buffering and ensure a consistently satisfying quality of service.

Making enough proven, beloved content created by others available to establish a satisfying service in itself represents a significant fixed cost. And the dominant scale player can set the bar for competitive content high enough that the smaller players will hemorrhage cash while it makes a good living. But the downside of huge global markets is that more players imagine they can achieve the scale required to survive. Netflix now faces at least six well-capitalized competitors chasing the same content, talent, and subscribers.

But the need to aggressively move into the business of creating unproven content—and the ongoing mix shift from the one type of content to the other—to continue to maintain relative scale is unambiguously bad financial news. The need to take creative risk as a core dimension of heightened competition ensures a deadweight loss to the system as value necessarily gets diverted from the collective competitors to the talent who play them off each other. Much of that loss will come from its shareholders' pockets.

The explosion of new entrants in a market where the well-run market leader struggles to generate cash flow reminds one of the joke about the best way to become a millionaire as a newspaper publisher—start as a billionaire. All the near-term noise around the mounting losses and launches can obscure the longer-term view of what a sustainable market equilibrium might look like. Given the structural attributes lending themselves to fixed-cost scale advantages buttressed by some customer captivity, itself reinforced by learning from data, it would be surprising if a small number of at least modestly profitable players of scale would not emerge.

The experience of the newspaper business is instructive of what a steady-state world might look like for Netflix. Although newspapers were mostly thought of as being solely in the continuous content creation business, they are in fact creators, aggregators, and distributors just like Netflix. If you pick up a typical newspaper, you may be surprised to discover that much of what fills its pages, between wire stories and advertisements, is aggregated content.

In chapter 3 we discussed in detail the sustainable digital economics of the *New York Times*. But if the nuanced story of the *Times* involved a number of puts and takes, for the local newspapers that had always represented the vast majority of newspaper circulation and profit, the impact has been uniformly devastating. In a digital environment, the aggregation and distribution functions have been commoditized and high-margin classified advertising has moved online, prompting a vicious cycle in which dramatically reduced revenues support less original content, further driving down revenues. Many of the digital-only content competitors, although successful in accelerating the decline of newspapers and attracting funding and eyeballs, have failed in the absence of meaningful barriers to entry to achieve consistent profitability.[94]

The pure online classified businesses that took significant market share from the newspapers have often fared only marginally better. Although some have managed to achieve multibillion-dollar public valuations, even with network effects—in the absence of any significant customer captivity and with limited fixed-cost requirements—they have eventually collapsed in the public markets as other competitive marketplaces have flooded many of these niches. Monster.com was the original online employment classified site and one of the earliest successful internet IPOs in

1996. After going public at $7, the stock reached a peak of $91 in 2000 at a valuation approaching $10 billion. It was bought by a global staffing company for a few hundred million dollars in 2016, having long been marginalized by direct broad-based and niche competitors like Career-Builder and dice.com as well as entirely new competitor categories like LinkedIn and Indeed.[95]

We saw, however, that the fate of the *New York Times*, the leading general interest national newspaper, in the face of digital disruption has been quite different for three primary reasons. First, the *New York Times*'s content, much like Netflix but unlike local newspaper content, had a significant untapped market that supported online subscriptions. Second, the larger addressable market supports further investment in content, upping the fixed cost price of entry for a credible subscription competitor. Third, the *New York Times* was never as reliant on advertising as local papers and relatively even less on the classified advertising that drove local paper profitability.

So the digital ecosystem has allowed the *Times* to radically expand its reach and improve its economic performance relative to the local newspapers whose profitability once dwarfed theirs. The sources of the *Times*'s historic competitive advantages—scale and captivity—have been enhanced in some ways. Its relative subscriber position and the relative size of its reportorial workforce has improved, and the concern about fake news has arguably increased the search costs associated with finding equally credible reporting. And the subscriber data it collects undoubtedly allows the company to allocate resources more intelligently and manage its customer relationships more effectively.

But the internet has created a broadly more competitive environment—whether from a resurgent *Washington Post* or Time Inc.—with billionaire backers, new digital-only players targeting narrow interest areas, or clever mega-aggregators like Apple, Google, or Facebook. So yes, the *Times* is well positioned to be one of only a small number of broad-based global English-language news services of scale, but as we saw, compared to the

New York Times of 2000, the *New York Times* of 2020 was still less profitable and less valuable.

What does this say for Netflix's prospects? Like the *Times*, it is the scale leader in a global content market that is unlikely to ultimately support more than a very few broad-based subscription services despite the digital medium's significant expansion of the overall market potential. In SVOD, Disney appears to have committed itself to this strategy and has the assets required to achieve scale, even if the financial returns realized on the road to getting there seem bleak. Amazon also has the financial wherewithal to keep its implicit pledge to Prime members to deliver expensive content along with fast free shipping indefinitely regardless of the economics. None of the other emerging competitors seems to have the combination of skills, resources, or commitment required to become a long-term global Netflix competitor. Some will persist and may carve out a sustainable geographic, psychographic, or demographic product niche.

That would represent a market structure in which Netflix should be able to thrive for the long term much like the *New York Times*. But in the short or maybe even medium term, Netflix faces a long list of mind-bogglingly deep-pocketed and possibly not fully economically rational competitors who have decided that they want to be in this business.

Thomas Hobbes described life in the state of nature as "poor, nasty, brutish, and short." There is no question that the first three adjectives accurately describe what competition will be like during this period. Whether it will be short, given the hundreds of billions of dollars of ready cash and available financing on the competitors' collective balance sheets, is open to question. Based on the behaviors of the analog moguls of yore, rather than beating a well-considered retreat, the movie is more likely to end when one of them decides they would be better off overpaying for Netflix rather than continuing to burn their shareholders' hard-earned money.

KEY CHAPTER TAKEAWAYS

1. Despite being derided by traditional media moguls as a mere re-seller of others' content or "rerun TV," Netflix always derived its historic advantages from supply-side scale and customer captivity. These are the same sources that allowed cable channels to drive media conglomerate profitability for decades. Netflix differs from these businesses, however, in its direct consumer relationships and its maniacal focus on operational excellence.

2. Netflix's shift from DVD distribution to online streaming was necessitated by the inevitable competitive influx of streaming competitors. By moving early and leveraging its customers, content relationships, and technological capabilities, Netflix did benefit from being a first mover to establish scale quickly in the SVOD environment.

3. Many have ascribed to Netflix's current streaming model strong network effects and the ability to select hit content based on its access to big data and AI. Although the data available to Netflix has enabled it to enhance its personalized recommendation engine, there is no evidence of significant new sources of competitive advantage.

4. Netflix's decision to invest aggressively in original content creation reflected both the intensity of new competition and the decision by many of the largest established content creators to no longer license to Netflix. While it was strategically sensible for Netflix, the business of taking creative risk has always yielded paltry long-term financial returns.

5. The combination of Netflix's structural advantages and commitment to operational excellence suggests a market equilibrium in streaming in which it and no more than a very few broad-based global players will ultimately survive. The road to equilibrium, given the large number of well-financed and committed competitors, will be bumpy and expensive.

GOOGLE:
LETTER-PERFECT ALPHABET

WHAT DO YOU GET THE company that has everything?[1] Alphabet is the unique franchise that seems to simultaneously benefit strongly from every relevant category of competitive advantage. Although the various "moon shots" like driverless cars, Google Glass, the health initiative Verily, and drones that emerged from the onetime "X" division are a source of endless fascination,[2] the company basically does one thing incredibly well: sell advertising. And the vast majority of that advertising is sold in connection with the core Google search capability. Throw in not just the moon shots, but also purchases made through the Google Play app store, various hardware devices like Nest home products and Pixelbooks and phones, YouTube subscription products, and even Google Cloud, and roughly 85 percent of Google's over $150 billion in revenues still persistently comes from advertising.

Google's longtime chief economist, Hal Varian, wrote a strange blog post a dozen years ago arguing that a single attribute explains the "secret sauce" behind its remarkable results: learning.[3] Although a much smaller company at the time, it had more than doubled its share of paid searches in the US in just the past four years, which already exceeded 75 percent in 2007. Today Google's global share is around 90 percent.[4]

A close reading of the blog post suggests that Varian does not really believe that this single quality explains Google's success. A cynic might be forgiven for thinking that Varian is intentionally playing semantic games to minimize the largest external risk to a company of its extraordinary resilience: regulatory risk. Antitrust authorities have a harder time attacking targets that can claim they owe their remarkable achievements to getting continuously smarter, and thus better for consumers, through the learning effects inherent in the business model.

Google's thoughtful approach to positioning its strengths, and its cautious approach to the use of internal emails, has been rewarded with a less far-reaching challenge from US antitrust authorities than the breakup being proposed to Facebook. Unfortunately for them, the state antitrust authorities have been less accommodating.[5] This relative success with the federal regulators was achieved despite the fact that Google represents the most impregnable competitive fortress among its FAANG brethren. What's more, some of its historic acquisitions—notably the $3.1 billion DoubleClick deal in advertising technology[6] and the $1 billion Waze deal in maps[7]—were arguably more problematic than those now targeted by the Federal Trade Commission for reversal at Facebook.

This is not to suggest that Google doesn't benefit from learning, only that this is simply one of a breathtaking number of mutually reinforcing advantages upon which the leviathan rests. Like Netflix, Google started life as a pure aggregator—as its corporate mission "to organize the world's information" makes clear. Unlike Netflix, however, the depth of Google's structural advantages ensured that it never needed to go into the content creation business in any serious way.[8]

The particular portfolio of competitive advantages that undergirds the Google franchise does not follow the traditional narrative of the Platform Delusion. Contrary to the views of some commentators who assign to network effects a role comparable to what Varian assigns to learning effects,[9] this is not the primary source of Google's overwhelming strength. And although Google does benefit from network effects, their true nature and consequences are different from what is widely assumed.

Google is the rare company that seems to have strong elements of all three of the most important sources of competitive advantage identified—economies of scale plus reinforcing demand and supply advantages. More remarkable is that Google displays multiple manifestations of each of these categories of advantage: the advantages of Google's scale flow from both the relative size of its fixed-cost base and network effects; it retains customer captivity of both consumers and advertisers because of habit, switching and search costs; and it secures major cost advantages through proprietary technology enhanced continuously by learning and data. Although these various advantages work together, it is still worth examining each individually in some detail to better understand precisely what makes Google's core franchise uniquely invulnerable to successful competitive attack.

SCALE

Notwithstanding Google's sometimes comical arguments over the years that search is not a market at all (you don't pay for it, so how can it be a market?) or just that it is not the relevant market (it competes against all advertising everywhere or, alternatively, all internet usage of any kind), at 90 percent of global search, Google's relative scale is not in doubt. If Microsoft couldn't make a dent with Bing after over a decade, it is small wonder that DuckDuckGo has fared no better. Those few who can still claim relevance in the market are restricted to a protected geography (Baidu in China or Yandex in Russia)[10] or niche search use case (Amazon in product search).

The greatest benefits of scale in search are of the old-fashioned supply-side variety and stem from the ability to spread the huge fixed-cost requirements over the larger user base. There are a variety of pieces to the fixed-cost infrastructure required to enable the basic search function at scale. Although it is not possible to identify which part of Google's more than $25 billion R&D budget is reflective of the fixed costs needed to support the continuous improvement of its search functions, its size both absolutely and relative to its FAANG peers is suggestive of the magnitude of the supply-side scale advantage in search.

Consider the fixed costs required to undertake the process of organizing the world's information and the value of having a large R&D budget to continuously improve each critical step in the chain that produces search results on an ongoing basis. Google's "crawler" programs automatically search the web and download pages to Google data centers. Google's technology in this area determines the completeness of search results. Google's "indexer" programs then organize the downloaded material into its databases and benefit from the design of the hardware and software of Google's massive data centers, including a not-so-secret massive flotilla of floating ones.[11] The efficient organization of Google's data centers is itself subject to a technology patent. This hardware and software together account for the superior speed of Google searches. Finally, Google's "query processor" organizes search results for presentation to users.

The combined effect of these investments and technologies make Google search results superior in completeness, speed, and, most important, relevance to those of other search engines.[12] And even if a potential competitor could match the investment in the hopes of splitting the market, the portfolio of complementary competitive advantages enjoyed by Google would thwart these efforts.

Although not as strong as scale effects on the supply side, Google benefits from a number of network effects as well. Because Google's search engine is ubiquitous, new users are likely to be introduced to it and trained to its use before even learning of its rivals. Other websites are also more likely to use Google because of its strong position with users. These tendencies, in turn, then increase the number of Google users, which is further reinforcing.

And one can't help noticing when starting to write a search query that Google's autocomplete feature often magically guesses what you might be planning to ask. This trick is based in part on the voluminous data the engine has about what other users are asking, suggesting a network effect from every incremental user improving the search experience of all users. More broadly, there is little question that Google's greater familiarity with prior search behavior drives a scale advantage on the demand side by facilitating the effective customization of the selection and presentation of search results for individual users.

But all prior experience is not equal. The incremental value of a new search query by one user for the results of another user is trivial. On the other hand, Google learns a lot about how to optimize results by looking at the same user's previous queries and clicks. So to the extent that there is a direct network effect on the user side of search, it is overwhelmingly driven by the number of one's own prior searches rather than the number of other searchers.

The more significant network effect flowing from Google's scale derives not from users but from the marketplace for advertising. In advertising, Google benefits from more than just the ubiquity-related network effects that apply to search. For example, its AdSense program, which places ads on blogs and other relatively small, decentralized sites, is especially attractive to advertisers because of its wide access to such sites and ability to customize placements based on extensive experience with these sites. At the same time, websites are drawn disproportionately to AdSense because that is where the greatest concentration of advertisers resides. AdExchange, Google's real-time bidding exchange for premium publishers and big brand advertisers, benefits from the same network effect dynamic. Many of Google's products in the area were rebranded as Google Ad Manager in 2018.

Notably, AdSense and AdExchange—collectively reported as Google Network Members' properties—Google's businesses that benefit most strongly from network effects, are a fraction of the size of the core search business that benefits predominantly from supply-side scale. The advertising revenue from this segment is less than a fifth of the revenue from Google's owned search properties, including Google.com, YouTube, Gmail, and Maps. And that proportion has been falling for years.

DEMAND

Customer loyalty, from both searchers and advertisers, to Google's search engine is a critical factor reinforcing the benefits of scale. Users become more effective at using particular search programs with experience, and that experience makes the incumbent search engine more effective at delivering relevant results. The sacrifice of this historic search investment by moving to a new search engine is a further source of loyalty to Google.

Experience with Google advertising and Google's automated programs for placing ads leads to advertiser loyalty in the same way that experience reinforces searcher loyalty. Much of the Justice Department's recent investigation of Google originally focused on whether this loyalty has been fairly earned or coerced by Google integrating software tools that dominate "every link in the complex chain between online publishers and advertisers."[13] Specifically, regulators looked at how Google links its leading products for websites to put their ad space up for sale with its leading digital advertising marketplaces. They also explored the propriety of the company's insistence that advertisers use Google's software tools when seeking placement on the Google-owned leading video website, YouTube.[14]

Google, for its part, insists that it is simply creating a more seamless and effective experience for both advertisers and publishers. Ironically, regulators' focus on Google's central role in the placement of digital display advertising has corresponded to the dramatic decrease in importance of this category of advertising generally and of these services to Google's profits specifically. As we discuss shortly, the Justice Department's 2020 antitrust suit ultimately decided to target an entirely different aspect of the business for the time being. Even if the federal government decides to revisit this topic later, or if the state lawsuit that focuses on it is successful, it will have little impact on the overall customer stickiness of Google's franchise or of its ability to invest more than anyone else to make the experience even better.

This multisided and multifaceted loyalty is enhanced by the ongoing product improvements in both the quality of search results and advertising effectiveness. The demand and supply advantages in the digital realm are often tightly linked in this way. An initially weak customer habit can quickly translate into product improvements, often with customized user applications, spawned by learning. These enhancements increase switching costs as users recognize the futility of finding equally satisfying search results elsewhere.

SUPPLY

On the supply side, technology and learning are themselves deeply intertwined advantages in digital environments where customer data facilitate continuous improvement. The very idea of someone developing a "better" technology in the abstract can seem impractical in use cases such as search where the application of well-established machine learning algorithms can quickly and demonstrably enhance results. How can Bing or Duck-DuckGo, no matter how much cleverer the coders and technologists they may attract, produce results as satisfying to me as Google if they have no experience with my search behavior? And of course, the presentation of paid advertising on Google is also determined by algorithms that are based on extensive response experiences and customized for advertising and individual users. The steady improvement in these proprietary algorithms over time has led to both increasing click-through rates for Google ads and steadily higher conversion rates for advertisers from clicks to sales. The latter improvements have, in turn, led to steadily higher advertising prices. In both areas, Google significantly outperforms its competitors and the gap is only increasing over time.

The speed with which learning-enhanced proprietary technology kicks in and grows over time varies widely by use case and can be a double-edged sword. For some digital businesses, the very speed with which customer data can be incorporated to improve or customize the product also enhances the ability of new entrants to catch up quickly. In applications where a little data goes a long way and the incremental value of a lot of data is marginal, proprietary technology and learning offer few structural advantages. The track record of Google, however, suggests that search represents a use case in which the integrated advantages of data-driven learning and technology are persistent and continue to grow without topping out.

The core scale advantages that come from the vast and growing investments in both search and advertising R&D reinforce these already tightly connected supply and demand advantages. This kind of virtuous cycle between Google's learning-enhanced proprietary technology and network effect supported customer captivity among both users and advertisers on the one hand and traditional cost–based economies of scale in R&D and other areas suggest that its remarkable economic performance is likely to endure. Google's "secret sauce" has many deeply interrelated ingredients, so the fact that Google founders Larry Page and Sergei Brin's original innovation embodied in their PageRank algorithm has long been fully available to their competitors is largely an economic irrelevance.

Despite this clear story about the real sources of competitive advantage, in *The Curse of the Mogul*, published over a decade ago, my coauthors and I noted some disturbing cultural parallels between Google and the media conglomerates whose systematic poor performance we sought to expose. Like these entertainment giants, Google maintained a studied mystique around its business strategies in the years following its 2004 IPO. Where media moguls explained all manner of shareholder value destruction in pursuit of the imperative that "content is king," in the early years after going public Google limited its public utterances to enigmatic high-level platitudes like "Don't be evil."[15] The company disclosed only the minimum legally required, carefully guarding as trade secrets not only its software algorithms but the nature and location of its facilities and even the precise responsibilities of its leading executives.[16]

One only slightly more specific core notion was a 70/20/10 rule under which 70 percent of workers' time is directed toward search, 20 percent toward adjacent areas, and 10 percent toward completely unrelated realms.[17] In theory, building adjacencies that genuinely leverage an existing competitive advantage to build a new franchise is both attractive in itself and serves to protect the core. In practice, for Google as much as others, the line between the supposedly adjacent and the clearly unrelated can be shifted to justify all manner of empire building. What's more, just as media moguls can't resist highlighting the hits and ignoring the flops, Google heavily promoted any successful product that came from the almost one third of employee time directed away from the core business without providing any metrics for assessing the returns on this massive investment.

There is little doubt that Google's ability to manifest such a compelling and comprehensive array of competitive advantages is in part a function of the fact that it has focused—as most successful companies do—in a highly specialized field. The fact that search broadly conceived turns out to be not only essential for most internet users but to have remarkably broad application to a variety of tools and services required by enterprises as well explains how the business has become much larger than anyone, including the founders, imagined possible. But this should not distract from the fact that it is the specialization that facilitates the advantages.

The fear that the company was diverting a significant fraction of its considerable resources into unrelated enterprises rather than digging the moat of competitive advantage ever deeper remained a real one for investors despite the substantial share appreciation during its first decade as a public company. The combination of grandiose initiatives and lack of financial transparency began to weigh on the stock, which actually fell slightly in 2014. The following year, the company hired a well-respected outsider as CFO[18] and announced the separation of search from its other initiatives under the newly established Alphabet holding company umbrella. It also, for the first time, imposed a time limit on its long-term research projects, many of which bear only the most tenuous connection to its core business.[19]

The restructuring was positioned more as an effort to unburden the sexy new innovative initiatives from the deadweight of the legacy business than as an effort to constrain their spending and narrow their focus.[20] But even Eric Schmidt, the original "adult supervision"[21] brought in to help Google move beyond its start-up roots, noted that much of the value of separating these initiatives would protect the golden goose simply by getting rid of the distracting moon shots. Until the restructuring, Schmidt conceded, "a disproportionate part of the day would be spent on moonshots."[22]

Although the shift to a holding company structure institutionalized the commitment to multiple enterprises unrelated to the core search franchise, the commitment to at least divulge "how much money is being poured into big new schemes"[23] was an important step forward. Although scant details were provided, investors felt that simply reporting results separately would force the leadership to keep its newly articulated commitment to "rigorously handle capital allocation and work to make sure each business is executing well."[24] Based on the positive stock price reaction, it appeared that the market was answering in the affirmative the metaphysical question posed by John Cassidy of the *New Yorker* in connection with the announcement, "Can Google Become a Normal Business?"[25]

The stock reacted with similar favor when it was announced in late 2019 that Sundar Pichai, the well-regarded CEO of Google, would replace the cofounders in the top job at the parent company. This change signaled an even sharper focus on both transparency and financial discipline rather than any fundamental change in the day-to-day operations at Alphabet.[26]

The promise of Pichai with respect to the former was quickly realized when he offered new detailed levels of disclosure on both YouTube and the cloud computing division on his first earnings call.[27] With respect to financial discipline, time will tell. Assurances were provided that a "sharper focus" would be applied to investments in the various moon-shot projects that continued to drain cash from the company.

Many questions remain with respect to the future of Alphabet. The *Economist* has expressed skepticism over whether the increasingly corporate management team has the vision to transition the famously engineering-centric culture through middle age.[28] The sentiment that "if it can be automated, it will be automated" was deeply ingrained at Google and had long applied even to areas like sales and customer service.[29] Among the existential questions facing the company are whether it can now embrace customer service in businesses like Cloud, where it is essential. Although Google and Microsoft both launched AWS competitors in 2008, a decade later Google's business was far less than half as large as Microsoft's.[30] Although with new leadership it has accelerated growth more recently, that Google Cloud remains a distant third is reflective of the deep challenges in building a sales culture from a standing start. Even if ultimately successful, the broader question is whether it can retain a culture of innovation in the context of a more structured operating environment.

And despite receiving plaudits from investors regarding Pichai's intentions with respect to how capital will be allocated in the future, Alphabet's stock price appreciation relative to the rest of FAANG suggests a wait-and-see attitude. At issue is not just the mix of future investment between moon shots and roof shots, but the criteria to be applied for either. As early as 2014, the company realized that an "over-glamorization" of moon shots at the expense of "methodical, relentless, persistent pursuit" of opportunities closer to home had been costly to the company.[31] And while progress had been made in shifting the emphasis, it is actually here that the Justice Department's recent lawsuit against Google could have the greatest impact.

Apart from Google's clever government and public relations efforts, the federal government's decision to tailor its challenge narrowly to Google's commercial deals with Apple and others to serve as the default search engine is likely driven by one primary consideration: it's a winner. Having recently suffered serial humiliations in court in its efforts to block AT&T's purchase of Time Warner,[32] the Justice Department "essentially copied the successful antitrust complaint it filed against Microsoft in 1998."[33] Given the limited scope of the suit and the fact that it will take years to wend its way through the system, the bigger danger to Google shareholders might be something that appears unrelated: a reacceleration of undisciplined moon shots.

Google has well over $100 billion on its balance sheet and is adding tens of billions more every year. Even with an aggressive buyback program, it can't spend anything near that amount in its core businesses, which display astounding returns—particularly if the government is successful in halting its payments for preferential distribution. And notwithstanding that, after over a year of review, its $2.1 billion purchase of Fitbit has finally closed, the US government apparently continues to monitor the transaction.[34] It seems unlikely that any significant new acquisitions could be in their future for some time.

Sadly, that only leaves the moon shots that had mercifully been scaled back in recent years. In its most recent 10-K, Google quietly removed its insistence that it would not pay a dividend "for the foreseeable future."[35] Based on the historic return on investment of Google's acquisitions and initiatives outside of its core—the $10 billion write-down of the Motorola Mobility business comes to mind as much as the stream of losses emanating from Google X—starting to systematically give the money back to shareholders seems a more prudent use of the mounting cash hoard.

All of this is speculation. What is clear, however, is the singular strength of the core Google franchise, built on a collection of mutually reinforcing competitive advantages of unparalleled breadth and depth. Future leaders of Alphabet can certainly find ways to squander the prodigious cash flows generated by the core business. It would take real sustained ingenuity, however, to undermine the structural resilience of the Google search business.

The very exceptionality of Google limits its usefulness as a template for either entrepreneurs or investors. Calling it a platform, which it is, adds little to understanding how it operates. Focusing on network effects, or any one of its myriad competitive advantages in isolation, risks fostering a fundamental misunderstanding of the business. Perhaps the most important lesson of a close study of Google is the most obvious one: wherever possible, at least when it comes to its core advertising franchise, avoid competing with it.

KEY CHAPTER TAKEAWAYS

1. Google has strong elements of all three of the most important sources of competitive advantage: economies of scale reinforced by demand and supply advantages. What's more, Google displays multiple manifestations of each of these categories of advantage.
2. Many have emphasized the importance of one or another entry barrier to explain the extraordinary resilience of the Google franchise. While there is value to analyzing the impact of each particular competitive advantage, this should not distract from the overarching insight that Google's singularity stems from the unparalleled breadth and depth of its collection of mutually reinforcing competitive advantages.
3. The remarkable structural strength of Google's core business led it to experiment in a wide number of unrelated domains without applying clear operating or financial discipline. In recent years, however, Google has both successfully transitioned its leadership and reorganized its structure to permit it to optimize its principle activities and more prudently invest in emerging opportunities. The result is an extraordinarily powerful combination of structural resilience and operational effectiveness.
4. Don't compete with Google if you can avoid it.

PART III

IN THE SHADOW OF THE GIANTS

Until now we have been occupied with two closely related enterprises.

First, we examined the underlying structural attributes of the digital ecosystem that has arisen over the last twenty-five years as the internet age flourished thanks to the development of technologies and infrastructure to support its full potential. Here the focus has been on the ways in which this environment has changed how competitive advantage is most likely to manifest itself in commercial enterprises. Although many have focused on how the digital era has facilitated the attainment of certain competitive advantages and expanded the potential scope within which they can operate, we show why other important advantages have become more ephemeral than ever.

Second, we analyzed in detail the sources of advantage enjoyed by FAANG, the five iconic companies that have come to represent a new generation of tech titans. Although they are not the only massive technology businesses to have been spawned by current conditions, this spotlight on the FAANG companies is justified by their collective stock performance and the unprecedented proportion of the overall market they have come to represent. What's more, for better or worse, the FAANG gang have secured a central role in the mythology of digital tech titans. What we have emphasized is that as notable as their collective significance are their individual differences. Although all are indeed powerful platforms, each company benefits from distinct portfolios of competitive advantage yielding stark differences in combined strength.

The next logical question is, What does this all mean for the rest of us? In other words, what are the implications for those who have not achieved tech titan status, at least so far? That is the topic to which we turn in part III.

For those companies that are not already among the select elite, this new world poses a double challenge. The lower break-even market shares and greater difficulties securing strong customer captivity in digital environments necessarily poses a real impediment to building a strong overarching competitive moat, even in a world where network effects and customer data are easier to access. And the fact that these efforts to construct and reinforce such a moat must be undertaken in the shadow of the extraordinary reach of the new awe-inspiring technology giants intensifies the difficulty of the task. Companies must confront the overwhelming influence of the tech titans not only in the core businesses where they dominate but also in a far wider range of adjacent sectors in which they still have an actual or potential competitive impact.

Several considerations have driven the selection of companies, sectors, and business models covered in part III. The goal is to paint a landscape of enough depth and breadth to provide the tools needed to trace how those beyond the borders of FAANG can successfully chart a course through the shoals of that double challenge. In discussing FAANG, particularly the more focused players like Netflix, we have already touched on a number of the direct competitors. In this section, however, we examine the obstacles and opportunities more broadly in sectors that have particular economic relevance, incorporate business models central to the digital economy, were not otherwise addressed, or highlight an important aspect of the Platform Delusion.

Although we have already discussed the strengths and weaknesses of Amazon in detail, the unique breadth of its articulated ambition—to sell anything to anyone, anywhere—requires a deeper dive into e-commerce. Chapter 9 identifies some commonalities of the categories and companies that have managed to thrive in the face of "the everything store" as well as those that have struggled.

Chapters 10 and 11 are dedicated to travel and tourism, which contribute something approaching $10 trillion to world GDP.[1] Although it is not, as sometimes falsely claimed, the world's largest industry,[2] it does display a number of other characteristics that justify two full chapters. The diversity of network effects business models, some of which exceeded their early promise and others of which have profoundly disappointed, is exceptionally useful in highlighting the most important drivers of success. What's more, the fact that some of the most successful network effects businesses in the sector both predate the internet and have been surprisingly unaffected by it challenges an essential element of the Platform Delusion.

The sharing economy is responsible for a disproportionate number of the highest-profile digital IPOs of recent years. The companies that fall under its rubric represent quintessential platform companies that create value by connecting holders of excess capacity with potential users of it.

Chapter 12 documents the huge variations in the attractiveness of some of these businesses, despite the obvious similarities, particularly between the two largest—Airbnb and Uber.

Google and Facebook are to digital advertising what Amazon is to e-commerce. But there are far more viable independent online retailers and marketplaces than there are sustainable business models of size reliant solely on online advertising. Chapter 13 follows the plight of the once mighty advertising agencies and the fate of the hundreds of failed adtech start-ups. More broadly we consider where in the sector there is still white space left to develop defensible business models in the face of Google's and Facebook's near duopoly (increasingly an oligopoly with Amazon) in digital advertising and adtech.

The FAANG companies have one significant attribute in common beyond size and performance—they overwhelmingly serve consumer markets (Amazon's AWS division is the most notable exception). In recent years, dozens of lower-profile but more consistently resilient multibillion-dollar cloud-based software platforms have been established to serve specific business sectors or functions. Chapter 14 uses the emergence of this more than trillion-dollar software-as-a-service (SaaS) sector to contradict several predictions central to the Platform Delusion—the tendency toward winner-take-all markets, the critical role of network effects in achieving digital success, and the decline of the relevancy of specialization. The SaaS industry case study also highlights the role of faulty assumptions about the power of artificial intelligence and big data in fueling these core conceits of the Platform Delusion.

Without attempting to be comprehensive, together the topics covered in part III provide a road map to identify the key characteristics of the winners and losers in the age of tech titans.

E-COMMERCE:
IF AMAZON IS THE EVERYTHING
STORE, WHAT'S LEFT TO SELL?

AMAZON HAS BEEN ACCUSED OF "destroying the fabric of America"[1] because of the effects of its apparent indomitability on local communities and the retail sector. Such fears are reinforced by the breathtaking scope of its own articulated ambition to serve as "the everything store": to be the leading purveyor of anything to anyone anywhere.[2] "Anything with a capital A," CEO Jeff Bezos has been saying for over twenty years.[3]

It is not just Bezos's fondness for the rhetoric of the Platform Delusion but the reality of Amazon that elicits such strong reactions. Amazon is responsible for close to 50 percent of e-commerce sales in the US; its closest competitors—Walmart and eBay—each have well under 10 percent. The company certainly has the feel of a category killer.[4] Although grandiose pronouncements may accurately describe the world-dominating objectives of the company, they do not properly describe an actual category of commerce.

Consumer proclivity to shop online varies dramatically by product and Amazon's relative success online varies as starkly by category. It is notable that two of the relatively small number of large-cap consumer internet companies are e-commerce retailers in categories that one would have expected Amazon to dominate if the Platform Delusion were true.[5]

As mentioned in chapter 5, in earlier times and under less scrutiny, Amazon would likely have been able to eliminate this apparent anomaly by simply buying Wayfair and Chewy as it did Diapers.com, Zappos, and other pesky vertical leaders.[6] What's more, there is a wide range of diversity in the extent to which Amazon's transactions in a particular category represent its own product, sales of others' product, or managing others' sales through its marketplace.

E-commerce Penetration by Sector: Current and Projected (2025)

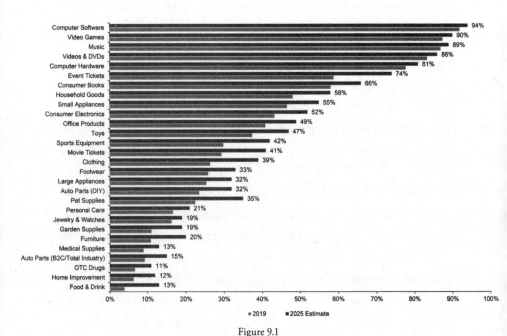

Figure 9.1

Source: Forrester, Evercore ISI Research

We have already looked at the multibillion-dollar automotive category, where there are crowded online marketplaces in which Amazon does not and is not likely to play a leading role. As noted, while the transaction volumes in these markets have continued to swell, the economics have deteriorated. These platforms are squarely in line with the long-term underperformance of e-commerce platforms generally.

Notwithstanding the performance of online automotive commerce, a wide range of other "marketplace" businesses have managed to not only grow but thrive either in the shadow of Amazon or where actual or potential competition from Amazon is not a meaningful driver of economics. Earlier we defined marketplaces as online platforms that facilitate transactions between buyers and sellers without ever taking ownership of the good or service. Some of these have achieved impressive results not only in the face of Amazon's generalized "everything store" but also where more focused Amazon efforts—either through an acquisition or branded organic product launch—have simply been ineffective at displacing a market leader.

Since online marketplaces passed $1 trillion in sales in 2016, Internet Retailer (now Digital Commerce 360) has been tracking the growing prevalence of this model.[7] During the three years leading to 2018, the percentage of e-commerce activity overall represented by marketplace models grew by over 50 percent—jumping from only 30 percent in 2015 to approaching half of all online retail transaction value. This growing share of the digital pie was reflected in the fact that fifty-five of the seventy-five largest marketplace companies (73 percent) grew faster than the 16 percent rate at which the overall e-commerce sector was expanding. And many of these grew far faster than Amazon's own marketplace business. Since 2018, this trend has continued. As of 2019, marketplaces represented 57 percent of the global e-commerce market.[8]

The apparent success of such a wide range of e-commerce competitors may come as a surprise given the presumption of indomitability often ascribed to (and promoted by) Amazon. Research firm BTIG has noted that investors in independent marketplaces are "perpetually petrified of competition from Amazon, Facebook, and Google." After reviewing the data, however, they concluded that "investor concerns are largely unwarranted."[9] Specifically they found that when one of these three titans announced their entry into a new marketplace, the stocks of the incumbent uniformly and immediately declined. We saw this phenomenon earlier with Zillow, whose stock dipped because of the mere rumor of a competitive Amazon launch. Within a year, however, not just Zillow but over 70 percent of these incumbents "were trading above their pre-news price."[10] As further evidence of Amazon's vulnerability, BTIG surveyed sixteen hundred of the company's own marketplace sellers and found that most of them planned to sell on competing marketplaces as well.[11]

BTIG's overall conclusions are best captured by the subtitle to its digital marketplace report: "Opportunities Abound Even in a World of Online Giants." The underlying reasons proffered by BTIG, however, as to "why the internet majors do not prove as disruptive as feared,"[12] are unlikely to lend much comfort either to investors or independents. The explanations provided relate overwhelmingly to flawed execution—whether because of an "uncompetitive offering" or simply "losing interest" in the targeted segment—rather than structural issues. These conclusions suggest that if only Amazon or another internet giant got its act together it really could dominate everything.

The closest thing to a structural impediment identified are the risks associated with "biting the hand that feeds" the internet giants, citing Google's reluctance to compete directly with Booking and Expedia, who provide billions in advertising revenues. But as we discuss in the next chapters, the case of online travel agencies is extreme and not nearly as black and white as this implies. What's more, Amazon has demonstrated a consistent willingness to bite down pretty hard on the hand that feeds it if the result is a more compelling consumer offering, as reflected in its initial decision to display low-priced marketplace product alongside its retail offerings and subsequently to offer its own competing branded product. Indeed one of the most serious charges against Amazon that is subject to regulatory scrutiny is that it actually used data from its own sellers to launch competing products—hardly an indication of an unwillingness to offend vendors on its platform.[13]

The breadth of instances BTIG identifies in which independent marketplaces have prospered often even in the face of aggressive attack by Amazon suggests that more fundamental structural issues are at play. A closer look at a few of those independent marketplace businesses that have managed to establish clear defensible franchises will suggest some of the key relevant market and industry attributes. An examination of one of the instances where Amazon did succeed in disrupting what had seemed like a secure market position will be similarly instructive about where Amazon's advantages are most formidable.

THE POWER OF SPECIALIZATION
AND COMPLEXITY: ETSY AND 1STDIBS

At first glance, Etsy and 1stDibs seem to have a lot in common. Both have established leading horizontal marketplaces that span a wide range of retail verticals, and the distinguishing feature of the products that they offer is their uniqueness. In 2020, Etsy generated well over $1 billion in revenues on gross merchandise sales of over $8 billion. The company was started in a Brooklyn apartment in 2005 as a hipster platform for handmade goods. 1stDibs was founded four years earlier in Paris as an online luxury marketplace for antiques. Since it moved to a pure marketplace model from a mostly classified advertising—lead generation business in 2016, transactional activity on its platform has exploded, reaching $343 million in 2020 according to its 2021 IPO filing.[14]

Other commonalities in the businesses are the ways in which they have subtly changed their identities, offered new services and functionality to buyers and sellers, and incrementally added adjacent commerce categories over time. Etsy began quite militantly as handmade only—the Etsy "Handmade Pledge" was often framed and displayed proudly by buyers and sellers—but has since broadened to encompass vintage items and craft supplies. Since 2013, it has allowed sellers to use outside manufacturers as long as the design was original.[15] And although the vast majority of its sales have remained in the same six categories for a while—apparel/accessories, home, jewelry, craft supplies, art/collectibles, paper/party supplies—the company has opportunistically added verticals on the fly, like the booming business it did around homemade COVID-19 masks.[16] In the case of 1st-Dibs, in addition to transforming its entire business model, it has moved well beyond antiques and vintage furniture so that today half of its business is in jewelry, art, and contemporary design.[17]

Despite these apparent similarities, and even playing in some of the very same product verticals, Etsy and 1stDibs each confront vastly different markets and industry structures that have propelled very different paths for first establishing and then protecting and reinforcing competitive advantage.

Etsy was founded a decade after eBay and both the market for and technology requirements of selling handmade goods were well known. The primary tool employed by Etsy for quickly gaining scale versus eBay's well-established market leadership position was a well-worn one—dramatically lower prices: 3.5 percent (plus a small twenty cents per item listing fee) versus a 12 percent commission on average. What made this strategy so effective—beyond the magnitude of the price differential—was the identification of a distinct segment of buyers and sellers who would respond readily to the call and for whom a specialized service designed around their needs would be attractive. Fostering a sense of community around this segment has been a continuing focus of the company's efforts.

One core challenge of building scale in marketplaces is maintaining balance between buyers and sellers as they grow. Low commissions for sellers in the absence of enough interested buyers does not deliver value—and attracting a critical mass of buyers to a new, unintuitively named start-up like Etsy can be a prohibitively expensive proposition. But in the world of artisans, it turns out that there is a significant overlap between buyers and sellers—more than 50 percent in the early years.[18] This in turn facilitated—and still facilitates to a degree—both even growth and a remarkably low level of marketing expense for the company.[19] At the time of its IPO a decade later, almost 90 percent of Etsy's traffic was still secured organically rather than through search or paid channels.[20]

When 1stDibs began in 2001, by contrast, no significant e-commerce was being undertaken for items as unique and valuable as it sought to sell. Sotheby's, arguably the leading off-line brand for expensive antiques, had lost millions trying to build an online platform—including through failed joint ventures with Amazon[21] and later with eBay.[22] It would be a decade before a professional CEO would take over from the founder and aggressively push 1stDibs to embrace a marketplace model.[23] But in the meantime, even as it operated as a traditional online classified business, the company undertook the painstaking process of vetting both the dealers themselves and, in selected instances, the items listed so that it quickly attracted serious antique buyers and created growing demand from dealers to be "approved" merchants on 1stDibs.

As purveyors of singular items in deep proven markets, Etsy and 1stDibs both benefit from strong network effects at scale. The challenges for a competitor to attract enough activity to establish a viable marketplace are substantial. Having the broadest selection continuously attracts more buyers and makes it more likely that they will transact. What's more, both are many-to-many marketplaces where the risk of collusion by participants on either side of the market would seem to pose limited risk to an operator.

But there are important differences as well. Although both have a long tail of sellers on their platform, in each case a core group are responsible for a disproportionate share of activity. In the case of Etsy, this concentration of activity among "power" or "super" sellers is particularly strong.[24] But with over 3 million active sellers on Etsy in 2020,[25] even if only 10 percent of these were responsible for 90 percent of the transactions, that would still represent hundreds of thousands of sellers. The total number of 1stDibs certified dealers is only in the thousands, by contrast, so the prospect of a critical mass of the most important ones working together is not so far-fetched. On the other hand, the concentration among top sellers is not nearly as high as at Etsy.

That said, when 1stDibs decided in 2016 to require its dealers to transact exclusively on the platform and pay a commission, there was a real risk of revolt.[26] By contrast, when Etsy raised its commission from 3.5 percent to 5 percent, the stock soared despite predictable seller grousing based on investors' correct prediction that it would have no negative impact on the number of merchants.[27] As a precaution, 1stDibs established a "Recognized Dealer" program that gave significant marketing benefits to its one hundred most valuable sellers to guarantee their continued buy-in to the platform. Despite some highly publicized grumbling, the company ultimately lost only 2 percent of its dealers.

While the strategic efforts required by 1stDibs to ensure that its most important sellers do not feel exploited restricts its pricing flexibility, the level of investment required to get them to commit to the platform in the first place provides a substantial impediment to potential insurgents. Both 1stDibs and Etsy must undertake fixed R&D and technology investments to provide the functionality and infrastructure needed to support a robust marketplace business. 1stDibs's success, however, also required building a global network of specialists to certify the dealers (today across fifty-five countries) in order to build credibility with buyers over time. What's more, a trusted network of shipping and insuring partners had to be developed to make online transactions seamless and secure. Together these investments reduce risk and complexity for buyers and the resulting substantial additional fixed-cost layer dramatically increases the volume of transactions needed to break even.

In addition to smoothing the way to achieving scale and enhancing the benefits once acquired, the combination of specialization and complexity often lends itself to a reinforcing competitive advantage critically important to maintaining a strong franchise: customer captivity. Marketplace buyers display notoriously little loyalty given the ease of considering and comparing other online alternatives. Amazon has demonstrated through Prime the ability to cultivate digital habit, but only at a huge financial cost. That said, when consistently offering the broadest selection of genuinely unique items, the search costs involved in finding satisfactory substitutes do provide some protection to the incumbent leader.

Etsy has a particular challenge in instilling buyer captivity. Frequency of activity is the key driver of habit, and Etsy has been positioned as a venue for "special" purchases. By definition, if it is a special occasion, it's not every day. Most Etsy buyers only use it once a year, and the company has begun to ramp up costly general brand advertising to increase purchasing frequency by repositioning the company as a destination for special and unique items rather than just for exceptional celebrations. 1stDibs faces a similar challenge in that much purchasing activity occurs around major moves, which only happen occasionally. Even avid collectors only shop so often. That said, its core interior designer audience, which represented 27 percent of the purchases in 2020, virtually lives on the site.

It is with sellers, however, that strong captivity most often manifests itself in specialized markets. In the case of 1stDibs, it was the painstaking work establishing its certified member dealer network undertaken during the decade leading up to the push into an e-commerce model that made its success possible in the face of aggressive competition—not only from the digital giants but also from the off-line leaders and well over a dozen well-financed online insurgents. By the time 1stDibs actually required all transactions to be executed on its platform, referrals through 1stDibs represented the vast majority of many of these dealers' sales, particularly in its original product categories. In addition, they had come to rely on software tools provided to upload, display, and market their inventory. And since 1stDibs had become the first stop for the most important buyers—not just professional interior designers and architects but individual collectors—sellers saw a significant downside to failing to reach this global network of repeat customers of size.

Although not as strong as 1stDibs's, Etsy also enjoys strong captivity with its sellers, as reflected in the fact that many do not list their wares on alternative platforms and have stuck with the platform through multiple controversial changes.[28] For the predominantly smaller businesses that compose much of Etsy's user base, even the logistics of loading, displaying, and managing their inventory is a significant undertaking that the company works hard to simplify.[29] Etsy's fastest-growing revenue streams are services that it provides to sellers that facilitate their ability to effectively reach buyers, while at the same time strengthening their reliance on the platform.

The ability of a niche commerce player like Etsy or 1stDibs to secure a sustainable competitive advantage on the supply side through proprietary technology vis-à-vis much larger broad-based competitors like Amazon, by contrast, may seem fanciful on its face. This has not stopped specialized marketplaces from touting these capabilities[30] and undertaking acquisitions[31] to enhance them. More realistically, such investments seem essential to avoid being put potentially at a significant competitive disadvantage relative to companies whose R&D budgets just in these areas often exceed the total revenues of more focused competitors. That said, even inferior technology when combined with unique and highly probative data sets can yield superior insights. While these tools play an important role in ensuring that sellers are matched with the most likely buyers in the most effective manner possible, there is little evidence to date that these platforms have developed a significant supply-side advantage.

Although both 1stDibs and Etsy succeeded in the face of competition from Amazon, the nature of that challenge and the balance of their respective competitive landscapes are quite different.

Amazon's joint venture with Sotheby's collapsed shortly before the launch of 1stDibs and around the same time that Amazon introduced its own marketplace business in 2000. Other than a brief underwhelming 2013 push into the fine art category,[32] Amazon has not subsequently focused on antiques. Today, much of the competing product is simply found under Amazon's "Collectibles and Fine Arts" tab or embedded within the general relevant product category like jewelry or furniture. In 2020, Amazon attempted another push into high-end product with the launch of a Luxury Stores platform, initially focused on fashion.[33] Regardless of whether this is extended to additional product categories, the fate of this latest effort is unlikely to be different from those that came before, for reasons we will soon discuss.

eBay, by contrast, has aggressively continued to look for ways to extend its collectibles franchise from Beanie Babies to high-end products like art and jewelry after the collapse of its own venture with Sotheby's. In 2014, it launched a program to allow its members to participate in live auctions by brick-and-mortar auction houses.[34] None of the major houses ever participated and it seems that this has been discontinued. Then in 2017, eBay launched its "Authenticate" program to attract sellers of high-value items—initially handbags[35] but extended to other categories like jewelry and watches—by having them mail in the items to be authenticated.[36] This also appears to have been effectively discontinued. 1stDibs does not "authenticate" every item listed like this program or, for that matter, like the off-line auction house business model. They instead, much more efficiently, authenticate sellers and then rely primarily on the threat of their being kicked off the platform in the event of complaints of counterfeit goods or fraudulent practices.

Neither Amazon nor eBay has much chance of ever attracting a critical mass of dealers or other purveyors of truly luxury items to their platforms because of the negative halo that emanates from the distinctly un-luxurious nature of the bulk of what they sell. Much more direct competition has come from a continuing stream of other much smaller online platforms, the most durable of which have mostly focused on a particular geography or product category or both. The power of specialization within nuanced product categories has been demonstrated again and again. Ironically, competitors are able to use Amazon's very strengths in delivering a breathtakingly consistent and reliable broad-based service against it. The playbook involves copying those attributes Amazon has now established as the price of entry in e-commerce (e.g., service and shipping) but overlaying a deeply customized variation for a product category and community that is challenging for Amazon to effectively replicate. The ability of

Wayfair to challenge Amazon as the leader in online furniture sales more broadly is further evidence of this.[37]

The biggest competitors to 1stDibs are high-end retailers that can serve as substitutes and the off-line auction houses that compete directly for product with the off-line dealers that sell on its platform. Both have struggled to establish significant digital businesses.

Luxury retailers' e-commerce strategies have been highly uneven, which is unsurprising given their focus on the in-store experience and personalized service. For instance, Tiffany's frustration with anemic sales on its own website led to an e-commerce partnership with Net-a-Porter.[38] After a bumpy start,[39] the arrangement has led to some online growth, but e-commerce still represents a single-digit percentage of overall sales.[40]

The largest auction houses have made some progress since the time of the early failed digital forays, but none of these players have ever been able to gain significant virtual traction beyond attracting distance bidders to their off-line auctions.[41] They continue to try, however, and have accelerated their online strategies in the face of COVID-19. Sotheby's, in particular, has established two online marketplaces—it most recently signed up a group of prominent New York art galleries to participate in an online high-end art marketplace called the Sotheby's Gallery Network.[42]

Whether or not these and other digital auction house initiatives are more successful than those of the past, their off-line businesses remain strong (although, unlike online marketplaces which grew, they fell as much as 40 percent during the pandemic).[43] The ultimate size of 1stDibs will depend more on the ability of its private dealer partners to take share from auction houses, its own ability to continue to successfully expand the range of luxury items its platform offers, and whether it moves into direct competition with the dealers by taking luxury consignments directly like The RealReal or thredUP.

Etsy confronted a much more direct attack with the launch of Amazon Handmade in 2015, just months after its IPO. Its shares struggled for years as it took incremental hits with every new announcement from Amazon—

for instance, establishing the "Amazon Handmade Gift Shop"[44] and the availability of Handmade product for immediate Prime Now delivery in certain cities.[45] Performance only turned around when investors noticed that Etsy's organic growth was actually accelerating in the face of the Amazon onslaught.[46] This suggested the surprising possibility that Amazon's marketing efforts served mostly to draw attention to the category, benefiting Etsy as the category leader! Unlike Etsy, little of Amazon Handmade's product is exclusive, and their efforts to recruit Etsy sellers have yielded mixed results at best.[47] The various shipping and other benefits Amazon provides to buyers simply cannot make up for a significant disadvantage on the supply side in a network effects business. Etsy stock price more than doubled from the beginning of 2018 to the beginning of 2020. It proceeded to quadruple during that year, becoming the single best-performing company in the S&P 500 stock index—to which it was added in September 2020.[48]

Beyond Amazon and eBay, the breadth of competitors that Etsy faces reflects the somewhat amorphous definition of the categories within which it sells. Vertical online and off-line competitors offer handmade-style products with an artisanal flavor, including West Elm Handcrafted or even Target's Pillowfort or Opalhouse lines.[49] Individual geographies have developed local competitors, including Aftcra in the United States,[50] but these suffer from being subscale based on the inability to spread the necessary fixed costs. More fundamentally, these can neither offer international wares to buyers or a global customer base to sellers. Probably the most serious emerging competitors are the technology platforms like Shopify that can provide an alternative ready-made technology platform on which to create and market an independent storefront. A number of payments and other technology companies serving small- and medium-sized businesses (SMBs) are increasingly broadening the range of services they offer their customers along these lines. To date, these efforts have been unable to deliver the level of buyer interest and number of transactions generated by the Etsy platform.

Notably, neither Etsy nor 1stDibs operate in markets that support incumbent off-line competitors of dominant scale. Sotheby's and Christie's together sell over $10 billion worth of luxury collectibles, which is plenty big, but the global market for luxury collectibles is in the hundreds of billions and fragmented across local auction houses and dealers. Etsy provides reach for sellers obviously not available from local flea markets and views itself as a complementary if also somewhat competitive channel to analog alternatives. It is in Etsy's interest for its seller community to be financially secure, and the availability of these off-line channels support that objective. In the case of 1stDibs, it is the dealers who are both their competitors (along with auction houses) on the demand side and customers on the supply side.

Where there are not just large off-line incumbents in the ecosystem, but ones who together constitute anything like a majority of all sales, they can themselves become direct online competitors (although this is often complicated both by inherent channel conflict and limited digital capabilities). Even if they decline to compete directly, the mere possibility can disrupt the many-to-many dynamic that enhances the benefits to marketplace operators of network effects. In some instances, however, the existence of dominant off-line competitors plays to Amazon's relative strengths in the digital realm and facilitates its ability to displace digital marketplace incumbents.

THE LIMITS OF POWER: AUTO PARTS

If Etsy and 1stDibs demonstrate how the combination of strong network effects bolstered by product complexity and fragmented buyers and sellers can yield remarkably resilient digital marketplace franchises, their example does not demonstrate that these qualities necessarily imply invincibility. Indeed, a single counterexample can disprove that: Amazon's displacement of eBay's previous leadership position in the online automotive parts market.

There are few product categories as complex as the car parts that make up what is known as the automotive aftermarket. According to the research firm Hedges & Company, "in the entire automotive aftermarket, including specialty parts and accessories, branded replacement parts and private label replacement parts, there are approximately 8 million base part numbers."[51] Given the diverse universe of engaged car hobbyists and local garages and repair chains that might have use for a difficult-to-find part, it is not surprising that digital markets for aftermarket parts quickly emerged.

Car parts were among the earliest items that found their way onto AuctionWeb, eBay's predecessor company founded in 1995. eBay launched eBay Motors as its first vertical marketplace in 2000[52] on the back of the strength of this franchise. Amazon, by contrast, did not launch an auto parts marketplace until 2006, by which time eBay was established as the clear leader. Yet today, Amazon's automotive parts marketplace is meaningfully larger than eBay's. To understand how this happened in a sector that would seem to lend itself to powerful network effects driven incumbent competitive advantages, a closer look at the specific nature of the market and the products is required.

Despite the intuitive appeal of selling auto parts online, as a category overall, it is one of the least e-commerce enabled. Obviously, the size and weight of certain parts don't lend themselves to easy marketplace transactions (ever try to mail a bumper or a car battery?). But the more fundamental reason is because the most prevalent use cases of auto parts purchases do not lend themselves to marketplace transactions. In what is an almost $150 billion market, only a third is dedicated to the do-it-yourself (DIY) B2C sector that easily accommodates a purely online transaction. The balance of the market (or around $100 billion) is in the do-it-for-me-market, which is made up of B2B sales mostly to dealers and repair shops that often need the part not in two days or even overnight, but immediately.

This B2B market is dominated by four brick-and-mortar retailers

(Advance Auto Parts, AutoZone, Genuine Parts Company, and O'Reilly Auto Parts) that support a national network of warehouses dedicated to "need it now" use cases. The fixed costs required to maintain this level of local parts density has established a long-standing market equilibrium in which these four behemoths—whose collective market value exceeds $100 billion—capture around 50 percent of the retail market. Even in the DIY market, there is strong customer preference for being able to speak with a knowledgeable salesperson before purchasing an important part. This is unsurprising given that data suggest DIYers often buy the wrong part and install it wrong.[53]

The fact that only 10 percent of automotive parts are transacted online does not mean that these traditional incumbents can ignore the online threat. Online has been consistently growing at rates approaching 20 percent, with Amazon taking a disproportionate share of that growth. More important, 90 percent of parts buyers do research online before making a buying decision, even if the purchase is still ultimately made off-line. Amazon launched a vehicle portal in 2016 that offers increasingly complex tools to identify the right part for specific models along with reviews and advice.[54] This level of functionality has become table stakes for anyone looking to compete in the sector. What's more, even the line between B2C and B2B has become muddy as most professional mechanics now keep their smartphones with them in the bay as they work on cars and determine what parts they need to order.

Amazon will remain at a competitive disadvantage with respect to these specialized retailers. Unless it empties its warehouses of most of its other nonautomotive products, there is no way it can provide the level of speed required for many professional use cases. But next day delivery could suffice for at least some such use cases. What's more, through its Amazon Home Services unit—and associated alliances with Sears Auto Center, Pep Boys, and Monro,[55] as well as mobile mechanic services like Wrench[56]—it has been able to shift some part of what would have been a B2B sale to a B2C one.

The four giant retailers would make a huge mistake if they simply rested on their structural advantages. With smart investments that leverage their unique assets, they should be able to maintain long-term growth and above-average financial returns—even as pure digital continues to capture some more market share. To date, however, all four have done only an average job digitally, maybe reflecting an institutional inertia that often infects businesses that get used to seemingly impermeable competitive advantages. The best of these, as reflected in the level of digital traffic,[57] is AutoZone, which has also partnered with FedEx to establish a next-day delivery service for the DIY market.[58] AutoZone's relative digital chops today could reflect its acquisition twenty-five years ago of a small software company that integrated parts catalog information into the repair shop workflow.[59]

With respect to competing pure digital players—not just eBay, in the marketplace model, but RockAuto in the online retail model—Amazon has been able to displace the incumbents' long-established leadership position. It has achieved this result by its unique ability to integrate both marketplace and retail models. Retail businesses by themselves are not network effects businesses, but often benefit from traditional supply-side scale. When combined with a marketplace business, however, they can augment existing network effects by broadening the range of both product and delivery options. This improves the chance that prospective buyers will find something that will meet their needs and transact. The vast majority—probably two thirds[60]—of Amazon's aftermarket sales are through its marketplace with the balance in retail sales.

The data Amazon collects regarding not just purchasing frequency but also which parts are more likely to be purchased when overnight delivery is offered allows it to optimize which unique items to stock and sell itself and which to rely on its marketplace for. The resulting, more comprehensive, offering attracts a broader range of potential buyers and provides the advantage over a pure marketplace—even the once leading one. That, along with some level of customer captivity associated with Prime membership and its broader maniacal focus on customer service and a seamless experience, explains how Amazon overtook eBay's marketplace position even while charging a higher commission.

Overtaking, however, is not the same as vanquishing. Some estimates suggest that Amazon and eBay divide a $10 billion marketplace business 60-40, and in certain product and customer categories, eBay probably remains the leader. The fact that the retail side of the business enhances its marketplace business doesn't make the retail side any more attractive on its own. Not only is Amazon competing there with the four giants, it must confront the long-standing leader in pure online retail, family-owned RockAuto, founded in 1999. RockAuto does not have the infrastructure costs of Amazon and "operates a drop ship model, shipping parts from a network of over three hundred manufacturers."[61] And while Amazon may have displaced it as the leading pure e-commerce retailer in the sector, the company and a slew of other e-commerce competitors are not going anywhere. RockAuto has continued to grow at double-digit percentages for over fifteen years, significantly constraining Amazon's pricing flexibility and potential profitability.

eBay's total auto parts business may be less than half the size of Amazon's—$4 billion versus $9 billion (on top of Amazon's $6 billion in Marketplace revenues, it has $3 billion of e-commerce sales). It remains likely, however, that eBay's business is more profitable. Based on its overall margins of around 30 percent, eBay would generate at least $1 billion in the automotive aftermarket. With Amazon's integrated marketplace and e-commerce margin unlikely to be greater than 5–10 percent, it would struggle to generate eBay's level of profit.

Well beyond the auto parts vertical, the conventional wisdom has long been that onetime online commerce leader eBay is guilty of inexcusable corporate malpractice by allowing Amazon to displace it from that lofty perch. When you compare Amazon's over trillion-dollar valuation with eBay's sub $50 billion valuation it is hard to conclude otherwise. And to be sure, over the years, eBay has made well-documented strategic mistakes[62] and suffered from poor execution.[63] But to conclude that eBay should have tried to become a second everything store is not justified by the numbers.

Amazon was in a bad, chronically unprofitable business and made a strategically brilliant move to leverage that position to give it a leg up on diversifying into the far more attractive marketplace business. The wisdom of this, however, does not suggest eBay shareholders would have been better off if eBay had used its position as the leader in attractive, profitable marketplace businesses to diversify into the uninviting retail sector.

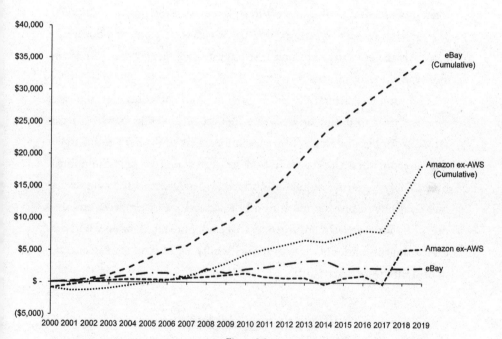

Amazon ex-AWS vs. eBay Reported Operating Income (2000–2019) Annual and Cumulative

Figure 9.2

Source: FactSet, Company filings

Amazon is obviously a force to be reckoned with, but its inability to displace online incumbents in a wide range of marketplace verticals despite the breadth of its offerings, the attractiveness of Prime, the quality of its service and execution, and the ability to offer complementary services is a testament to the power of strong network effects when paired with significant reinforcing advantages. Where the strength of Amazon's collective value proposition—integrating both marketplace and retail offerings—is most disruptive to incumbents tends to be in markets within which off-line players of scale continue to play a significant role. Even in categories where Amazon's relative strengths are greatest, however, there is no real evidence supporting the Platform Delusion.

The auto parts example highlights that Amazon's hybrid offering is most compelling in markets characterized by diverse products and use cases. Yet in such environments, Amazon itself faces stiff competition from more focused online and off-line players with their own advantages, at least with respect to certain product or customer segments. So, ironically, Amazon's relative position is strongest in segments where the availability of superior returns is weakest.

Amazon has plenty of room to grow in retail and continues to pose a serious threat to online and off-line incumbents. But as Amazon faces attack from broad-based off-line incumbents like Walmart and Target, who are pursuing their own hybrid strategies, and Google Shopping's increasingly aggressive online-only attack,[64] specialization and complexity will continue to provide meaningful protection for incumbents and opportunity for innovative insurgents. That said, pure retail models, without a meaningful marketplace feature, will continue to struggle to generate consistently superior returns.

KEY CHAPTER TAKEAWAYS

1. Online commerce is increasingly dominated by marketplace models, which now represent a majority of online retail transactions. Many of these often vertically focused marketplace businesses have continued to grow faster than the overall online market even in the face of aggressive competition from Amazon.

The attractiveness of the economics of these businesses varies widely based on the strength of the underlying network effects and reinforcing advantages.

2. The success of Etsy and 1stDibs highlights the relevance of two particularly important attributes in establishing durable market-place franchises: the extent to which the market lends itself to specialization and the degree of product complexity. Specialization facilitates the establishment of relative scale as well as customer captivity and learning. Product complexity enhances the increasing strength of network effects at scale, drives higher required break-even market shares, and improves the usefulness of applying technology to data.

3. Amazon sometimes has been effective at displacing digital marketplace incumbents. Amazon Vehicles has done just that in the automotive parts sector, where its retail product and service selection significantly improve upon what can be provided by a pure marketplace. Amazon's integrated retail and marketplace product offering is particularly potent where, as with car parts, important product use cases require delivery options that would be unavailable without Amazon's physical distribution infrastructure.

4. The existence of significant off-line competitors is indicative of where Amazon's hybrid retail/marketplace model is most impactful. The overall sector economics, however, are likely most challenging precisely where Amazon has the greatest advantage relative to pure digital peers. As Amazon faces attack from broad-based off-line incumbents like Walmart and Target, who are pursuing their own hybrid strategies, specialization and complexity will continue to provide meaningful protection for incumbents and opportunity for innovative insurgents.

FLY ME TO THE MOON:
WHO MAKES MONEY WHEN AIR
TRAVEL GOES DIGITAL?

ONE MASSIVE PIECE OF THE economy in which Amazon does not play a meaningful role is consumer services. This does not stem from an inherent inability to sell services rather than things. Indeed, its most profitable and fastest-growing businesses are the services it provides to businesses through AWS and third-party services to its marketplace participants.[1] But in the consumer realm, Amazon's services are often provided free or bundled with an inexpensive Prime subscription as a means to encourage the purchase of actual stuff.

This is not for want of trying. The earliest of its major forays into traditional consumer services was Amazon Home Services, launched in 2015.[2] Given the importance of home products to the core franchise, the category at least makes some sense. This focus on the home led Amazon to also purchase a video doorbell company and launch a home security service. Yet despite the strategic logic and potential support from these somewhat related businesses, Amazon remains far behind industry leaders Angie's List and Yelp in home services.[3]

In the larger consumer services sectors, Amazon's track record is even weaker. Its financial services initiatives in payments, lending, and credit cards have at best failed to make a dent and often, as in the case of Amazon Wallet, have completely collapsed. A variety of health care initiatives, launched either internally or through acquisitions, continue but remain a big question mark.[4] The most recent disappointment in this area was the dissolution of Haven, its high-profile partnership with Warren Buffet and JP Morgan to disrupt employee health care that featured celebrity doctor and author Atul Gawande.[5] And in the multitrillion-dollar travel and tourism sector, Amazon's foray was unambiguously disastrous but mercifully brief. Amazon launched Destinations shortly after Home Services to offer hotel bookings and information on dining and attractions, focusing on weekend road-trippers.[6] The service was shut down before the end of the year.[7]

The digital travel space is a mystery on several levels. On the one hand, the inherent transparency of the internet suggests that there would be few barriers to entry when it comes to offering or comparing ticket and room prices, leaving little opportunity for superior profits. The dramatic decline in the number of travel agents and agencies reflects the introduction of digital economics to the sector and is consistent with expectations.

On the other hand, the largest online travel company—Booking Holdings—is worth more than the equity value of Delta, United, and American Airlines combined. What's more, multiple other substantial and profitable digital travel companies with diverse business models have regularly gone public during the last twenty-plus years, from Expedia (1999) and Trivago (2016) to TripAdvisor (2011) and Ctrip (2003), now just Trip. And that does not include the sharing-economy businesses like Airbnb that have targeted the travel sector or the well over a dozen[8] other travel related unicorns, like TripActions,[9] that continue to regularly emerge. What's more, a variety of other unexpected trends—like the recent reversal in the steady decline in off-line travel agents[10]—adds to the mystery of the sector.

Air travel, in particular, is a huge and, at least until the coronavirus pandemic brought it to a temporary halt, fast-growing sector of the economy that both online and off-line has mostly delivered tears and sorrow to investors. Airlines themselves have attracted more scorn over decades from Warren Buffett than almost any other business. Buffett suggested at one point that it was a shame that a foresighted capitalist hadn't shot down Orville Wright.[11] But Buffett has nonetheless, like a moth to a flame, been repeatedly drawn back to the industry—only to be burned. Most recently, he unloaded his entire stake in the sector in the face of the COVID-19 crisis, admitting he had again been "wrong about the sector."[12]

One would generally not think that an off-line sector with such a track record of uneven results would be likely to feed a steady, resilient digital counterpart. In fact, within the air travel ecosystem there is just such an industry and, indeed, one whose strong network effects and long-standing winner-take-all attributes are more consistent with the Platform Delusion than the FAANG companies.

Yet, despite these remarkable results, this sector exhibits one core characteristic fundamentally at odds with the Platform Delusion. The basic conceit of the Platform Delusion is that the internet has enabled the emergence of these all-powerful business models. This industry, however, is over fifty years old. Its success has nothing to do with the internet, and the emergence of the internet has had surprisingly little impact on the strength of its competitive advantages. Although the sector may be a little obscure, it is not anachronistic. Many of the strongest network effects driven electronic franchises—the massive credit card industry is another prime example that we will discuss more later—both predated and have been largely unaffected by the internet.

Like with any good mystery, to unravel it, you need to go back to the beginning. The industry being referred to is one whose history and characteristics are not widely appreciated by the general public. It was born of a collaboration between the era's largest technology company and American Airlines.

THE BIRTH OF ELECTRONIC TRAVEL PLATFORMS

Decades before there was an internet, airlines and travel agents struggled with the problem of how to effectively communicate and transact on behalf of customers. In the earliest days, an agent called a booking office who would literally check a box on an index card representing the particular flight. Even after American Airlines automated its inventory tracking in the 1940s with the development of the first computerized reservation systems (CRS), interactions between the airlines and the sales agents remained decidedly low tech. It was only when American partnered with IBM over a decade later to introduce SABRE (an acronym meaning the Semi-Automatic Business Research Environment, now just Sabre)[13] in 1960 that the beginnings of the modern global distribution systems (GDS) that still power commercial aviation were established.

The other US airlines soon followed in developing these capabilities, as did international carriers. But it wasn't until the 1970s that reservation systems really became global distribution systems through software that facilitated electronic connections to travel agents. By the 1990s, these systems had coalesced into just a handful of industry consortia and the historic airline ownership dissipated as the increasingly independent GDS giants went public, spun off, sold out, or some combination of these (Sabre did all three at different points). The last major combination[14] was of Worldspan (formed in the 1990s by Delta, Northwest, and TWA) and Galileo (originally a British Airways–led group that merged with United Airlines–founded Apollo), both of which were private equity owned when they became Travelport in 2007. The last private airline–owned GDS, the long-standing European leader Amadeus, went public in 2010. Amadeus, Sabre, and Travelport remain the only truly global GDS competitors.

Once these GDS platforms began connecting pricing and inventory availability from airlines to travel agents almost fifty years ago, the businesses began to exhibit classic two-sided network effects. The more relevant content was available from airlines, the more travel agents would look to connect; the more connected travel agents the platform boasted, the more airlines would want to tap into these deep sources of distribution.

The economics of the industry revolve mostly around a fee per flight segment per booking that the airlines pay the GDS and that the GDS shares with the travel agents. This fee has on average remained around $5 but both the size of the fee and the nature of the split varies widely based on the relative bargaining power in the relationship.[15] So fees are lower for larger airlines and for segments purchased in the airline's home country where the carrier might easily have attracted the customer directly. Similarly, although on average a GDS splits the fee evenly with travel agencies, smaller agencies secure far less and larger ones far more.

Volume discounts aside, only the largest travel agencies "multi-home" among GDS providers. This is because each GDS charges a subscription fee and this, along with the burden of installation, maintenance, and staff training on multiple systems, makes it uneconomic to support more than one. But the downside, particularly given the nontrivial switching costs, is that the GDS has the upper hand in setting fee cuts. By contrast, the biggest global airlines almost always multi-home, showing all of their content on each of the three GDSs. Although it did not start out this way, as a result of litigation, regulation, ownership changes, and competitive moves, that has largely been the industry status quo for decades. And the very fact that the major airlines multi-home is the reason why most travel agents don't bother to as, bargaining leverage notwithstanding, there is little incremental benefit from doing so.

The tight cadre of GDS players have managed to consistently capture 10 percent of airline industry profits in good years while still doing well in the bad and have served as expensive but indispensable partners for most travel agencies. Their contracts are long term, and although a slowdown in travel will hit their bottom line, they are mostly immune to the spikes in oil prices, employee actions, crashes, regulatory challenges, and public relations nightmares that systemically plague the airlines themselves. This uninterrupted GDS track record of plenty has led to a variety of complaints from airlines and agencies.[16] A number of these grievances, as we will discuss shortly, have some validity.

It is hard to argue, however, that this long-standing industry equilibrium has not served its constituents well over time. Airlines have access to the collective reach of the travel agencies aggregated by the GDSs without needing to build their own marketing and distribution networks to replicate that. Even small travel agencies in distant lands can quickly offer their clients the same view of global flight availability as a large agency in an urban center. This electronic infrastructure, which has supported the exponential growth in global travel since the end of the Second World War, has been a key driver of the overall economy.

The highly profitable steady-state of these electronic network effects driven platforms predated the widespread adoption of the internet by consumers and businesses alike. So how did the introduction of the ultimate disruptive technology impact the cozy oligopoly? Less than you might think.

THE INTERNET CHANGES EVERYTHING AND NOTHING

The emergence of the internet and technological advances generally have posed three threats to the GDS dominated established order. The ability of the GDS industry to thrive in the face of these very real structural challenges demonstrates the nature and resilience of its competitive advantages.

Threat #1: Airlines go direct to travelers

The internet provided a new and efficient means for airlines to communicate and transact directly with travelers. This technology radically enhanced the previously limited direct channel to the public that entirely disintermediates the indirect channel (travel agents). The fundamental purpose of the GDS is to service the network connecting the indirect channel with the airlines, so anything that disintermediates the travel agents disintermediates them as well.

Of course, individual customers always had a direct line to the airlines, either by phone or by visiting what were once ubiquitous, smart-looking ticket offices often found in the most expensive real estate of major cities around the country. The advantages to both the airline and the traveler of being able to book online without waiting to interact with a customer service agent are obvious. Almost as soon as the e-ticket became available in 1994, the number of ticket offices began to fall. American Airlines once had 120 such offices in the US.[17] Today it keeps three, all in Florida.[18] But direct sales even during the heyday of airline ticket offices represented barely 20 percent of ticket sales. Thanks to the internet, airlines now sell well over half of their tickets directly.

Threat #2: The rise of the OTAs

The internet has enabled the establishment of dozens of online travel agencies (OTAs) through which travelers can book themselves after comparing different travel options. Microsoft established one of the first and most durable OTAs[19] with Expedia in 1996. And a proliferation of OTAs spawned a proliferation of metasearch companies, like Skyscanner and Kayak, that compared the offerings of the various OTAs.[20] These developments offered an entirely new level of price transparency to consumers who no longer needed to rely on the word of a travel agent or the cumbersome process of visiting multiple airline websites or calling multiple reservation offices.

Online travel agencies don't actually compete with either GDSs or airlines—they compete with off-line travel agencies. But their introduction into the ecosystem had significant implications for both. By potentially aggregating substantial demand, OTAs could gain leverage in negotiating the share of the airline fee the GDS gets to keep for itself. And airlines' preference is for the online opportunity to be captured by the online direct channel rather than a strengthened online indirect one. As a result, at least initially, both GDSs and airlines sought to themselves play a role in the emerging OTA sector. For instance, Travelocity was founded as a joint venture with Sabre, and two major OTAs were founded by consortia of airlines—Orbitz in the US and Opodo in Europe.

Notably, both Orbitz and Opodo were ultimately sold to GDSs, but the GDSs all eventually divested their interests in affiliated OTAs.[21] So why, if it seemed like such a good idea originally for both airlines and GDSs to get into the OTA business, did both get out? The answer is sometimes just what it seems: the OTA business, when it comes to air travel, is neither a very good nor very strategic business for either GDSs or airlines.

The ability of so many dozens of competing OTAs to enter the market over the years is the best indicator of a lack of barriers to entry. Sure, some differentiated themselves in one way or another, by business model or market positioning, but, at the end of the day, they all relied on the same GDSs to deliver largely the same content. And as the number of OTAs multiplied, all looking to attract the very same travelers, marketing costs loomed particularly large. In addition to the substantial offline investment required to establish and maintain a consumer brand, all of these businesses needed to dedicate substantial resources to secure a favorable relative position at the gateway to most consumer journeys: Google.

The need to develop effective search engine optimization (determining where an offering appears in organic search results) and search engine marketing (enhancing search visibility through paid advertisements, typically pay-per-click) has become a core operating discipline for any consumer product or service. There are sectors where being particularly innovative in search engine optimization and marketing (SEO/SEM) strategies is what distinguishes the best-in-class operator. The problem, however, is that this skill rarely represents a sustainable competitive advantage. Such innovations are eventually copied and Google is notorious for changing its algorithms just when a business thinks it has cracked the code. *The Huffington Post* and *BuzzFeed*, both founded by the same pioneering online marketer, grew dramatically, achieved profitability for a time, and fundamentally changed how news sites monetize content. As every other news site imitated their most effective strategies, neither business made money for an exceptionally long time and growth at both stalled.

What's more, the OTAs' willingness to spend in their desperate efforts to entice users is part of what attracted metasearch companies into the mix, further squeezing the available margins of the OTAs. And when Google bought its own metasearch company, ITA Software, in 2011 to power its flight-search tools, this accelerated the increasing importance of the metasearch channel.[22] This has three negative implications for OTAs. First, it impedes their efforts to acquire organic traffic. Second, it further bids up the cost of inorganic traffic acquisition. Third, it increases the likelihood that travelers will be sent directly to an airline site rather than an OTA.

These increasing marketing costs caused by increasing competition have driven a structural incentive to consolidate the sector. The advantages of traditional scale here are realized from both spreading the fixed costs and gaining bargaining leverage within the value chain. And, as we will see shortly, dozens of OTAs have been consolidated into just two massive scale players who represent close to 90 percent of that market. But if these players benefit from economies of scale, why doesn't that necessarily make them good businesses, at least with respect to air travel?

Supply-side scale, as we have said, provides limited benefits without reinforcing competitive advantages. There are no other significant demand- or supply-side advantages available to flight OTAs. On the demand side, the ultimate customers are generally only looking to secure the best deal on a flight as easily as possible, and they exhibit little loyalty. On the supply side, the narrow use case of securing the lowest price on a pre-identified point-to-point trip does not lend itself to leveraging big data or proprietary technology for superior results.

But OTAs benefit from network effects—demand-side scale to complement the supply-side scale. And air travel is a many-to-many market of the kind that lends itself to potentially powerful network effects; OTAs can connect many airlines to many more fliers. The trouble is that on both sides of its network, the OTAs have been disintermediated by other networks: the three GDS networks on the supply side and Google plus the metasearch networks on the demand side. That leaves the OTAs squeezed in between. And even the supply-side scale enjoyed by the OTAs is less overwhelming than it seems in air travel. The nearly 90 percent share of the two largest noted is only within the OTA category. That category in total still competes both with off-line travel agents and the airlines themselves and represents only 25 percent of airline bookings globally.[23] Direct bookings have exploded as airlines pour more of their marketing muscle into this category, and the collapse of leisure off-line travel agents has begun to turn around as millennials increasingly embrace the joys of personalized service.[24]

So, what has the combined impact of the explosive growth of direct channel disintermediation on the one hand and intensified negotiating leverage from OTA consolidation on the other done to the economics of GDSs? The numbers speak for themselves. Let's look at the decade of performance at Amadeus, the last GDS to go public, from its IPO in 2010 through the beginning of 2020, just before the coronavirus pandemic devastated the travel industry broadly.

Amadeus has been the strongest performer in the industry. By virtue of its strategy of investing for the long term and signaling an unwillingness to engage in destructive price competition, it has been the beneficiary of a slow steady share shift from the weakest GDS. What is most striking, however, is how well the three GDSs have held up collectively in light of these structural changes to the industry. This result has been driven primarily by the source of overall sector profitability and the breadth and intensity of GDS competitive advantage.

It is true that because of the more generous splits, leisure air bookings

Market Performance of Amadeus Since IPO

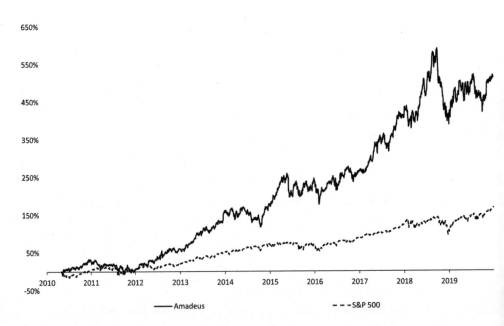

Figure 10.1

Source: S&P Capital IQ

from an OTA are half as profitable to a GDS as a booking from an off-line agent. But where the airlines make their money, and where the GDSs are an indispensable partner, is business travel. The corporate market relies primarily on off-line travel agents known as travel management companies (TMCs)—American Express Global Business, BCD, and CWT are the biggest—and make little use of either the direct channel or OTAs. What's more, the TMC sector is less consolidated. Those top three vendors control a majority of the market, but less than Expedia and Booking do in the OTA market.[25] Although these larger off-line agencies do leverage their size to secure better terms from the GDSs than smaller agencies, it is a much more even share than commanded by the OTAs and has been relatively stable over time.

The overall growth in air travel—consistently a multiple of GDP growth—combined with the mix shift away from lower-margin leisure travel bookings has more than made up for the loss of volume to airlines and the pricing pressure from OTAs. This is all the more remarkable given how dramatic the shift away from GDSs has been—since 2000, the portion of air travel booked through GDSs has fallen from well over half globally to only about 30 percent.[26] Of course, newspapers were also able to outperform the overall market for decades as their readerships declined due to the strength of their structural advantages—until they weren't. Although this is still a relevant cautionary tale, as we note shortly, a key difference is that most GDSs aggressively built new software businesses, leveraging their unique access to and knowledge of their installed base.

The structural superiority of the GDS platform to the OTA platform in the air travel ecosystem is profound. The supply-side scale advantages of the three industry leaders are supported by a business model dominated by substantial fixed costs. The value of the network effects is enhanced both by the lack of dominance of any single or small group of participants on either side of the market and the importance of access to the long tail of smaller players only available easily through the platform.

Unlike OTAs, GDSs' scale advantages are strongly reinforced by strong customer captivity on both sides of the market. Remember that GDSs started life as among the first enterprise software companies on record, an industry characterized by long-term contracts and high switching costs. What's more, the GDSs over time have developed additional Passenger Service Systems software applications—driving everything from the pricing and allocation of inventory to the management of the back end of their own websites—both to further embed themselves in the airline workflow and improve the content delivery on their core GDS offerings. Amadeus, the overall leader in this segment as well as the industry, now earns over 40 percent of revenues from IT solutions. It is not a coincidence that the historically weakest player, Travelport, has been the slowest to develop these sticky applications. Customer captivity with the travel agents who are not software customers is more straightforward. Other than for the very largest of these, single sourcing is a financial necessity, and making changes to their GDS provider would be a major undertaking involving significant cost and disruption to their business.

Threat #3: Airlines go direct to travel agents

The extent and depth of GDS competitive advantage is demonstrated by the third, and potentially most dangerous, threat to their business model. Airlines picking off low-margin leisure customers is one thing. Airlines and travel agents collaborating directly and going around the GDSs entirely goes to the heart of their value proposition.

Over the years, frustration with a combination of the cost and functionality of GDSs has promoted new entrants and alternatives to the current order. As the airlines have consolidated, particularly in the US, they have succeeded in putting some pressure on GDS pricing. But none of the proposed structural alternatives have gotten any meaningful traction. The only other GDS to gain meaningful adoption in the last decade has been the Chinese-government-controlled TravelSky, which is largely limited to domestic Chinese travel.

In the past, various low-cost carriers have eschewed the GDS platforms entirely to rely exclusively on direct bookings, but even these have mostly relented to ensure access to the valuable business traveler channel.[27] The first major frontal assault on the GDS incumbents from a major carrier came from Lufthansa, which in 2015 began imposing a surcharge on bookings made through the indirect channel.[28] More significantly, the establishment of a new industry-wide XML-based communication standard (called NDC)[29] to facilitate airlines' content distribution to agents around the GDSs allowed Lufthansa to establish direct connections through which it offered preferential rates and availability.[30]

Lufthansa's strategy required it to change its agreements with the GDSs under which it commits to fare and content parity across channels in exchange for lower booking fees. The problem with this approach is that the GDS volume losses were overwhelmingly experienced in the local market, where GDS fees are lowest, but the revised content agreement resulted in higher fees across the global network of remaining bookings. A number of analysts concluded that the net impact of the changes on GDS profitability "may actually be beneficial."[31] A number of other carriers have pursued a variety of hybrid strategies establishing select direct channels utilizing the GDS infrastructure.[32] None, however, have taken the extreme measures of Lufthansa—and apparently for good reason.

All of this begs the question of why Lufthansa would have pursued this aggressive strategy and escalated the conflict.[33] Given the combination of questionable economics and the impact on relations with its travel agent and GDS partners—who have pushed the EU to launch an antitrust probe into its practices[34]—there seems to be very little upside. To be sure, the charge that the very apparent unassailability of the GDSs' competitive moats made them slow to modernize technology and innovate has some validity. In particular, the periods of time where GDSs were owned by private equity firms in highly leveraged transactions that constrained investments were not marked by great progress in the GDS product road map. Proving the point, Travelport is still owned by private equity and needed to restructure during the COVID-19 crisis, and its share losses to Amadeus appear to have accelerated. But the straw man of green screen technology and general customer unresponsiveness is unfair, as the more recent growth in the IT solutions businesses of these firms attest. Indeed, some have suggested that the "main catalyst" for the radical nature of Lufthansa's approach was the preexisting "problems with Lufthansa's own distribution strategy" rather than the failings of the GDS providers.[35]

That said, the lessons of the GDS case study are not just about the resiliency of intense mutually reinforcing advantages. It is about the fact that time and technology and changes to industry structure are threats to even the strongest competitive advantages and vigilance remains essential. This vigilance relates not just to continuously reinforcing the advantages through aggressive product and marketing investment but to how to most constructively interact with others in the ecosystem. This includes establishing a culture that avoids destructive competition among oligopolists—say through the perfectly legal reciprocal avoidance of trying to "steal" travel agency customers from each other's areas of respective geographic strength.

But equally important is the dealings with upstream and downstream partners. Those blessed with such competitive advantages as the GDS sector should play the long game and share the benefits in a way that makes their continued success in the interest of others in the value chain as well. Short-term milking strategies, combining aggressive pricing with constrained R&D, are an invitation to long-term threats. Indeed, whether the establishment of NDC ultimately undermines the GDSs' collective franchise will be as much a function of their behavior as the power of the technology.[36] The shorter investment horizons of certain private equity firms—characterized on occasion as an ethos analogous to the "pump-and-dump" schemes of boiler room traders[37]—has sometimes encouraged long-term value destructive behavior.

Far from being an anachronism, the GDS history closely mirrors other sectors where long-established electronically based network effects businesses have not just survived but thrived in the face of internet-enabled disrupters. Credit card networks connecting merchants and banking institutions are an even more dramatic example of the phenomenon. Like the airlines' establishment of the GDSs, the original credit card companies were created and owned by the banks themselves.

Although these companies did well after they achieved their independence, many expected that Visa and Mastercard would be disintermediated with the birth of the online payments industry. In the early days of first mover PayPal, the company tried to do just that by incentivizing customers to use their bank account information rather than credit card numbers. But in 2016, PayPal eventually realized that trying to go around rather than leveraging the incumbent credit card networks would dramatically slow its own growth—and most significantly was creating opportunities for fast followers like Apple Pay and Android Pay.[38]

The resulting growth of PayPal[39] and of the broader online payments sector that has emerged has only served to accelerate the value appreciation of the credit card networks. The shares of both Visa and Mastercard appreciated more than ten times over just the last decade. And while the new online payments sector has exploded, with not just PayPal but dozens of internet unicorns created, none of these new platforms come close to the value of either of these two over fifty-year-old incumbents. Indeed, that entire industry is probably smaller than the combined value of Visa and Mastercard.[40] That said, Visa's unsuccessful $5.3 billion effort to acquire fintech disrupter Plaid—thwarted by the Justice Department—suggests that even these juggernauts are not impervious to changes in the ecosystem.[41]

Returning to the massive travel sector, there are other important lessons to explore that highlight cracks in the foundation of the Platform Delusion. Given the unfavorable comparison between OTAs and GDSs in the commercial aviation ecosystem, it may seem a little surprising that the title of the next chapter is "'To Travel Is to Live': How Priceline Became Worth $100 Billion." Priceline is most definitely an OTA and the value of the entire GDS industry—at its peak before the coronavirus pandemic ravaged the travel industry—was barely half that of this single company. In light of the structural observations about the air travel sector, one aspect of Priceline's success should be obvious: despite its origins in the sector, the company's success has very little to do with air travel.

KEY CHAPTER TAKEAWAYS

1. The GDS industry has been the only reliable, substantial money-maker in the air travel sector. Airlines themselves have had a long history of volatile results, often driven by factors outside their control. Although recent consolidation has improved the consistency of results, as the coronavirus pandemic demonstrated, the industry is far from immune to shocks.

2. An electronic network that substantially predates the internet, the GDS industry is a powerful network effects driven oligopoly with reinforcing supply-side scale and customer captivity.

3. Even as the percentage of travel booked through GDSs has declined precipitously as airlines have increasingly gone direct to consumers and sometimes established direct connections to travel agencies, GDS revenues, profits, and profitability have continued to grow. This unexpected result is supported by the inherent power of their network effects, their indispensability to the highly profitable corporate travel market, their unique ability to deliver incremental value-added services, and the uninterrupted growth in air travel until COVID-19.

4. Even extraordinary franchises supported by multiple sources of competitive advantage are subject to threats and pressures over time. The GDSs have addressed this by building adjacent businesses that leverage their structural advantages. The perception that the potential franchise benefits are being fully realized and fairly shared diminishes any incentive to disintermediate the incumbent or otherwise encourage new competitors. Weaknesses on these fronts may ultimately shorten the reign of the GDSs, but it is unlikely to happen any time soon.

"TO TRAVEL IS TO LIVE!":[1]
HOW PRICELINE BECAME
WORTH $100 BILLION

WHAT IS NOW BOOKING HOLDINGS started life in 1997 as Priceline .com, the "Name Your Own Price" business made famous by commercials starring William Shatner. Although the company only changed its name in 2018, almost two decades after it went public, the reliance on the original sketchy business model had been minor for over a decade and the connections to the sketchy founder completely severed for even longer.

Also gone is Priceline's overwhelming reliance on air travel. When he was not writing copy for the original Shatner radio ads, founder Jay Walker was giving away equity in the company to get airlines to provide discounted tickets. While Walker touted the marketing gimmick as "absolutely revolutionary" and assured the public that "a significant amount of the global economy"[2] would ultimately be priced using the Name Your Own Price mechanism, "sale of leisure airline tickets," according to the company's prospectus for its March 1999 IPO, "represented essentially all of the Company's revenues."[3] Although the tiny money-losing company had also launched products, at least on a test basis, covering the sale of new automobiles, home mortgages, and hotel room reservations, and had ambitions well beyond these categories, potential investors who read the public disclosure were informed that Priceline's "near term, and possibly long-term prospects" would continue to rely on airline ticket sales.[4]

Priceline impresario Walker was an unlikely guru for the digital age. A labor relations major who took a break from college to launch a failed local newspaper, the serial entrepreneur started with actual businesses and then, with the launch of think tank Walker Digital in 1994, moved to ideas. In addition to being mostly unsuccessful, what many of the businesses seemed to have in common was being "usually based on some kind of low-tech, cross-marketing scheme."[5] His only real financial success prior to Priceline was a business that used monthly credit card statements and other channels to sell discounted magazine subscriptions. Like Priceline, this business— ultimately branded as Synapse—positioned itself as a consumer-friendly (once-in-a-lifetime opportunity!) while using questionable claims and marketing techniques (auto-renewing the subscription perpetually). Walker sold Synapse to Time Inc., whose subsequent owners paid $5 million to settle a class action lawsuit relating to the business's deceptive practices.[6]

Walker attracted highly respected executives to join Priceline, blue chip investors to back it, and the leading internet research analyst of the era, Morgan Stanley's Mary Meeker, to sponsor it. Despite the various red flags, notably Priceline's own financials, the momentum behind the venture led to great expectations.[7] And these were not disappointed. On the day of its IPO, the stock closed at over four times its opening price and increased over ten times a month later.

Priceline's stock drifted down from its early spike before the internet bubble peaked in March 2000. Things didn't start to get really bad, however, until the company reported in September that it expected to dramatically miss expectations and fail to break even as planned. Revenues would actually be down sequentially in the quarter because of a shortfall in airline ticket sales.[8] At the same time, the state of Connecticut announced it would launch a consumer fraud investigation into its practices.[9] Barely a week later, Walker announced that he was pulling the plug on an affiliated business licensing the Priceline "technology" to sell food and gasoline.[10] The venture, launched with much fanfare the previous year,[11] had consumed hundreds of millions in cash with little to show for it. The following month, layoffs and the departure of the well-regarded CFO were announced, bringing the stock to an all-time low of $4.28 from its all-time high of $165.

Within a couple of weeks, a company filing revealed it would need to take a charge for fees and litigation expenses in connection with a lawsuit alleging that Walker had actually stolen the Name Your Own Price idea. Walker Digital had provided an indemnity that Priceline now doubted Walker could satisfy.[12] By the time Walker left the company and resigned from the board at the end of the year, Priceline's shares had sunk to little over $1.[13] He sold most of his remaining stake in the company over the next summer, largely severing his ties.[14]

Litigation had frequently characterized Walker's early business ventures. For instance, during Carl Icahn's stewardship of TWA, he had sued one of Walker's ventures for making improper bulk sales of coupons to travel agents. Icahn's continuing enmity for Walker led him to be one of the few winners from Priceline's stock collapse; he shorted it all the way down.[15] After leaving Priceline and returning to Walker Digital, however, litigation more or less became Walker's actual avocation, filing dozens of patent lawsuits against over a hundred companies, including the likes of Amazon and Google.[16] Walker found himself more likely viewed as a patent troll[17] than the "Edison for a new age"[18] he had been called during Priceline's early years.

Priceline shares would remain stubbornly in the single digits for years after Walker's departure. So anemic was the stock that the company announced a 1 for 6 reverse stock split in 2003 to avoid the risk of delisting.[19] The tragedy of 9/11 extended Priceline's operational distress but had one significant positive unintended consequence—it shifted the company's focus away from air travel to hotels. As hotels came to account for over half of booking services, Priceline took a stake in Travelweb, a hotel reservation network owned by major hotel groups. Between 2002 and 2004, non-air segments, predominantly hotel reservations, moved from one third to two thirds of revenues.

THE BIRTH OF BOOKING.COM

By 2004, Priceline had stabilized its stock price and diversified its reliance on both air travel and its quirky business model. Less than 10 percent of travel inventory is distributed through off-price channels like the original Priceline. These include various ticket consolidators as well as other competitive online "opaque" pricing services like Hotwire. By entering the traditional online retail travel segment, Priceline significantly expanded its potential addressable market.

But Priceline remained a fraction of the size of three much larger competitors that had already begun to roll up the online industry. The biggest of these, IAC Travel, owned not just Expedia but Hotwire and Hotels.com. It was one thing to announce the intention of moving from niche to broad-based travel service provider. It was another to execute such an insurgency in the face of multiple incumbent players with vastly greater resources. At the time, IAC Travel's marketing budget approached half a billion dollars, while Priceline's was well under a hundred million dollars.

Given these financial demands in its home market, Priceline had launched in Europe through a joint venture with private equity firm General Atlantic to help fund the anticipated losses. The trouble was that no one in Europe or elsewhere had ever heard of Name Your Own Price, and the capital required to not just build a brand but educate the public about a new way of purchasing was overwhelming. Shortly after 9/11, General Atlantic pulled the plug on funding. The failure of these organic efforts laid the groundwork for the transactions that would transform the company.

The acquisition of the Dutch hotel site Booking.nl in March 2005 was not the signal event in the history of Booking Holdings. Rather, it was a larger transaction made the previous September by UK-based Active Hotels that enabled the dramatic turnaround.[20] Active and Booking had identical business models and complementary footprints. Each was the largest in its respective geography (Active in the UK and Booking in continental Europe) and had signed up a similar number of hotels, primarily smaller independents not otherwise easily accessible. The potential revenue lift from combining the networks, by offering new continental options to UK consumers and new UK options to those on the continent, was clear. And the increased attractiveness to hotels of working with a service offering a wider pool of vacationers was equally obvious. The logic of a combination had led the two companies to discuss a merger before either had been approached by Priceline.

Current Booking Holdings CEO Glenn Fogel ran Priceline corporate development at the time and was actually shutting down their London operation when he identified the Active acquisition and followed it up with Booking.nl. The two companies' operations were combined, rebranded as Booking.com, and extended beyond Europe. The total price of the two deals together was under $300 million.

The effect of these transactions on the company's results and share performance was swift once the two acquisitions were integrated in 2005. The stock appreciated 500 percent in 2006 and 2007, with revenue and profit margins growing significantly faster than peers over the period. Priceline first exceeded Expedia's market capitalization in 2009[21] and exceeded its gross bookings in 2013.[22] Over the years, the company made a number of other acquisitions that dwarf these two, but even collectively the subsequent transactions have not had anything like the seismic impact of Active and Booking.

Later deals strengthened a geographic position (Agoda in Asia in 2007), added a technological capability (Buuteeq for digital marketing capabilities, Hotel Ninjas for property management software, and Pricematch for hotel data analytics, all in 2014 and 2015) or built a logical adjacency (TravelJigsaw for car rentals in 2010 and Kayak and Momondo for metasearch in 2013 and 2017, respectively). Although most of these were not terribly successful, they were mercifully few and generally modest—only Kayak cost more than $1 billion. Unfortunately, the company's largest acquisition, restaurant reservation software platform OpenTable for $2.5 billion in 2014, was the most strategically tenuous. It was the subject of an initial $941 million impairment charge in 2016 and another smaller one in 2020.[23]

Although the company now operates under a number of major brands, the vast majority of revenues and profits are associated with Booking.com itself. The Priceline brand actually discontinued its Name Your Own Price bidding process for airfare and car rental deals, and now primarily operates as a traditional US OTA, a majority of whose bookings are hotel reservations.[24] On July 26, 2017, the year before Priceline changed its name to Booking Holdings, the company's market value rose above $100 billion.[25]

A ROOM WITH A VIEW: WHAT MAKES HOTEL RESERVATIONS SO MUCH BETTER THAN SELLING AIRLINE SEATS FOR OTAS?

We have described in detail the path taken by Booking Holdings to transform itself from an unprofitable niche US air travel focused OTA to, according to the *Economist*, "the world's largest online travel company."[26] But Booking, although it has diversified into metasearch and some mostly related software businesses, is still overwhelmingly an OTA. The ability of this single company to dwarf the size not only of the entire GDS industry but all the other public companies in the OTA sector combined is attributable primarily to one factor: the difference between hotels and airlines.

The relevant distinctions relate to the nature of the product itself as well as the industry structure.

OTAs have network effects, but as we observed in chapter 9, product complexity is a key characteristic determining the likely impact of these effects. The greater the number of relevant attributes a buyer is likely to consider before making a purchase, the more diverse the pool of supply needs to be for a network operator to offer an acceptable service. What's more, once a level of viability is achieved, the value of incremental supply is similarly driven by the importance of product nuance. In leisure air travel, convenience—and since the elimination of the Concorde, all non-stop flights take about the same amount of time, although departure and connection times vary significantly—and cost dominate all other considerations. Sure, we all have some preferences within the full-service airline and the low-cost carrier categories and a sense of how much we value the overall difference between the two groups. But these considerations simply impact our selection between otherwise close substitutes. For most routes, there are less than a handful of options in any case, which is why there are hundreds of flight OTAs and it is so easy to establish a new one.[27]

When it comes to product complexity, hotels are a different matter altogether. Visiting New York for a romantic getaway? There may be only a few airlines flying your route, but once you arrive, there are almost seven hundred different hotels, of which almost five hundred are in Manhattan. And these hotels have more than a hundred thousand rooms, only some with a view. This is a context in which the depth of alternatives, particularly as the focus is narrowed not just by price, but by part of the city, type of hotel, characteristics of the room, and availability of personally salient amenities, really matters.

The dramatic impact of product complexity in otherwise identical business models can be seen in a wide variety of industries far beyond OTAs. For example, there are many drivers of the respective fates of the world's two largest financial data providers, Reuters (later Thomson Reuters and now Refinitiv) and Bloomberg. But the single most important factor that enabled Bloomberg to overtake Reuters even with a century-long head start was that Bloomberg targeted fixed-income markets while Reuters's historic core franchise was foreign exchange. Although there are almost two hundred world currencies, only ten represent 99 percent of the trading volume. By contrast, there are many more outstanding debt issuances than even the many thousands of listed public companies. A single public company—or private company or governmental entity—can issue dozens of different debt securities. Not only do the number of outstanding bonds dwarf the number of stocks, but the number of financially relevant terms of each—from call dates and premiums to indentures and change of control terms—is vast. Notably, this very complexity lends itself to the development of sticky software and analytic tools to track, manage, and compare the various securities.[28]

Turning to industry structure, we have discussed the impact of airline consolidation, particularly notable in the US.[29] International carriers, after a period of liberalization and the emergence of new competitors, have also begun to consolidate in recent years.[30] Hotels have experienced comparable consolidation trends as independent hotels have either sold outright or affiliated with major groups to benefit from their marketing might.[31] Unlike in the case of airlines, however, an enormous long tail of independent hotels remain. The Hotel Association of the City of New York represents more hotels than the International Air Transportation Association represents airlines globally. What's more, this understates the continuing level of fragmentation, as even among those hotels that have affiliated with one of the giant hotel brands, there are often still distinct ownership and/or management groups involved with significant independent decision-making authority.

In addition, unlike the history of the airline industry in which the original GDSs grew out of early homegrown enterprise software initiatives and airline consortia, the diversity of hotels has spawned a correspondingly diffuse collection, both regional and global, of software providers that manage reservations and facilities as well as customer acquisition and connections to online travel agents. This last function is called a "channel manager," for which there are many dozens of competing options. The optimal channel managers will depend on the size, complexity, location, and target market of a particular hotel as well as the other software being used that needs to be integrated. This disparate set of software providers and connections to the fragmented hotel industry simply did not lend itself to the establishment of a GDS-like utility that managed overall room supply, leaving a much bigger potential opportunity for the OTAs to play a valuable marketplace role.

The closest counterpart to GDSs in the history of the hotel industry that might have disintermediated the OTAs is The Hotel Industry Switch Company (THISCO), established by seventeen hotel chains in 1989. The differences from the GDSs, however, are far greater than the commonalities. The driving force behind THISCO, established decades after the original GDSs, was not the hotel chains themselves—indeed they each only grudgingly contributed $100,000 after much heated debate. Rather the primary backer was actually Rupert Murdoch, who at the time owned a bunch of travel publications, including the Hotel and Travel Index used by travel agents describing hotels around the world.[32] Murdoch wanted hotel company support in his efforts to migrate the content to an exciting new technology—not the internet but CD-ROMs. Murdoch saw THISCO— and its flagship product forever known as the UltraSwitch—as an interface to sell CD-ROMs by establishing an interface between what was then still seven GDSs and the various hotel reservation systems.[33]

In the thirty years since the birth of THISCO, the business has undergone numerous name and ownership changes, gone public and back to private, and been passed around between a head-spinning number of private equity firms seeking to turn it around. But at the end of the day, despite still having billions of transactions pass through the "switch" every month, the number of inexpensive alternative paths ensured that the business will always struggle to maintain revenue and profitability. The most recent sale of the re-renamed DHISCO (in between, it was called a number of things with the word Pegasus in it) was to another private equity backed company for not much more than $10 million.[34]

Given the GDSs' established connections to hundreds of thousands of travel agents from their historic position with the airlines, one might assume that they would be able to extract the same value from the hotel ecosystem as from the airline ecosystem. To be sure, they have all expanded their services to hotels. But the plethora of inexpensive alternative channels through a complex web of extranets, APIs, DSPs, and new emerging solutions[35] have ensured that pricing is low and that this remains a small percentage of GDS revenues.[36]

More important, because of the relative fragmentation of both the hotel market and the market for distribution channels, travel agencies are able to keep a far bigger portion of a much larger commission. Where airlines are able to enforce a roughly flat $5 per flight fee, with the GDSs able to retain at least half from all but the largest travel agents, hotels typically pay travel agent commissions of between 15–30 percent with the GDSs receiving a tiny portion for the use of their distribution infrastructure. Indeed, the GDS focus on acquiring hospitality reservation systems to build their IT services businesses is in part an effort to establish the kind of indispensability on the hotel side that they have long enjoyed with airlines.

The bad news for the OTAs is that the largest hotel chains keep commissions closer to 10 percent. But the reality is that relatively few of these hotel brands' bookings come through the OTAs—like the airlines, they have been increasingly focused on securing direct bookings—and a minority of the OTA's hotel bookings are affiliated with these chains.[37] The good news is that the top five hotel brand companies only control around half the US's hotel rooms (the top four airlines control two thirds of the market) and far less internationally.

This greater fragmentation of hotels themselves and the networks that connect them to travel agents ensures that the two increasingly dominant OTAs represent an increasingly greater portion of the value in the lodging ecosystem. In the absence of any credible scale intermediary between the hotels and the OTAs, they have been able to enjoy the advantages associated with true many-to-many marketplaces with multiple structural advantages. Morgan Stanley analysts pointed out that for the decade ending in 2016, Expedia and Booking Holdings went from being one fourth the size of the five largest hotel brands' market caps to double their size.[38]

Not surprisingly, this has been a source of frustration to the largest hotel brands, jealous of the relative clout of their airline counterparts. They are aggressively trying to build their direct channel through massive marketing campaigns, big discounts, and promotion of their loyalty programs, all of which make sense. But they have also repeatedly tried to create OTA and metasearch competitors, which is a fool's errand. Priceline's first significant acquisition in the hotel space was picking up the carcass of Travelweb for $29 million. Travelweb had been the industry's failed 2002 attempt to gain leverage against the OTAs.[39] Priceline had been an investor in the venture (the $29 million headline price in 2004 included its original $8 million investment)[40] and when the partners declined to make the marketing investments needed to turn it into a credible player, Priceline saw it as a vehicle to accelerate the pivot away from airlines and the Name Your Own Price model. Thus, ironically, the hotels played an important role in strengthening what has become their most expensive and aggravating source of room demand.

A decade later, the major hotel groups tried again, this time without Priceline.[41] The idea was to create a portal that combined the advantages of metasearch with the benefits of direct booking.[42] The new consumer destination site Room Key attacked Booking and Expedia, who invest billions in marketing to sustain their positions, without a meaningful marketing budget of its own. And although Room Key visitors can benefit from the same low rates available from the hotels' own websites (if they are loyalty members), the service lacks the breadth of options and ease of use offered by traditional OTA and metasearch competitors. Best Western CEO David Kong conceded, "We basically repeated the same mistake again."[43]

The primary problem with Room Key and its predecessor wasn't execution, both having recruited highly credible industry CEOs. The basic

issue is industry structure. The relative fragmentation of the hotel industry and the relative consolidation of the OTA industry suggest the impos-
sibility of creating a compelling product on a financially sensible basis.
Harvard Business Review published a thinly veiled fictionalized case study
that highlighted the misguided nature of establishing a "third way" that
diverts hotel industry resources from optimizing marketing spend on direct and third-party channels.[44]

WHY BOOKING IS WORTH SO MUCH MORE THAN EXPEDIA

We mentioned earlier that Priceline surpassed Expedia in market value
and gross bookings in 2009 and 2013, respectively. Expedia, however,
retook the mantel of largest OTA by bookings when it purchased Travelocity, Orbitz, and HomeAway in 2015 for $280 million, $1.6 billion, and
$3.9 billion, respectively.[45] Nonetheless, Expedia never again exceeded its
competitor's market capitalization. For two businesses that look so much
like each other—operating in almost all the same categories globally and
with almost identical gross bookings today—the disparity in performance
over the last decade is striking. From the end of 2009, the year that it
permanently overtook Expedia's equity value, until the end of 2019, just
before COVID-19 disproportionately devastated all the travel-related
equities, Booking Holdings shares had grown almost tenfold. That's more
than double the compound growth rate of the overall market. Meanwhile,
Expedia actually lagged the market over this period.[46]

The dramatic value disparity is driven by a number of factors. At the
highest level, subtle differences in product mix can combine to have a significant impact on results. So it is not surprising that, although air travel
is a small fraction of Expedia's total bookings, it still represents relatively
more of its total business than at Booking. Both companies have similar
numbers of total bookings, but Booking Holdings reports twice as many
room nights, suggesting that Expedia relies more on low-margin airline

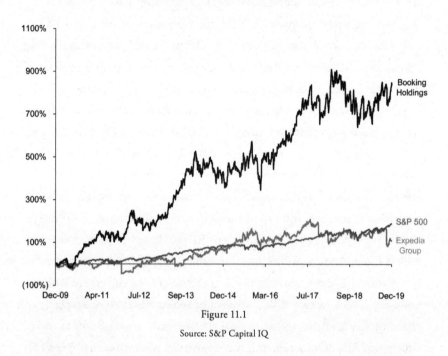

Figure 11.1

Source: S&P Capital IQ

bookings. Expedia's revenues are also much more derived from the US, the market in which both the airline and hotel industries are most concentrated. The size of commission rates OTAs can negotiate tend to decrease with industry concentration.

Two other aspects of how these respective businesses grew played a meaningful role in their respective value appreciation.

First, although both companies have done plenty of acquisitions, Expedia has relied far more on these for its growth. With a few exceptions, Booking's acquisitions have been smaller and designed to provide a beachhead in a new category, geography, or capability from which to build internally. Many more of Expedia's deals have been larger traffic consolidation plays. It is possible to get a bargain in an acquisition, but where the auction process is highly competitive—which most of Expedia's bigger deals appear to have been—the bulk of potential value creation goes to the seller while the risk of successful integration remains with the buyer.

Although both companies represent a portfolio of travel-related services, the reliance on inorganic deals has made Expedia's consumer facing brands more diverse and more diffuse. The resulting greater number of individual brands to manage and market and the lack of a flagship driving the vast majority of revenues impact the potential efficiency of operations. Booking is organized around six major brands, of which Booking .com represents the overwhelming majority, while Expedia has over twenty brands, none of which represents the majority of revenues. The fact that Booking has been able to use its core brand to organically build a business that is far larger than the portfolio of alternative accommodation brands (Vrbo is the largest) Expedia purchased as part of the $3.9 billion HomeAway acquisition reflects the power of Booking's model.[47]

A subtler but equally notable distinction between the two businesses, however, relates to two different ways of selling hotel rooms—the merchant model and the agency model. In the early days of online travel, which was US dominated, the way it usually worked is that the OTA negotiated a steeply discounted bulk rate with the hotels and would sell the rooms at whatever price it could get. The OTA would keep the money until the guest completed the stay, at which point it would remit the net price to the hotel. This is the merchant model, so-called because the OTA is the merchant of record. In the agency model, the OTA simply facilitates a reservation between the hotel and the guests, who don't actually pay until they stay. The hotel sets the price and remits a commission once the stay is completed.

There has always been an active debate about which model is "better" in the abstract.[48] On the one hand, the agency model has higher margins as it is a true "asset light" approach to aggregating supply. On the other hand, the merchant model captures the cash sooner, but more importantly ensures control of the room inventory, which is hugely valuable in times of high demand.

But in historic context, the most relevant issue turned out to be how much easier it was in the early days to sign up hotels, particularly smaller long-tail ones, using the agency model. With the agency model, all that needs to be agreed on is the commission, but merchant deals involve negotiating a more detailed contract covering the net price and the inventory that will be made available. When trying to build scale quickly in a business characterized by network effects, speed is critical. In Europe, where both Active and Booking were launched, neither consumers (who were still reticent to provide their credit cards to OTAs) nor hotels were used to payment at the time of booking. So, as both competed for the land grab for independent hotels in their respective geographies, Booking had a significant advantage over companies like Expedia who were committed to the merchant model as the "superior" approach.

Expedia had looked at both Active and Booking but passed because, as former CEO Dara Khosrowshahi conceded, "we were attached to the merchant model."[49] Specifically, the company had become used to benefiting from the attractive working capital characteristics of holding on to travelers' money and the higher room markups available. By the time Expedia realized their mistake and purchased an alternative agency-based European OTA—Italy's Venere in 2008—Booking had an entrenched relative scale advantage in Europe and much of the rest of world where the markets also primarily used the agency model.

Although most hotels multi-home, the smaller independents are more likely to stick with one that has consistently delivered traffic. These also are the most likely to require outsourced support. Booking has built a significant business supporting the management and marketing needs of hoteliers. These standalone B2B businesses leverage their wide hotel customer footprint while strengthening the stickiness of the core consumer booking platform.[50]

Today, both Expedia and Booking Holdings use a mixture of merchant and agency models for different markets and different products.[51] And just as Amazon's success in the auto parts space is based on the unique breadth of its offerings using a combination of retail and marketplace product, Booking's and Expedia's basic advantage over competitors is the higher likelihood they will present site visitors with an option that meets their needs regardless of whether the room is "merchant" or "agency" based. But the legacy of the companies' respective histories have given Booking a persistent substantial share advantage in most markets outside the US, where the agency model still dominates. The hotel industry is significantly more fragmented in these markets than in the US, leading to better terms and higher profits. Similarly, Booking's relative strength with smaller hotels and independents as well as geographies with greater hotel fragmentation generally supports stronger financial results. Expedia, by contrast, has more than double the relative exposure[52] to bookings with the largest chains, which can exert the greatest leverage with the indirect channel.

Regardless of their relative positions, it is clear that the OTA sector, and the dominant position these two play in it,[53] represents the closest analogy in hotels to the position held by GDSs in airlines. As a sector that, unlike the GDSs, clearly does owe its existence to the emergence of the internet, these companies come closer to aligning with the industry structures and dynamics predicted by the Platform Delusion. The only problem with this narrative is that Booking, even as it dramatically outperformed Expedia, actually has not managed to secure the position as the leading digital travel company.

GOOGLE, TRIPADVISOR, AND THE LIMITS OF SEO

Booking Holdings has built a powerful franchise benefiting from both demand- and supply-side scale and reinforced by the customer captivity of those hotels who have come to rely on its marketing might and various software tools to attract and manage customers. But it turns out that even Booking, which dwarfs the entire GDS industry and all of its OTA competitors combined, is not the biggest kid on the travel industry value chain block. That moniker belongs to our old friend Google. If Amazon has not managed to play any significant role in this vast sector of the economy, Google sits squarely at the top of the funnel where travel dreams begin and has used that enviable position to take a bigger and bigger slice of the pie over time.

Google has not taken the step of moving up the value chain and directly attacking the OTAs for two reasons. First, it is always worth thinking twice before killing the golden goose. Booking and Expedia each spent around $5 billion in marketing in 2019—most of which went to Google.[54] Second, and more important, being a travel agent, even an online one, requires undertaking a variety of functions—customer service notably among them—that are not Google's business. Google's entire model is built on leveraging scalable technology rather than managed services. But this does not mean that Google isn't happy to chip away at the parts of the OTAs' businesses that do lend themselves to Google's core competencies.[55] And the OTAs remain vulnerable to minor changes in Google's search algorithm, as was seen when Expedia blamed just such changes on a quarterly earnings shortfall that cut its market value by 25 percent in a single day.[56]

Indeed, as the case of travel metasearch demonstrates, Google is happy to compete head-on with customers when the business model is synchronous with its own. The vast majority of Google's travel revenues come from its core AdWords franchise. But the opportunity to take more of the overall advertising pie by doubling down on the metasearch segment through the ITA acquisition proved irresistible. And as the sad tale of TripAdvisor that follows will reveal, when Google has a bull's-eye on your business, you have every reason to be very afraid.

The early days of metasearch saw lots of capital attracted to the intuitive appeal of the category. On the one hand, this investing euphoria seemed justified based on the inevitable growth in usage—it is estimated that three fourths of travelers now use metasearch engines along the way.[57] What's more, some of the first movers developed clever SEO and SEM strategies to complement their clever brand campaigns. On the other hand, sitting squarely between a few dominant OTAs and Google seems structurally precarious to say the least. In addition, the relatively low fixed costs required to develop a functional metasearch engine suggests a low break-even market share with plenty of potential competition.

Within what quickly became a crowded space,[58] TripAdvisor stood out for the intrinsic power and ingenuity of its model. Founded in 2000, by the time it went public in 2011, the site boasted over 50 million reviews and had established itself as an indispensable content destination for prospective travelers. The overwhelming traffic demonstrated the network effects of the model—travelers want the most recent relevant reviews of properties they are considering and reviewers want to share with the widest possible audience. As recently as 2018, the *Guardian* newspaper said, "TripAdvisor is to travel as Google is to search, as Amazon is to books, as Uber is to cabs—so dominant it is almost a monopoly."[59]

But neither reviewers nor travelers pay for the privilege to participate on the platform. TripAdvisor remains a metasearch company and it relies on advertisers (of whom Booking and Expedia are by far the largest) who want access to the users planning to take a trip. And although the strength of its unique network effects driven review content helps its position in organic search results, nothing provides a long-term solution to sitting between Google[60] and your two biggest customers,[61] all of whom have their own competing metasearch capabilities.

TripAdvisor shares rose steadily for about two and a half years from when it began trading at $30/share as an independent company on December 20, 2011.[62] Traffic continued to grow 50 percent year over year through 2013 and the shares hit an all-time high of $110 on June 27, 2014, after which they began their long inevitable decline in the face of the structural infirmities identified. TripAdvisor shares ended 2019—

before the coronavirus pandemic hit—at almost the exact same price at which they began their journey eight years earlier.

This does not mean that TripAdvisor is a bad company with no competitive advantages. It does have network effects that enable it to amass compelling content that other metasearch companies have not. Trivago, another metasearch company, had a splashy IPO in 2016 almost exactly five years after TripAdvisor went public.[63] After more than doubling in value in the first six months, its shares began an uninterrupted downward journey[64] to the present, significantly underperforming TripAdvisor.

Trivago is an interesting case of a misguided attempt to create a differentiated competitive advantage exclusively based on brand—in this case primarily through expensive television commercials featuring the insufferable "Trivago Guy." Brand can provide powerful reinforcement to advantages like scale and captivity. But where such structural advantages do not exist in the first instance, investment in brand is unlikely to yield superior returns. The failure of TripAdvisor as a network effects driven digital platform to deliver the kind of performance predicted by the Platform Delusion highlights the critical importance of other structural attributes—here the lack of diversity of key network participants and low switching costs—in determining success.[65]

This also does not mean that there is no place left in digital travel for enterprising entrepreneurs to profitably disrupt the status quo. These last two chapters demonstrate that the digital travel ecosystem has spawned a wide range of good and bad businesses. What determines which are most likely to succeed are where within the ecosystem they sit, whether they have a credible path to scale, and what other structural attributes the business can be expected to exhibit at scale.

That said, given the size and strength of the incumbents all along the value chain, with a particularly intimidating Google keeping guard at the front door, it feels likely that a very small number of the dozens of start-ups targeting the sector every year will endure.[66] Some, however, have managed to target market segments where the owner of an intelligently designed digital platform could establish defensible barriers.

Business travel management companies (TMCs), we noted earlier, are not as consolidated as leisure OTAs, are still predominantly off-line, and deliver customers who are far less price sensitive and far more important to the bottom line of many hotels and travel providers. TripActions has raised almost $800 million dollars—nearly half of it during the pandemic—to build a scale competitor in this space providing an end-to-end digital solution to businesses encompassing the services provided by both expense management software companies like Concur and corporate travel agencies like American Express.[67] One could imagine at scale a sticky service leveraging technology but with human support that delivers businesses a variety of cost and administrative benefits while providing greater satisfaction to employees.

The incumbents, of course, are not sitting still. And there are other start-ups trying a different version of the same idea.[68] Expedia purchased an earlier venture-backed online corporate travel business, Egencia, in 2004 without driving any fundamental change in the market.[69] Whether the product and technology have arrived at a place that could drive enough adoption to secure defensible scale is still a question for TripActions. But unlike, say, the next niche metasearch company or any app that focuses on air travel, one can understand the potential path to sustainable superior returns.

KEY CHAPTER TAKEAWAYS

1. The complexity and number of relevant attributes in selecting a hotel room and breadth of options in any location supports far stronger network effects in a platform of scale connecting potential guests and properties than one connecting potential fliers and airlines.

2. Although, as in the airline industry, there has been significant consolidation in the hotel industry, it remains far more fragmented. The diversity of hotels and their very different history has made GDS operators play a less important role in this ecosystem. These structural distinctions have doomed repeated efforts by large hotel groups to develop a compelling alternative to the dominant OTAs.

3. The massive fixed costs required to attract hotel demand, overwhelmingly through Google, reinforces the value of network effects driven scale on the supply side for OTAs. These scale advantages are reinforced by other demand and supply advantages. The data amassed by the largest OTAs gives them advantages vis-à-vis smaller competitors in optimizing marketing spending on Google and other digital channels.

4. Metasearch companies sit between Google and the dominant OTAs in the ecosystem and cannot expect to sustainably retain most of the value their networks create. Even TripAdvisor, with unique network effects generated content, cannot fully mitigate this structural infirmity. Other points in the travel value chain better lend themselves to the establishment of digital competitive advantage.

12

IT'S NICE TO SHARE, SOMETIMES: WHY AIRBNB WILL ALWAYS BE A BETTER BUSINESS THAN UBER

THE *FINANCIAL TIMES* RECENTLY IDENTIFIED the sharing economy as "one of the most important online phenomena of the decade."[1] Richard Waters, the publication's US West Coast editor, noted, however, that "for a sector that is already getting long in the tooth, there are a surprising number of unresolved questions." The one he identifies as of "particular interest": Are these good businesses?

Part of the challenge in assessing the strength of this increasingly ubiquitous category is the lack of agreement about the characteristics that define its contours. The term "sharing economy" has been used without great precision to describe a broad range of commercial and noncommercial transactions. Sometimes it is presented as simply encompassing all peer-to-peer business models, whether what is being "shared" is one's money—as in the case of LendingClub or Kickstarter—or one's time—as in the case of various gig economy businesses like TaskRabbit or Sittercity. Sometimes it is extended to include exchanges involving businesses and not just between individuals. Similarly, there is disagreement as to whether the definition should encompass transactions that entail an actual transfer of ownership.

The basic economic problem of how to optimize asset utilization is not new. In the case of assets under shared ownership, this topic captured the attention of economists almost two hundred years ago under the rubric of the "tragedy of the commons."[2] What is new, however, is the ability of internet-based connections to dramatically improve the efficiency of resource allocation and the corresponding proliferation of companies dedicated exclusively to this function. From parking spaces (JustPark) to recreational vehicles (RVshare), these businesses allow assets that are only used part of the time to be enjoyed more of the time.

What these businesses have in common is that they are platforms that provide access to the excess capacity of these assets. Some have argued, accordingly, that the sharing economy is a misnomer and that it is better termed the "access economy."[3] The point is that the value in these businesses does not primarily flow from any social aspect of the transaction, but from making easily available a good or service that would otherwise lie fallow.

These sharing platforms exhibit the classic indirect network effects that characterize all manner of marketplace businesses. Owners of the excess capacity are interested in making it available on the platform that attracts the greatest demand, and potential renters of that capacity are looking for the broadest selection and lowest price. We have seen time and again, however, that the existence of network effects in itself tells an investor relatively little about the attractiveness of a particular business. Given the breadth of competing views of what constitutes a "sharing economy" business, it should come as no surprise that there are dramatic differences in resilience among such enterprises. But even between apparently similar business models within a relatively narrow definition of sharing platforms, there is significant variability in quality.

This is most easily demonstrated by comparing the two most well-known and valuable sharing platforms that have had the most dramatic impact on the overall economy: Uber and Airbnb. Uber lets car owners share their vehicles and their time to create a competitor to cabs, car services, car rentals, and even car ownership. Airbnb facilitates the rental of all or part of private residences. The vast new pool of accommodations made available competes with hotels and more traditional rentals, and the platform competes with online and off-line travel agents and realtors. Although both businesses have expanded the use cases to which the platform is applied—for instance, Uber now sometimes buys the car for a driver and Airbnb now works with professional property managers—the sharing paradigm remains both businesses' core proposition. Uber went public in May 2019 at a valuation of over $80 billion. Even at the height of the pandemic, its valuation was over $50 billion and by the end of the year had crept back to $100 billion. Airbnb had been valued at just over $30 billion in a private round raised in 2017.[4] When it was forced to delay its public offering because of the pandemic and raise new private capital in April 2020, the valuation fell below $20 billion.[5] The top of the IPO valuation range filed by Airbnb's bankers toward the end of the year was still $35 billion, well less than half of Uber's value at the time.[6]

Although Uber had consistently been valued at a multiple of Airbnb, the key market and product attributes that drive sustainable franchise value suggest that it is Airbnb that has always been the better business.

Template for Assessing Competitive Advantage

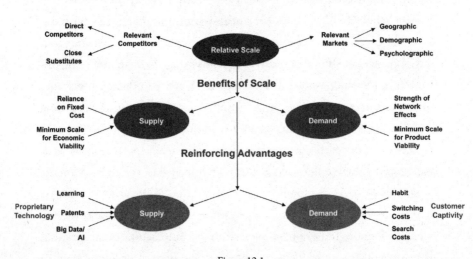

Figure 12.1

When the company finally did go public in December 2020, the valuation surged past $100 billion.[7] By the end of the year, Airbnb's value exceeded Uber's despite earning less than half its revenues. The public market's apparent view of the relative attractiveness of the two businesses is supported by a closer examination of the respective strength and sources of the collection of competitive advantages enjoyed by each.

RELATIVE SCALE AND MINIMUM VIABLE MARKET SHARE

In assessing the competitive advantage of scale, there are two interrelated topics that must be addressed. First, the extent of the advantage relative to others is quantified and, second, the nature of the benefits that flow from this relative advantage is considered.

Both Uber and Airbnb are the biggest global players in their respective "sharing" markets—ride sharing and space sharing. In these global markets, both companies represent market shares in the twenties.[8] In addition, they are both likely 40–50 percent larger than their next-largest competitor—Chinese Didi for Uber and Booking for Airbnb. But, as we shall discuss shortly, it is far from clear that the ride-sharing market—unlike the space-sharing market—is really global. As a result, in any given market, Airbnb is likely to face the same handful of players while Uber is more likely to also confront significant local or regional champions.[9]

Even if one concludes that Uber, still with more than double the share of Lyft, its closest direct competitor in the US, enjoys at the moment somewhat greater relative scale than Airbnb in at least some markets, this is only the beginning of the analysis. Far more impactful is the extent to which the relevant market and product characteristics turn scale into tangible economic benefits. It is here that the differences between the two companies are most stark.

Two primary attributes are responsible for the superiority of Airbnb over Uber: product/service complexity on the demand side and the fixed-cost requirements on the supply side. The former determines how many network participants are needed for a viable product and the extent to which additional network participants continue to enhance the product. The latter determines basic break-even economics and the relative financial advantage of being larger than competitors.

In any given city, the product viability of both companies is a function of local density—of drivers on the platform on the one hand and property inventory on the other. A key distinction between Uber's and Airbnb's respective marketplaces, however, is how the level of intrinsic product complexity drives the marketplace liquidity required to establish a viable service in a locality. In ride hailing, other than price, the ability to deliver a car within three to five minutes dominates all other customer considerations. How many drivers it takes to satisfy this level of service will depend on both the geography and activity level in a given market. But any service that can attract enough drivers to achieve this threshold, if priced correctly, would be competitive with any other. In the short-term lodging market, by contrast, there are many more salient product characteristics and market segments. An acceptable service would need to secure an adequate pool of alternative accommodations across these dimensions to attract broad interest. Although it is again impossible to know in the abstract how many providers could meet this minimum level, the need to satisfy such a nuanced profile of demand suggests that it would be fewer than for a more homogeneous product or service.

Once the minimum product-viability requirements have been met, complexity also impacts the value to users of increasing available supply beyond this point. Having so many drivers that cars arrive sooner than the optimal three to five minutes is not useful. Riders often can't get to the car that fast. In the short-term lodging market, however, the wide range of relevant product characteristics ensures that the value of higher incremental density in local listings does not top out in the same way. Indeed, evidence suggests that more listings not only attract more travelers but also drive higher occupancy rates. This dynamic reinforces the value of relative network scale on the demand side for Airbnb that is far greater than for Uber.[10]

On the supply side, the biggest distinction between Uber and Airbnb is that ride-hailing service customers primarily use them in a single city. In contrast, customers of short-term lodging services use those services in and hail from many different locales. As a result, people choosing platforms on which to list their primary residences are not just concerned about the density of listings in their home cities—density of listings as well as awareness of the platform in multiple popular destination cities is also important to attracting travelers to a platform. Thus, the collective fixed costs associated with a national or global network of local market leadership positions, which in turn benefit from spreading the central fixed overhead, become a significant obstacle to new entrants.

The importance of the global footprint to the competitiveness of an alternative accommodations provider is highlighted by the respective fortunes of Airbnb's two biggest competitors, Expedia and Booking.com. Although both are global, Expedia acquired a portfolio of locally focused brands while Booking uses its core brand globally. As Expedia belatedly realized, the ability to attract international demand from vacationers for a local listing placed on a service unknown outside of its home country is limited. After five years, Expedia retired its HomeAway brand in the US and established Vrbo as its global brand in 2020, although it still maintains multiple local brands like Abritel in France, Stayz in Australia, Bookabach in New Zealand, and FeWo-direkt in Germany. Despite spending $3.9 billion for the HomeAway portfolio, Expedia generates less than half the revenue of Booking's organically generated business.

Uber, like Airbnb, is global, although it operates in less than half as many countries as Airbnb. But Uber competitors don't need to be global in order to offer a compelling alternative. It may be that in some markets, the level of fixed operating costs won't sustain more than one or two ride-hailing services. But in larger metropolitan areas, multiple robust offerings are always available, and viability sometimes can be achievable at market shares of less than 20 percent. This effectively translates to a permanent pool of four or more Uber competitors, severely limiting returns. What's more, niche providers targeting segments like children (HopSkipDrive) and women (Safr) have emerged that can potentially establish viability at much lower overall market shares. Local incumbent taxi companies have increasingly adopted their own competing "sharing" apps.[11] In some markets, like Brazil, competitors number in the hundreds, representing a mix of global giants like China's Didi and low-cost services with basic homegrown apps.[12]

Ironically, in some larger markets, like New York City, costly local regulations designed to cripple the ride-sharing sector have raised the minimum viable market share so that the level of competition beyond the two market leaders is artificially low.[13] Indeed, by being a fast follower, Lyft historically has been able to free-ride on Uber's investments to clear the regulatory way for the service. More recently, the services have worked together to successfully pass a California ballot initiative allowing them to use gig workers.[14] But what regulation gives it can take away; it is unlikely to support a broad-based sustainable advantage. Despite such high-profile victories as in California, Uber has painfully seen in London that regulation is a double-edged sword. The number and speed of competitors ready to take advantage of Uber's legal challenges in London reflect the generally low entry barriers in the sector.[15]

Conversely, the greater fixed-cost needs in short-term lodging mean that Airbnb competitors can break even only at far higher market shares. It is not a coincidence that while Uber may face competition from dozens of local and regional ride-hailing services, Airbnb has far fewer direct competitors of size in any given market—and the serious ones have generally attempted a more global footprint. To help spread the fixed-cost requirements, Airbnb's primary competitors have become part of larger international travel companies. For example, HomeAway Inc. (which has half as many listing as Airbnb) was acquired by Expedia Inc., and FlipKey

Inc. (with one third as many listings as Airbnb) was purchased by Trip-Advisor Inc. Booking, Airbnb's largest alternative accommodations competitor, as noted, used its global footprint to build its business organically.[16]

CUSTOMER CAPTIVITY

The nature and durability of customer relationships is a key determinant of the speed at which share can move in a particular marketplace. When combined with minimum viable market share, the level of customer captivity enables a potential new entrant to quickly calculate how long it can expect to lose money before achieving a break-even market share. So, for instance, in an industry where customer loyalty limits annual share movement to a couple of points and break-even market share is 20 percent, an insurgent can expect at least a decade of losses before establishing financial viability.

Customer captivity is an attribute of incumbents and by definition only applies to existing customers. As a result, the structural advantage is far greater in well-penetrated businesses where the number of new customers annually represents a relatively small portion of the overall opportunity. In a market that is doubling in size every year, even where existing customers are entirely captive, if an insurgent is able to split new customers evenly it could achieve a 25 percent share in the first year—well in excess of the 20 percent break-even market share that would take a decade to achieve in the previous example.

Many of the product qualities that make users unlikely to switch are also likely to play a role in attracting new ones as well. That said, in emerging industries, strong customer captivity is rarely available because users look to keep their options open until a sector finds its footing. Over time, however, as legacy customers represent an increasing percentage of annual industry revenues, the ability to retain users in the face of potentially competitive offerings becomes both more essential and more valuable. Both ride sharing and space sharing now experience wide and increasing adoption, particularly among younger demographic groups.[17]

Just because customer captivity is important doesn't mean it is easy. By enhancing the ability to easily search out, compare, and switch between sellers, the internet has set the bar far higher for businesses to articulate truly compelling reasons for customers to stay put. What's more, customers and business partners operating in an environment characterized by swift technological change, even in well-established markets, are generally wary of long-term commitments. Nonetheless, robust captivity is still achievable when service quality, breadth of offerings, the verification of nuanced counterparty credentials, and seamless buying processes are central to the ultimate decision to transact.

Unfortunately, even the best-run ride-hailing company will struggle to encourage loyalty among drivers and riders. Over 80 percent of drivers overall work with two or more services, and this percentage has been increasing.[18] Moreover, although a small minority of riders overall currently use multiple ride-hailing apps, that percentage is growing fast and varies widely by geography and demographic.[19] Among my MBA students in New York City, it is already greater than 90 percent.

There is a difference between an individual's willingness to entrust short-term rentals of his or her home to multiple companies and a professional driver's willingness to drive for multiple ride services. And, as we've discussed, for the customer, price and speed are the overwhelming factors influencing the decision about which ride service to use for a short trip, but many other factors play a large role in the decision to stay in a stranger's house. And the downside of making a mistake in connection with your only vacation is much greater than in connection with one of many crosstown journeys.

More broadly, the importance of trust and thus a platform's verification capabilities—that is, its ability to reassure both parties in a transaction by providing detailed information about with whom they are doing business and what they are getting into—is a much more critical factor in reaching a decision about a short-term rental than it is in choosing which service to use for a brief ride. Homeowners want to know who will be staying in their homes, and guests want to know the experiences of others who have used those homes. A single good experience will make customers much less likely to take a chance with an alternative platform even if it seems to offer a comparable or even a slightly better proposition.

When Airbnb establishes a leadership position in a market, competitors are at a disadvantage in terms of inventory availability. Many of Airbnb's listings are exclusive and as long as adequate occupancy rates are achieved, it is not worth listing a property on multiple sites. However, the same is not true for Uber's competitors in the ride-hailing market, because most drivers use multiple apps. Drivers engage in a regular ritual in which they review the weekly promotional offers available from competing services before deciding which app to favor in the subsequent days. Furthermore, while a driver can easily manage multiple apps in real time, a homeowner (and the vast majority of Airbnb listings come from primary homeowners rather than professionals) most likely will need to enlist a "channel manager" service to do the same. That often entails incremental expense and definitely involves greater complexity.

The observance of ride-hailing market-share shifts of greater than 5 percent over a matter of months nationally (and of even more in some localities) suggests a future filled with a steady stream of new competitors for Uber.[20] This is not the case for Airbnb in the short-term lodging market, where the time required to recruit and sign up new units significantly slows the potential rate of market-share shifting and the resulting time it would take a new entrant to break even.

Uber's decision to begin to offer a broader range of services, notably Uber Eats food delivery,[21] and a subscription service, Uber Pass,[22] reflects attempts to build customer loyalty in a category without much. Neither has had much impact on captivity in the core service and both have had a questionable influence on the overall economics of the business. When the pandemic lowered ride-hailing activity by as much as 85 percent, the explosion in food delivery certainly mitigated Uber's revenue losses. But food delivery is even more competitive and unprofitable with lower break-even market shares than ride hailing. As a result, the business lost hundreds of millions of dollars more despite the superior top-line performance. The focused US competitor Lyft has eschewed both international and service-line expansions, but it quickly established its own aggressive subscription service, Lyft Pink, in response to Uber Pass. Neither Pink nor Pass has gotten much traction or fundamentally changed the low loyalty exhibited toward these services.

LEARNING, DATA, AND AI

Finally, the fortunes of network effects businesses depend on the value of the data that they can elicit in their respective markets. Some transactions generate data that is proprietary and, when combined with appropriate analytics and technology, yield hugely valuable predictive insights. Zillow Inc.'s continued dominance in the online real estate marketplace, for instance, is in part a function of its ability to use its unique access to data to continually improve its automated valuation models and its home search and recommendation engines.[23] In contrast, as we highlight in chapter 14, peer-to-peer (P2P) lenders discovered that, for most borrowers, their proprietary data yielded little more insight than was readily available elsewhere from sources such as credit scores.

I pore over the reviews of previous visitors before I book a stay in a stranger's apartment, and an absence of reviews makes it unlikely that I will take the plunge, no matter how nice the pictures. By contrast, Uber driver reviews are not primarily used by riders to select cars (I rarely even note whether a driver's rating is 4.5 or 4.8) but rather by the company to manage its fleet quality over time.[24] Similarly, what information is more valuable for marketers: the fact that on most days I use Uber to travel from home to office, or the name of the city I am planning to visit and how much money I am planning to spend to stay there? And while feedback on drivers will assist Uber in culling those who undermine the service and facilitate training those who join, the nuanced picture that emerges from travelers around the world allows Airbnb to direct regular users to the most appropriate venues and help those listing their homes to deliver a satisfying experience. The resulting high level of satisfaction among Airbnb users reinforces customer captivity, and the company is able to use the data on satisfaction to encourage both rebooking and referrals.[25]

Uber has built a remarkable business and is today the clear leader in the US ride-sharing market and the largest player overall globally. The structural attributes discussed, however, suggest that ride sharing will always be intensely competitive in large local markets. In many international markets, Uber is the insurgent and its US market position provides limited advantage elsewhere. More broadly, the resilience of its position hinges on a relentless aggressiveness rather than an inexorable tendency toward a global winner-take-all or -most equilibrium.

By contrast, Airbnb's strong network effects are paired with significant customer captivity. The intensity of competition even at the local level is likely to be less than Uber's given the advantages afforded by the global fixed-cost base. And the data its leadership position delivers should allow its managers to further entrench and monetize its unique position.

Expedia's acquisition of HomeAway in 2015 and Booking.com's continued focus on building its alternative accommodations inventory suggests that Airbnb will continue to face competition globally. Both of these competitors' ability to offer a combination of traditional and alternative options is clearly a differentiator compared to Airbnb's. In response, Airbnb has quietly begun to add boutique hotels to their listings to ensure that they are not left at a competitive disadvantage vis-à-vis these broad-based travel giants.[26]

But the fact that Booking claimed in 2018 to have surpassed Airbnb in alternative accommodations listings[27] but generated only $2.8 billion of revenue from them that year compared to Airbnb's $3.6 billion suggests the inherent value of specialization within the category. Travelers may consider shared accommodation as a fundamentally different kind of experience and look for different kinds of attributes and rely on different kinds of assurances to establish trust. Home and apartment owners may value dealing with a platform that is focused primarily on managing their very different needs rather than negotiating with hotel chains and property managers.

A number of new Airbnb competitors that target niche market needs will continue to attract capital and survive, if not thrive, despite the failure of many such start-ups recently in the face of COVID-19.[28] And regardless of any advantages from specialization, the outperformance of short-term rentals relative to Expedia and Booking's traditional hotel businesses during the pandemic is likely to intensify the OTAs' competitive focus on the segment.[29] But Airbnb seems to have the potential to be one of the minority of network effects businesses that genuinely may have the opportunity to maintain a winner-take-most market position globally. That said, the significantly different quality of Uber's business, despite the superficial similarities, highlights how the flawed assumptions of the Platform Delusion lead investors to make ill-considered decisions.

KEY CHAPTER TAKEAWAYS

1. There is no generally agreed upon definition of the "sharing economy," but the ability of the internet to facilitate a wide range of transactions that increase the productivity of assets that are only used part of the time is clear. Uber and Airbnb have become global market leaders in two now-massive "sharing" subsectors: ride hailing and short-term lodging.
2. Despite the obvious similarities, the ultimate economics of the respective businesses will be quite different. Airbnb's valuation is now comparable to Uber's despite being a fraction of the size. Longer term, structural considerations suggest that Airbnb can build a stronger and more durable franchise.

3. The value of density of supply in any given city drives the network effects of both Uber and Airbnb. But because visitors looking for rooms come from all over, while ride sharing is a predominantly local business, effective competitors to Airbnb need to establish global operations whereas Uber faces hundreds of local competitors. What's more, the large number of highly relevant attributes in choosing a place to stay, in contrast to just price and speed for rides, substantially enhances the incremental value of relative network scale.

4. Although the internet facilitates switching only a click away, the relevance of trust to a service can still create strong network stickiness. Entrusting one's home to a stranger or picking a location for your family's annual vacation requires far greater trust than that involved in a short crosstown journey. Service complexity also enhances customer captivity by increasing search costs and lends itself to useful applications of data science in ways not available to more commodity-like services.

5. The existence of network effects should represent the beginning rather than the end of the analysis of overall potential franchise value.

MAD MEN, SAD MEN:
ADVERTISING AND ADTECH MEET
THE INTERNET

THE EMERGENCE OF THE INTERNET offered up a virgin and fast-growing advertising medium that launched hundreds, even thousands, of new ad-supported businesses. It also created the possibility that technologies could ultimately deliver advertisers their holy grail—a one-to-one relationship with their potential customers. Even better, with a seemingly infinite supply of web page views, this nirvana would enable brands to reach their target audience wherever they happen to travel on the internet at ever lower prices. This prospect attracted even more capital to an even larger number of tech start-ups addressing some aspect of the complicated digital road that links marketers to consumers. Both opportunities have largely been a bust for all but a tiny few.

Initial euphoria over how ad-reliant incumbents might benefit from the new medium ultimately gave way to more clear-eyed assessments best reflected by CNN president Jeff Zucker's famous 2008 admonition to avoid "trading analog dollars for digital pennies."[1] But there remained an expectation, or maybe just a hope, that these threats could eventually be overcome by supplementing their existing analog assets with some magical combination of technological innovation and organic digital growth. Even Zucker upped his estimate of digital pennies to "digital dimes" the following year.[2]

The unrealistic expectations of the media giants can easily be dismissed as delusional fantasies of dinosaurs from a now bygone era. But the same structural challenges that doomed the flawed strategies of the incumbents also undermined the validity of business plans for which billions in funding was provided to eager insurgents by professional investors. As it turns out, much of the advertising and ad tech sectors lend themselves alternatively to winner-take-most dynamics for a handful of scale players (in a rare instance where the Platform Delusion seems not so delusional) or an absence of significant structural advantage with unhindered entry. This state of affairs has obvious implications for investors and entrepreneurs. But it also raises important questions for policy makers given the historic dependence on advertising of those news businesses that our democratic institutions rely on to produce an informed electorate.

THE DIGITAL ADVERTISING BOOM AND BUST

Outside of search and social media, dominated by Google and Facebook respectively, the fundamental economic challenge facing advertising businesses is that no conceivable level of sustainable growth in online eyeballs can possibly keep up with the speed of decline in advertising rates. The precipitous fall in how much an advertiser will pay for a digital impression corresponds to the exponential expansion in available online advertising inventory.[3] What's more, now that technology allows users to be followed around the internet by advertisers, attracting a unique audience only gets you so far: programmatic advertising software can deliver the exact same users when they are on some other site at a lower price. As we saw in our discussion of the *New York Times* in chapter 3, even the highest-quality content attracting a growing number of subscribers has trouble maintaining even flat advertising revenues—the price the *New York Times* can charge approaches the lowest price offered by any website that happens to be visited by a *New York Times* reader.

As these dynamics became obvious in one category of advertising, initially digital display or banner advertising, enterprising digital publishers were able to find successive new avenues of growth. Each of the green shoots of potential continued advertising growth, whether native, video, mobile, or performance, in turn would become subject to the same inevitable economics that plagued simple display ads in the first place. And yet investors continued to pour hundreds of millions of funding into entirely new ad-driven start-ups, sometimes at billion-dollar or even multibillion-dollar valuations, well into 2016—long after it should have been clear that the jig was up for these enterprises.[4] The downward reforecasts of these digital publishers had already begun by that year, and the predictable wave of layoffs, write-downs, and bankruptcies would soon follow.[5]

Online advertising on both desktop and mobile had been facing a relatively steady decline in their respective rates of growth for almost a decade[6] by the time digital came to overtake traditional media in 2019.[7] More concerning is the extent to which the growth has been disproportionately captured by Google and Facebook. Some analysts have tried to demonstrate that in some years, *all* of the net growth in digital has accrued just to these two players—or that the rest of the digital advertising universe was actually shrinking.[8]

Given the structural observations regarding the effectively bottomless supply of advertising inventory on the internet, how is it that Google and Facebook have been able to thrive in largely ad-based businesses? The short answer is that the portfolio of quite different but comparably compelling mutually reinforcing competitive advantages detailed in chapters 4 and 8, respectively, allows both to offer value that the rest at a competitive disadvantage simply can't match.

The slightly longer answer is that these two businesses operate in exceptional domains where technology provides the ability to leverage their relative scale to deliver continuous, uncapped improvements in the effectiveness of the advertisements that they deliver. It is not just that they both have loads of data, it is that they have data of the kind that is uniquely relevant to advertisers. Netflix, with almost 200 million sub-scribers glued to their screens around the world, generates lots of data. But it historically hasn't bothered with advertising not only because of the risk of alienating its customer base but also because the data about what shows and movies you like is just not that pertinent to advertisers.[9] What you search for and what you click on is known only to Google. Your web of social interactions and communications (and increasingly what you buy online and off-line)[10] is the exclusive province of Facebook. This is the kind of data that machine learning and, yes, artificial intelligence can transform into increasingly accurate predictions about which ads will be most impactful to which users.

So Google and Facebook dominate online advertising because they deliver an increasingly more effective product than anyone else can. This doesn't mean that others cannot play or even take a little share if they find a way to attract an audience whose demographics or activities can yield equivalent impact with less data. Amazon, which now leads Google in the product search category, has been taking market share even though it re-mains not much more than a tenth of its larger competitor's size in ad-vertising.[11] And the much smaller Snap and Pinterest—the former having unique traction with a younger demographic and the latter attracting com-mitted buyers in certain core product categories—have also made tiny dents in the ad duopoly's dominance.[12] But given the structural advan-tages outlined, it seems unlikely that Google and Facebook have any sig-nificant risk of falling below 50 percent of the growing digital advertising market for the indefinite future. Indeed, COVID-19 appears to have "su-percharged" these structural tendencies.[13]

This state of affairs raises a number of difficult public policy ques-tions related to antitrust and beyond. To be sure, there is more to be done to define and police anticompetitive actions. Inexplicably, unlike its Eu-ropean counterpart, US antitrust law does not include a blanket prohibi-tion on "abuse of a dominant position." Beyond policing bad behavior, however, it is hard to know what to do given that what provides these giants with such an immovable market position is the inherent ability—at least with respect to delivering advertising effectively—to do anything others can do, but better. A number of proposed solutions would effectively require Google and Facebook to deliver a worse product in order to allow others to catch up. To the extent that antitrust law seeks to encourage innovation, regulation in such a vein seems like a strange way to achieve that end.

One area that introduces conflicting public policy aims and no small degree of irony is privacy. We have noted that a significant source of Google's and Facebook's continuing competitive advantage is the nature of the information about their massive user bases. These companies maintain huge repositories of so-called first-party data—information provided directly by their customers—that is both highly proprietary and extraordinarily valuable. And they have developed sophisticated tech stacks to protect their data from outsiders. That is why the companies are referred to as "walled gardens" with respect to customer data.

Others who have less robust or less relevant user information must supplement it with so-called third-party data to improve the effectiveness of their advertising. Third-party data are collected or purchased from other websites or platforms or commercial aggregators of such data. In addition, to enhance the value of their own limited first-party data, websites install so-called third-party cookies to be able to track where and what their users do once they leave.

Much of the focus of privacy policy has understandably been on the use of third-party data. But these restrictions, although good for privacy, will strengthen the relative competitive position of those whose reliance on third-party data is limited because of the relative strength of their own first-party data—namely the internet giants whose inviolable market positions are the subject of separate public policy concerns. In 2020, Google announced that it intends to eliminate third-party cookies from its dominant Chrome browser by 2022. This may be good for your privacy but it is also definitely good news for Google's business.[14]

US antitrust law does not explicitly incorporate privacy considerations. This significantly complicated, for instance, the government's review of Google's acquisition of Fitbit where traditional market analyses
provided little basis for concern. What's more, US law does not directly
address privacy issues at all. The FTC reviews privacy issues based on
the generic authority over consumer protection. This thin, disconnected
patchwork of regulation seems hardly equipped to address the complex
interrelated policy questions raised by the emergence of these technology-
enabled media leviathans. The most interesting policy proposals involve
requiring these companies to share at least some aspects of their proprietary data.[15] Whether the US political system has the capacity to fill the
various interrelated regulatory lacunae in a manner that sensibly balances
the competing interests seems very much open to question.

THE ADTECH BOOM AND BUST

Of all the mini-busts of internet 2.0, the adtech bust was among the most
spectacular. So painful was the wreckage that many venture funds have
instituted formal or informal prohibitions on future investments in the
sector.[16] Early-stage adtech businesses peaked in 2015, attracting over
$3 billion in funding.[17] By January 2017, Fred Wilson of Union Square
Ventures was predicting that the "adtech market will go the way of search,
social and mobile as investors and entrepreneurs concede that Google and
Facebook have won and everyone else has lost."[18]

The growing challenges faced by the sector in attracting capital reflects more than the powerful tool set created by Google, Facebook, and
increasingly Amazon. Investor caution is reinforced by the current and
prospective regulatory constraints on data use in designing innovative
products and the inherent challenges in developing technology-based sustainable advantage in ecosystems dominated by incumbent tech giants.
And if the long shadow of Google and Facebook has cast a pall on adtech
investing, the only slightly less intimidating likes of Oracle, Salesforce,

and Adobe have had a comparable impact on the flow of funds to a closely related category of investing—marketing technology start-ups.[19]

Adtech and martech are distinct if highly interconnected markets. The former focuses on how to create, distribute, and manage paid campaigns while the latter involves free campaigns designed to reach individuals directly through, for example, email, social media, and various personalization techniques. In dealing with Google, search engine marketing (SEM) tools designed to help bidding on keywords are considered adtech, while search engine optimization (SEO) tools assisting in placement of free search results is the province of martech. Although there are plenty of such products and platforms that clearly fall in one bucket or the other—an advertising exchange or network is clearly adtech and a customer relationship management (CRM) or social media management system is clearly martech—the lines can be blurry and the tools are increasingly converging as companies look to manage the overall consumer experience.

Martech spending is significantly greater than adtech spending, and the declines in funding have not been quite as dramatic. Historically, the distinction between adtech and martech was sometimes defined by whether the tools were used by advertising agencies or by in-house teams. No industry has been more impacted by the transformation of the advertising industry landscape than the giant advertising agencies. As they face their collective existential crisis, the sector has overwhelmingly decided to literally bet its future on the anticipated adtech-martech convergence. To understand whether this is likely to have been a good or bad bet, we need to consider the key drivers of the agencies' decline.

MAD MEN, SAD MEN

A quick snapshot of the advertising agency business taken from a distance in 2019 might suggest a fundamentally healthy sector. The top five agency holding companies that dominate the industry collectively generated over $60 billion in revenue for the year, with most of them reporting stable or improving margins. Although it wasn't growing like it used to, the sector overall, as represented by these five stalwarts, was not shrinking either. And a few years earlier, the holding companies had reached an important milestone in making the digital transition when they reported that these revenues accounted for a majority of their business.[20]

Underneath the surface calm, however, was an industry in turmoil, forced to confront changing customer needs, new aggressive competitors, and a fundamental identity crisis regarding the nature of its core value proposition and economic model. These pressures had emerged well before the 2020 pandemic would accelerate the very shift to digital that was at the root of the sector's challenges.

The iconic mad men of yore were the slick storytellers who designed the creative advertising campaigns for the biggest consumer brands. They were generally compensated by receiving a commission for placing the advertisements in connection with the campaign. Like most creative businesses, the bad news was that there was limited financial leverage from the core functions. But the good news is that in a downturn, the cost structure was flexible enough that the agencies were able to manage continuing profitability. The benefits that holding companies secured from aggregating far-flung agencies primarily came from centralizing their ad placement operations and being able to offer the broadest range of global clients the broadest possible array of services.

By the 2000s, much had changed about advertising agencies. Compensation on a cost-plus-fee basis had overtaken commissions by the late '90s. Digital offerings were expanded through a combination of acquisitions and internal investment in a digital arms race among the traditional agencies.[21] New products and services were offered to customers. But the core of advertising agencies' value proposition, built around designing and executing creative media brand campaigns, remained mostly unchanged.

And that is where the shift of media from off-line to online has eaten away at the indispensability of the agencies. Clients still need great branding campaigns. But branding campaigns are precisely those for which department store magnate John Wanamaker's famous observation—"Half the money I spend on advertising is wasted; the trouble is I don't know which half"—still to some extent applies. Google CEO Eric Schmidt offered up a modern (and more self-serving) version of the same sentiment about such traditional marketing: "The last bastion of unaccountable spending in corporate America."[22]

For performance-based advertising, by contrast, clients can attribute success easily and project return on investment (ROI) quickly—click-through and conversion rates are not hard to calculate. And as we have seen, it is in the area of performance-based advertising that the internet not only excels but keeps getting better. So the relative growth of online has driven and continues to drive decreases in the relative share of advertising going to branding rather than performance campaigns.

Big data offers relatively modest assistance in assuring the success of a branding campaign. Sure, data can be helpful at figuring out what matters to people and what their proclivities are. And we have gotten far better at figuring out quickly if something has worked. But at the end of the day an ad campaign is a creative crapshoot. This is the same reason that Netflix, with all its user data, and despite the oft-repeated tale about *House of Cards*, is really not inherently better positioned to make great shows. Advertising executives exhorting their teams to produce ads that will go viral in a digital age are no more effective than the studio executives of old who shouted, "I want hits!"[23] By contrast, as the cost effectiveness of one broad category of advertising has continuously improved while the other has remained relatively stagnant, the resulting shift in resources has been highly predictable. All categories of brand advertising have represented a minority of global paid media spending for over a decade and the proportion has continued to shrink.

As you can see, brand advertising has always represented a small fraction of online media spend, so it is not surprising that the agencies' share of digital media spend is a small fraction of their corresponding share of off-line spend. What should be particularly concerning, however, is that

The Declining Importance of Global Brand Spending (2010–2020)
(in $ billions)

	2010	2020E	Change 2010–20	Compound Annual Growth Rate
Brand Advertising				
Off-line	381.3	401.1	5.1%	0.5%
Online	10.0	83.5	835.0%	23.6%
Total	**391.3**	**484.6**	**23.8%**	**2.2%**
Performance Based				
Off-line	404.9	625.6	54.5%	4.4%
Online	52.6	274.6	522.0%	18.0%
Total	**457.5**	**900.2**	**96.8%**	**7.0%**
Total Media Spend	848.8	1384.8	63.1%	5.0%
Brand Share of Media Spend	**46.1%**	**35.0%**	**(11.1%)**	

Figure 13.1

Source: Daniel Salmon et al., Digital Marketing Hub v4.1: Revisiting the TAM and
Examining Market Shares, BMO Capital Markets, June 2019

even in the off-line world, spending has shifted away from brand building to more immediate strategies for moving product off shelves. The significantly lower portion of revenue that the agencies represent in the digital media giants compared to the traditional media giants diminishes their relative leverage in securing their clients favorable terms—one of the few scale advantages highlighted in the agency holding company model.

A number of other related structural factors further explain the declining relevance of the holding companies in the advertising ecosystem. First, Google and Facebook and digital media generally have democratized the availability of advertising. Whereas the options were once pretty limited if you couldn't afford to get on TV or into a newspaper, the internet has radically broadened the playing fields. So Fortune 500 companies that dominate ad holding companies' client lists—the CPG giants remain a quarter of their revenues—themselves now represent a much smaller fraction of overall advertising.

Second, the inherently transparent structure of digital media and the dramatically lower cost of producing commercial messages for it lowered the barriers to entry while undermining agency economics in the now predominantly cost-plus-fee business model. The competition comes not just from an endless stream of new digital agencies but increasingly from the holding companies' core customer base itself. As noted, that customer base is made up predominantly of precisely those companies whose size would justify bringing these digital capabilities in house. Increasingly, brands themselves—most recently these include McDonald's, Nike, PayPal, and Walmart—are making adtech and martech acquisitions.[24]

Finally, the crowded and complex web of competing platforms and software solutions that sit between marketers and their online targets does not play to agencies' historic strengths. Yes, these are often "platform" businesses—demand- and supply-side platforms, SEO and SEM platforms, ad servers, exchanges, and on and on—but all of these segments typically support dozens of competitors. This is true even in the few instances where an incumbent giant—as Google's DoubleClick is in ad exchanges—is the clear leader. This confusing cacophony of technologies seems a tailor-made opportunity for a different kind of business from ad agencies to exploit: consultants. Since 2018, the digital consultancies Accenture, PWC, Deloitte, Cognizant, and IBM were already hard on the heels of the holding companies in rounding out the list of ten largest global advertising agencies.[25] What's more, they are growing far faster than the traditional agencies both organically and through aggressive acquisitions.

As one commentator described the problem, "Here's the brutal truth: Agencies may have storytelling, but consultants have problem-solving."[26] More ominous for the holding companies is that, more recently, the consultant's inorganic growth has not just been through technology buys but through the purchase of creative agencies as well.[27] So maybe the consultants will get storytelling after all.

DON'T GET MAD OR SAD, GET EVEN

Based on the frantic succession of "bet the company" deals undertaken since 2015 by at least three of the five advertising holding companies, it appears that much of the industry decided that its best strategy was to become problem solvers before the consultants became storytellers. Interpublic, Publicis, and Dentsu have collectively spent well over $10 billion dollars—in the case of Publicis, almost as much as all of their previous acquisitions combined—on data-driven marketing solutions companies.[28]

These deals represented a diverse collection of first- and third-party data, analytics, and consulting as well as industry or function-specific technology tools and creative capabilities. The acquired assets had been aggregated by the various targets and integrated with varying degrees of success over many years. What all the transactions had in common was their objective of shifting from serving as creative advertising brand managers to indispensable partners in managing the overarching relationship between these companies and their customers.

The case of Publicis is particularly instructive. In 2015, the company purchased digital marketing consultant Sapient for $3.7 billion. At the time, Publicis claimed that the combination would represent the "agency of the future" by establishing itself as "a leader at the convergence of marketing, commerce, consulting, and technology."[29] Less than two years later, the company would be forced to write down $1.5 billion of the purchase price after the hoped-for benefits failed to materialize.[30] This did not dissuade the company from an even larger $4.4 billion purchase of Epsilon in 2019, this time emphasizing the value of the target's data assets.[31]

The contrast to this approach by the other two giant holding companies could not be starker. Omnicom has broadly eschewed large acquisitions and funded its data-driven strategies internally, supported by partnerships and smaller bolt-on acquisitions.[32] Since the departure of its controversial long-serving CEO Martin Sorrell in 2018, the world's largest ad agency, WPP, has aggressively pursued the divestiture of not only control of its core data analytics subsidiary, Kantar, but the far-flung collection of minority stakes in media and technology companies it had accumulated over decades. The new CEO announced a "radical evolution" of its approach, which encompassed both a "renewed commitment to creativity" and the importance of "leveraging the strengths of our unique technology partnerships."[33]

The decreasing importance of branding relative to overall marketing spending is an unfortunate but inevitable structural reality that advertising agencies must face. But the need for effective brand management is not going away and the creative capabilities that are advertising agencies' core strength are not going to be disintermediated by the internet. There can be no debate about the importance of modern advertising agencies' creative efforts reflecting and optimizing the increasingly complex technology and media environment. But racing to beat technology consultants at their own game rather than focusing on more effectively leveraging the agencies' own unique creative capabilities feels like a losing proposition. So does spending billions on proprietary technology and data to compete with trillion-dollar companies with way more of both.

Time will tell whether the path chosen by WPP or Publicis will prove more successful. Of course, success will likely be determined as much by execution as by strategy. But a flawed strategy, particularly one focused on securing sustainable advantage where even achieving parity is unlikely, makes effective execution all the more challenging.

WHAT'S LEFT IN ADTECH?

Just as niche advertising players have found ways to build businesses around the dominant Facebook-Google duopoly—and Amazon has shown that some of those niches, like product search, can be quite large—within adtech and, more often, martech, a number of companies have been able to build defensible moats around functions or segments that lend themselves to structural advantage.

In adtech, the opportunity to create a scale player to aggregate the fragmented inventory outside of the two massive walled gardens has been realized by the largest demand-side platform (DSP), The Trade Desk (TTD). Founded by two former Microsoft executives, TTD outflanked competitors by positioning itself as a friend to the advertising holding companies, eschewing efforts to disintermediate them by going directly to their clients.[34] This allowed TTD to quickly gain relative scale by aggregating these massive sources of advertising demand and attracting publishing partners offering placement. The resulting network effects were reinforced by the supply-side scale benefits from continuous investment in enhanced software tools, the captivity of close customer relationships reflected in 95 percent customer retention, and clear opportunities to leverage their transactional data to drive continuous improvement.

In little more than a decade, TTD's market value has grown to exceed $20 billion and dwarfs the dozens of competing independent DSPs.[35] But for all its success and structural advantages, TTD in 2020 generated far less than $1 billion of revenue. Its platform placed only about $4 billion of digital advertising spending out of 2020 US spending in the category of over $150 billion.[36] While this suggests a large potential untapped market, it also highlights how limited the opportunity outside of the massive walled gardens (which have their own huge competing DSPs) really is today in adtech.[37] One related area that has driven a recent minor renaissance in adtech has been the explosion in the number of connected TVs, where Google and Facebook do not have the same lock on the market. This has spawned a sudden burst of both deal activity[38] and significant new investments from independents like TTD and venture firms.[39]

In martech, the potential opportunities for independents are greater, as the number of distinct functions encompassed by the term is far broader than simply optimizing media spend. The wide range of differentiated domains that benefit from focused expertise lends itself to the establishment of defensible niches. Possibilities include website optimization, marketing automation, customer tracking, analytics tools, content management, loyalty programs, and email and SMS marketing. But while the number of potential areas of specialization is far wider, so is the list of giant software companies whose installed bases provide them a significant leg up in delivering an incremental marketing solution.

One interesting success story is that of the standalone software business that remained after Acxiom sold its marketing solutions business to ad giant Interpublic for $2.3 billion in 2018. At the time the company had under $300 million of revenue. Now called LiveRamp and in 2021 with closer to $500 million of revenue, the company provides a contributory data platform that allows brands, agencies, publishers, and other technology partners to resolve consumer identity. This enables corporate clients to determine whether marketing messages are reaching their intended audiences across digital and traditional channels like email and even TV, and it allows them to integrate and connect diffuse data sets without compromising privacy. LiveRamp has prospered because companies are loath to provide the sensitive customer information needed to create this kind of industry utility to multiple parties or to a business (like one of the tech titans) that may have other interests or incentives. By positioning itself as the neutral and indispensable partner that exists solely to manage the integrity of this shared identity data resource, the value of LiveRamp alone quickly exceeded what all of Acxiom had ever been worth *before* selling its $2.3 billion marketing solutions division.

LiveRamp is emblematic of the continuing opportunity to build independent scalable marketing services niches.[40] Other examples of successful vertically focused public companies are HubSpot in inbound marketing and content management and more recently Sprout Social in social media management. The ability of massive marketing cloud providers Adobe, Oracle, and Salesforce to add additional functionality as a one-stop marketing platform, however, poses a high bar to establishing a successful independent. The incremental value delivered by specialized scale and product focus must be so great in the context of the particular use case and industry structure, that it overwhelms the efficacy of an integrated offering. As we explore in the next chapter though, the consistent proven ability of specialization to facilitate the development of defensible software franchises—even in the face of much larger competitors who can apply artificial intelligence to their massive databases—extends far beyond martech.

KEY CHAPTER TAKEAWAYS

1. The explosion of digital advertising in the internet era, worth $130 billion just in the US, has attracted thousands of ad-supported start-ups looking to share in the bounty, and technology start-ups looking to manage it.

2. The initial euphoria proved misplaced as the vast majority of the growth in spending has been absorbed by Facebook and Google. Even the most compelling publishers struggle to grow ad spending as ad rates decline with endless new inventory and technology allows marketers to reach targeted consumers anywhere on the internet with startling efficiency.

3. Efforts to regulate the Facebook-Google ad duopoly must take care not to undermine the fundamental source of their success: the ability to use data to continuously improve the effectiveness of the advertising they deliver.

4. Advertising agencies' core value proposition of effective storytelling to establish and enhance brands has become relatively less important in the digital era. In response, many agencies have tried to reposition themselves as technology or consulting companies, competing against much larger specialized enterprises.

5. The opportunities for adtech firms in an ecosystem dominated by Google and Facebook are slim. Within the broader martech universe, the opportunities for independents to successfully specialize are far wider, but so is the list of giant software companies like Adobe, Oracle, and Salesforce competing to deliver new solutions to their massive installed bases.

BIG DATA AND ARTIFICIAL INTELLIGENCE: WHEN THEY MATTER AND WHEN THEY DON'T

DIGITAL PLATFORMS AND THEIR ASSOCIATED networks spawn data. Lots of data. The amount of information generated from an anonymous cash transaction at a store is trivial compared to the multiple interconnected algorithms lit up by every electronic transaction, whether on the internet or even using a credit card in person. The prospect of turning the mounds of data created by our collective digital footprints into actionable intelligence that improves business performance has obvious intuitive appeal.

The use of smart software, sometimes described as machine learning, or—more futuristically—artificial intelligence (AI), to turn big data into gold is routinely touted by everyone from entrepreneurs seeking funding to established (or aspiring) public companies seeking higher valuations. The FAANG companies have all to a greater or lesser degree—whether through acquisitions in the sector or promoting themselves as an "AI company"—touted the importance of artificial intelligence in their respective strategic visions.

The current fervor mirrors successive waves of AI-related exuberance dating back to the 1950s, all of which have one thing in common—they have been "long on promise, short on delivery."[1] In their book, *Rebooting AI: Building Artificial Intelligence We Can Trust*, renowned computer scientists Gary Marcus and Ernest Davis call the persistent enormous gap "between ambition and reality" in artificial intelligence "the AI Chasm."[2] In a business context, these limitations may partly explain the data confirming that "real managers in real companies are finding AI hard to implement."[3]

Software applications are not new, and the core algorithm design that underlies much of what passes for artificial intelligence has been around for decades.[4] There is no question that the increased availability of computing power, infrastructure bandwidth, and data sets have further empowered these technologies. But even in the relatively targeted domains of health care[5] and autonomous vehicles,[6] where the revolutionary potential impact of AI has been most heavily hyped, it has simply not delivered as promised.

The historic and more recent disappointments have not done much to cull the ranks or dampen the ardor of the futurists and AI cheerleaders that populate the sector. Within the realm of business strategy, Harvard Business School Professors Marco Iansiti and Karim R. Lakhani have emerged as leading evangelists for the growing power and ubiquity of the reinforcing advantages of network effects and artificial intelligence. And structurally, as discussed in chapter 3, this combination of supply-side learning advantages with demand-side scale advantages represents a logical pairing for the digital age.

In *Competing in the Age of AI: Strategy and Leadership When Algorithms and Networks Run the World*, Professors Iansiti and Lakhani outline a vision of the new age that isn't too far from now-conventional wisdom among not just academics but investors and the general public. They maintain that the "self-reinforcing loops"[7] of network and learning effects facilitated by digital environments drive accelerating returns with scale and that the "algorithm-driven operating models" of the AI economy are "almost infinitely scalable."[8] They argue that the resulting economic impact is "many times as great"[9] as the Industrial Revolution, leading to a "winner-take-all world."[10] Professors Iansiti and Lakhani are hardly alone in their belief in this coming revolution, an AI-centric version of the Platform Delusion.

Given the enthusiastic promotion of these ideas and the validity of the broad structural observations underlying them, the ubiquity of investor pitch decks extolling the benefits of "big data" is not surprising. Over-whelmingly, however, these particular PowerPoint slides typically appear toward the end of these investor presentations, often in a section called "growth opportunities." What is usually being sold is the potential to en-hance monetization or competitive advantage once either enough data is collected and/or algorithms to effectively exploit it are developed. But a notable characteristic of network effects businesses is just how few really benefit from actual—as distinguished from potential—strong supply-side advantages along these lines.

The chasm between theoretical potential and practical reality is partly explained by the limited value of the data in the context of many use cases on the one hand and the nascent state of many of the technologies that might be able to profitably exploit the data on the other. "Artificial intelli-gence" may be the buzzwords of the moment, and they have certainly played a central role in separating a long line of investors from their money, but proven internet business models where these have been the primary source of sustainable competitive advantage are notably scarce.

Take the case of the emergence of the multibillion-dollar P2P lend-ing market. Established first in the UK in 2005, the simple idea was to harness the power of the internet to establish platforms to match borrow-ers and lenders directly without the overhead of traditional banks. The platform typically assesses an origination fee for the initial match and a servicing fee for the ongoing management of the relationship.

It is not hard to see how the P2P marketplace benefits both borrow-ers and lenders. A diversified portfolio of such loans would undoubtedly yield significantly better returns than a savings account. And individuals and small businesses would now have access to liquidity that traditional banks (or even relatives) might not make available on any terms. Less clear is how competing P2P platforms could profitably distinguish them-selves beyond charging lower fees. Borrowers presumably want the lowest rates and lenders want the opposite. If different platforms yielded mean-ingfully different rates for borrowers of comparable risk, presumably one side or the other of any prospective transaction would balk. The result should be relatively similar financial offerings.

This is where data could come in. A platform that has more information about similarly situated borrowers' actual risk profile because it has serviced more of these loans should be better at pricing the risk of a given borrower. A less sophisticated platform might attract borrowers by offering better terms than their risk justifies but, once the resulting default rates become evident, lenders will flee the platforms. Over time as the relative superiority becomes clearer and relative market share follows, this data advantage should grow.

This was precisely the narrative that supported the wildly successful IPO of LendingClub, the largest (but notably not the first) P2P marketplace in December 2014. LendingClub raised almost $1 billion, making it the largest tech IPO of the year, and the stock rose over 50 percent on the first day of trading. Within weeks the company was valued at over $10 billion, making it the first large-cap fintech company. Research published by lead underwriter Goldman Sachs initiating coverage of the company explained that LendingClub demonstrated "meaningful competitive advantages . . . similar to other Internet marketplace models" that drive "winner-take-most dynamics."[11] Although, at the time of the IPO, LendingClub's adjusted EBITDA margins were under 10 percent, Goldman Sachs assured investors that the structural marketplace characteristics described should generate margins "over 40 percent" longer term.

Goldman's confidence was based on the belief that the proprietary data elicited from a greater number of loan originations had allowed LendingClub to develop superior dynamic credit models. As a result, "more high-quality borrowers are attracted to LendingClub's platform due to the lower interest rates [due to the lower risk premium required by lenders], creating a positive-feedback loop of better loan performance and increased investor trust."[12]

The problem with Goldman's prognosis was that, for most borrowers, readily available information like credit scores provide perfectly adequate predictive capabilities. The incremental proprietary borrower data, even when massaged by painstakingly developed proprietary technology, simply does not yield significant incremental value.

In the early days of the new marketplace, the ability to attract demand, either from early adopter lenders or borrowers, could differentiate a platform. As P2P lending became established, however, major institutional investors began to participate and scale aggregators of demand emerged, both of which limited the ability of P2P lending platforms to retain much excess value for themselves.

The sector thought of itself as an attractive vehicle to benefit from the network effects that would flow from connecting participants in a classic "many-to-many" marketplace. But in place of disparate lenders and borrowers, LendingClub and its peers found themselves wedged between enormous institutional private wealth managers like Goldman Sachs itself and giant consumer finance portals like LendingTree and Credit Karma as well as Google. Much as the metasearch travel companies are limited by their reliance on Expedia and Booking for demand and Google for supply, in the absence of significant supply advantages from learning, this was never going to be a very good business.

The collapse of LendingClub's stock was driven by a wide variety of factors, some very specific to the company.[13] But the failure of even industry stalwarts—including Prosper Marketplace, the US first mover in the P2P lending sector—to maintain consistent profitability much less Goldman's promised 40-percent-plus margins while literally dozens of new entrants have found a way to operate in some segment of the market, suggests that the barriers to entry imposed by "big data" and AI are illusory.

Interestingly, in one segment of the market, it appears that there is meaningful incremental value from data beyond simple credit scores. For borrowers with lower credit scores, additional data analysis can yield significant insight into the probability of repayment. Yet, ironically, LendingClub sought to distinguish itself by operating exclusively in that portion of the market where big data add no appreciable value—borrowers with credit scores above 640.[14] A number of other businesses have emerged targeting this niche of borrowers with low credit scores—LendUp and Applied Data Finance—using a variety of business models but all emphasizing the role of data analytics. These face their own challenges, but at least there is a case to be made for being able to develop a supply-side advantage.

The failure of LendingClub does not repudiate entirely the opportunity to accelerate the move down the learning curve by leveraging proprietary data and technology on the internet. Ancestry.com and Zillow are just two examples we highlighted earlier of companies for which this phenomenon is at least partly responsible for their continued dominance of their respective niches. It does highlight, however, the importance of determining whether the particular use case at issue lends itself to such benefits and whether those same dynamics allow others to catch up quickly. Where the predictive relevance of the data or its applicability to product improvement or customer management is limited, the mere existence of big data is not a differentiator. Similarly, the very power of machine learning to draw useful conclusions from relatively small data sets means that any advantage will come only when significant incremental pertinent knowledge can be gleaned from much larger data sets.

The case of LendingClub underlines the challenges facing network effects businesses seeking to rely predominantly on big data as their primary reinforcing advantage at scale. But the potential for the marriage of network effects and artificial intelligence to supercharge competitive advantage is neither the sole nor the most revolutionary influence on industry structure highlighted by AI evangelists like Professors Iansiti and Lakhani. They contrast the efficiencies of the Industrial Revolution, which relied on the benefits of vertical specialization, with the Age of AI, which entails breaking down what they view as now anachronistic organizational silos. According to them, becoming an AI-driven company "is about fundamentally changing the core of the company by building a data-centric operating architecture"[15] that cuts horizontally across the organization. As a result, "competitive advantage is shifting away from vertical capabilities toward universal capabilities in data sourcing, processing, analytics and algorithm development," leading in their view "to the gradual demise of traditional specialization."[16]

Exhibit A for this view of the coming horizontal world order presented in *Competing in the Age of AI* is the remarkable turnaround at Microsoft engineered by CEO Satya Nadella. The company had lost half of its value from its highs of 1999 to the lows of 2009. The shares grew almost tenfold over the subsequent decade, becoming in 2019 the third company (after Apple and Amazon) to reach a trillion dollars in market capitalization. In the chapter called "Becoming an AI Company," Professors Iansiti and Lakhani demonstrate how Nadella reoriented and refocused the company during this period.[17] The result was the successful transition from an enterprise made up of largely disconnected business lines, many still built on shipping discrete software CDs, to an integrated AI-enabled cloud-based software powerhouse.

When he took the reins in 2014, Nadella inherited two business lines that were structurally at war with each other: a cloud-based infrastructure business, Azure, that competed with market leader Amazon Web Services, and a series of traditional "on-premises" enterprise applications businesses that increasingly faced competition from open-source and other cloud-based alternatives. That structural divide was reinforced by a cultural one, as Azure continued to develop its own incompatible software. What's more, porting Microsoft enterprise applications onto Azure was notoriously difficult. Nadella bridged these divides by articulating a unitary corporate mission around being the leading productivity platform for enterprises and embracing both cloud computing and open-source technologies as central to that vision. A series of dramatic organizational changes, capital investments, product initiatives, and acquisitions consistent with this articulated change in direction provided the internal and external credibility needed for successful execution.

Breaking down the silos between infrastructure and applications and establishing a unitary software design across the organization gave Microsoft access to previously unimaginable quantities of information about its customers, projects, and products. This in turn exposed a variety of promising use cases on which to apply the magic of machine learning and artificial intelligence, which the company pursues aggressively. As Professors Iansiti and Lakhani note, in addition to facilitating improvements "on a continuous basis based on constant feedback from users," the data flow provides a "level of customer intimacy [that] opens up all kinds of opportunities for analytics."[18] The new and improved Microsoft is the archetype of what they believe it means to be an "AI company": "It is about fundamentally changing the core of the company by building a data-centric operating architecture supported by an agile organization that enables ongoing change."[19]

Microsoft's achievement is impressive and demonstrates the potential positive impact of centralizing a wide range of key functions to enhance decision-making by leveraging data. Rather than being limited to just software or technology businesses, *Competing in the Age of AI* argues that this "same transformation is happening at an accelerated pace across all industries."[20] Indeed, citing Google's entry into the auto industry, Iansiti and Lakhani argue that traditional industry boundaries are fast disappearing and that the power of AI will drive the emergence of massive enterprises with continuously increasing, mutually reinforcing competitive advantages of "scale, scope, and learning."[21] In this new world of "unprecedented scale," "specialized capabilities" will necessarily become "less relevant and less competitive."[22]

To examine whether this prediction is true, it is worth looking at the development of the industry that should be ground zero for the core trends described in *Competing in the Age of AI*: SaaS software. The ability of software providers to host solutions themselves rather than requiring installation at the client site offers huge potential benefits and spawned a vast industry seeking to disrupt the legacy software sector. The cloud-computing revolution that drove Microsoft's strategic rebirth reflects the growing ascendance of SaaS models over traditional on-premises solutions. It would be hard to imagine a sector more disposed to the factors driving the predicted increasing irrelevance of specialization. This history and the current reality, however, tell a very different story.

THE SAAS REVOLUTION: WHY NEITHER ORACLE NOR SALESFORCE TOOK OVER THE WORLD

The SaaS revolution, although a creature of the internet revolution, did not hit its stride until well after the first internet boom had crashed and burned. The national buildout of broadband capacity combined with dramatic improvements in computing and storage capacities facilitated the explosive growth of "on-demand software," as the sector was often originally described. The idea of providing software as a service was not a new one. Service bureaus targeting small- and medium-sized businesses (SMBs) had provided central hosting applications dating back to the 1960s. And a variety of so-called application service providers (ASPs) emerged in the late 1990s to provide hosted software for an affordable monthly charge, sometimes delivered over the internet.

But these software implementations were typically "single tenant"—only one company could use them at a time. What was truly revolutionary about the SaaS model was that it allowed a single instance of the software to serve multiple clients simultaneously, a so-called multitenant architecture. And what vastly expanded the market potential was the increasing acceptance, and ultimately preference, of even global multinational businesses for SaaS applications.

The enterprise software market targeted by the emerging SaaS competitors was dominated by entrenched giants with a powerful business model. Under their traditional approach, the software is deployed "on-premises" in a client/server environment. The customer pays for an upfront perpetual software license based on the number of users but is also charged for ongoing maintenance and upgrades. The initial implementations can take many months or even years and are highly customized and notoriously expensive affairs involving armies of internal and external consultants, some of whom never seem to leave. That process involves extensive training and support, dedicated hardware, and a variety of associated middleware so that in the end the software itself represents a fraction of the total cost to the customer.

The challenge for new-entrant SaaS businesses attacking these incumbents was twofold. First, even if a potential customer were intrigued by the flexibility and cost savings offered by a SaaS solution—customers were charged a monthly subscription fee based on users, and the applications often deployed without third-party help in weeks—the switching costs for an existing enterprise client were enormous. And depending on how critical the software's function was, the risk of faulty execution of the changeover could be substantial. Second, despite the argument that the modular design of SaaS products actually facilitated the ability to customize and integrate with other providers, potential clients were skeptical that a single instance of distributed software could have the needed sophistication for complex applications. In addition, for particularly sensitive tasks, many companies were nervous about the security implications of not maintaining direct control of the software and associated data within their physical plant. As a result, the earliest customers for SaaS products were emerging and smaller businesses that adopted relatively simple discrete applications where there was no incumbent to displace.

One of the earliest SaaS companies was Salesforce. The company was founded in 1999 by a voluble and brilliant former Oracle employee, Marc Benioff, who had been inspired to build a company that delivered business software as securely and reliably as Amazon delivered consumer products.[23] It initially focused exclusively on customer relationship management (CRM) products, which at the time represented a $10 billion market. Competition came from the three largest broad-based enterprise software providers, who integrated CRM into their suite of products. In addition, Salesforce faced a range of specialist players some of whom, like Siebel, focused on large customers, while others targeted SMBs, like Best. At the time of Salesforce's successful 2004 IPO, it was one of a handful of public SaaS companies and had less than $100 million in sales.

Despite the modest size of the SaaS industry at the time, the incumbent software leaders were very aware of the threat it posed. A year after the Salesforce IPO, Oracle announced the acquisition of Siebel for $5.8 billion, making it the largest CRM company in the world. Both Oracle and Siebel had developed "on-demand" offerings, primarily targeted to the SMB market, but continued to pursue a hybrid approach, protecting their core business model. On the announcement of the deal, Benioff sent an email to employees observing that "even dinosaurs mate a few times before they die." For his part, Oracle CEO and founder Larry Ellison, who had been an early Salesforce investor, expressed the hope that the value of his stake would "dwindle to zero."[24]

Ellison's wish was not fulfilled. In 2020, the value of Salesforce equity eclipsed Oracle's and approached $200 billion.[25] The broader SaaS sector represented well in excess of a trillion dollars of market capitalization. The only other pure SaaS company that is even more valuable is Adobe, a legacy software leader that, going beyond even Microsoft, has not only embraced the cloud strategically but actually transitioned its entire business to SaaS from an enterprise license model. Adobe's ability to execute its dramatic transformation reflects the widespread acceptance of SaaS, as the effectiveness of the model has been demonstrated in a wide array of highly complex and sensitive applications.

The relative ascendancy of SaaS over legacy enterprise software since 2000 can legitimately be termed a revolution. The stunning success of SaaS models has fostered much conventional wisdom both about the nature of SaaS businesses as well as the speed and inevitability of their ultimate world domination. For instance, it is widely assumed that, after twenty years, SaaS at this point represents a majority of software deployments and at least plays a meaningful role in all significant vertical sectors. On-premises enterprise software players, by contrast, are assumed to be shrinking in the face of the irreversible secular trend toward cloud. The multitenant nature of the SaaS architecture promotes the availability of demand-side network effects, which are supposed to more than compensate for the reduction in

supply-side scale benefits that results from the lower absolute fixed-cost requirements of SaaS businesses. And, as suggested by Professors Iansiti and
Lakhani, although the early SaaS applications were specialized, as the industry develops, the superiority of horizontal applications becomes increasingly clear by applying AI to centralized capabilities across vertical use cases.

Like the conventional wisdom underlying the Platform Delusion itself, the truisms of the SaaS revolution are all demonstrably false.

It is true that, since around 2010, a majority of incremental software
revenue has been cloud-based and that this percentage has continued to
grow. In 2020, an estimated 62.6 percent of new software sales have been
for SaaS applications. But despite this relative trend, the absolute level of
new enterprise license deployments has continued to grow, even if at a
modest rate. The result is that in 2020, SaaS applications represented not
that much more than a quarter of total application software spend and are
only expected to equal enterprise license spend by 2025 at the earliest—a
full quarter century after the SaaS revolution began.

What's more, in a number of multibillion-dollar vertical markets,
SaaS applications have failed to gain any meaningful traction at all. And
this is true not just in sectors where sensitivities over data ownership and
control predominate. For those use cases, SaaS companies have often structured deployments that allow data to remain on servers literally owned by
the customers. For automotive dealerships, to name one example, the market for dealer management systems (DMS) continues to be as dominated
by the same two traditional industry leaders (CDK and Reynolds and
Reynolds) today as it was in 2000.

The point here is that the competitive power of strong customer captivity when paired with scale advantages is substantial, and often underestimated. The other surprise is the nature of that scale. Although the
absolute fixed-cost requirements of on-premises enterprise software businesses often far exceed that of their SaaS counterparts, the relative dependence on fixed costs is far lower. The variable consulting and maintenance
expenses associated with traditional software businesses represents a far

SaaS Leads the Growth of Enterprise Applications

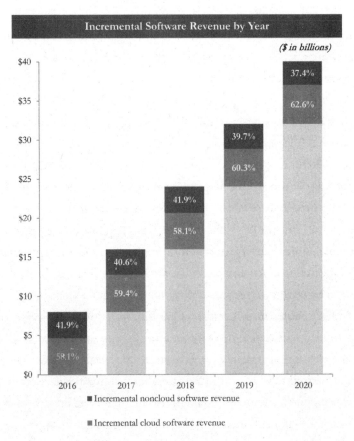

Figure 14.1

Source: Christine Dover, research director, Enterprise Applications and
Digital Commerce, IDC

greater proportion of the overall cost structure than in SaaS businesses. As a result, the supply-side benefits of scale are actually greater for SaaS businesses because so much more of their cost structure is fixed.

But do the stronger supply-side scale effects make SaaS businesses inherently "better?" Not necessarily. The lower absolute fixed-cost requirements in many cases significantly lowers break-even market shares, supporting a greater number of viable competitors. What's more, the very flexibility of the SaaS architecture and business model that attracts customers in the first place makes it easier for them to leave later if offered a more compelling alternative. This doesn't mean that there is not significant customer captivity in these businesses, only that it is often less than in traditional software. On average, traditional software businesses have higher overall margins than SaaS, even if their gross margins are lower. And even if Salesforce won the battle with Oracle in CRM, Oracle has continued to grow and has remained much more profitable than Salesforce.

But what about network effects and the age of AI?

SaaS companies do not typically have network effects; these are old-fashioned supply-side scale businesses. The last thing a customer embracing the benefits of a multitenant software wants is for the other tenants—particularly competitors—to be able to use its data. There are a few exceptions to this rule. A SaaS software company called Turnitin is the leading provider of anti-plagiarism software to educational organizations around the world. As sophisticated cheating often involves sharing papers between students at different schools, participating institutions benefit by contributing all submitted materials to a common proprietary anonymized database. This SaaS application benefits from both supply- and demand-side scale and has margins well above traditional software applications reflecting this fact. But it is an unusual SaaS use case that lends itself to this powerful combination of competitive advantages.

The anticipated AI and learning advantages highlighted by Professors Iansiti and Lakhani appear to manifest themselves more vertically than horizontally, contrary to their predictions. The SaaS revolution has spawned hundreds of vertically oriented applications of adequate scale to achieve profitability, with all verticals able to support multiple competitors. The three largest traditional enterprise software players—Microsoft, Oracle, and SAP—all of which now operate in both the on-demand and on-premises realms, have continued to play across verticals. But the continuously proliferating number of pure SaaS companies have largely remained vertically focused, and any consolidation has taken place mostly within verticals or with close adjacencies. At this point there are more than eighty public SaaS companies of which almost seventy are worth at least $1 billion and twenty are worth over $10 billion.

SaaS Software Market Capitalization Growth

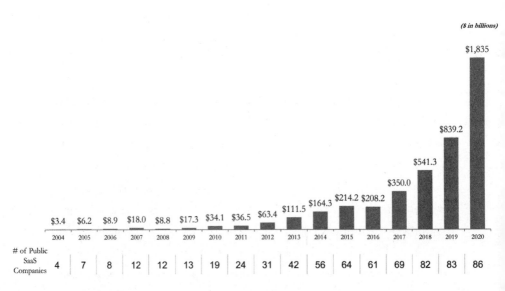

Figure 14.2

Source: S&P Capital IQ

Salesforce, the largest and most influential of the new breed of SaaS companies, in contrast to most of its smaller peers, has been on an acquisition rampage that in some years has exceeded that of the notoriously voracious Oracle. But although some of these have increasingly added to horizontal capabilities and new verticals—for example, app development tools like Heroku to strengthen its homegrown Force.com platform and, most dramatically, its $28 billion megadeal for Slack to complement its much smaller 2016 acquisition of Quip in the "enterprise productivity" category[26]—the vast majority have directly reinforced its position in the CRM market or the closely related digital marketing space.

The increasingly fragmented and vertically organized SaaS sector suggests that specialization may actually enhance the value of AI because specialized data sets allow machine learning to yield the most compelling insights. This is consistent with the observation that successful applications of AI to date are characterized by the very narrowness of the domains targeted.[27] If so, rather than rendering specialization obsolete, the emergence of the cloud may be sparking a renaissance in vertically focused software enterprises, in contrast to the largest integrated cross-functional providers that dominated the traditional enterprise software landscape. To understand why this could be true, it is worth following the path of one of the eighty public SaaS companies that has managed to thrive in this dynamic ecosystem.

BlackLine targeted a market that at first glance would seem to offer little opportunity for an insurgent start-up. Rather than identifying an industry with distinctive needs, starting in 2005, BlackLine offered a product that performed a task central to any complex company's accounting activities. The reason such a specialty seemed perilous is that accounting represents a central function of the massive enterprise resource planning (ERP) businesses that dominated the software industry. Nonetheless, BlackLine's software undertook to automate the monthly financial close process, starting at the divisional level and then rolling up to the consolidated company financials.

Up until then, the ERP vendors simply took the monthly company financials as an input and had not automated the process of closing the monthly books. BlackLine identified a functionality that was largely being performed manually with predictably error-prone results. This was a corporate pain point not just because of the costly, labor-intensive nature of the Excel-based process but also because increasing regulatory scrutiny required a higher degree of transparency and accountability in developing these financial reports. And although the addressable market for such a narrow capability was probably only one to two billion dollars in the US, globally the market for this and other adjacent accounting applications was probably ten times that amount.

When BlackLine launched its initial product in 2005, the top five ERP companies represented almost three fourths of the market. In addition to SAP, Oracle, and Microsoft, Sage and SSA Global (since acquired by Infor) rounded out the group.[28] The utility of the BlackLine product was greatest with large complex organizations that were these companies' core customers, rather than the SMBs that were the focus of many of the earliest SaaS applications. When BlackLine sold a majority stake in the company to outside investor Silver Lake Sumeru in 2013, it had just over $25 million in revenues and was still unprofitable, but it had a loyal blue chip client list that included AT&T, AIG, Boeing, and United Health. By the time BlackLine went public in 2016, revenues were expected to exceed $100 million for the year. In 2020, BlackLine generated over $350 million and is solidly profitable.

How could the broad-based ERP companies allow BlackLine to develop into what is now an almost $10 billion market cap company? It wasn't for want of trying to stop it. Oracle hired a former BlackLine employee and developed its own product that is effectively given away for free to buyers of the broader suite of Oracle products. The value of specialized knowledge, particularly regarding complex processes like the financial close and associated activities, stems precisely from the difficulty in replicating it. As Therese Tucker, founder and executive chair of BlackLine, told me when I asked the secret of their continued success, "this is a platform developed specifically for accounting and finance that integrates fifteen years of deep knowledge in the domain."[29] Generic horizontal capabilities are no match for the ability to use cloud-generated data to continuously improve a specialized product.

It is true that the switching costs are not as high for SaaS solutions as for on-premises applications. But the use of artificial intelligence and machine learning to not just identify and correct but predict potential problems for a relatively inexpensive but still mission-critical application would give a customer pause before agreeing to adopt a less costly offering from a horizontally integrated ERP provider.

BlackLine is in the very early innings of applying true AI technologies; it is doing so in very narrow specific use cases like transaction matching where the potential benefits are clear. Tucker gave two reasons why she was not worried that larger horizontal software players would gain a relative advantage as AI became more powerful and ubiquitous. First, her own experience convinced her that the specialized players would continue to be able to frame the most relevant questions upon which to apply the new technologies effectively. Second, although by definition larger software companies would have access to greater absolute quantities of data, the leading specialized players will still have more of the relevant data within the relevant topic areas. What's more, the willingness of customers to allow a specialized player to use the data is probably greater than is the case with technology giants whose reputations in this area have been under attack.[30]

Oracle continues to bundle its financial close offering with its accounting suite, but hundreds of Oracle's customers use BlackLine's Connector for Oracle to automatically integrate into its E-Business Suite rather than use Oracle's cheaper homegrown product.[31] In 2018, the leading global ERP provider, SAP, announced that it was effectively giving up any attempt to compete in the arena by agreeing to serve as a BlackLine reseller.[32] And BlackLine continues to grow quickly both through geographic expansion and incrementally broadening its suite of products into an increasing number of adjacent functions.

The BlackLine case highlights not only the continuing, perhaps even increasing, value of specialization in the age of AI but also the essential role of human judgment in deciding when applying machine learning techniques is a good use of corporate resources and when it is a costly distraction. The euphoria over the promise of artificial intelligence has led many executives and investors to ignore the importance of carefully formulating the right questions to elicit useful answers. The increasing corporate tendency to throw data at problems as a way to avoid difficult decision-making gets the potential of big data exactly backward. As AI pioneer Judea Pearl has noted, it is "easy to understand why some people would see data mining as the finish rather than the first step," but the most important questions will always require us to engage in the "work of having to consider and articulate substantive assumptions about how the world operates."[33] To do that effectively and avoid many dry AI holes being dug to little purpose or effect, specialized knowledge will remain essential.

KEY CHAPTER TAKEAWAYS

1. Software applications are not new, and the core algorithm design that underlies much of what passes for artificial intelligence has been around for decades. What is new is the massive quantity of data that flows through the proliferating digital platforms upon which these established techniques can be applied.

2. The ability of AI to substantially reinforce competitive advantage at scale is a function of the potential value of the unique insights it can yield in the context of a particular use case. Where the predictive relevance of the data or its applicability to product improvement or customer management is limited, the mere existence of "big" data is not a differentiator. Similarly, the very power of machine learning to draw useful conclusions from relatively small data sets means that any advantage will come only when significant incremental pertinent knowledge can be gleaned from much larger data sets.

3. The potential ability of AI applications to enhance decision-making across an organization by leveraging centralized data resources has led some to suggest that specialization is becoming irrelevant. Yet often it is in the context of specialized data sets that machine learning can yield the most compelling insights.

4. The explosion of cloud-based solutions and the increasing adoption of SaaS-based software has both upended the software industry and increased the volume of real-time data available to the sector. The overwhelmingly vertically focused nature of the over-trillion-dollar SaaS software industry that has emerged reinforces the continuing value of specialization in the age of AI.

EPILOGUE

START-UP FEVER:
IS IT A CURE OR A DISEASE?

IT IS HARD TO PINPOINT the genesis of an idea. Equally difficult is to pinpoint when a novel concept settles into conventional wisdom. Most often these phenomena are the collective result of a variety of disconnected causes. More often than not, however, those who have a vested interest in its adoption—in the case of the Platform Delusion, the enormous platforms and their financial backers—play a disproportionate role in establishing the informal consensus. The goals of increasing valuations and discouraging competitors represent powerful incentives to promote the big lie.

What is unambiguous is that the Platform Delusion has resulted in massive value destruction. Investors have backed misguided business plans and strategies on a grand scale. Incumbents have misallocated precious capital and diverted management attention to pursue impractical schemes and unachievable objectives. The culprit is a fetishization of network effects, and to a smaller extent, other buzzwords like "big data" and "AI," that feed the Platform Delusion without a deeper respect and appreciation for the fundamental tenets of competitive advantage.

Those most committed to the Platform Delusion have a tendency to swing wildly from dark pronouncements about the inevitability of a global takeover by a handful of invincible platforms to euphoric predictions about the riches available to venture capitalists who invest in platforms.

But how is one to reconcile the notion that the economy is increasingly dominated by "a small number of digital superpowers" who are able to capture a "large and expanding share of the value generated" with the assertion that "the Age of AI has possibly created the greatest entrepreneurial opportunity in the history of civilization"?[1] What I have tried to show in the preceding pages is that neither extreme of this schizophrenic ideology is true.

Part III profiled dozens of valuable young but now well-established companies that came of age in the era of tech titans. Their success was far from inevitable, their paths diverse and the roads taken littered with the carcasses of other aspirants who lost their way. Although they targeted a wide variety of markets using a broad array of business models and strategies, there are important commonalities that distinguish this group from the much larger class that ran out of steam.

What these businesses mostly share is a laser focus on relieving a very specific and urgent customer pain point. This discipline enabled them to develop the two characteristics that have proven most ephemeral in digital business models—customer captivity and relative scale. The reality that alternatives are one click away and that break-even market shares are lower than ever casts a pall over all new technology-enabled ventures. Being a platform or having network effects does nothing to mitigate these existential risks. Targeting a narrow market with acute demands facilitates the development of loyalty on the one hand and the rapid establishment of scale within that niche on the other.

Product and service attributes like complexity and trust that increase the cost of switching and searching are the foundation of many of the best new franchises highlighted here, from Etsy to Airbnb. And the ability to integrate usage into the customer's daily life as so many of the successful SaaS companies have ingrains that customer captivity even more deeply.

Specialization reinforces captivity and expedites the attainment of relative scale, and it also enhances learning and increases the chances that valuable use cases for AI and big data can be developed. The ability of Wayfair to thrive in the shadow of Amazon in the relatively mundane online furniture market reflects the value of specialization versus absolute size. And sometimes just not being one of the tech titans can be a source of advantage by establishing the alternative independent source, as in the case of The Trade Desk, or where trust and data security is critical, as in the case of LiveRamp.

Some may complain that this approach is limited to small, niche markets and that investors are obsessed with massive global opportunities. But we all started as babies. Both online and off-line, the strongest, biggest, baddest franchises began by dominating a niche and growing relentlessly like ringworm as they devoured each successive adjacency. Booking started by dominating independent hotels in Holland, then continental Europe, and now so much more around the world. BlackLine, like many of the dozens of multibillion-dollar, vertical SaaS software companies, started with a shockingly narrow use case. By quickly demonstrating the indispensability and efficacy of its product, however, the company has been able to continuously expand its TAM.

There are very few massive markets, most notably search, that lend themselves to winner-take-most dynamics. Even social media, which in the form of Facebook has many of the same structural barriers as Google, has shown itself to be much more vulnerable to targeted geographic-, demographic-, and product-based competitive attack. It is notable that where fears of global domination seem most justified is in product categories that essentially did not exist previously. Search and social are entirely new industries. In sectors where there were already analog incumbents of scale, it is difficult to think of a single one where a new digital monolith has conquered all. Finally, the fact that the most dominant platform company, Google, owes its resilience primarily to competitive advantages other than network effects undermines the assumptions of the Platform Delusion.

Any structural tendency toward winner take most in truly vast markets has exhibited two notable characteristics: it is rare and it is substantially driven by uncapped improvements in efficiency from learning and technology at scale. This has implications for the proper regulatory approach to the phenomena where it occurs. Namely, regulators must establish clear criteria to constrain potential abusive behavior of these few, without undermining the benefits made available to the many from these powerful scale-driven advantages.

The collective belief in limitless opportunities for start-ups may not be justified, but what is unambiguously true is that venture capitalists have succeeded in raising more money off the back of this conviction than ever before "in the history of civilization." The most successful venture capital firms have historically demonstrated a remarkable persistence in their returns, reflecting the network effects inherent in venture capital.[2] These network effects are spawned by the fact that the value in early-stage companies is overwhelmingly reflected in the quality of their people and ideas. The leading firms have unmatched relationships with proven founders and offer unparalleled access to resources and expertise through their web of friends and affiliates.

But the most epochal funds of the most iconic firms were at most a few hundred million dollars. The most successful investments at the seed or early-stage rounds rarely amounted to more than $10 million.[3] Today these same firms are raising funds of over $1 billion. It is hard to see how any firm could effectively manage the number of start-up investments implied by funds of this size.

Take Sequoia Capital, founded in 1972. Founder Don Valentine's $150,000 1978 investment in Apple is the stuff of legend.[4] More recently, the firm famously took the entire 2011 $8 million Series A round of WhatsApp. When Facebook purchased the company for $22 billion in 2014, Sequoia netted close to $3 billion. But the firm's latest flagship fund is $8 billion. By contrast, the founder of what has been characterized as the best-performing venture fund in history[5]—Chris Sacca's 2010's Lowercase Ventures Fund I, an $8.4 million seed fund with investments in Uber, Instagram, and Twitter—followed a different path altogether. After raising one additional modestly sized fund in 2015, Sacca announced he was closing the fund and simply continuing to support the existing portfolio.[6]

To be fair, successful venture capital funds make most of their money, and expend most of their capital, on follow-on commitments to their most promising investments. So, for instance, the initial Sequoia WhatsApp investment was followed by a subsequent $52 million tranche before the ultimate takeout. And as tech companies stay private longer before tapping the public markets, the size of the subsequent rounds has gotten meaningfully larger. But calling billion-dollar late-stage rounds (and some of these have been multibillion dollar rounds) "start-up" investments feels disingenuous. Indeed, many of these rounds have been shared with traditional private equity or growth investors and mutual or sovereign wealth funds. The returns of these categories of investor do not share the persistence characteristics of the best venture firms. Total venture investing in both 2018 and 2019 exceeded a mind-boggling $130 billion and was dominated by the largest funds.[7] Whether the historic persistence in returns continues as they essentially move into a different line of business remains to be seen.

Entirely distinct from the financial pitfalls of misjudging the relative attractiveness of early-stage investing, the romanticization of start-up opportunities raises broader cultural, economic, and even regulatory concerns. When I got my MBA in the late 1980s, around half of graduates of the top programs trundled off to investment banks and consulting firms. At the time, it seemed both troubling and unfortunate on a number of levels that so much high-powered talent was being directed toward two such narrow service professions. First, it seemed intuitively obvious that society would be better off if a few more of our best and brightest actually decided they wanted to produce something or otherwise improve the world. Second, it is highly unlikely that so many graduates made this choice in the first place out of a profound interest in either calling rather than that McKinsey and Goldman jobs were collectively viewed as the greatest indicia of business school "success."[8]

Well, the good news and the bad news is that the ambitions of the most-sought-after MBA graduates have changed dramatically.

Today over 50 percent of Harvard Business School's graduates join small, earlier stage businesses, with over 10 percent of the class of 2020 for the first time electing to do something on their own. Almost 20 percent of Stanford MBAs actually start their own businesses and fewer than 1 percent go into investment banking anymore.[9] Given the conventional wisdom about small businesses being the engine of growth and the general excitement about the endless potential of the digital economy, what is not to like about this start-up fever that has taken over during the last thirty years? Plenty.

First, it is no more likely that such a high percentage of graduates had always secretly pined to be entrepreneurs than that they dreamed of life as a banker or consultant. Far more probable is that the profound desire to follow whatever path is perceived at the moment as most associated with success fatally impedes the ability of many to clearly consider what they might actually enjoy. But at least in banking or consulting, when the inevitable epiphany comes for many that this is not their life calling, they will have acquired many broadly applicable skills as well as exposure to many professional roles and industries. The corresponding experiences at early-stage ventures may end with a similar epiphany or, more likely, when the business fails, as most do. At that point, however, the odds that meaningful expertise will have been developed or that life within that start-up bubble will have delivered broader lessons, is significantly lower.

Second, there is significant evidence that, despite the conventional wisdom about small businesses being the primary engine of innovation and economic growth, our most valuable human capital resources can make a greater impact by improving the productivity of the assets of more established enterprises. Some research suggests that "it takes forty-three start-ups to end up with just one company that employs anyone other than the founder after ten years."[10] Even the oft-repeated statistics about the central role of new businesses in overall job creation—described by some as "the small business job creation myth"[11]—are questionable when the focus is put on net job creation after subtracting the job losses from the overwhelming number of small businesses that go bust.

As issues relating to misogyny and racism in the workplace rightfully come to the foreground, it is also worth noting that Title VII of the 1964 Civil Rights Act, first extended by the Supreme Court to cover sexual harassment in 1986[12] and more recently to LBGT rights,[13] does not even apply to businesses with fewer than fifteen employees. More broadly, research suggests that "on virtually every meaningful indicator, including wages, productivity, environmental protection, exporting, innovation, employment diversity and tax compliance, large firms as a group significantly outperform small firms."[14] This is not to suggest that students for whom starting a new business is a genuine passion should not pursue the calling, only that the assumptions about its intrinsic economic and social superiority as a corporate form are not justified.

If it is neither true that a handful of digital giants are taking over the world or that it has never been easier to start a profitable online disruptor, where does that leave investors? The answer is in a digital economy that offers new avenues to build sustainable barriers but where historic sources of advantage are more difficult to preserve. The net impact of an environment that is characterized by a radical level of transparency that favors users over producers is that it has never required more ingenuity to establish or maintain strong business franchises.

But it can and has been done. Even in the long shadow of FAANG, new innovative enterprises consistently emerge and old dogs develop new tricks to reinforce their core advantages. The specialized many-to-many marketplaces that embrace product complexity, the vertical SaaS platforms that use customer data to drive continuous improvement, the indispensable leaders in online travel who manage to drive unique customer value despite Google's ubiquity and relentlessness, the data-sharing platforms that provide their participants powerful decision-making tools—all of these have created powerful moats, but they all require continuous digging to sustain.

What all these success stories have in common is that for each of these companies, it took some combination of additional structural advantages to secure its position once scale was achieved. No single explanatory factor is shared among these, but all have found tools to instill at least some customer captivity in the brutally competitive digital ecosystem. The ability to do so typically requires an element of specialization that supports valuable product or service attributes that even much larger broad-based competitors simply cannot match.

So neither the unthinking embrace of the start-up ethos nor the paralyzing fear of FAANG, both of which are deeply associated with the Platform Delusion, is warranted. The fetishization of network effects, artificial intelligence, or start-ups generally distracts from building the continued respect for the unchanging fundamental tenets of competitive advantage required to thrive in the age of digital disruption. The failure of investors to appreciate both the continuing relevance of these principles and the changing nature of their likely application will have predictable implications for their returns. More consequentially, if the simplistic assumptions about the indomitability of FAANG and the inherent attractiveness of start-ups are not rejected, our collective financial and human resources will not be effectively employed to realize the full social and economic potential of the digital era.

ACKNOWLEDGMENTS

This book derives most immediately from a class called Digital Investing that I have been teaching since 2015 at Columbia Business School. The conceit of the course is to examine the sources of competitive advantage of once disruptive but now established digital leaders in varied industries to inform potential investments in the next wave of disruptors targeting the same sectors. This exercise revealed an unexpectedly wide diversity of advantages enjoyed by the digital incumbents on the one hand and attractiveness of the digital insurgents on the other. That in turn highlighted the inadequacy of conventional wisdom regarding the appeal of digital business models generally that *The Platform Delusion* aims to remedy. My initial attempt to synthesize these observations appeared in the *MIT Sloan Management Review*, thanks to the encouragement of editors Ted Kinni and Paul Michelman, under the title "All Platforms Are Not Equal."[1]

Given these origins, I am particularly in debt to Jeremy Philips, a Founder and General Partner at Spark Capital Growth, who has taught Digital Investing with me from the beginning, as well as to the students, teaching assistants, and guest speakers who have supported this effort. The course, the article, and the book owe a massive intellectual debt to Bruce C. N. Greenwald, the Robert Heilbrunn Professor Emeritus of

Finance and Asset Management at Columbia Business School and a regular guest in the early days of the Digital Investing class. The framework used to analyze digital industry structures is the same one we used in *The Curse of the Mogul*[2] to analyze media industry structure. Both *The Curse of the Mogul* and *The Platform Delusion* rely heavily on Professor Greenwald's earlier work on competitive advantage, *Competition Demystified*.[3] That book demonstrates the fundamental connection between strategic and financial analysis that lies at the heart of the current enterprise.

Writing a book is not possible without honest feedback along the way to maintain intellectual and emotional equilibrium—particularly during a pandemic. I have come to rely on Myra Kogen, the former long-time director of the Brooklyn College Learning Center, to review anything I write before submission. My friends Ethan Berman, Darren Carter, Gordon Crovitz, John Edward Murphy, Cameron Poetzscher, and Xiaoying Zhong also read the entire manuscript and provided valuable commentary. I want to thank a longer list of friends, relatives, academics, and industry participants who provided encouragement, comments on some part of the manuscript, or just shared their perspective on some aspect of the book's thesis. This group includes Lanny Baker, David Eisenberg, Beth Ferreira, Reed Hastings, Warren Jensen, Jeff Jordan, David Knee, Larry Kutscher, Chaille Maddox, Lance Maerov, John Martin, Flip Maritz, James Miln, Brian Murray, Judea Pearl, Varsha Rao, Andrea Reichenbach, Clare Reihill, David Rosenblatt, Jason Shames, Richard Siklos, Sheila Spence, and Therese Tucker.

At Columbia, I have benefited from the generous input of my colleagues Wouter Dessein, Bruce Greenwald, Michael Mauboussin, Jonah Rockoff, and Miklos Sarvary at the business school, Tim Wu at the law school, Sudhir Venkatesh in the sociology department, and James B. Stewart at the journalism school. Ajit Sunil Akole from Columbia College served as a particularly enthusiastic and creative research assistant. More generally, Hollis O'Rorke and Jamie Chandler at the business school's media and technology program made sure I didn't go too far off the rails.

At Evercore, where I remain a senior adviser, Nathan Graf and Jason Sobol have put up with me for over a decade and still agreed to critique the entire book with the same thoughtfulness that makes them indispensable to their clients. Outside of these two colleagues with whom I work most closely, I have also shamelessly exploited my access to a wide range of deep subject matter expertise at Evercore, both in banking and equity research, relating to most topics covered. John Belton, Michael Caldwell, Marty Cicco, Vinay Kameswaran, Greg Melich, Jeff Reisenberg, Jaison Thomas, and David Togut have all shared important insights upon which I have relied. I somehow tricked the talented associate Michael Lizza to perform research and analysis that underpins much of this work on top of his already highly demanding job responsibilities. Laura Holden, my remarkable executive assistant at Evercore, effectively served as another research assistant.

I also want to thank my agent Jim Levine for taking me and this on and for his thoughtful counsel throughout. Finally I must thank my marvelous editors at Portfolio. Adrian Zackheim supported the idea from the start and delivered on everything he promised, which is as much as an author can ask. Merry Sun was assigned this project after the original editor changed jobs and quickly made it her own and definitely made it better.

None of those who have offered me assistance or support should be held accountable for what I have actually produced, nor should any agreement with my conclusions be imputed.

NOTES

INTRODUCTION

1. See John Kennedy, "How Digital Disruption Changed 8 Industries Forever," *Silicon Republic*, November 25, 2015.
2. Karen Jacobs, "Circuit City Files for Bankruptcy," Reuters, November 11, 2008; Phil Wahba and Tom Hals, "Borders Files for Bankruptcy, to Close 200 Stores," Reuters, February 16, 2011.
3. Saul Hansell, "Toys 'R' Us Sues Amazon.com Over Exclusive Sales Agreement," *New York Times*, May 25, 2004.
4. Mary Pat Gallagher, "Breach of Online-Marketing Deal Will Cost Amazon $51M," Law.com, June 24, 2009.
5. Michael Corkery, "Toys 'R' Us Files for Bankruptcy, Crippled by Competition and Debt," *New York Times*, September 19, 2017.
6. Tim Arango, "Time Warner Views Netflix as a Fading Star," *New York Times*, December 12, 2010.
7. Cynthia Littleton, "HBO to Launch Standalone Over-the-Top Service in U.S. Next Year," *Variety*, October 15, 2014.
8. Edmund Lee and Cecilia Kang, "AT&T Closes Acquisition of Time Warner," *New York Times*, June 14, 2018. At the time that the $85.4 billion deal closed, Netflix was worth almost $100 billion more.
9. During 2020, Nasdaq grew 43.6 percent, almost precisely ten times more than the NYSE, which grew a paltry 4.4 percent.
10. See Stephanie Yang, "The Pandemic Turned My Parents into Day Traders," *Wall Street Journal*, October 23, 2020. Small-scale speculators are estimated to now account for as much as a quarter of overall trading volume.
11. See Adrian Daub, *What Tech Calls Thinking: An Inquiry into the Intellectual Bedrock of Silicon Valley* (New York: FSG Originals, 2020) for a broader critique of a variety of questionable Silicon Valley–generated concepts "made plausible and made to seem inevitable."

12. An exception to this is that winner-take-all businesses are indeed exceptional in every sense of the word—they are astoundingly profitable and exceedingly rare, in both the digital and analog realms. Way more often than not, winner-take-all is an aspiration rather than a description, never to be realized.

13. Jason Dean and Katherine Bindley, "One Word Defined Tech Companies' Growth. It is Now 'Exploding in Their Face,'" *Wall Street Journal*, December 27, 2019.

14. Paul Tough, *How Children Succeed: Grit, Curiosity, and the Hidden Power of Character* (Boston: Houghton Mifflin Harcourt, 2012), 96–98.

15. According to Prequin, in 2000 AUM (assets under management) were $646 billion. By June 2020, this figure was over $5.5 trillion.

16. The acronym IBG YBG, which stands for "I'll be gone, you'll be gone," was used to justify all manner of selfish short-term decision-making by investment bankers and came to represent the ethos of the sector. Jonathan A. Knee, *The Accidental Investment Banker: Inside the Decade That Transformed Wall Street* (New York: Oxford University Press, 2006), 156.

17. Marco Iansiti and Karim R. Lakhani, *Competing in the Age of AI: Strategy and Leadership When Algorithms and Networks Run the World* (Brighton, MA: Harvard Business Review Press, 2020), 207.

CHAPTER 1: THE FOUR PILLARS OF THE PLATFORM DELUSION

1. Michael A. Cusumano, Annabelle Gawker, and David Yoffie, *The Business of Platforms: Strategy in the Age of Digital Competition, Innovation, and Power* (New York: Harper Business, 2019), 13.

2. Burt Helm, "Can Any Company Be a Tech Company? Inside the Unlikely Journey of Cult Salad Brand Sweetgreen," *Inc.*, May 2019. In addition to Professor Youngme Moon, the board includes major backer Steve Case, who, it will be remembered, convinced Time Warner that a combination with AOL was a good idea.

3. See Sienna Kosman, "The History of Credit Cards," The Balance, August 8, 2019; Merrill Fabry, "Now You Know: What Was the First Credit Card," *Time*, October 19, 2016.

4. "40,000 Visitors See New Stores: Weather-Conditioned Shopping Center Opens," *New York Times*, October 9, 1956.

5. Jean-Charles Rochet and Jean Tirole, "Platform Competition in Two-Sided Markets," *Journal of the European Economic Association* (June 2003): 990–1029.

6. Rochet and Tirole, "Platform Competition," 990. The authors cite Marc Rysman's work on the yellow pages industry as "the first empirical paper to estimate network effects in a two-sided market." Rysman's paper was not published until 2004: "Competition Between Networks: A Study of the Market for Yellow Pages," *Review of Economic Studies* 71, 483–512. Not referenced is the much earlier work on middlemen by Asher Wolinsky and Ariel Rubenstein, "Middlemen," *Quarterly Journal of Economics* 102, no. 3 (August 1987): 581–94. They

do, however, mention some later articles on competition between intermediaries. Rochet and Tirole, 994, n.4.

7. Rochet and Tirole, "Platform Competition," 992.

8. Claire Cain Miller, "How Jean Tirole's Work Helps Explain the Internet Economy," *New York Times*, October 14, 2014.

9. Diane Labrien, "5 Common Reasons Why Ecommerce Companies Fail," Tech .co, October 24, 2016. One prominent study of one thousand UK e-commerce start-ups found that 90 percent failed within the first ninety days; Paul Skeldon, "90% of E-commerce Start-ups End in Failure within the First 120 days," InternetRetailing, July 17, 2019.

10. The more successful high-end malls have continued to enjoy net operating margins over 70 percent. See Brian Sozzi, "After Christmas Your Mall Might Vanish—But It May Also Be Reborn," *Yahoo Finance*, December 26, 2020.

11. Carol Ryan, "Online Retailers Can Head to the Mall," *Wall Street Journal*, October 8, 2019.

12. Lena Rao, "Why Flash Sales Are in Trouble," *Fortune*, December 16, 2015.

13. Alistair Barr and Clare Baldwin, "Groupon's IPO Biggest by US Web Company Since Google," Reuters, November 4, 2011.

14. Ciara Linnane, "Groupon and Blue Apron's Real Problem: Neither Business Model Works, Experts Say," MarketWatch, February 22, 2020.

15. Guadalupe Gonzalez, "Airbnb, GitLab, and 13 Other Unicorn Startups Potentially Going Public in 2020," *Inc.*, January 8, 2020.

16. See Aaron Elstein, "Casper IPO Suffers from a Lack of FOMO," *Crain's New York Business*, January 14, 2020 ("Casper's problems start with the economics of the business not making any sense").

17. Kate Rooney, "Hedge Fund Manager Einhorn Likens Chewy to Dot-com Bubble Poster Child Pets.com," CNBC, July 26, 2019. But see Ryan Cohen, "Chewy Founder: We're No Pets.com," CNBC, July 26, 2019. The dramatic rebound of Chewy's share price has spawned the inevitable entry of other pet-oriented retail businesses into the market. Charity Scott, "BarkBox to Go Public in $1.6 Billion Deal," *Wall Street Journal*, December 16, 2020.

18. Claudia Assis, "Online Marketplace Poshmark Confidentially Files for IPO," MarketWatch, September 25, 2020; Elizabeth Segran, "Poshmark's Explosive IPO Bodes Well for the Resale Industry, But How Sustainable Is Secondhand?," *Fast Company*, January 19, 2021.

19. In terms of overall returns, of the seventy-seven companies considered (IPOs of less than $10 million were excluded), Amazon is the clear outlier. A $100 investment in the May 1997 Amazon IPO would have been worth over $166,000 by the end of 2020. This is more than twenty-five times greater than the next most successful e-commerce IPO. But as we highlight in chapter 5, the profits of Amazon in 2020—and for the indefinite future—derive overwhelmingly not from consumer retail but from the B2B AWS cloud services division. Excluding

Amazon from the group of seventy-seven yields overall returns that are less than half of that available from the S&P 500.

20. See David S. Evans and Richard Schmalensee, *Matchmakers: The New Economics of Multisided Platforms* (Brighton, MA: Harvard Business Review Press, 2016), 203 ("network effects power all multisided platforms").

21. See Jonathan A. Knee, Bruce C. Greenwald, and Ava Seave, *The Curse of the Mogul: Whats Wrong with the World's Leading Media Companies* (New York: Portfolio, 2009), 176–80.

22. See Andrei Hagiu and Julian Wright, "How Defensible Are Zoom's Network Effects?," *Platform Chronicles*, December 15, 2020.

23. Geoffrey Parker, Marshall W. Van Alstyne, and Sangeet Paul Choudary, *Platform Revolution: How Networked Markets Are Transforming the Economy and How to Make Them Work for You* (New York: Norton, 2016), 225.

24. Cusumano et al., *The Business of Platforms*, 16. It is worth mentioning that the authors also subscribe to the notion that all platform businesses exhibit network effects, although they concede that these "can be strong or weak, positive or negative."

25. Cusumano et al., *The Business of Platforms*, 24.

26. Cusumano et al., *The Business of Platforms*, 109.

27. Chinese-government-controlled PetroChina briefly became the first trillion-dollar company in 2007 after shares skyrocketed on the day it debuted on the Shanghai Stock Exchange. It has since lost 80 percent of that value. Many ascribe the previous lofty valuation to a combination of Chinese capital controls and speculation. Andrew Batsin and Shai Oster, "How Big Is PetroChina?," *The Wall Street Journal*, November 6, 2007.

28. Sinead Carew, "Microsoft Market Cap Touches $1 Trillion, Pulls above Apple," Reuters, April 25, 2019.

29. Amrith Ramkumar, "Alphabet Becomes Fourth US Company to Reach $1 Trillion Market Value," *Wall Street Journal*, January 16, 2020.

30. Jack Nicas, "Apple Reaches $2 Trillion, Punctuating Big Tech's Grip," *New York Times*, August 19, 2020.

31. Software companies are dealt with separately in chapter 13 to reflect the impact of the internet and greater bandwidth on the emergence of SaaS businesses.

32. Large cap is defined as greater than $10 billion. Pure software companies are excluded.

33. Priyamvada Mathur, "Which US Companies Had the Biggest IPO Haircuts?," *PitchBook*, September 11, 2019.

34. Begum Erdogan et al., "Grow Fast or Die Slow: Why Unicorns Are Staying Private," McKinsey and Company, May 11, 2016; Eric Griffith and Mike Isaac, "With the Economy Uncertain, Tech 'Unicorns' Rush Toward I.P.O.," *New York Times*, December 9, 2018; John Divine, "IPO Delays: Why Unicorns Push Back Public Debuts," *U.S. News & World Report*, September 24, 2019.

35. Yves Smith, "Fake 'Unicorns' Are Running Roughshod over the Venture Capital Industry," *New York*, November 14, 2018. The article discusses the surprising lack of reaction to the claims made in the academic paper by Will Gornall and Ilya Strebulaev, "Squaring Venture Capital Valuations with Reality," ultimately published in *Journal of Financial Economics* 135, no. 1 (January 2020): 120–43.

36. Sam Shead, "Uber CEO Says He's Leaving It as Late as Humanly Possible to Go Public," *Business Insider*, June 9, 2016.

37. Karl Russell and Stephen Grocer, "Uber Is Going Public: How Today's I.P.O.s Differ From the Dot-Com Boom," *New York Times*, May 9, 2019.

38. *PitchBook*.

39. *PitchBook*

40. Maureen Farrell, "Record IPO Surge Set to Roll On in 2021," *Wall Street Journal*, December 30, 2020.

41. Epistle 1, lines 70ff.

42. Michael Porter, *Competitive Strategy: Techniques for Analyzing Industries and Competitors* (New York: Free Press, 1980). Professor Porter's book on competitive advantage as such did not appear for another five years. Michael Porter, *Competitive Advantage: Creating and Sustaining Superior Performance* (New York: Free Press, 1985).

43. I borrow both this definition and the perspective on Porter from Bruce Greenwald and Judd Kahn, *Competition Demystified: A Radically Simplified Approach to Business Strategy* (New York: Portfolio, 2005), 4–6.

44. In practice, there are many different metrics representing the profitability of a company to which a valuation multiple is applied. The most frequently cited, p/e, EBIT, EBITDA, and OCF, and others are in turn subject to a mind-numbing number of inconsistent adjustments. This alphabet soup of benchmarks is theoretically meant to reflect (some would argue that certain of these metrics are actually designed to obscure rather than reflect) the cash-generating capabilities of the business. Ari Levy, "Why Charlie Munger's 'Bulls—t Earnings' Metric Is Used by So Many Tech Companies," CNBC.com, February 15, 2020.

45. See Bruce Greenwald et al., *Value Investing: From Graham to Buffett and Beyond*, 2nd ed., (New York: Wiley: 2020).

46. Fred Wilson, "Negative Gross Margins," AVC.com, October 21, 2015.

CHAPTER 2: NETWORK DEFECTS

1. See R. Preston McAfee and John McMillan, "Organizational Diseconomies of Scale," *Journal of Economics & Management Strategy* 4, no. 3 (September 1995): 399–426.

2. Michael Schrage, "Arthur Ochs Sultzberger Jr.," *Adweek*, June 1999.

3. James Currier, "The Network Effects Manual: 13 Different Network Effects (and Counting)," NfX.com, January 15, 2018.

4. Bharat Anand, *The Content Trap: A Strategist's Guide to Digital Change* (New York: Random House, 2016), 22–23.

5. There have been a number of legendary debates over the size of emerging total addressable markets, most famously the one between venture capitalist Bill Gurley and Professor Aswath Damodaran over the size of the ride-sharing market. See Aswath Damodaran, "Uber Isn't Worth $17 Billion," FiveThirtyEight, June 18, 2014; Bill Gurley, "How to Miss by a Mile: An Alternative Look at Uber's Potential Market Size," *Above the Crowd* (blog), July 2014.

6. D'Arcy Coolican and Li Jin, "The Dynamics of Network Effects," *Andreesen Horowitz* (blog), December 13, 2018; https://a16z.com/2018/12/13/network-effects-dynamics-in-practice/. ("Platforms with relatively commoditized inventory . . . are more likely to see their network effects asymptote once they reach a base level of liquidity.")

7. Verisk, "ISO Proposes Change to For-Profit; Part of Managed Evolution to Better Meet Customer Needs," press release, September 25, 1996. https://www.verisk.com/archived/1996/insurance-services-office-proposes-change-to-for-profit-part-of-managed-evolution/.

8. For history of Early Warning, see the company website at https://www.earlywarning.com/about.

9. Ravi Kumar, "What Makes Marketplace Business Models (Many to Many) So Attractive Compared to Classic Businesses (One to Many)?," Medium.com, July 20, 2018 (summarizing talk by Andreesen Horowitz General Partner Jeff Jordan).

10. Erik Davis, "Databases of the Dead," *Wired*, July 1, 1999.

CHAPTER 3: IT TAKES A VILLAGE

1. For an early article highlighting some factors driving the diversity of outcomes in network effects businesses, see Andrei Hagiu and Simon Rothman, "Network Effects Aren't Enough," *Harvard Business Review*, April 2016.

2. Marshall W. Van Alstyne, Geoffrey G. Parker, and Sangeet Paul Choudary, "Pipelines, Platforms and the New Rules of Strategy," *Harvard Business Review*, April 2016.

3. Edmund Lee, "*New York Times* Hits 7 Million Subscribers as Digital Revenue Rises," *New York Times*, November 5, 2020.

4. *New York Times* shares achieved a high of $52.79 in June 2002 and had not reached that level again by the end of 2020. In early 2021, the stock did briefly surpass this previous high-water mark.

5. Thomas Yeh and Ben Swinburne, "Start Spreading the News—Initiate OW," Morgan Stanley Research, October 14, 2020.

6. The *New York Times* previously operated a number of other businesses including television, magazines, a local newspaper group, *Boston Globe*, and About.com, all of which have been sold. In 2000, the core *New York Times* Media Group, which corresponds to the company today, generated $1.927.4 billion in revenues.

7. amNewYork, "amNewYork and METRO Join Forces to Become New York City's Top Daily Paper," January 6, 2020; Kathy Roach, "Metro Is Manhattan's Highest Daily Circulation Paper," *Metro*, February 21, 2018.

8. David D. Kirkpatrick, "International Herald Tribune Now Run Solely by The Times," *New York Times*, January 2, 2003.

9. Keach Hagey, "*New York Times* to Rename International Herald Tribune," *Wall Street Journal*, February 25, 2013.

10. *The Washington Post* eliminated what had been a national weekly edition in 2009, after more than twenty-five years of operation. Although at one point the product had a circulation as high as 150,000, by the time it was discontinued its national circulation had fallen to 20,000. Andy Alexander, "Post's National Weekly Edition to Close," *Washington Post Ombudsman* (blog), August 10, 2009. In 2000, the *Washington Post*'s circulation was 56,000. The *Los Angeles Times* had launched a daily four-section national edition in 1998, hoping to significantly expand the 40,000 circulation reach of an early slimmer version. Lisa Bannon and Wendy Bound, "*Los Angeles Times* Heats Up the National Newspaper Game," *Wall Street Journal*, November 5, 1998. It ceased publication six years later. Frank Ahrens, "*L.A. Times* to End National Edition," *Washington Post*, December 3, 2004.

11. Stephen Nellis, "Apple's News Service Reaches 100 Million Users, App Store Sales Expand," Reuters, January 8, 2020.

12. Alex Sherman, "Apple News+ Has Struggled to Add Subscribers Since the First Week of Launch, Sources Say," CNBC.com, November 14, 2019.

13. Lucia Moses, "To Get to 10 Million Subscribers, the *New York Times* Is Focusing on Churn," Digiday, October 26, 2017.

14. John Belton et al., "(Not) the Failing *New York Times*: Initiating Coverage of NYT at Outperform," *Evercore ISI*, December 13, 2018. An argument can be made that a high-quality real-time news service with a distinctive voice should achieve sustainably lower churn than even the best streaming entertainment service, but the sheer number of news alternatives makes this seem challenging.

15. In *The Business of Platforms*, the authors identify "four fundamental drivers of platform market dynamics," 50. Barriers to entry is treated as one of these, while multi-homing and network effect are treated as two other distinct drivers, 49–58. The final category proffered is "the impact on differentiation and niche competition," 54. Michael A. Cusumano, Annabelle Gawker, and David Yoffie, *The Business of Platforms: Strategy in the Age of Digital Competition, Innovation, and Power* (New York: Harper Business, 2019).

16. Jeremy Peters, "Some Newspapers, Tracking Readers Online, Shift Coverage," *New York Times*, September 5, 2010.

17. This inherent leverage in the digital operating model suggests that even relatively modest improvements in key metrics like subscription pricing, customer churn, and subscriber additions could yield 2025 profit above 2000 levels in either the base or pure digital case.

18. The recent aggressive efforts by both individual states and countries to extract an increasing toll on the FAANG companies from operating within their borders does lend some credence to these complaints. See Tony Romm, "Silicon Valley-backed Groups Sue Maryland to Kill Country's First-ever Online Advertising Tax," *Washington Post*, February 18, 2021; Gerrit De Vynck, "Australia Wants Facebook and Google to Pay for News On Their Sites. Other Countries Think It's a Good Idea Too," *Washington Post*, February 19, 2021.

19. Deborah D'Souza, "Tech Lobby: Internet Giants Spend Record Amounts, Electronics Firms Trim Budgets," Investopedia, June 25, 2019. Increasingly even digital start-ups have turned to regulatory strategies both to facilitate disruption and establish their own regulatory barriers. See Bradley Tusk, *The Fixer: My Adventures Saving Startups from Death by Politics* (New York: Portfolio, 2018).

20. There is still some controversy on this topic. Gordon Crovitz, "Who Really Invented the Internet?," *Wall Street Journal*, July 22, 2012. But see Michael Moyer "Yes, Government Researchers Really Did Invent the Internet," *Scientific American*, July 23, 2012.

21. Lavonne Kuykendall, "Buffett Trims Moody's Stake, Could Sell More," *Wall Street Journal*, July 23, 2009. Buffett continued to sell through the following year. Alex Crippen, "Warren Buffett Sells More Moody's after Stock Rebounds," CNBC.com, November 1, 2009; Alex Crippen, "Warren Buffett's Berkshire Hathaway Trims Moody's Stake Again," CNBC.com, December 22, 2009; Alex Crippen, "Warren Buffett Resumes Sales of Moody's after Stock Price Rebounds," CNBC.com, September 15, 2010. He resumed his sales in 2013. Phil Wahba, "Berkshire Sells Off More Moody's Shares, Stake Down to 11.1 Percent," Reuters, May 6, 2013.

22. Nick Kostov and Sam Schechner, "GDPR Has Been a Boon for Google and Facebook," *Wall Street Journal*, June 17, 2019.

23. Jonathan A. Knee, *Class Clowns: How the Smartest Investors Lost Billions in Education* (New York: Columbia University Press, 2017).

24. Chris Isidore, "Amazon to Start Collecting State Sales Taxes Everywhere," CNN Business, March 29, 2017.

25. Tim Wu, *The Curse of Bigness: Antitrust in the New Gilded Age* (New York: Columbia Global Reports, 2018), 123. In fairness, Professor Wu does acknowledge that a few of Google's 214 allowed acquisitions had some conditions placed on them.

26. This loophole is an open secret in the technology industry and had been exploited for decades by a broad range of companies well beyond FAANG. See, e.g., Jeffrey Young, "Blackboard Buys Another Rival, to Customers' Dismay," *Chronicle of Higher Education*, May 15, 2009.

27. Tim Fernholz, "How Google Dodged Anti-trust Law to Buy Waze," Quartz, June 19, 2013.

28. Eric Savitz, "Trump's FTC Declares War on Amazon, Facebook, Other Tech Giants with a Probe of Ten Years of Deals," *Barron's*, February 11, 2020.

29. Brent Kendall, "Justice Department to Open Broad, New Antitrust Review of Big Tech Companies," *Wall Street Journal*, July 23, 2019.

PART II: IN THE LAND OF THE GIANTS

1. Lee Brodie, "Cramer: Does Your Portfolio Have FANGs?," CNBC.com, February 5, 2013. For the full video go to https://www.cnbc.com/id/100436754. Lang is a private trader and public speaker who contributed regularly to Cramer's various media ventures and started his own online service called Explosive Options.

2. 24/7 Wall St., "BC Has 5 Red-Hot Stocks to Buy for 2016," MarketWatch, December 18, 2015.

3. Robert Boroujerdi et al., "Tactical Considerations: Is 'FANG' Mispriced?," Goldman Sachs Equity Research, June 9, 2017.

4. Abigail Stevenson, "James Cramer Renames FANG FAAA: Your Key to Long-term Growth," CNBC.com, February 27, 2016. Cramer has subsequently happily reembraced FAANG, James Cramer, "Who in a Million Years Would Ever Think That FAANG Would Be Value?," Real Money, March 4, 2019.

5. James Mackintosh, "The Agony of Hope Postponed, by a Value Investor," *Wall Street Journal*, July 14, 2019.

6. Tae Kim, "Warren Buffett Believes This Is 'the Most Important Thing' to Find in a Business," CNBC.com, May 7, 2018.

7. Brian Nowak et al., "Alphabet Inc.: Ready to Join the Big Tech Sum of the Parts Club?," Morgan Stanley Research, January 23, 2021.

8. Sigmund Freud, *The Future of an Illusion* (London: Hogarth Press, 1927), 52.

9. See Charles Duhigg, "How Venture Capitalists Are Deforming Capitalism," *The New Yorker*, November 23, 2020. ("Venture capitalists had become co-conspirators with such hype artists, handing them millions of dollars and encouraging their worst tendencies.")

10. Available at https://judiciary.house.gov/online-platforms-and-market-power/. See Tim Wu, "What Years of Emails and Texts Reveal about Your Friendly Tech Companies, *The New York Times*, August 4, 2020.

11. Although Amazon does not break out its R&D by division, it does reveal in footnotes to its financials that the $25.8 billion of costs to operate AWS in 2019 were primarily classified in this way. Even if only $13 billion of the $25.8 billion were so classified, the percentage of overall costs for the balance of Amazon dedicated to R&D—or in Amazon's nomenclature, Technology and Content—falls to under 10 percent.

12. Justin Fox, "Amazon's Great R&D Gift to the Nation," Bloomberg, April 5, 2018; Rani Molla, "Amazon Spent $23 Billion on R&D Last Year—More Than Any Other US Company," Recode, April 9, 2018.

13. Timothy Green, "How Much Does Amazon Spend on R&D? Less Than You Think," Motley Fool, June 13, 2018.

14. See Sally French and Jessica Shaw, "The No. 1 Social Network by Country Isn't Always Facebook," MarketWatch, February 19, 2016.

15. Marty Swant, "Facebook Wants to Compete with LinkedIn by Adding a Job Application Feature," *AdWeek*, February 15, 2017.

16. Andrew Perrin and Monica Anderson, "Share of US Adults Using Social Media, Including Facebook, Is Mostly Unchanged Since 2018," Pew Research Center, April 10, 2019.

17. Chris Hughes, "It's Time to Break Up Facebook," *New York Times*, May 9, 2019.

18. Priit Kallas, "Top 10 Social Networking Sites by Market Share Statistics (2020)," DreamGrow Digital, January 2, 2020; Leo Sun, "Analysis: Are Social Media Users Abandoning Facebook and Instagram?," *USA Today*, September 12, 2019; Mera Jagannathan, "Why Did Facebook Lose an Estimated 15 Million Users in the Past Two Years?," MarketWatch, March 7, 2019.

CHAPTER 4: FACEBOOK

1. Niall Ferguson, *The Square and the Tower: Networks and Power from the Freemasons to Facebook* (New York: Penguin Press, 2018).

2. Facebook's original mission, "making the world more open and connected," was officially changed to "Give people the power to build community and bring the world closer together" in 2017. Josh Constine, "Facebook Changes Mission Statement to 'Bring the World Closer Together,'" *TechCrunch*, June 22, 2017. Several years earlier the company had officially retired its informal motto of Move Fast and Break Things. Nick Statt, "Zuckerberg: 'Move Fast and Break Things' Isn't How Facebook Operates Anymore," CNET, April 30, 2014.

3. John Gramlich, "10 Facts About Americans and Facebook," Pew Research Center, May 16, 2019. Usage among teens, however, is lower and declining.

4. There is great variability based on what is being measured (site visits, active users, time spent, or advertising revenue) and what services are considered social (there is debate as to whether YouTube is a social network). The highest share (typically around 90 percent) is based on ad revenues and the lowest is number of site visits (under 60 percent) with most other metrics hovering around 70 percent. Compare A. Guttmann, "Social Network Advertising Revenue in the United States in 2019, by Company," Statista/eMarketer, March 13, 2020; K. Clement, "U.S. Market Share of Leading Social Media Websites 2020," Statista, June 18, 2020. Facebook share includes Instagram.

5. Douglas MacMillan and John McKinnon, "Google to Accelerate Closure of Google+ Social Network after Finding New Software Bug," *Wall Street Journal*, December 10, 2018.

6. Charlie Osborne, "Facebook's Latest Privacy Scandals Open Regulator Floodgates," ZDNet, April 26, 2019.

7. Michael Arrington, "It's Official(ish): MySpace Is Biggest Site on the Internet," *TechCrunch*, December 12, 2006.

8. Herb Weisbaum, "Trust in Facebook Has Dropped by 66 Percent Since the Cambridge Analytica Scandal," NBC News, April 18, 2018; Evan Osnos, "How Much Trust Can Facebook Afford to Lose?," *New Yorker*, December 19, 2018.

9. Emerging Technology from the arXiv, "An Autopsy of a Dead Social Network," *MIT Technology Review*, February 27, 2013.

10. Joseph Gallivan, "Titans in Chat Wars—AOL and Microsoft Fight over Open Access," *New York Post*, July 27, 1999.

11. Michael Arrington, "Facebook Launches Facebook Platform: They Are the Anti-MySpace," *TechCrunch*, May 24, 2007.

12. Neil Vidyarthi, "A Brief History of Farmville," *AdWeek*, January 25, 2010; Allison Lips, "Farmville: The Craze That Changed Facebook Forever," *Social Media Week*, April 23, 2018.

13. Catherine Clifford, "How Mark Zuckerberg Keeps Facebook's 18,000+ Employees Innovating: 'Is This Going to Destroy the Company? If Not, Let Them Test It,'" CNBC, June 5, 2017.

14. Kristi Oloffson, "Why Is It So Hard to Delete Your Facebook Account?," *Time*, May 14, 2010.

15. Jason Cipriani, "How to Completely Delete Your Facebook Account, Loose Ends and All," CNET, June 5, 2020.

16. Aja Romano, "How Facebook Made It Impossible to Delete Facebook," *Vox*, December 20, 2018.

17. Minda Zetlin, "Facebook Doesn't Make It Easy to Delete Your Account. Here's How to Do It," *Inc.*, March 14, 2018.

18. Yongzheng Zhang and Marco Pennacchiotti, "Predicting Purchase Behaviors from Social Media," In *Proceedings of the 22nd International Conference on World Wide Web (WWW)*, New York, NY: Association for Computing Machinery, 2013, 1521–32.

19. See Dan Gallagher, "Big Tech's Growth Comes with a Big Bill," *The Wall Street Journal*, July 17, 2018.

20. This is reflected in Zuckerberg's letter to potential investors at the time of Facebook's IPO: "The Hacker Way is an approach to building that involves continuous improvement and iteration. Hackers believe that something can always be better, and that nothing is ever complete." *Wired* staff, "Mark Zuckerberg's Letter to Investors: The Hacker Way," *Wired*, February 1, 2012.

21. As discussed in chapter 12, the ability to effectively target advertising continues to improve, but this is primarily driven by incremental usage by an individual rather than incremental network size.

22. Diane Bartz et al., "Facebook Faces U.S. Lawsuits That Could Force Sale of Instagram, WhatsApp," Reuters, December 9, 2020.

23. Michelle Meyers, "How Instagram Became the Social Network for Tweens," CNET, September 8, 2012; Henry Blodget, "Everyone Who Thinks Facebook Is Stupid to Buy WhatsApp for $19 Billion Should Think Again," *Business Insider*, February 20, 2014.

24. House Committee on the Judiciary, "Online Platforms and Market Power: Examining the Dominance of Amazon, Apple, Facebook and Google," July 27, 2020. Documents available at https://judiciary.house.gov/online-platforms-and-market-power/.

25. Tim Wu, *The Curse of Bigness: Antitrust in the New Gilded Age* (New York: Columbia University Press, 2018), 123.

26. Daisuke Wakabayashi et al., "Justice Department Opens Antitrust Review of Big Tech Companies," *New York Times*, July 23 2019.

27. Mike Isaac, "How Facebook Is Changing to Deal with Scrutiny of Its Power," *New York Times*, August 12, 2019.

28. Georgia Wells, Jeff Horwitz, and Aruna Viswanatha, "Facebook CEO Mark Zuckerberg Stoked Washington's Fears about TikTok," *Wall Street Journal*, August 23, 2020.

29. Mike Isaac and Cecilia Kang, "'It's Hard to Prove': Why Antitrust Suits against Facebook Face Hurdles," *New York Times*, December 10, 2020.

30. Jeff Horwitz and Deepa Seetharaman, "Break Up Facebook? It's Complicated, Tech Experts Say," *Wall Street Journal*, December 10, 2020.

31. Jeff Horwitz, "Zuckerberg's Deal Making for Facebook Is Central to Antitrust Cases," *Wall Street Journal*, December 10, 2020.

32. The success of WeChat, China's "app for everything," provides the strongest counterargument. Eveline Chao, "How Social Cash Made WeChat the App For Everything," *Fast Company*, January 2, 2017.

33. Lauren Feiner, "Zuckerberg Blasts Elizabeth Warren's Plan to Break Up Facebook and Says It's an 'Existential Threat,'" CNBC, October 1, 2019.

34. In 2021, Facebook did start requiring WhatsApp users to share data with the mothership. Lily Hay Newman, "WhatsApp Has Shared Your Data With Facebook for Years, Actually," *Wired*, January 8, 2021; Arjun Kharpal, "WhatsApp Delays Privacy Update Over User 'Confusion' and Backlash About Facebook Data Sharing," CNBC, January 18, 2021.

35. Given the losses, Facebook would need to contribute significant cash to the business before it was spun. The case for a forced separation of Instagram is both stronger from an antitrust perspective and more complex from a separation perspective.

36. Meera Jagannathan, "Why Did Facebook Lose an Estimated 15 Million Users in the Past Two Years?," MarketWatch, March 7, 2019.

37. Siraj Datoo, "Mark Zuckerberg Loses $7 Billion as Companies Drop Facebook Ads," Bloomberg, June 27, 2020.

38. Issie Lapowsky, "The 21 (and Counting) Biggest Facebook Scandals of 2018," *Wired*, December 20, 2018; Ryan Mac, "Literally Just a Big List of Facebook's 2018 Scandals," *BuzzFeed*, December 20, 2018.

39. Michelle Castillo, "Mark Zuckerberg's Personal Challenge for 2018: Fix Facebook," CNBC.com, January 4, 2018.

40. Salvador Rodriguez, "Facebook Apologizes after Employees Complain about Racist Company Culture," CNBC.com, November 8, 2019.

41. Sheera Frankel et al., "Facebook Employees Stage Virtual Walkout to Protest Trump Posts," *New York Times*, June 1, 2020.

42. Salvador Rodriguez, "Inside Facebook's 'Cult-like' Workplace, Where Dissent Is Discouraged and Employees Pretend to Be Happy All the Time," CNBC.com, January 8, 2019. This report, based on "more than a dozen" anonymous former Facebook employees who left as early as 2016, became the basis of widespread reporting and commentary.

43. Squawk Alley, "Facebook Nears $100/share," CNBC.com, July 21, 2015.

44. Rip Epson, "Ben Horowitz: 'Facebook Is the Best-run Company in Technology,'" *TechCrunch*, October 18, 2011.

45. Rachel Gillett, "Seven Reasons Facebook Is the Best Place to Work in America and No Company Can Compare," *Business Insider*, December 7, 2017.

46. Salvador Rodriguez, "Facebook Is No Longer the 'Best Place to Work,' According to New Glassdoor Survey," CNBC.com, December 5, 2018.

47. Salvador Rodriguez, "Facebook Is No Longer One of the 10 Best Places to Work, According to Glassdoor," CNBC.com, December 11, 2019.

48. Hunt Allcott, Matthew Gentzkow, and Chuan Yu, "Trends in the Diffusion of Misinformation on Social Media," Research & Politics (April–June 2019) 1–8.

49. Davey Alba, "On Facebook, Misinformation Is More Popular Now Than in 2016," *New York Times*, October 12, 2020.

50. Said to Peter Parker by his soon-to-be-murdered uncle Ben, in the original Sam Raimi–directed version of *Spider-Man* (Sony, 2002).

CHAPTER 5: AMAZON

1. Brad Stone, *The Everything Store: Jeff Bezos and the Age of Amazon* (Boston: Little, Brown, 2013), 48.

2. There were a number of unsuccessful predecessors to Marketplace: Amazon Auctions launched in March 1999 and morphed into something called zShops. Marketplace launched exclusively for used books in the US in 2000 and more broadly for other product categories and geographies in later years. See Business Wire, "Amazon Marketplace a Winner for Customers, Sellers and Industry," March 19, 2001.

3. Precise commission rates vary based on product category, price, and other factors. Meaghan Brophy, "Amazon Seller Fees: Cost of Selling on Amazon in 2020," *Fit Small Business*, September 1, 2020.

4. Alexandra Berzon, Shane Shifflett, and Justin Scheck, "Amazon Has Ceded Control of Its Site. The Result: Thousands of Banned, Unsafe, or Mislabeled Products," *Wall Street Journal*, August 23, 2019.

5. Stone, *The Everything Store*, 129–30.

6. Stone, *The Everything Store*, 187.

7. Colin Bryar and Bill Carr, *Working Backwards: Insights, Stories, and Secrets from Inside Amazon* (New York: St. Martin's, 2021), 190.

8. See Jonathan A. Knee, "What's Amazon's Secret?," *New York Times*, February 13, 2021.

9. Costco was founded in 1983, although competitor Price Club (with which Costco subsequently merged) opened its first warehouse store in 1976. Adam Bryant, "Costco Set to Merge With Price," *New York Times*, June 17, 1993.

10. "Overstock Launches Online Discount Club—Club O," PR Newswire, March 11, 2004.

11. Bryar and Carr, *Working Backwards*, 188.

12. Bethany McLean, "Is Overstock the New Amazon?," *Fortune*, October 18, 2004.

13. Will Oremus, "Alexa Is Losing Her Edge," *Slate*, August 23, 2018.

14. Constance Grady, "The 2010s Were Supposed to Bring the eBook Revolution. It Never Quite Came," *Vox*, December 23, 2019.

15. Although the original platform was established in 2002, the integrated suite of services that is the basis of what AWS sells today was relaunched in 2006.

16. "Can Amazon Keep Growing Like a Youthful Startup?," *Economist*, June 18, 2020.

17. Brandon Butler, "The Myth about How Amazon's Web Services Started Just Won't Die," Network World, March 2, 2015.

18. The authors of *Working Backwards* by contrast identify an earlier product that allowed third-party developers to create programs to facilitate the sale of Amazon products as the true genesis of AWS. This is equally unbelievable as an explanation as many large tech companies had similar programs to encourage third-party developers and none saw any particular connection to establishing a cloud computing business. Colin Bryar and Bill Carr, *Working Backwards*, 250.

19. Stone, *The Everything Store*, 213–15.

20. Both Google (with App Engine) and Microsoft (with Azure) launched two years after Amazon in 2008, but neither could really make it work until years later. In this case, the first-mover advantage was significant even though the technology was still being developed. Cloud computing was a new type of IT service and AWS in its early days had many issues but the potential benefits for early clients like Netflix led them to work with Amazon to solve the problems. The fact that these original customers often had to create extensive "patches" or customized workarounds to make the platform work actually created significant switching costs once the competitors' products became more comparable.

21. Rani Molla, "Amazon Spent Nearly $23 Billion on R&D Last Year—More Than Any Other U.S. Company," Recode, 2018.

22. Nandita Bose, "Amazon Dismisses Idea Automation Will Eliminate All Its Warehouse Jobs Soon," Reuters, May 1, 2019.

23. Iansiti and Lakhani, *Competing in the Age of AI*, 41.

24. Jay Greene, "Amazon Now Employs More Than 1 Million People," *Washington Post*, October 19, 2020.

25. Iansiti and Lakhani, *Competing in the Age of AI*, 41. See also Nick Statt, "Amazon Says Fully Automated Shipping Warehouses Are at Least a Decade Away," *The Verge*, May 1, 2019.

26. Emma Cosgrove, "Amazon's Shipping Costs Continue to Climb with No End in Sight," Supply Chain Dive, January 30, 2020.

27. Sarah Perez, "Walmart Launches Free, 2-day Shipping without a Membership on Purchases of $35 or More," *TechCrunch*, January 30, 2017.

28. Nancy Messieh, "Not Just Amazon: 27 Online Shipping Sites with Free 2-day Shipping," makeuseof.com, December 18, 2018.

29. Lauren Feiner, "Amazon Starts to Roll Out Free One-day Delivery for Prime Members," CNBC.com, June 3, 2019.

30. One-click ordering was actually the subject of a 1999 patent, recently expired, so that it could not be literally copied without paying a license fee, which some did. "Why Amazon's '1-click' Ordering Was a Game Changer," Knowledge@Wharton, September 14, 2017.

31. Stone, *The Everything Store*, 187.

32. Aishwarya Venugopal, "Members Only: US Retailers Revamp Loyalty Schemes for Amazon Era," Reuters, May 14, 2019.

33. Kaya Yurieff, "Everything Amazon Has Added to Prime over the Years," CNN Money, April 28, 2018.

34. It is also impossible to identify from the outside what other Amazon initiatives may be responsible for any increased spending by members. Morgan Quinn, "12 Ways Amazon Gets You to Spend More," CBS News, June 20, 2016.

35. Between 2005 and 2020, Prime's subscription price grew from $79 to $119, reflecting a compounded annual growth rate of just over 2 percent. The CPI grew just under 2 percent over the same period. In addition, more recent additions to Prime have been far more likely to enroll in the monthly rather than annual option, suggesting that they are running out of potential new customers in their core markets. Don Reisinger, "Amazon Prime's Numbers (and Influence) Continue to Grow," *Fortune*, January 16, 2020.

36. Eugene Kim, "Bezos to Shareholders: Its 'Irresponsible' Not to Be Part of Amazon Prime," *Business Insider*, May 17, 2016.

37. Todd Spangler, "Amazon Spent $11 Billion on Prime Video and Music Content in 2020, Up 41% From Prior Year," *Variety*, April 15, 2021.

38. Brooks Barnes, Nicole Sperling, and Karen Weise, "James Bond, Meet Jeff Bezos: Amazon Makes $8.45 Billion Deal for MGM," *New York Times*, May 26, 2021.

39. Nathaniel Meyersohn, "It's Only $4.99. But Costco's Rotisserie Chicken Comes at a Huge Price," CNN Business, October 11, 2019.

40. Bryar and Carr, *Working Backwards*, 239.

41. Tony Romm et al., "Justice Department Announces Broad Antitrust Review of Big Tech," *Washington Post*, July 23, 2019; John McKinnon and Deepa Seetharaman, "FTC Expands Antitrust Investigation into Big Tech," *The Wall Street Journal*, February 11, 2020.

42. Tim Wu and others argue for a fundamental reconception of antitrust law for precisely these kinds of reasons. See Tim Wu, *The Curse of Bigness: Antitrust in the New Gilded Age* (New York: Columbia University Press, 2018), 135. Now, not only has Wu been appointed as President Biden's special assistant for technology and competition policy, another aggressive Amazon critic has been nominated to the

FTC. Lauren Feiner, "Biden Is Loading Up His Administration with Big Tech's Most Prominent Critics," CNBC, March 9, 2021. Professor Lina Khan, also of Columbia Law School, first came to prominence with a a law school note that argued for novel approaches to subjecting Amazon to antitrust scrutiny. Lina M. Khan, "Amazon's Antitrust Paradox," *Yale Law Journal* 126 (January 2017): 710.

43. Roger Blair and Christina DePasquale, "'Antitrust's Least Glorious Hour': The Robinson Patman Act," *Journal of Law and Economics* 57, no. S3 (February 2014): S201.

44. Michelle Castillo, "Amazon Is Number Three in Online Ads, Closing in on Google and Facebook," CNBC.com, September 19, 2018.

45. Nandita Bose, "Exclusive: Walmart to Make First Direct Pitch to Big Corporate Ad Buyers at New York Event," Reuters, May 21, 2019.

46. Stone, *The Everything Store*, 341.

47. Jason Del Rey, "Why Amazon's Explanation for Shutting Down Diapers.com and Quidsi Stunned Employees," *Vox*, April 2, 2017.

48. Jonathan Sheiber, "Walmart Is Buying Jet.com for $3 Billion," *TechCrunch*, August 6, 2016. After three years, Walmart integrated the remains of Jet.com into its own website. Nandita Bose, "Jet.com Falls by Wayside as Walmart Focuses on its Website, Online Grocery," Reuters, June 12, 2019.

49. Stone, *The Everything Store*, xvi.

50. Stone, *The Everything Store*, 88.

51. Bryar and Carr, *Working Backwards*, 26, 79.

52. Bryar and Carr, *Working Backwards*, 190.

53. Bryar and Carr, *Working Backwards*, 13.

54. Dana Mattioli and Sebastian Herrera, "Jeff Bezos Exits as CEO, but His Role at Amazon Will Likely Be Little Changed," *Wall Street Journal*, February 3, 2021.

55. Aaron Tilley, "Who is Andy Jassy? Jeff Bezos Acolyte Moves from Cloud to Amazon CEO," *Wall Street Journal*, February 2, 2021.

56. Jonathan A. Knee, Bruce C. Greenwald, and Ava Seave, *The Curse of the Mogul: Whats Wrong with the World's Leading Media Companies* (New York: Portfolio, 2009), 8.

57. Amazon, "Amazon.com Acquires Three Leading Internet Companies," press release, April 27, 1998.

58. Courtney Reagan, "What's Behind the Rush into the Low-Margin Grocery Business," CNBC.com, June 6, 2013.

59. Cecilia Fernandez, "Retail Trade in the U.S.," IBISWorld U.S. Industry (NAICS) Report, June 2020, 44–45.

60. Alison Griswold, "The UK Led the World in Online Grocery Delivery—Until Coronavirus Happened," Quartz, March 21, 2020.

61. Gina Acosta, "The Predictable Rise of Instacart," *Progressive Grocer*, October 9, 2020; Russell Redman, "Report: Instacart Planning $30 Billion IPO," *Supermarket News*, November 16, 2020.

62. Nathaniel Meyersohn, "Coronavirus Will Change the Grocery Industry Forever," CNN Business, March 19, 2020.

63. Bill Bostock, "How Ocado Went from Understated British Grocer to an $18.4 Billion Tech Giant, as the Coronavirus Pandemic Confirms the Future of Grocery Shopping Is Online," *Business Insider*, July 12, 2020.

64. Alana Semuels, "Why People Still Don't Buy Groceries Online," *Atlantic*, February 5, 2019.

65. Alexia Elejalde-Ruiz, "Peapod, Based in Chicago, Is Shutting Down Grocery Delivery in the Midwest and Cutting 500 Jobs," *Chicago Tribune*, February 12, 2020.

66. Emma Vickers, "Morrisons Learns from New York Home Delivery Success Story," *Guardian*, February 18, 2013. The UK supermarket chain that took a stake in FreshDirect to learn from its "success" ultimately sold the position back to FreshDirect after two years of unsuccessfully looking for a buyer. Sarah Butler, "Morrisons Sells Stake in US Grocer Delivery Service FreshDirect," *Guardian*, August 16, 2016.

67. Jennifer Smith, "FreshDirect Delivers Apologies as Grocery Shipments Stumble," *Wall Street Journal*, September 21, 2018.

68. Hayley Peterson, "The Grocery Wars Are Intensifying with Walmart and Kroger in the Lead and Amazon Poised to Cause Disruption,'" *Business Insider*, January 31, 2020.

69. Mounica Vennamaneni, "Whole Foods Market, Marketing Strategies and Programs Analysis," Medium, July 15, 2017.

70. James Del Rey, "Amazon Is Shutting Down Its Fresh Grocery Delivery Service in Parts of at Least Nine States," *Vox*, November 3, 2017; Russell Redman, "First Amazon Fresh Store Opens to Public," *Supermarket News*, September 17, 2020.

71. Monica Nickelsburg, "Zillow Shares Slump as Amazon Webpage Hints at Expansion into Real Estate Referrals," GeekWire, July 17, 2017.

72. Melody Hahm, "Why the Housing Industry Should Fear Amazon," Yahoo Finance, October 1, 2018.

73. Catey Hill, "Amazon Is Selling Entire Houses for Less than $20,000—with Free Shipping," MarketWatch, June 30, 2019.

74. Michael Tobin, "Cars.com Completes Strategic Review but Finds No Buyer," *Wall Street Journal*, August 5, 2019.

75. Bruce Greenwald and Judd Kahn, "All Strategy Is Local," *Harvard Business Review*, September 2005.

76. Mark Mahaney et al., "Amazon Inc: How 'The Five' Could Boost Amazon's Revenue Growth," RBC Capital Markets, August 5, 2019.

77. Jeffrey Dastin and Akanksha Rana, "Amazon Posts Biggest Profit Ever at Height of Pandemic In U.S.," Reuters, July 30, 2020.

78. "Amazon.com Announces Financial Results and CEO Transition," Business Wire, February 2, 2021.

79. Courtney Reagan, "Grocer Aldi Targets Nearby Rivals in Its Bid to Boost Its US Footprint," CNBC.com, August 9, 2018.

80. Julia Finch, "Tesco's American Dream Over as US Retreat Confirmed," *Guardian*, December 5, 2012.

81. Julia Kollewe, "Sainsbury-Asda Merger in Doubt over 'Extensive Competition Concerns,'" *Guardian*, February 20, 2019. While the merger is still pending, Walmart's Asda overtook Sainsbury as the number two player in the market. "Asda Overtakes Sainsbury's to Become Second Largest Supermarket," BBC News, April 2, 2019.

82. Deirdre Hipwell, "Walmart's UK Retreat Leaves Asda With a New Owner, Old Problems," Bloomberg, October 2, 2020; Alistair Gray and Jonathan Eley, "How Walmart's UK Invasion Fizzled Out," *Financial Times*, October 5, 2020.

83. Don Davis, "Where in the World Will Amazon Go Next?," Digital Commerce 360, September 2, 2020.

84. Sarah Perez, "Amazon Prime Launches in China," *TechCrunch*, October 28, 2019.

85. "Amazon Plans to Shut Down China Marketplace in Rare Retreat," Bloomberg, April 19, 2019.

86. "India Poised to Become Third-largest Consumer Market: WEF," *Economic Times*, January 9, 2019.

87. Rajiv Rao, "What Amazon's Rare Defeat in China Could Mean for Its Tough Slog Ahead in India," ZDNet, April 24, 2019.

88. "Bezos Says Amazon to Up India Investment to $5 Billion," Reuters, June 7, 2016.

89. Jason Del Rey, "Amazon's Invincibility Showing Some Cracks—and a Big One in India," Recode, February 1, 2019.

90. Jon Russell, "Walmart Completes Its $16 Billion Acquisition of Flipkart," *Tech-Crunch*, August 20, 2018. Walmart later sold its own Indian operations to Flipkart, consolidating these operations. Sarah Nassauer, "Walmart Sells Its Indian Stores to Flipkart," *Wall Street Journal*, July 23, 2020.

91. Isobel Hamilton, "Amazon Plans to Invest $1 Billion in India and CEO Jeff Bezos Said a US-India Alliance Will Be Most Important This Century," *Business Insider*, January 15, 2020.

92. Ananya Bhattacharya, "A Few Biggies' Failure Hasn't Ended the Clamour for Indian Food-tech. Ask Amazon," Quartz India, March 5, 2020.

93. Vindu Goel, "Welcome to India, Mr. Bezos. Here's an Antitrust Complaint," *New York Times*, January 13, 2020.

94. Manish Singh, "Amazon's Fresh $1B Investment Is Not a Big Favor, Says India Trade Minister," *TechCrunch*, January 16, 2020.

CHAPTER 6: APPLE

1. A third founder, Ron Wayne, was initially given 10 percent to serve as a tie-breaker to resolve the inevitable conflicts between the very different Jobs and Wozniak. He ultimately decided life was too short and took $2,300 for his stake, which today could be worth close to $100 billion. Walter Isaacson, *Steve Jobs* (New York: Simon & Schuster, 2011), 64–65.

2. Mathew Honan, "Apple Drops 'Computer' from Name," Macworld, January 9, 2007.

3. Jobs died on October 5, 2011, a few days into the start of Apple's fiscal year 2012. In that year, iPhones exceeded 50 percent of revenues for the first time, reaching as high as two thirds of revenue in 2015. It is generally anticipated that the iPhone will remain the source of at least half of Apple's revenues until 2022.

4. Isaacson, *Steve Jobs*, 332.

5. Louise Kehoe, "Why Technical Wizardry Needs a Hard Sell/Launch of Latest Apple Computer Product," *Financial Times*, October 9, 1986.

6. Carmax survey can be found at https://www.carmax.com/articles/ranking-car-brands-most-and-least-loyal-owners.

7. Trent Gillies, "Car Owners Are Holding Their Vehicles for Longer, Which Is Both Good and Bad," CNBC, May 28, 2017. (Citing IHS Markit data.)

8. Lauryn Chamberlain, "86% of Car Shoppers Conduct Research Online Before Visiting a Dealership," *GeoMarketing*, March 27, 2018.

9. IBM introduced the PC in August 1981. Apple achieved a 12 percent operating margin for its fiscal year ending September 1981. It would not achieve a margin above 10 percent again until FY 2007.

10. Isaacson, *Steve Jobs*, xix.

11. Apple's efforts to litigate to protect its creative ideas were largely unsuccessful, as courts generally found these not eligible for patent or copyright protection, most notably in the case brought against Microsoft. See "Today in 1988: Apple Sues Microsoft for Copyright Infringement," *Thomson Reuters Legal* (blog), March 17, 2019.

12. Shortly after returning in 1997, Jobs had announced an alliance with Microsoft under which the company would both invest in Apple and develop versions of its core software for the Mac. The decision to actually support Windows represented a much more fundamental shift. Vikas Bajaj, "Apple Allows Windows on Its Machines," *New York Times*, April 5, 2006.

13. Interestingly, during Jobs's first stint at Apple, the operating systems of the various computing products, like the Lisa, Macintosh, and Apple II, were all incompatible.

14. The ability to establish playlists that could be posted on the iTunes Store and shared, creating a potential network effect, did not come until several years after the iPod was a big hit. Christopher Breen, "iMixing It Up," *Macworld*, September 17, 2004. The more sustained effort even later to produce a music-based social network, Ping, was a clear failure and quickly shut down.

15. Notably, unlike its computer operating system, Apple did ultimately license iTunes to other manufacturers like HP and Motorola.

16. Apple, "Apple Reinvents the Phone with iPhone," press release, January 9, 2007.

17. Walter Mossberg, "Newer, Faster, Cheaper iPhone 3G," *Wall Street Journal*, July 9, 2008.

18. Brian X. Chen, "June 29, 2007: iPhone, You Phone, We All Wanna iPhone," *Wired*, June 29, 2009.

19. Chaim Gartenberg, "10 Years Ago, the App Store Still Didn't Understand What It Meant to Be Mobile," *The Verge*, July 10, 2018.

20. Apple, "Apple Launches iPad," press release, January 27, 2010.

21. Some workaround software has been developed to allow Android phones to iMessage but it is not easy. Sam Costello, "iMessage for Android: How to Get It and Use It," Lifewire, September 9, 2019. No such hack is available for Face-Time.

22. Karen Turner, "Developers Consider Apple's App Store Restrictive and Anti-competitive, Report Shows," *Washington Post*, June 15, 2016. See also Kif Leswing, "Inside Apple's Team That Greenlights iPhone Apps for the App Store," CNBC.com, June 22, 2019.

23. When Jobs returned to Apple in 1997, one of his first decisions was to kill the Apple clones that had been approved during his absence, even as he was announcing a truce with Microsoft that expanded the range of applications available on the Mac. Isaacson, *Steve Jobs*, 336.

24. Jeff Smykil, "Android Overtakes Apple in the US Smartphone Market," Ars Technica, May 10, 2010.

25. Ariel Michaeli, "App Stores Growth Accelerates in 2014," *Appfigures* (blog), January 13, 2015. https://blog.appfigures.com/app-stores-growth-accelerates-in-2014/.

26. Isaacson, *Steve Jobs*, 565.

27. Something like this seems to be the view of Steve Wozniak, "Think of what we could have done to improve the Apple II, or how much could have been done to give us products in IBM's market," interview of Wozniak by Greg Williams and Rob Moore for *Byte* magazine, 1984.

28. Peter Burrows of *BusinessWeek* quoted in "Apple iPhone's Huge First Mover Advantage over Google's Android," MacDailyNews, September 25, 2008. See also Tom Kaneshige, "Why Apple Owns the High-End: First Mover Advantage," CIO, August 6, 2009.

29. John Markoff and Laura Holson, "Apple's Latest Opens a Developers' Playground," *New York Times*, July 10, 2008.

30. David Nield, "Some Notable Mobile Phone Firsts in History," Gizmodo, January 1, 2019. Nokia's efforts to launch a more traditional app store in direct competition with Apple were late and fraught. Priya Ganapati, "Nokia Ovi App Store Faces Turbulent Start," *Wired*, May 26, 2009.

31. Jenna Wortham, "App Makers Take Interest in Android," *New York Times*, October 24, 2010.

32. Joshua Topolsky, "Hello, Google Play: Google Launches Sweeping Revamp of App, Book, Music and Video Stores," *The Verge*, March 6, 2012.

33. Flurry Analytics 2014 Mobile App Store Report.

34. A comparison of https://appfigures.com/top-apps/google-play/united-states/top-overall to https://appfigures.com/top-apps/ios-app-store/united-states/iphone/top-overall confirms that only 3.13 percent of Android apps in the top 100 paid, free, and grossing (each) are not on the Apple App Store and similarly 2.84 percent of all iOS apps in the top 100 paid, free, and grossing (each) are not on the Google Play store.

35. Roberto Baldwin, "This Is How Apple's New iPhone Trade-in Program Works," *Wired*, August 30, 2013.

36. Lucas Mearian, "iOS vs. Android: When It Comes to Brand Loyalty, Android wins," *Computerworld*, March 9, 2018. (Citing research by Consumer Intelligence Research Partners. Loyalty is defined as percent of activations with the same operating system.)

37. John Authers, "Value Investors See Tech Stocks Coming of Age," *Financial Times*, October 23, 2013; Michael Schrage, "The Myth of Commoditization," *MIT Sloan Management Review* (Winter 2007); Rob Walker, "Not Necessarily Toast," *New York Times Magazine*, April 8, 2007.

38. See, most recently, Reed Hasting and Erin Meyer, *No Rules Rules: Netflix and the Culture of Reinvention* (New York: Penguin Press, 2020).

39. Isaacson, *Steve Jobs*, 558.

40. Isaacson, *Steve Jobs*, 458.

41. Tripp Mickle, "John Ive Is Leaving Apple, but His Departure Started Long Ago," *Wall Street Journal*, June 30, 2019.

42. Jack Nicas and Don Clark, "Apple Introduces New Macs with the First Apple Chips," *New York Times*, November 10, 2020; see also Matthew Buzzi, "Should You Skip the Apple M1 Chip?," *PC Magazine*, November 19, 2020.

43. Adam Levy, "The Biggest Sign Yet the Apple Watch Is Failing," *Motley Fool*, May 17, 2017; Daniel Kline, "Apple's Homepod Failure Is a Reflection of Its Bigger Problem," *Motley Fool*, April 11, 2019; Matthew Panzarino, "Apple Discontinues Original HomePod, Will Focus On Mini," *TechCrunch*, March 12, 2021.

44. Kif Leswing. "The Tech Industry Is Looking to Replace the Smartphone—And Everybody Is Waiting to See What Apple Comes Up With," CNBC, February 20, 2021.

45. Stephen Nellis et al., "Apple Targets Car Production By 2024 and Eyes 'Next Level' Battery Technology, Sources Say," Reuters, December 22, 2020. As of this writing, Apple's efforts to find a production partner have been unsuccessful. Charles Riley, "Who Could Make the iCar? Apple Is Running Short of Options," CNN Business, February 8, 2021.

46. Daisuke Wakabayashi, "Apple Targets Electric Car Shipping Date For 2019," *Wall Street Journal*, September 21, 2015; Lora Kolodny et al., "Apple Just Dismissed More Than 200 Employees from Project Titan, Its Autonomous Vehicle Group," CNBC, January 24, 2019.

47. Lizzy Gurdus, "Tim Cook: Apple's Greatest Contribution Will Be 'About Health,'" CNBC, January 8, 2019.

48. Jim Edwards, "Apple Will No Longer Report iPhone Numbers after Growth Went to 0%, and Analysts Are Now Worried iPhone Sales May Decline," *Business Insider*, November 2, 2018.

49. Evan Niu, "How Apple's Services Business Has Evolved over the Past Decade," *Motley Fool*, December 24, 2019.

50. Timothy B. Lee, "How Apple Became the World's Most Valuable Company," *Vox*, September 9, 2015.

51. Apple, "Apple Launches Mac," press release, July 17, 2002.

52. Adam Lashinsky, "Inside Apple," *Fortune*, May 23, 2011.

53. Philip Elmer-DeWitt, "Apple's MobileMe Is Dead—but You Can Still Retrieve Your Files," *Fortune*, July 1, 2012.

54. Ellis Hamburger, "Apple's Broken Promise: Why Doesn't iCloud 'Just Work?,'" *The Verge*, March 26, 2013.

55. Nick Statt, "Apple's Cloud Business Is Hugely Dependent on Amazon," *The Verge*, April 22, 2019.

56. Matthew Panzarino, "Apple Is Rebuilding Maps from the Ground Up," *TechCrunch*, June 29, 2018.

57. Rebecca Greenfield, "Why Nobody Will Miss iTunes Ping," *The Wire*, June 13, 2012.

58. Jeriel Ong and Ross Seymore, "iHold. Initiating Coverage with a $205 P/T," Deutsche Bank Research, June 19, 2019.

59. Tim Higgins, "Apple's Booming Services Business Could Be Hit in Google's Antitrust Battle," *Wall Street Journal*, October 25, 2020.

60. Higgins, "Apple's Booming Service Business."

61. Mike Murphy, "The Apple iPhone Violates All the Rules about the Price of Technology Coming Down over Time," Quartz, November 5, 2018.

62. See e.g., Mergen Reddy and Nic Terblanche, "How Not to Extend Your Luxury Brand," *Harvard Business Review*, December 2005.

63. Adam Levy, "Apple Music Tops 60 Million Subscribers, but Can It Catch Spotify?," *Motley Fool*, June 30, 2019.

CHAPTER 7: NETFLIX

1. Google does have a few subscription services, although these are not really direct competitors to Netflix. YouTube Premium is an ad-free version of its core YouTube and YouTube Music products. YouTube TV by contrast is one of a number of largely undifferentiated OTT "skinny bundles" designed to compete as a lower-cost alternative to the basic cable channel package. Facebook for its part has been declaring that it is a "video first" company since at least 2016. Jessica Guynn, "Mark Zuckerberg Talks Up Facebook's 'Video First' Strategy," *USA Today*, November 2, 2016. Although this has included some halting efforts to finance long-form scripted and unscripted projects, Facebook's efforts have largely focused on video as a means to share, communicate, and monetize through video ads, live streaming, video calling, and most recently content such as Instagram Reels to compete with TikTok.

2. It is not clear when Sumner Redstone first started saying it, but he did enjoy claiming authorship. Sumner Redstone, interview by Kai Ryssdal, Marketplace Morning Report, American Public Media, May 15, 1996. Although Redstone is correct that he first used the phrase before Bill Gates wrote his brief 1996 essay

of the same name, lower-profile mogul Gerald Levin of Time Warner had been saying it prior to either of them. See https://www.craigbailey.net/content-is-king -by-bill-gates; Barry Layne, "Levin: No Seat for Seagram," *Hollywood Reporter,* January 26, 1994. The phrase, however, had appeared well before moguls of any variety began using it.

3. Sumner Redstone, *A Passion to Win* (New York: Simon & Schuster, 2001), 109.

4. Redstone, *A Passion to Win,* 109.

5. Today, AMC, Regal, and Cinemark represent over half of the total US screens. Brett Lang and Matt Donnelly, "Inside Indie Movie Theatres' Battle to Survive," *Variety,* March 26, 2019.

6. See Jonathan A. Knee, Bruce C. Greenwald, and Ava Seave, *The Curse of the Mogul: Whats Wrong with the World's Leading Media Companies* (New York: Portfolio, 2009), 177. They also benefited from the ability to spread fixed regionally based marketing and overhead costs.

7. The first Netflix original series was actually *Lilyhammer,* which debuted the previous year on February 6, 2012.

8. Austin Carr, "Netflix Now Boasts More Subscribers than Showtime, Starz, HBO Next?," *Fast Company,* January 26, 2011.

9. Tom Petruno, "Netflix CEO Takes on 'Short Sellers,'" *Los Angeles Times,* December 20, 2010.

10. Daniel Strauss, "A Notorious Short-seller Pulls Back on Its Bet Against Netflix," Markets Insider, November 8, 2019.

11. Andrew Wallenstein, "Netflix Surpasses HBO in U.S. Subscribers," *Variety,* April 22, 2013.

12. NBCUniversal was initially a joint venture of General Electric and Comcast, with Comcast contributing a number of its own cable channels as part of the initial purchase price.

13. John Belton et al., "The Song of the Summer: Initiating Coverage of WMG at Outperform," Evercore ISI Research, June 29, 2020.

14. Janko Roettgers, "Netflix Culture Document: Five Insights on the Way It Works," *Variety,* June 21, 2017. See also Patty McCord, "How Netflix Reinvented HR," *Harvard Business Review,* January/February 2014.

15. Hastings and Meyer, *No Rules Rules.*

16. Daniel Kline, "Customer Satisfaction with Cable, Internet Service Providers Drops Again," *USA Today,* May 24, 2018. See www.theacsi.org.

17. Craig Moffett et al., "Web Video: Friend or Foe . . . and to Whom," Bernstein Research, October 7, 2009.

18. Todd Spangler, "Netflix Tops 200 Million Streaming Subscribers, Handily Beats Q4 Subscriber Forecast," *Variety,* January 19, 2021.

19. Todd Spangler, "Netflix Targeting 50% of Content to Be Original Programming, CFO Says," *Variety,* September 20, 2016.

20. Daniel Frankel, "Netflix Originals Spiked from 4% of Catalog to 11% from 2016–18," *Multichannel News,* March 21, 2019.

21. Jason Lynch, "495 Scripted Shows Aired in 2018 as Streaming's Output Surpassed Basic Cable and Broadcast," *AdWeek*, December 13, 2018.

22. Andrew Ross Sorkin et al., "Quibi's Quick End," *New York Times*, October 22, 2020.

23. "TV's Golden Age Is Real," *Economist*, November 24, 2018.

24. George Foster and Victoria Chavez, "FOX Sports and News Corp.'s Sports Empire," Stanford Graduate School of Business Case SPM-10, September 3, 2003. See also James Fallows, "The Age of Murdoch," *Atlantic*, September 2003.

25. See e.g., Elaine Low, "Bidding War for 'South Park' U.S. Rights Could Hit $500 Million," *Variety*, October 18, 2019.

26. Lucas Shaw, "The Hollywood Empire Strikes Back against Netflix," *Bloomberg Businessweek*, October 8, 2018; Brooks Barnes and John Koblin, "J. J. Abrams Said to Be Near $500 Million Deal with Warner Media," *New York Times*, June 17, 2019.

27. Private equity firm Providence was also an original JV partner but sold its stake in 2012.

28. Amy Chozick and Brian Stelter, "An Online TV Site Grows Up," *New York Times*, April 16, 2012.

29. "Amazon Prime Members Now Get Unlimited, Commercial-free, Instant Streaming of More Than 5000 Movies and TV Shows at No Additional Cost," *Business Wire*, February 22, 2011. Amazon had a separate video service called Unbox dating back to 2006, but it never had much traction. Pamela Statz, "Amazon Unbox Gets It All Wrong," *Wired*, September 8, 2006.

30. Todd Spangler, "Step Aside, Netflix: Amazon's Entering the Original Series Race," *Variety*, October 22, 2013.

31. Matt Brian, "Amazon Spins Out Prime Video and Launches It Globally," Engadget, December 14, 2016.

32. Todd Spangler, "Hulu Tops 25 Million Subscribers," *Variety*, January 8, 2018; Sara Salinas, "Hulu Loses in the Neighborhood of $1.5 Billion a Year, and Disney Is Set to Double Its Stake," CNBC.com, August 11, 2018.

33. Georg Szalai, "Hulu Now Worth $25B, up from $15B, Analyst Says," *Hollywood Reporter*, May 23, 2016.

34. Todd Spangler, "Disney Assumes Full Control of Hulu in Deal with Comcast," *Variety*, May 14, 2019.

35. Todd Spangler, "Hulu Sale Called Off," *Variety*, July 12, 2013. After Disney purchased Fox's stake in Hulu, AT&T, which by then owned Time Warner, sold its stake back to the company at a $15 billion valuation. Todd Spangler, "Hulu Acquires AT&T's 10% Stake in Streaming Venture for $1.43 Billion," *Variety*, April 15, 2019.

36. Brad Stone, "What's in Amazon's Box? Instant Gratification," *Bloomberg Businessweek*, November 24, 2010.

37. Jeffrey Dastin, "Exclusive: Amazon's Internal Numbers on Prime Video, Revealed," Reuters, March 14, 2018.

38. Adam Levy, "Here's Exactly How Much Amazon Is Spending on Video and Music Content," *Motley Fool*, April 30, 2019.

39. Natalie Jarvey, "'Older, Broader, Edgier': What to Expect from Hulu Under Disney's Control," *Hollywood Reporter*, May 22, 2019.

40. The relaunch of CBS All Access as Paramount+ in 2021 put further pressure on Netflix in this regard. Travis Clark, "New Data Shows How Much of Paramount Plus' TV and Movie Catalog Is Exclusive," *Business Insider*, March 22, 2021.

41. Claire Groden, "Netflix Announces Release Dates for Its First Original Movies," *Fortune*, July 7, 2015.

42. Michael Rukstad, David J. Collis, and Tyrell Levine, "Walt Disney Co.: The: Entertainment King," Harvard Business School Case 701-035, Exhibits 1 and 8, March 9, 2001.

43. Stephen Battaglio, "Netflix Acquires the Global Streaming Rights to 'Seinfeld,'" *Los Angeles Times*, September 16, 2019.

44. Scott Roxborough, "International Streamers Investing Millions to Take on Netflix Overseas," *Hollywood Reporter*, April 2, 2019.

45. Notably, however, some of the "original" content does not actually come with either global or perpetual rights. Even with *House of Cards*, which Netflix licensed from Media Rights Capital, the rights in a number of jurisdictions that Netflix did not yet operate in were licensed to others. These included China, India, Australia, and New Zealand. Ashley Rodriguez, "Netflix Didn't Make Many of the 'Originals' That Made It Famous. That's Changing," Quartz, February 26, 2019.

46. "Where Netflix Sees Potential—and Risks," *Wall Street Journal*, October 30, 2016 (Reed Hastings interview with Dennis Berman).

47. R. T. Watson and Ben Fritz, "Netflix Splurges on Big-Budget Movies," *Wall Street Journal*, July 29, 2019.

48. Edmund Lee, "Netflix Appoints Ted Sarandos as Co-Chief Executive," *New York Times*, July 16, 2020.

49. Bryan Kraft and Clay Griffin, "Netflix: Upgrading to Buy," Deutsche Bank Research, April 15, 2019.

50. Geoffrey Parker, Marshall W. Van Alstyne, and Sangeet Paul Choudary, *Platform Revolution: How Networked Markets Are Transforming the Economy and How to Make Them Work for You* (New York: Norton, 2016), 225.

51. Kraft and Griffin, "Netflix: Upgrading to Buy."

52. Duncan Sheppard Gilchrist and Emily Glassberg Sands, "Something to Talk About: Social Spillovers in Movie Consumption," *Journal of Political Economy* 124, no. 5 (2016): 1339.

53. Duncan Gilchrist and Michael Luca, "How Netflix's Content Strategy Is Reshaping Movie Culture," *Harvard Business Review*, August 31, 2017.

54. Chris Yeh, "CS183C Session 16: Reed Hastings," Medium, November 12, 2015 (conversation between Reid Hoffman and Reed Hastings).

55. Todd Spangler, "Netflix Says It Never Accessed Facebook Users' Private Messages," *Variety*, December 19, 2018.

56. Daniel Terdiman, "What Are Good Friends For? Perhaps for Recommending DVD's," *New York Times*, December 30, 2004.

57. Jared Newman, "Netflix Quits Social Networking—Again," PCWorld, January 13, 2011.

58. Sarah Pavis, "Watch This, Friends: Netflix Already Built and Killed an Amazing Social Network," *The Verge*, March 15, 2013.

59. Spangler, "Netflix Says It Never Accessed Facebook Users' Private Messages."

60. Todd Spangler, "Netflix Has Deleted All User Reviews from Its Website," *Variety*, August 17, 2018.

61. Reed Hastings, interview with the author, May 28, 2020.

62. Quoting Joris Evers, Netflix director of global corporate communications in David Carr, "Giving Viewers What They Want," *New York Times*, February 24, 2013.

63. Steven Brown, "Netflix Tells SEC 'Churn Rate' Doesn't Matter," *San Francisco Business Times*, September 16, 2011.

64. Patrick Campbell, "What Is a Good SaaS Churn Rate and Average Churn Rate by Industry," ProfitWell, August 8, 2020.

65. A range of estimates are cited in Jamie Powell, "The Quality of Quantity at Netflix," *FT Alphaville*, October 19, 2018. The more recent estimate by Second Measure is 34 percent.

66. Kathryn Rieck, "Netflix Has Unparalleled Customer Retention. Can Disney or Apple Shake It?," Second Measure, September 18, 2019.

67. Cynthia Littleton, "CBS All Access, Showtime to Reach 16 Million Streaming Subscribers by Year's End," *Variety*, February 20, 2020.

68. Cynthia Littleton, "Paramount Plus to Launch March 4 in US and Latin America," *Variety*, January 19, 2021.

69. Tim Wu, "Netflix's Secret Special Algorithm Is a Human," *New Yorker*, January 27, 2015.

70. Paul Bond, "Netflix Outbids HBO for David Fincher and Kevin Spacey's 'House of Cards,'" *Hollywood Reporter*, March 15, 2011.

71. David Carr, "Giving Viewers What They Want," *New York Times*, February 24, 2013.

72. Emily Steel, "How to Build an Empire, the Netflix Way," *New York Times*, November 29, 2014.

73. Leslie Goldberg, "It's Official: Netflix Orders 'Marco Polo' to Series," *Hollywood Reporter*, January 14, 2014.

74. John Kobin, "Netflix, in Rare Cancellation, Is Ending 'Marco Polo,'" *New York Times*, December 13, 2016.

75. Todd Spangler, "Netflix Execs Defend Cancellations, Saying 93% of Series Have Been Renewed," *Variety*, July 17, 2017. A more recent analysis suggests that the average life span of a series on Netflix is actually shorter than traditional television: Travis Clark, "Your Favorite Netflix Shows Are More Likely to Be Canceled After 2–3 Seasons Than on Traditional TV," *Business Insider*, April 9, 2019.

76. Sahil Patel, "Nielsen Sets Timeline for Big Change in TV Ratings," *Wall Street Journal*, December 8, 2020.

77. Janko Roettgers, "How Netflix Wants to Rule the World: A Behind-the-Scenes Look at a Global TV Network," *Variety*, March 18, 2017.

78. See Thomas Simonet, *Regression Analysis of Prior Experiences of Key Production Personnel as Predictors of Revenue from High Grossing Motion Pictures in America* (New York: Arno Press, 1980).

79. See Knee et al., *The Curse of the Mogul*, 107–11 for a more detailed discussion of these approaches.

80. Tom Huddleston Jr., "A Computer Is Deciding What Movies You're Going to Watch Next," *Fortune*, April 21, 2017.

81. Tatiana Siegel, "Warner Bros. Signs Deal for AI-Driven Film Management System," *Hollywood Reporter*, January 8, 2020.

82. Brad Stone, *Amazon Unbound: Jeff Bezos and the Invention of a Global Empire* (New York: Simon & Schuster, 2021), 135–58.

83. *Birdbox* was slightly above average for critics that year as calculated by Rotten Tomatoes (64 percent versus an average score of 57.8 percent) and below average by Metacritic's calculation (51 percent versus 62.1 percent). *Murder Mystery* was well below the average for critics on both services (43 percent and 38 percent, respectively). Audience scores on Rotten Tomatoes were slightly worse than critics' and slightly better on Metacritic.

84. Some have multiplied average ticket prices by the number of subscribers who clicked on these films to argue that they would have been blockbusters. See Mike Reyes, "Netflix's Murder Mystery Might Have Made a Ton of Money in Theaters," Cinema Blend, June 20, 2019. Just like we used to speak of movies you would wait to see on an airplane, there is no reason to imagine that a theater ticket would have otherwise been purchased for most films watched on a Netflix subscription. Dan Reilly, "Netflix's 'Murder Mystery' Would've Killed with a $120 Million Opening Weekend—If the Adam Sandler Comedy Ran in Theaters," *Fortune*, June 19, 2019.

85. Ben Fritz, *The Big Picture: The Fight for the Future of Movies* (Boston: Houghton Mifflin Harcourt, 2018).

86. Dan Gallagher, "Netflix Movies Could Use More Thumbs Up," *Wall Street Journal*, October 21, 2019.

87. Hastings and Meyer, *No Rules Rules*, 147.

88. Hastings and Meyer, *No Rules Rules*, 233.

89. Todd Spangler, "Netflix Licensed Content Generates 80% of U.S. Viewing, Study Finds," *Variety*, April 12, 2018.

90. Jon Swartz, "Netflix Has Biggest Quarter with Nearly 16 Million Subscribers Signing On," MarketWatch, April 22, 2020.

91. Sarah Perez, "Pandemic Accelerated Cord Cutting, Making 2020 the Worst-Ever Year for Pay TV," *TechCrunch*, September 21, 2020.

92. The outlier here is Disney film studio, which has essentially gotten out of the business of making original films and almost exclusively exploits its owned brands. That this achieves margins more akin to brand licensing is not that surprising, although they have done a superior job of turning already proven intellectual property into marketable films. The underlying brands being exploited, however, did not come cheaply. In addition to the various owned Disney brands, including the animated hits that are being systematically remade into live-action versions, the purchase of Marvel (and the repurchase of rights that Marvel had licensed elsewhere), Lucasfilm, and Pixar, not to mention the Muppets and Winnie-the-Pooh, collectively cost something like $20 billion.

93. Marc Graser, "Epic Fail: How Blockbuster Could Have Owned Netflix," *Variety*, November 12, 2013.

94. See e.g., Edmund Lee, "Digital Media: What Went Wrong," *New York Times*, February 1, 2019.

95. Chris O'Brien, "The Disruptor Disrupted: Why Monster Had to Sell Itself to Randstad for $429 million," VentureBeat, August 6, 2019. Automotive classified, once a very high-flying sector in public and private markets, has seen comparable pressure and competition. See Michael Tobin, "Cars.com Completes Strategic Review But Finds No Buyer," *Wall Street Journal*, August 5, 2019

CHAPTER 8: GOOGLE

1. This chapter borrows from the description of Google's sources of competitive advantage in Jonathan A. Knee, Bruce C. Greenwald, and Ava Seave, *The Curse of the Mogul: Whats Wrong with the World's Leading Media Companies* (New York: Portfolio, 2009), 98–102.

2. Nina Zipkin, "8 of the Coolest Projects to Come Out of X, Google's Moonshot Factory," *Entrepreneur*, January 23, 2019.

3. Hal Varian, "Our Secret Sauce," Official Google Blog, February 25, 2008.

4. There are multiple services that track search share, all of which place Google just over or just under 90 percent globally. One particularly useful analysis by country is Matthew Capala, "Global Search Engine Market Share in the Top 15 GDP Nations," Alphametic, March 19, 2020.

5. Rob Copeland and Keach Hagey, "Why Google Is Facing Antitrust Lawsuits from All Sides," *Wall Street Journal*, December 17, 2020.

6. Steve Lohr, "This Deal Helped Turn Google into an Ad Powerhouse. Is That a Problem?," *New York Times*, September 21, 2020.

7. Erin Black, "How Google Came to Dominate Maps," CNBC, December 5, 2020. Video available at https://www.cnbc.com/2020/12/05/how-google-maps -came-to-dominate-navigation-.html.

8. Shortly after the purchase of YouTube, Google provided some financing and marketing support for a number of niche original content channels. Claire Miller, "YouTube to Serve Niche Tastes by Adding Channels," *New York Times*, October 7, 2012. More recently, the company launched a subscription product that mixed

ad-free access to user-generated content, a music service, and some originally produced content. Conor Dougherty and Emily Steel, "YouTube Introduces YouTube Red, a Subscription Service," *New York Times*, October 21, 2015. After changing the name, they changed the strategy, pulling back significantly on original content. Alex Moazed, "YouTube Decides It Doesn't Want to Be Netflix," *Inc.*, March 28, 2019. None of the content initiatives amounted to more than a few hundred million dollars, in contrast to the multibillion-dollar commitments of Netflix, Amazon, and now Apple. Facebook, like Google, has so far mostly eschewed funding much original content. Although its programming budget for Watch Video now does exceed $1 billion, much of this is licensed from TV networks and sports leagues. Tom Dotan and Jessica Toonkel, "Facebook Cuts Back on Original Programming for Watch Video," The Information, January 29, 2020.

9. Steve Lohr, "Google, the New Master of Network Effects," *New York Times*, July 7, 2008.

10. One can argue that Yahoo and Naver are still "relevant" in Japan and Korea, respectively, but with market shares stuck in the teens they remain a tiny fraction of Google.

11. Rory Carroll, "Google's Worst-kept Secret: Floating Data Centers Off US Coasts," *Guardian*, October 30, 2013.

12. Ironically, the technology that allowed Google to monetize its superior search results—manifested in the Google AdWords program under which advertisers bid on keywords to secure prominent placement—was not developed by Google at all. The company was ultimately forced to pay hundreds of millions in a settlement to the owner of the original pay-per-click business. Will Oremus, "Google's Big Break," *Slate*, October 13, 2013.

13. Keach Hagey and Rob Copeland, "Justice Department Ramps Up Google Probe, with Heavy Focus on Ad Tools," *Wall Street Journal*, February 5, 2020. Texas has led the state antitrust suit that focuses on their advertising businesses and alleges a conspiracy with Facebook to monopolize the sector. Lauren Feiner, "Texas and Nine Other States File New Antitrust Suit Against Google—Here Is the Full Complaint," CNBC, December 16, 2020.

14. Paresh Dave and Sheila Dang, "Explainer: Advertising Executives Point to Five Ways Google Stifles Business," Reuters, September 11, 2019.

15. Chris Gaither, "The One Bit of Info Google Withholds: How It Works," *Los Angeles Times*, May 22, 2006; Chris Ayres, "Shrouded in Secrecy: An Awe-Inspiring Fount of Information," *The Times* (London), June 15, 2006.

16. Adam Lashinsky, "Who's the Boss?," *Fortune*, October 2, 2006.

17. "The 70 Percent Solution: Google CEO Eric Schmidt Gives Us His Golden Rules for Managing Innovation," *Business 2.0*, November 28, 2005. The original source for this formulation is a 1996 book that had nothing to do with technology. Indeed, in that work, although the numerical splits are the same, what they were meant to be dedicated to is entirely different: 70 percent from on-the-job experiences, 20 percent from feedback, and 10 percent from courses

and reading. Michael Lombardo and Robert Eichinger, *The Career Architect Development Planner* (Minneapolis, MN: Lominger, 1996).

18. Nathaniel Popper and Conor Dougherty, "Google Hires Finance Chief Ruth Porat from Morgan Stanley," *New York Times*, March 24, 2015.

19. Alistair Barr, "Google Lab Puts a Time Limit on Innovations," *Wall Street Journal*, March 31, 2015.

20. Conor Dougherty, "Google to Reorganize as Alphabet to Keep Its Lead as an Innovator," *New York Times*, August 10, 2015.

21. Scott Austin, "About Eric Schmidt's 'Adult Supervision' Comment," *Wall Street Journal*, January 20, 2011.

22. Eric Schmidt and Jonathan Rosenberg, "How Alphabet Works," in *How Google Works* (New York: Grand Central, 2017), xxiv.

23. Richard Waters, "Google Sets Out Plan for the Long Term," *Financial Times*, August 11, 2015.

24. Larry Page, "G Is for Google," Google Official Blog, August 10, 2015.

25. John Cassidy, "Can Google Become a Normal Business?," *New Yorker*, August 11, 2015.

26. Eric J. Savitz, "Google Parent Has a New CEO. Why That's Good for the Stock," *Barron's*, December 4, 2019.

27. Richard Waters, "Alphabet Chief Lifts the Covers on Earnings," *Financial Times*, February 4, 2020.

28. "Google Grows Up," *Economist*, July 30, 2020.

29. John Battelle, *The Search: How Google and Its Rivals Rewrote the Rules of Business and Transformed Our Culture* (New York: Portfolio, 2005), 148.

30. Brent Thill et al., "Mega Cloud Update: Still in the First Inning," Jefferies Equity Research, May 18, 2020.

31. A Google employee published an influential Roofshot Manifesto: "We choose to go to the roof not because it is glamorous, but because it is right there!" *How Google Works*, xxviii.

32. Brent Kendall, "U.S. Appeals Court Rejects Justice Department Antitrust Challenge to AT&T–Time Warner Deal," *Wall Street Journal*, February 26, 2019.

33. Tim Wu, "Google, You Can't Buy Your Way Out of This," *New York Times*, October 22, 2020.

34. Max Cherney, "Google Is Getting Closer to Buying Fitbit. Here's What It Means for Competitors," *Barron's*, September 29, 2020; Dan Sebastian, "Google Proceeds with Fitbit Deal, but Government Review Continues," *Wall Street Journal*, January 14, 2021.

35. Andrew Bary, "Alphabet Stock Is Worth 35% More Based on a Sum of Its Parts, Analyst Says," *Barron's*, July 28, 2020.

PART III: IN THE SHADOW OF THE GIANTS

1. World Travel & Tourism Council, Travel and Tourism: Global Economic Impact & Trends 2020, June 2020.

2. Rosie Spinks and Dan Kopf, "Is Tourism Really the World's Largest Industry?," Quartz, October 11, 2018.

CHAPTER 9: E-COMMERCE

1. Sara Salinas, "Greycroft's Patricof Says Amazon Could Be Helping to Destroy 'the Fabric of America,'" CNBC.com, April 6, 2018.
2. Karl Russell and Ashwin Seshagiri, "Amazon Is Trying to Do (and Sell) Everything," *New York Times*, June 16, 2017.
3. Joshua Quittner, "An Eye on the Future," *Time,* December 27, 1999. In his *Time* Person of the Year interview from 1999, the thirty-five-year-old Bezos did allow for exceptions for "animals and armaments."
4. Wayne Duggan, "Latest E-Commerce Market Share Numbers Highlight Amazon's Dominance," Yahoo! Finance, February 4, 2020.
5. Market capitalization of Wayfair and Chewy as of 12/31/20 were $25 billion and $39 billion, respectively.
6. David Gewirtz, "15 Companies You Might Not Know Are Owned By Amazon (and One That Got Dumped for a Huge Loss)," ZDNet, July 31, 2017.
7. Fareeha Ali, "Online Marketplaces: A Global Phenomenon," *Internet Retailer*, July 11, 2017.
8. 2020 Internet Retailer's Online Marketplaces Report, 5th edition, https://www .digitalcommerce360.com/article/infographic-top-online-marketplaces.
9. Marvin Fong, "Digital Marketplace: The Business Model of the Digital Age," BTIG, November 2018.
10. Fong, "Digital Marketplace," 16.
11. Fong, "Digital Marketplace," 15.
12. Fong, "Digital Marketplace," 17.
13. Dana Mattioli, "Amazon Scooped Up Data from Its Own Sellers to Launch Competing Products," *Wall Street Journal*, April 23, 2020. Amazon has also been accused of similarly using information gleaned from companies it invests in. Dana Mattioli and Cara Lombardo, "Amazon Met with Startups about Investing, Then Launched Competing Products," *Wall Street Journal*, July 23, 2020.
14. 1stdibs.com, Inc., Form S-1 Registration Statement, May 17, 2021.
15. See Elizabeth Wayland Barber, "Etsy's Industrial Revolution," *New York Times*, November 11, 2013.
16. Anne VanderMey, "Etsy Rallies Its Artisinal Troops: 'Start Making Face Masks,'" Bloomberg, April 7, 2020.
17. Sissi Cao, "The E-Commerce of the World's Most Beautiful Things: 5 Questions with 1stDibs CEO," *Observer*, March 22, 2019.
18. Beth Ferreira (who was at Etsy from 2007 to 2012 and ran finance and operations), interview with the author, September 17, 2020.
19. Rob Walker, "Handmade 2.0," *New York Times Magazine*, December 16, 2007. ("The luck or genius of the site is that Kalin and the other founders encountered

in the D.I.Y./craft scene something that was already social, community-minded, supportive and aggressively using the Web.")

20. Etsy, Inc., Form S-1, March 4, 2015.

21. Ken Bensinger and Nick Wingfield, "Amazon, Sotheby's to Shut Joint Web Site as Online Art Industry Retrenches," *Wall Street Journal*, October 11, 2000.

22. Brooks Barnes and Nick Wingfield, "With Online Art Auctions a Bust, Sotheby's Logs Out of eBay Deal," *Wall Street Journal*, February 5, 2003.

23. "1stDibs Names David Rosenblatt as CEO; Benchmark Invests," PR Newswire, November 3, 2011.

24. eBay established the concept of PowerSellers and Etsy is testing a comparable "Super Seller" program. Ina Steiner, "Etsy Tests Super Seller Badge Not Unlike eBay PowerSellers," eCommerce BYTES, October 26, 2018.

25. Fareeha Ali, "Sales Spike 146% on Etsy's Marketplaces in Q2," Digital Commerce 360, August 7, 2020.

26. Steven Kurutz, "Antique Dealers Protest New 1stDibs Rules," *New York Times*, March 11, 2016.

27. Aisha Al-Muslim, "Etsy Raises Fees, Angering Sellers but Sending Stock Soaring," *Wall Street Journal*, June 14, 2018.

28. Kaitlyn Tiffany, "Was Etsy Too Good to Be True?," *Vox*, September 4, 2019. ("Etsy has hardly ever made a decision that didn't make *someone* furious, and still—in spite of *repeated predictions*—it has never actually alienated a substantial number of its sellers to the point where they've walked away.")

29. See 2019 Etsy Seller Census, "Celebrating Creative Entrepreneurship around the Globe," Spring 2019. Eighty percent of sellers are businesses of one and 97 percent operate the business from home. https://extfiles.etsy.com/advocacy/Etsy_GlobalSellerCensus_4.2019.pdf.

30. Sara Castellanos, "Etsy Accelerates AI Experimentation Thanks to Cloud," *Wall Street Journal*, February 19, 2020. The chief technology officer brought on at 1stDibs in connection with its 2012 funding round previously worked in the AI Laboratory at Lockheed Martin. Nick Summers, "1stDibs Raises $42m from Index Ventures, Spark Capital and Benchmark to Boost Global Expansion," thenextweb.com Insider, December 3, 2012.

31. Ingrid Lunden, "Etsy Buys Blackbird Technologies to Bring AI to Its Search," *TechCrunch*, September 19, 2016.

32. Greg Bensinger, "Amazon's Next Move: Fine Art," *Wall Street Journal*, June 28, 2013. The initiative never gained much traction. Sarah Cascone, "Amazon Art Struggles to Lure Collectors Online, as Expected (Right?)," Artnet News, March 27, 2014. The site has also been plagued by charges of rampant copywrite infringement; Nicole Nguyen, "Stolen Artwork Is All over Amazon—and Creators Want the Company to Do Something about It," *BuzzFeed*, January 23, 2019.

33. James Vincent, "Amazon Launches Luxury Stores to Separate the Hoi Polloi From the Haute Couture," *The Verge*, September 15, 2020.

34. "eBay Launches Live Auctions for Premium Art and Collectibles," Business Wire, October 6, 2014.

35. "Launch of eBay Authenticate Boosts Shopper Confidence for Luxury Handbag Purchases," PR Newswire, October 16, 2017.

36. Amir Ismael, "eBay Launches an Authentication Program That Makes It Safer to Buy and Sell Big-Ticket Items like Watches, Designer Handbags, and Collectibles on the Site—Here's How it Works," *Business Insider*, November 21, 2019.

37. April Berthene, "Wayfair.com Dominates Online Furniture Sales," Digital Commerce 360, February 13, 2020.

38. Phil Wahba, "How Tiffany Plans to Sell a Lot More Jewelry," *Fortune*, April 12, 2016.

39. Stuart Lauchlan, "Tiffany Sees e-commerce as a Small, but Valuable Gem," diginomica, March 20, 2017.

40. Aishwarya Venugopal and Melissa Fares, "Tiffany Sticks to 2019 Targets, Helped by e-commerce," Reuters, March 22, 2019.

41. Sotheby's pure online sales in 2018, the last year it was public, were only $72 million, representing a mix of true online marketplace sales and transactions on its wine and home goods e-commerce websites. Sotheby's 2018 Annual Report.

42. Fang Block, "Sotheby's Launches a New Digital Sales Channel," *Barron's*, April 28, 2020. The earlier initiative was an online consignment marketplace, Sotheby's Home: "Sotheby's Launches Sotheby's Home: Luxury Design Marketplace," PR Newswire, October 10, 2018.

43. Eileen Kinsella, "Sotheby's and Christie's Place Hundreds of Workers on Furlough and Cut Executive Pay as Art Business Feels the Impact of Coronavirus Postponements," *Art News*, April 2, 2020.

44. Chris Dieterich, "Etsy Shares Clobbered by Amazon's Latest Crafts-selling Effort," *Wall Street Journal*, October 23, 2017.

45. Sarah Perez, "Amazon Brings Its Handmade Items to Prime Now Through the Holidays," *TechCrunch*, December 5, 2017.

46. Daniel Sparks, "Etsy Earnings: Growth Accelerates Yet Again," *Motley Fool*, August 8, 2018.

47. See Roni Jacobson, "How Etsy Dodged Destruction at the Hands of Amazon," *Wired*, October 7, 2016; Sarah Kessler, "How Amazon Lures 'Artisanal' Sellers and Hangs Them Out to Dry," oneZero, July 13, 2020.

48. Matt Phillips and Gillian Friedman, "Etsy Was a Twee Culture Punchline. Now It's a Wall Street Darling," *New York Times*, December 8, 2020.

49. See Phil Wahba, "Target's New Kids Collection Isn't for Boys or Girls," *Fortune*, February 8, 2016; Corinne Ruff, "Target Debuts 'Eclectic' Home Brand Opalhouse," *Retail Dive*, February 21, 2018.

50. A wide variety of niches other than purely geographical ones have emerged, but none have had a significant impact on the handmade market. Sig Ueland, "13 Marketplaces for Handmade Goods," *Practical Ecommerce* (blog), February 24, 2020.

51. Hedges & Company, "Automotive Data Questions Answered: ACES and PIES Data, Is There an Auto Parts Fitment Database, Automotive Part Numbers," September 1, 2012, https://hedgescompany.com/blog/2012/09/total-auto motive-part-numbers.

52. eBay company website, "Our History," retrieved at https://www.ebayinc.com /company/our-history/.

53. Mark Hughes, "DIY Car Repairs on the Rise but Drivers End up Paying 170 Pounds to Fix Their Mistakes, Study Says," Garage Wire, March 19, 2019; Bengt Halvorson, "Five Car Problems You Shouldn't Fix Yourself," *Washington Post*, June 20, 2012.

54. Ben Fox Rubin, "Amazon Offers Up Car Advice with Amazon Vehicles," CNET, August 25, 2016.

55. Alex Kwanten, "Amazon Partners with Aftermarket on Sales and Repair," *Automotive News*, August 18, 2019.

56. Alex Kwanten, "Mobile Mechanics Blaze Trail for Amazon in Service at Customer Homes, Offices," *Automotive News*, August 18, 2019.

57. Oliver Wintermantel, Greg Melich, and Michael Montani, *Retail Broadlines and Hardlines Web Traffic Tracker* (New York: Evercore ISI, 2020), 11.

58. Meagan Nichols, "FedEx Launches New e-commerce Service—and One of Its First Customers Is AutoZone," *Memphis Business Journal*, December 17, 2018.

59. "Autozone Inc. to Buy Alldata Corp for $56.75M in Stock," Dow Jones Newswires, February 6, 1996.

60. Ryan Sigdahl and Matt Wegner, "U.S. Auto Parts Network, Inc.—Buy," Craig-Hallum Capital Group, January 8, 2020 (Exhibit 8).

61. Michael Doyle et al., "E-Commerce Revs Its Engine in the Automotive Aftermarket," William Blair Research, April 2019.

62. See e.g., Derek Thompson, "Why Did eBay Sell Skype?," *Atlantic*, September 1, 2009; Helen Wang, "How eBay Failed in China," *Forbes*, September 12, 2010.

63. Julia La Roche, "Carl Icahn Shreds the eBay Board, and Demands that eBay and PayPal Split," *Business Insider*, February 24, 2014.

64. Daisuke Wakabayashi, "Google Takes Aim at Amazon. Again," *New York Times*, July 23, 2020.

CHAPTER 10: FLY ME TO THE MOON

1. Amazon.com Inc (AMZN.NASD)—Financial and Strategic SWOT Analysis, GlobalData, August 20, 2020.

2. Darrell Etherington, "Amazon Home Services Gets Its Official Launch," *TechCrunch*, March 30, 2015.

3. See Lydia DePillis, "Amazon Can Sell You Stuff. But Can It Clean Your House?," CNN, October 24, 2018; Julie Bort, "Homeadvisor CEO Explains the Secret to Besting Amazon," *Business Insider*, July 8, 2018.

4. Christina Farr, "Tech Giants Have Big Ambitions in Health, but Do Best When They Stick to What They Know," CNBC, December 31, 2019. Amazon's big-

gest recent initiative has been the launch of Amazon Pharmacy, which has had a predictable impact on the shares of traditional pharmacies. Christina Farr, "Amazon Jumps into the Pharmacy Business with Online Prescription Fulfillment, Free Delivery for Prime Members," CNBC, November 17, 2020. Whether they will ultimately succeed even here, where the service is much more analogous to its core retail business, is very much open to question. Vitaliy Katsenelson, "These Drug Distribution Stocks Have a Built-in Defense against Amazon Pharmacy," MarketWatch, November 19, 2020.

5. Emily Flitter and Karen Weise, "Amazon, Berkshire and JP Morgan Will End Joint Health Care Venture," *New York Times*, January 4, 2021.

6. Erika Owen, "Amazon Launches Curated Travel Booking," *Travel and Leisure*, April 27, 2015.

7. Eugene Kim, "Amazon Just Shut Down a Travel Site It Launched 6 Months Ago," *Business Insider*, October 14, 2015. Amazon had previously offered hotel discounts as part of its daily deal site, Amazon Local, but this had been discontinued and the entire Amazon Local operation eventually discontinued as well. Sarah Perez, "Amazon to Exit Daily Deals with Closure of Amazon Local," *TechCrunch*, October 30, 2015.

8. Rafat Ali, "The Unicorns: These Are the 15 Most Valuable Private Companies in Travel," Skift, October 29, 2015.

9. Olivia Carville, "New Tech Unicorn TripActions Aims to Bring AI to Business Travel," Bloomberg, November 8, 2018.

10. Jamie Biesiada, "How Many Travel Agents in the U.S.? Depends on Whom You're Asking," Travel Weekly, February 6, 2018; Richard D'Ambrosio, Travel Agent Popularity on the Rise Yet Again," *Travel Market Report*, August 9, 2019.

11. Adam Levine-Weinberg, "7 Ways Warren Buffett Blasted the Airline Industry before Investing Billions in It," *Business Insider*, March 8, 2017.

12. Mark DeCambre, "Buffett Says He Dumped Entire Stake in Airline-sector Stocks: 'The World Has Changed for Airlines' Amid Coronavirus," MarketWatch, May 3, 2020.

13. Sabre company website, "The Sabre Story," retrieved at https://www.sabre.com/files/Sabre-History.pdf.

14. In 2015, Sabre completed a much smaller transaction—the $411 million acquisition of Abacus International, a 1998 joint venture with a regional consortium of eleven Asian carriers in which it already had a 35 percent stake. PR Newswire, "Sabre to Acquire Abacus International," May 14, 2015.

15. Amadeus, "Powering Better Journeys through Travel Technology, presentation, January 2021, page 15. https://corporate.amadeus.com/documents/en/investors/all-years/financial-information-and-presentations/2017-amadeus-introductory-presentation.pdf.

16. John King and Kash Rangan, "Global Distribution System (GDS) Primer," BofA Merrill Lynch Global Research, September 26, 2014.

17. Barbara Peterson, "The Death of the Airline Ticket Office," *Conde Nast Traveler*, September 29, 2017. All of the major airlines closed all but a few US ticket offices over a decade ago. See e.g., "Delta to Close All Area Ticket Offices," AviationPros.com, December 3, 2007.

18. American Airlines company website, "Ticket Sales Centers," retrieved at www .aa.com/i18n/customer-service/contact-american/ticket-sales-centers.jsp.

19. The first was the Internet Travel Network in 1995, which pivoted to a business-to-business service under the name GetThere and was ultimately purchased by Sabre in 2000 for $757 million. Jay Campbell, "Sabre to Get GetThere," *Business Travel News*, September 4, 2000.

20. Although the first metasearch engines were developed around the same time as the earliest OTAs, it would be several years before this technology was applied specifically to the travel domain. Several were established in the late 1990s, notably Sidestep, FareChase, and Qixo, although their functionality and efficacy remained quite limited. See Craig Stoltz, "Faring Better—and Worse," *Washington Post*, November 5, 2000 (noting inconsistency of performance of early metasearch services). Over time, however, metasearch has come to represent an increasing share of travel search.

21. Amadeus sold Opodo to eDreams for 450 million euros in 2011 while Travelocity and Orbitz were each sold to Expedia in 2015 for $280 million and $1.3 billion, respectively.

22. In addition to having a consumer-facing metasearch business, ITA Software actually licensed the technology that many of the other metasearch companies relied on. In approving the acquisition, the Justice Department required ITA to continue to develop products and offer them to competitors. Claire Cain Miller, "U.S. Clears Google Acquisition of Travel Software," *New York Times*, April 8, 2011.

23. David Togut et al., "Upgrading Amadeus to Outperform; Downgrading Sabre & Travelport to Underperform," Evercore ISI Research, January 4, 2018, 9.

24. Christopher Tkaczyk, "Millennials Are Relying on Travel Agents in Record Numbers," *Travel and Leisure*, August 29, 2017.

25. Travel Weekly, "2019 Power List," June 24, 2019.

26. Germán Bou and Fernando Pujadas, "Rocky Amadeus. Coverage Initiated with Neutral, JB Capital Markets," September 9, 2019, 10. The biggest loss of share is from direct bookings to the airlines, which by themselves account for roughly half of US bookings. In addition, several large, fast-growing domestic travel markets, notably Russia and China, have their own exclusive GDSs. Finally, as discussed below, the establishment by IATA of a new industry-wide XML-based communication standard has allowed airlines to selectively establish direct connections with certain travel agents. Thomas Poutieux, "Soft Landing," Kepler Cheuvreux Equity Research, November 20, 2018, 61.

27. See e.g., Michael Baker, "At Long Last, Southwest to Enable GDS Bookings," Travel Weekly, August 5, 2019.

28. Johanna Jainchill, "Lufthansa's GDS Fee, Designed to Cut Costs, Will Penalize Agents," Travel Weekly, June 7, 2015.

29. This New Distribution Capability (NDC) was developed by the International Air Transportation Association, which represents 290 airlines and over 80 percent of total air traffic: http://www.iata.org/en/programs/airline-distribution/ndc.

30. Ben Ireland, "Lufthansa and Corporate Travel Agents Agree First Direct Connect Deals," Travolution, April 27, 2017.

31. Julian Serafini and Paul Krantz, "Amadeus: Gaining Altitude—Initiating at Buy," Jeffries Equity Research, July 22, 2019.

32. Robert Silk, "Private-channel Airline Distribution Deals Spark Concern," Travel Weekly, November 17, 2017. See, more recently, Sean O'Neill, "New Wholesale Model Could Shake Up Airline Distribution Thanks to American Airlines Test with Sabre," Skift, April 17, 2020.

33. Linda Fox, "Lufthansa Group Airlines to be Removed from Sabre as Pair Fail to Reach Distribution Agreement," PhocusWire, May 14, 2020.

34. Foo Yun Chee, "Travel Agents Seek EU Antitrust Probe into Lufthansa Pricing," Reuters, December 19, 2018.

35. Serafini and Krantz, "Amadeus: Gaining Altitude."

36. Altexsoft Team, "New Disribution Capability (NDC) in Air Travel: Airlines, GDS and the Impact on the Industry," Travel Daily Media, March 3, 2019.

37. John Kosman, "Why Private Equity Firms like Bain Capital Really Are the Worst of Capitalism," Rolling Stone, May 23, 2012.

38. Daphne Howland, "PayPal, Visa Declare Truce, Sign Digital Payments Partnership," Retail Dive, July 22, 2016.

39. PayPal's shares, which had been stagnant, began an extended climb once the Visa deal was announced, more than tripling in value over the next four years. In 2020, the company extended and significantly expanded the Visa partnership. Eric Volkman, "Visa and PayPal Partnership Deal Extension Promises More Instant Pay Options for Users," Motley Fool, September 13, 2020.

40. The combined market value of Visa and Mastercard was $750 billion as of the end of 2020. PayPal, with a market value above $250 billion at the end of 2020, is the biggest public online payments company by far.

41. Brent Kendall et al., "Visa Abandons Planned Acquisition of Plaid After DOJ Challenge," Wall Street Journal, January 12, 2021.

CHAPTER 11: "TO TRAVEL IS TO LIVE!"

1. Hans Christian Anderson, The Fairy Tale of My Life: An Autobiography (Lanham, MD: Cooper Square Press, 2000), 414.

2. Peter Elkind, "The Hype Is Big, Really Big, at Priceline," Fortune, September 6, 1999.

3. Priceline.com Incorporated, Amendment No. 1 to Form S-1, Securities and Exchange Commission, February 16, 1999.

4. Priceline.com Incorporated, Amendment No. 1 to Form S-1.

5. Elkind, "The Hype Is Big."

6. "California Synapse Magazine Auto Renewal Class Action Settlement," Top Class Actions, March 21, 2019.

7. Carrie Lee, "Priceline Is Expected to Soar, but Turbulence May Emerge," *Wall Street Journal*, February 19, 1999.

8. Business Wire, "Priceline.com Anticipates 3rd Quarter Revenues to Be Below Expectations," September 27, 2000.

9. Chris Woodyard and Matt Krantz, "Priceline Hits a Sour Cord as Connecticut Opens Consumer Fraud Investigation, Web Site Struggles to Please Investors, Customers," *USA Today*, September 29, 2000.

10. Saul Hansell, "Pricelines's WebHouse Club Abandoned as Investors Balk," *New York Times*, October 6, 2000; Julie Angwin and Nick Wingfield, "Priceline Offshoot Ate Millions in Costs to Subsidize Customers," *Wall Street Journal*, October 16, 2000.

11. Dana Canedy, "What's Your Bid on Peanut Butter? Groceries Join Big Items on a Name-Your-Price Web Site," *New York Times*, September 22, 1999.

12. Tribune News Services, "Priceline.com Hit by Charge as Think Tank Restructures," *Chicago Tribune*, November 23, 2000. Most of the underlying lawsuit was eventually dismissed on technical grounds, although not the charge that Priceline had falsely claimed it had actually invented Name Your Own Price (NYOP) bidding. "Judge Throws Out Most of Marketel's Case against Priceline.com," Dow Jones Business News, December 7, 2000.

13. Joseph Gallivan, "Priceline's Founder Jay Walker Quits," *New York Post*, December 29, 2000.

14. Cassell Bryan-Low, "Priceline Founder Jay Walker Sells Stocks at a Bargain Price," *Wall Street Journal*, August 22, 2001.

15. Jeff Opdyke and Jennifer Renwick, "For Priceline's Big Investors, the Stock Price Isn't Right," *Wall Street Journal*, September 29, 2000.

16. John Letzing, "Founder of Priceline Spoiling for a Fight over Tech Patents," *Wall Street Journal*, August 22, 2011.

17. Nitasha Tiku, "Priceline Founder Jay Walker Sure Has Filed a Lot of Lawsuits for Someone Who's Not a Patent Troll," *New York Observer*, August 22, 2011.

18. *Forbes*, "An Edison for a New Age?," May 16, 1999.

19. Business Wire, "Priceline.com Declares 1-For-6 Reverse Stock Split," June 16, 2003.

20. Dennis Schaal, "The Oral History of Travel's Greatest Acquisition," Skift, July 8, 2019.

21. Dennis Schaal, "Priceline Overtakes Expedia in Market Capitalization," PhocusWire, November 17, 2009.

22. Dennis Schaal, "Priceline Overtakes Expedia in Gross Bookings for the First Time," Skift, November 8, 2013.

23. The company has made subsequent small acquisitions into the underperforming unit. Business Wire, "Booking Holdings Agrees to Acquire Venga," May 2, 2019.

24. Name Your Own Price for some products survives under the "Express Deals" tab of Priceline. Dennis Schaal, "The Death of Priceline's Name Your Own Price Is Likely Drawing Near," Skift, March 26, 2018.

25. *Economist*, "The Priceline Party: The World's Largest Online-travel Company," July 29, 2017.

26. *Economist*, "The Priceline Party."

27. Scott Keyes, "The Complete Guide to Online Travel Agencies," Scott's Cheap Flights, November 14, 2019.

28. A more extensive comparison of Reuters and Bloomberg is found in Jonathan A. Knee, Bruce C. Greenwald, and Ava Seave, *The Curse of the Mogul: Whats Wrong with the World's Leading Media Companies* (New York: Portfolio, 2009), 148–59.

29. Thomas Pallini, "The Past 2 Decades Saw the Number of U.S. Airlines Cut in Half," *Business Insider*, March 21, 2000.

30. Natasha Frost, "European Airlines Are Confronting the Same Grim Reality Faced by their US Counterparts Decades Ago," Quartz, November 6, 2019.

31. Julie Weed, "Independent Hotels Are Disappearing as Chains Grow," *The New York Times*, October 21, 2019.

32. Murdoch sold the entire travel business to what is now RELX shortly after this venture was established. Geraldine Fabricant, "Murdoch Sells Travel Business," *New York Times*, May 6, 1989.

33. John F. Davis, "The Formation of THISCO," Hospitality.net, June 25, 2002.

34. Sean O'Neill, "RateGain Buys DHISCO to Expand Its Hospitality Distribution," Skift, August 2, 2018.

35. See e.g., "Age of Experience and Two New Distribution Disruptors," Reuters, November 27, 2019.

36. Bill Carroll and Judy Siguaw, "The Evolution of Electronic Distribution: Effects on Hotels and Intermediaries," *Cornell Hotel and Restaurant Administration Quarterly* 44, no. 4 (August 2003): 38–50.

37. Thomas Allen et al., "Hotel Brands vs. OTAs: Who Will Win the War?," Morgan Stanley Lodging and Internet Research, May 18, 2016.

38. Allen et al., "Hotel Brands vs. OTAs."

39. Hotel Business, "Hotels Rally around Travelweb.com Venture," November 7, 2002. An earlier European joint venture involving Accor, Forte, and Hilton, and book.com, had similarly ended in tears. Lee Winter, "Accor, Forte and Hilton Name Web Site Venture," Travel Weekly, November 9, 2000.

40. Jerry Limone, "Priceline to Acquire 100% of Travelweb," Travel Weekly, May 4, 2004.

41. Kevin May, "Hotel Giants Come Together to Launch Room Key Search Site," PhocusWire, January 11, 2012.

42. Dennis Schaal, "New Website RoomKey.com Competes with Online Travel Agencies," *USA Today*, May 30, 2012.

43. Deanna Ting, "The Disappointing Life of Hotel Booking Site Room Key," Skift, July 11, 2016.

44. Chekitan S. Dev and Peter O'Connor, "Case Study: Should a Hotelier Invest in a New Kind of Online Travel Agency?," *Harvard Business Review*, December 2015.

45. Danny King and Kate Rice, "With Orbitz Buy, Expedia to Become World's Largest OTA," Travel Weekly, February 12, 2015.

46. The ten-year compound annual growth rates for Booking, Expedia, and the S&P are 25.1 percent, 7.7 percent, and 11.2 percent, respectively.

47. In 2018, Booking had more than double the alternative accommodations revenue of Expedia. Jamie Biesiada, "In Homesharing, Booking Holdings Right up There with Airbnb," Travel Weekly, March 21, 2019.

48. Peng Liao, Fei Ye, and Xiaoli Wu, "A Comparison of the Merchant and Agency Models in the Hotel Industry," International Transactions in Operational Research, February 2017.

49. Schaal, "Oral History."

50. A number of the technology acquisitions noted earlier were integrated into BookingSuite, their B2B platform, along with a variety of internally developed products. See Linda Fox, "Booking.com Tests Marketplace Offering Third Party Technology," PhocusWire, July 19, 2018.

51. The increasing impact of an independent wholesale channel has led Booking and Expedia to both incorporate this model as well into their offerings. See César López, "Booking.com Is Now Offering Third-party Inventory with Booking.Basic," Mirai, September 7, 2018.

52. Allen et al., "Hotel Brands vs. OTAs."

53. In China, CTrip alone has a share approaching what Booking and Expedia enjoy collectively globally. Rashma Kapadia, "China's Largest Online Travel Agency Is Going Global," *Barron's*, November 1, 2019.

54. Steven Lerner, "Expedia Group, Booking Holdings Spent More than $11B on Marketing (Mostly to Google) in 2019," PhocusWire, March 6, 2020.

55. Christina Jelski, "Google's Travel Incursion Gradual, but a Threat to OTAs," Travel Weekly, September 3, 2018.

56. Luis Sanchez, "Why Expedia Blamed Google for Its Earnings Debacle," *Motley Fool*, December 1, 2019.

57. Pablo Delgado, "How Metasearch Became the Most Important Marketing Channel in Travel," PhocusWire, July 10, 2019. The list of once-hot metasearch companies that fell to earth, sometimes after having been bought or gone public, is a long one. See, most recently, Greg Kumparak, "Four Years after Being Acquired, Hipmunk Is Shutting Down," *TechCrunch*, January 14, 2020.

58. "Partnerships Key to Online Travel Search Survival," Reuters, November 24, 2005.

59. Linda Kinstler, "How TripAdvisor Changed Travel," *Guardian*, August 17, 2018.

60. Vikram Singh, "How Google Reviews Is Crushing TripAdvisor," HospitalityNet, April 10, 2019.

61. Dennis Schaal, "TripAdvisor Is on a Collision Course with Its Two Biggest Customers," Skift, March 24, 2015.

62. Tricia Duryee, "TripAdvisor Dips Lower on First Day of Trading," AllThingsD, December 21, 2011.

63. Reuters, "Hotel Booking Platform Trivago Jumps 10.7 Percent in IPO Debut," December 16, 2016.

64. Katrin Terpitz, "Just a Year After Its IPO, Trivago Caught in a Storm," *Handelsblatt*, December 18, 2017.

65. Interestingly, both TripAdvisor and Trivago were initially purchased by Expedia (in 2005 and 2012, respectively). Expedia ultimately spun off the former and took the latter public (while maintaining control). The OTAs' fascination with metasearch is reminiscent of the GDSs and airlines' initial investments in OTAs. In neither case did the imagined synergies materialize and the investments were later sold, spun, diluted, or simply marginalized within the companies.

66. Ian Cumming and Kevin O'Shaughnessy, "50 Travel Startups to Watch in 2020," Travel Massive, December 11, 2019.

67. Matthew Parsons, "TripActions Wants to Find Ways to Unite Dispersed Employees With $155 Million in New Funding," Skift, January 21, 2021.

68. Alice Hancock, "The Start-ups Trying to Shake Up Corporate Travel," *Financial Times*, July 2, 2019.

69. Dow Jones Newswires, "Expedia Bulks Up European Corporate Travel," September 7, 2004.

CHAPTER 12: IT'S NICE TO SHARE, SOMETIMES

1. Richard Waters, "Airbnb and DoorDash IPOs Leave Gig Economy Issues Unresolved," *Financial Times*, December 10, 2020.

2. The term was popularized by a 1968 paper that referenced William Forster Lloyd's 1833 example of the problem of managing shared grazing land. Garrett Hardin, "The Tragedy of the Commons," *Science* 162, no. 3859 (December 1968): 1243.

3. Giana Eckhardt and Fleura Bardhi, "The Sharing Economy Isn't about Sharing at All," *Harvard Business Review*, January 28, 2015.

4. Katie Benner, "Airbnb Raises $1 Billion More In a Funding Round," *New York Times*, March 9, 2017.

5. Joshua Franklin, "Airbnb New $1 Billion Investment Comes at Lower Valuation: Sources," Reuters, April 7, 2020.

6. Steve Kovach, "Airbnb Seeks Valuation of Up To $35 Billion in Its IPO," CNBC, December 1, 2020.

7. Noor Zainab Hussain and Joshua Franklin, "Airbnb Valuation Surges Past $100 Billion in Biggest IPO of 2020," Reuters, December 10, 2020,

8. Paul Yong, "The Rise of Home-Sharing Platforms," DBS, August 2019 (estimating Airbnb global share at 27 percent). Based on publicly disclosed or reported revenues of various ride hailing companies, it is likely that Uber is also in the 20s.

9. Not only Lyft, but companies like Yandex, Gett, and Grab all have over $1 billion in revenues. In alternative accommodations, outside of Airbnb and Booking, only Expedia has over $1 billion in revenues. What's more, even in local markets, the extent of competition from traditional incumbent alternatives—taxis and car services for Uber; hotels, short-term rentals, and real B&Bs for Airbnb—need to be considered in assessing the competitive environment. See Dan Cook, "Taxi and Limousine Services in the US," IBISWorld, July 2020.

10. SharesPost Company Report, "Airbnb: Unlocking Travel's Final Frontier," https://sharespost.com, 26. ("[W]e observed an interesting trend in the underlying data. As Airbnb was able to increase its listings in a given city, the number of guests per listing also increased.")

11. Jake Holmes, "Ride-sharing Apps: Taxis for the 21st Century," CNET, September 6, 2019.

12. Sergio Held, "How Didi Is Going Places in Latin America," *China Daily*, March 3, 2020.

13. Clayton Guse, "Ride-hailing App Juno Shuts Down in NYC, Blames New Regulations," *Daily News*, November 18, 2019.

14. Preetika Rana, "Uber, DoorDash Gig-Workers Victory in California Sets Tone for Other Fights," *Wall Street Journal*, November 4, 2020.

15. Ryan Browne, "Uber Rivals Mobilize as the Company's Future in London Becomes Uncertain," CNBC, November 27, 2019.

16. Dennis Schaal, "Booking Claims It Beats Airbnb with 5 Million Alternative Accommodations Listings," Skift, April 10, 2018.

17. See Jingjing Jiang, "More Americans Are Using Ride-hailing Apps," Pew Research Center, January 4, 2019. Based on results of the online travel agents, the pandemic has accelerated adoption of space sharing. Taylor Soper, "Expedia's Vrbo Vacation Rental Business Sees Significant Growth as Travel Giant Aims to Cut Costs," GeekWire, July 6, 2020.

18. See Harry Campbell, "Lyft and Uber Driver Survey 2019: Uber Driver Satisfaction Takes a Big Hit," Ride Share Guy, October 1, 2020. All surveys available at https://therideshareguy.com/uber-driver-survey. The percentage of drivers using more than one service was 67.7, 78.5, and 83.5 percent in the 2017, 2018, and 2019 surveys, respectively. Over the same time the percentage driving primarily for Uber fell from 75 percent to 50.8 percent.

19. See Kate Gessner, "Uber vs. Lyft: Who's Tops in the Battle of U.S. Rideshare Companies," Second Measure, May 19 2020, https://secondmeasure.com/data points/rideshare-industry-overview. The recent emergence of apps that allow riders to use multiple ride-sharing services through one screen will likely accelerate this trend. David Gutman, "New App Connects You to Multiple On-demand Ride Services Through One Screen," *Seattle Times*, August 31, 2017.

20. See Rani Molla, "Lyft Has Eaten into Uber's Market Share, New Data Suggests," *Vox*, December 12, 2018; Leslie Hook, "Uber Loses Ground in the U.S. as Rival Lyft Accelerates," *Financial Times*, June 18, 2017.

21. Uber recently doubled down on the sector through the acquisition of Postmates. Alex Sherman, "Uber Agrees to Buy Food-Delivery Service Postmates for $2.65 Billion in Stock," CNBC, July 7, 2020.

22. Josh Rivera, "Uber Expands Its Subscription Services Across the U.S., Now at $25 a Month," *USA Today*, August 19, 2020.

23. Frank DiPietro, "Why Data Is Powering Growth at Zillow Group Inc.," *Motley Fool*, Jan. 13, 2017.

24. James Cook, "Uber's Internal Charts Show How Its Driver-Rating System Actually Works," *Business Insider*, February 11, 2015.

25. Lisa Qian, "How Well Does NPS Predict Rebooking?," Medium, Dec. 10, 2015.

26. Katie Warren, "While You Were Still Using Airbnb to Spend a Weekend in a Stranger's Home, the Company Was Quietly Expanding into Boutique Hotels and Entire Airbnb-branded Buildings," *Business Insider*, December 9, 2019.

27. Schaal, "Booking Claims It Beats Airbnb."

28. Salvador Rodriguez, "Short Term Rental Market Faces Consolidation as Start-ups and Small Landlords Offload Properties," CNBC, May 30, 2020.

29. Jill Menze, "Booking Holdings Feels 'Full Impact' of Coronavirus as Gross Bookings Plunge 91% in Q2 2020," PhocusWire, August 6, 2020. See also Deirdre Bosa, "Airbnb Is Poised for a Comeback after a Brutal Spring," CNBC, June 16, 2020.

CHAPTER 13: MAD MEN, SAD MEN

1. Scott Kirsner, "Zucker Offers Insight to NBC's Future," *Variety*, February 27, 2008.

2. Variety Staff, "Rejoice! Your Digital Pennies Are Now Dimes!" *Variety*, March 19, 2009.

3. A phenomenon entertainingly detailed in Michael Wolff, *Television Is the New Television: The Unexpected Triumph of Old Media in the Digital Age* (New York: Portfolio, 2015).

4. Kara Swisher and Peter Kafka, "NBCUniversal Poised to Make Big Investments in *BuzzFeed* and Vox Media," Recode, June 30, 2015; Keach Hagey, "Disney Invests Another $200 Million in Vice Media," December 8, 2015; Todd Spangler, "Turner Leads $15 Million Round in Mashable," *Variety*, March 11, 2016.

5. Peter Kafka, "Disney Put More Than $400 Million into Vice Media. Now It Says That Investment Is Worthless," Recode, May 8, 2019.

6. PwC, "Internet Advertising Revenue Report," IAB, May 2020.

7. Kurt Wagner, "Digital Advertising in the US Is Finally Bigger Than Print and Television," Recode, February 20, 2019.

8. Peter Kafka, "Google and Facebook Are Booming. Is the Rest of the Digital Ad Business Sinking?," Recode, November 2, 2016.

9. Ashley Rodriguez, "Netflix Gave a Detailed Presentation of Why It Won't Sell Advertising. But It's Still Working with Brands In Other Ways," *Business Insider*, January 22, 2020. Netflix has, however, shown a consistent willingness to change direction quickly when it is financially or strategically compelling. See

Kelsey Sutton, "Media Buyers to Netflix: Take Our Money!," *Adweek*, February 4, 2020.

10. Aaron Holmes, "This Is How Facebook Learns What You Buy at Physical Stores in Order to Show You Relevant Ads—and How to Opt Out," *Business Insider*, December 11, 2019.

11. Jasmine Enberg, "Global Digital Ad Spending 2019," eMarketer, March 28, 2019.

12. Megan Graham, "The Google-Facebook Ad Duopoly Is Facing a Bigger Challenge from the Trio of Snap, Pinterest, and Amazon," CNBC, November 2, 2019.

13. Keach Hagey and Suzanne Vranica, "How Covid-19 Supercharged the Advertising 'Triopoly' of Google, Facebook, and Amazon," *Wall Street Journal*, March 19, 2021.

14. Sara Morrison and Rani Molla, "Google Chrome's Cookie Ban Is Good News for Google—and Maybe Your Privacy," Recode, January 16, 2020.

15. "Big Tech Will Have to Share Data Under EU Proposals," *Financial Times*, February 19, 2020.

16. Jason Rowley, "Advertising Giants Leave Little Room for Adtech Startups, and VCs Are Noticing," *TechCrunch*, June 13, 2017.

17. See Clare Ballentine, "Google-Facebook Dominance Hurts Ad Tech Firms, Speeding Consolidation," *New York Times*, August 12, 2018; Madhumita Murgia, "Adtech Funding Drops in Face of Facebook-Google Duopoly," *Financial Times*, January 3, 2017 (both citing CB Insights research).

18. Fred Wilson, "What Is Going to Happen in 2017?," AVC.com, January 1, 2017.

19. Adtech funding has experienced a 10 percent negative five-year compound annual growth rate while the corresponding martech decline was only 3.5 percent. Arman Tabatabai, "Where Top VCs Are Investing in Adtech and Martech," *TechCrunch*, January 22, 2020.

20. Bradley Johnson, "State of the Agency World: Digital Rules, Growth Slows, Consultancies Surge," *Ad Age*, April 30, 2018.

21. Eric Pfanner, "WPP Acquires AKQA to Beef Up Digital Marketing," *New York Times*, June 20, 2012.

22. John Battelle, *The Search*, 167.

23. See Duncan Watts, *Everything Is Obvious: How Common Sense Fails Us* (New York: Crown, 2011), 54–107, 118–22. Making the point that successful viral campaigns seem "obvious" after the fact but not only are they impossible to predict in advance, the attributed cause is often an example of the "post-hoc fallacy."

24. Jennifer Small, "Adtech M&A Deals Surge in 2019 but Holding Companies Hit the Brakes," *Campaign*, January 15, 2020.

25. *Ad Age*, Agency Report 2018.

26. David Gutting, "How to Rearm Creative Industry to Keep Consultants at Bay," *Fast Company*, September 17, 2019.

27. Megan Graham, "Accenture Just Bought an Indie Ad Agency, as Boardrooms Get Serious about Creative Marketing," CNBC, April 5, 2019.

28. Patience Haggin, "Big Ad Agencies Hope to Gain Edge by Buying Data Companies," *Wall Street Journal*, June 17, 2019.

29. This deal followed the failed combination of Publicis with Omnicom and was described by WPP's CEO as "the behavior of a jilted lover." Lara O'Reilly, "Publicis Groupe is Acquiring Sapient for $3.7 billion," *Business Insider*, November 3, 2014. This was not an entirely new strategic thrust at Publicis, however, as it had spent almost $2 billion before 2010 to purchase digital agencies Digitas and Razorfish. Brian Morrisey, "Publicis to Acquire Razorfish," *Adweek*, August 10, 2009.

30. Nick Kostov, "Publicis Books Heavy Write Down Sending Shares Lower," *Wall Street Journal*, February 9, 2017.

31. Megan Graham, "Publicis $4.4 Billion Acquisition Leaves Analysts Skeptical," CNBC, April 15, 2019.

32. Alexandra Bruell, "Amid Ad-Industry M&A, Omnicom Says It Isn't Looking for Big Deals," *Wall Street Journal*, April 16, 2019.

33. WPP, "WPP Presents Strategy for Growth," press release, December 11, 2018. See also WPP Analyst Presentation, "WPP Accelerating Growth Capital Markets Day," December 17, 2020. https://www.wpp.com/investors/calendar-and-events/investor-events-2020/accelerating-growth-investors-and-analysts-presentation.

34. Ronan Shields, "How Long Can the Trade Desk Ride Its Current Wave of Success?," *Adweek*, August 15, 2018.

35. The other major non-independent DSP aside from Google Marketing Platform (encompassing the old DoubleClick) is Amazon Advertising Platform. Erica Sweeney, "Amazon's DSP Jumps Ahead of Google's as Most Used by Advertisers, Study Says," *Marketing Dive*, November 6, 2018.

36. Daniel Salmon, "Digital Marketing Hub v4.1," Exhibit 55, BMO Capital Markets, June 2019.

37. Although Google and Amazon have their own directly competing DSPs, Facebook's Ad Manager only sells its own inventory. Isua Botman, "Is Facebook's Ad Manager a DSP?," The Drum, April 18, 2017.

38. Megan Graham, "AdTech Company Magnite Is Buying SpotX In Play to Deepen Its Strength in Streaming Ads," CNBC, February 5, 2021.

39. Megan Graham, "The Pandemic-fueled Boom in TV Streaming Has Paid Off in a Big Way for Ad Tech Firm The Trade Desk," CNBC, July 17, 2020.

40. The ability of Google and the other massive platforms to potentially impede independents like LiveRamp and TTD still remains. Kate Kaye, "'They Won't Enable Our Identifier': Identity Tech Providers Try to Make Sense of Google's Plan Not to Support Alternate Identifiers," *Digiday*, March 4, 2021. And advertising agencies see it in their interest to continue to support the efforts of the

independents. Alexandra Bruell, "Publicis Groupe Signs On to Use Trade Desk's Alternative to Cookies," *Wall Street Journal*, April 8, 2021.

CHAPTER 14: BIG DATA AND ARTIFICIAL INTELLIGENCE

1. Gary Marcus and Ernest Davis, *Rebooting AI: Building Artificial Intelligence We Can Trust* (New York: Pantheon Books, 2019), 3.
2. Marcus and Davis, *Rebooting AI*, 18–25.
3. Tim Cross, "An Understanding of AI's Limitations Is Starting to Sink In" *The Economist Technology Quarterly*, June 13, 2020.
4. See Judea Pearl and Dana MacKenzie, *The Book of Why: The New Science of Cause and Effect* (New York: Basic Books, 2018).
5. Christopher J. Kelly et al., "Key Challenges For Delivering Clinical Impact With Artificial Intelligence," *BMC Med* 17, no. 195 (2019). The most recent corporate acknowledgment of the limitations of AI in the field of health was the decision by IBM to explore the sale of its once vaunted Watson Health initiative. After spending at least $4 billion on acquisitions to support what had been described as a "bet the ranch" effort, the business never gained real traction and consistently lost key executives and money. Daniel Hernandez and Asa Fitch, "IBM's Retreat from Watson Highlights Broader AI Struggles in Health," *Wall Street Journal*, February 20, 2021.
6. Neal Boudette, "Despite High Hopes, Self-Driving Cars Are 'Way in the Future,'" *New York Times*, July 17, 2019.
7. Iansiti and Lakhani, *Competing in the Age of AI*, 161.
8. Iansiti and Lakhani, *Competing in the Age of AI*, 96.
9. Iansiti and Lakhani, *Competing in the Age of AI*, 206.
10. Iansiti and Lakhani *Competing in the Age of AI*, 174.
11. Heath Terry, Debra Schwartz, Perry Gold, and Tina Sun, "Initiation: Lending-Club Corp., Premium Marketplace with Premium Valuation," Goldman Sachs Equity Research, January 20, 2015.
12. Terry et al., "Initiation: LendingClub Corp."
13. Peter Rudegeair, "LendingClub CEO Fired Over Faulty Loans," *Wall Street Journal*, May 9, 2016.
14. See Peter Tufano, Howell Jackson, and Andrea Ryan, "Lending Club," Harvard Business School Case 9-210-052, December 17, 2010. Earlier competitor Prosper's FICO cutoff was 300.
15. Iansiti and Lakhani, *Competing in the Age of AI*, 101.
16. Iansiti and Lakhani, *Competing in the Age of AI*, 207.
17. Iansiti and Lakhani, *Competing in the Age of AI*, 99–123.
18. Iansiti and Lakhani, *Competing in the Age of AI*, 104.
19. Iansiti and Lakhani, *Competing in the Age of AI*, 101. To the extent that Microsoft's turnaround in the last decade is connected to the growth of Azure, there is a legitimate question about whether this has been driven more by data and AI or the pivot to embrace open-source technology. When Azure started, it was all

about Windows, but Linux was really the dominant OS for public cloud. It was only after Nadella decided to deprioritize Windows that Azure took off and Microsoft's rebirth really commenced.

20. Iansiti and Lakhani, *Competing in the Age of AI*, 205.
21. Iansiti and Lakhani, *Competing in the Age of AI*, 204–11.
22. Iansiti and Lakhani, *Competing in the Age of AI*, 206.
23. The *Economist*, "Software's Jolly Iconoclast," June 5, 2003.
24. See David Yoffie and Alison Wagonfeld, "Oracle vs. Salesforce.com," Harvard Business School Case 9-705-440, September 21, 2006.
25. Jordan Novet, "Marc Benioff's Salesforce Has Eclipsed Larry Ellison's Oracle in Market Cap," CNBC, July 10, 2020.
26. Ari Levy, "Salesforce Acquires Slack for Over $27 Billion, Marking Cloud Software Vendor's Largest Deal Ever," CNBC, December 1, 2020.
27. Marcus and Davis, *Rebooting AI*, 13–18.
28. Ann Bednarz, "SAP to Maintain ERP Dominance in 2005, AMR Says," *Network World*, June 15, 2005.
29. Theresa Tucker, interview with the author, August 20, 2020.
30. Natasha Lomas, "Oracle and Salesforce Hit with GDPR Class Action Lawsuits Over Cookie Tracking Consent," *TechCrunch*, August 14, 2020.
31. PR Newswire, "BlackLine Releases Oracle ERP Connector," October 30, 2018.
32. PR Newswire, "BlackLine Announces Reseller Agreement with SAP," November 1, 2018.
33. Pearl and MacKenzie, *The Book of Why*, 352.

EPILOGUE: START-UP FEVER

1. Iansiti and Lakhani, *Competing in the Age of AI*, 219.
2. Ramana Nanda, Sampsa Samila, and Olav Sorenson, "The Persistence Effect of Initial Success: Evidence from Venture Capital," *Journal of Financial Economics* 13, no. 1 (July 2020): 231.
3. CB Insights, "The Top 5 VC Bets of All Time," Medium, March 21, 2018.
4. According to Sequoia's website, this was the firm's second investment; Atari was the first; https://www.sequoiacap.com/companies/apple.
5. Dan Primack, "Exclusive: Is This the Best-performing VC Fund Ever?," *Fortune*, January 8, 2015.
6. Todd Haselton, "Chris Sacca Is Retiring from Venture Capital and 'Shark Tank,'" CNBC, April 26, 2017.
7. "US Venture Capital Investment Surpasses $130 Billion in 2019 for Second Consecutive Year," PR Newswire, January 14, 2020 (announcing publication of PitchBook–NVCA Venture Monitor).
8. Jonathan A. Knee, "Must I Bank?," *Wall Street Journal*, April 23, 2008.
9. Stanford Graduate School of Business 2020 MBA Employment Report; see also Harvard Business School Recruiting, Entrepreneurship, Data and Statistics at https://www.hbs.edu/recruiting/data/Pages/entrepreneurship.aspx.

10. Robert D. Atkinson and Michael Lind, *Big Is Beautiful: Debunking the Myth of Small Business* (Cambridge, MA: MIT Press, 2018), 88, citing research in Scott A. Shane, *The Illusions of Entrepreneurship: The Costly Myths That Entrepreneurs, Investors, and Policy Makers Live By* (New Haven, CT: Yale University Press, 2010).

11. Atkinson and Lind, *Big Is Beautiful,* 81.

12. Meritor Savings Bank v. Vinson, 477 US 57 (1986).

13. Bostock v. Clayton County, 590 US TK (2020).

14. Atkinson and Lind, *Big Is Beautiful,* 15.

ACKNOWLEDGMENTS

1. Jonathan A. Knee, "All Platforms Are Not Equal: Why Airbnb Will Always Be a Better Business Than Uber," *MIT Sloan Management Review* 54, no. 2 (winter 2018). Chapter 12 draws extensively on this work.

2. Jonathan A. Knee, Bruce C. Greenwald, and Ava Seave, *The Curse of the Mogul: What's Wrong with the World's Leading Media Companies* (New York: Portfolio, 2009).

3. Bruce Greenwald and Judd Kahn, *Competition Demystified: A Radically Simplified Approach to Business Strategy* (New York: Portfolio, 2005).

INDEX

Page numbers in *italics* refer to figures.

Abacus International, 333n14
Abrams, J. J., 138
Accenture, 260
acquisitions, 76, 95
 by Amazon, 51, 92–93, 97–98, 178
 by Expedia, 226, 228, 247
 by FAANG companies, xx
 by Facebook, 51, 59, 65, 73, 76–78, 290
 by Google, 51, 52, 160, 170, 255
 by marketplace businesses, 186
Active Hotels, 218–19, 229
Acxiom, 264
Adobe, 256, 264, 276
advertising, 11, 43, 49–50, 176, 250–65,
 309n21
 adtech, 255–56, 260, 262–65, 342n19
 agencies, 256–60, 343n40
 Amazon and, 92, 176, 343n35
 boom and bust of digital advertising,
 251–55
 branding and, 258, *259*, 262
 classified, *see* classified advertising
 data and, 252–53
 Etsy and, 185
 Facebook and, 73, 176, 252–54
 Google and, 159–61, 163–65, 176, 180,
 231, 252–54, 260, 327n12
 marketing technology (martech), 256, 260,
 263–64, 342n19
 newspaper, 98
 streaming services and, 148

Aftcra, 189
Agoda, 219
AI, *see* artificial intelligence
AIG, 282
Airbnb, xx, 199, 237–43, 245, 247–48, 288,
 340n9
airlines, 48–49, 199–201
 American Airlines, 200, 201, 204
 consolidation of, 210, 222
 direct connection with travel agents,
 210–13
 direct connection with travelers, 203–4
 global distribution systems (GDS) and,
 see global distribution systems
 Lufthansa, 210–11
 travel agents' seat sales on, vs. hotel
 reservations, 220–26
 see also travel sector
Aldi, 100
Alibaba, 56, 87, 101, 102
Alphabet, 14, 56, 57, 59–60, 159, 167–70
 R&D spending of, *64*
 see also Google
Amadeus, 201, 207, *208*, 209, 211, 334n21
Amazon, xii, xv, xx, xxi, 7–9, 13, 14, 45, 55,
 59, 63, 83–105, 175, 177–81, 186–90,
 195–96, 217, 272, 289
 acquisitions by, 51, 92–93, 97–98, 178
 advertising and, 92, 176, 343n35
 antitrust probe of, 91–92
 art market and, 186, 330n31

Amazon (*cont.*)
  Auctions, 311n2
  auto parts market and, 190–94, 230
  competitive advantages of, *61*, 87–103
  content creation and, 91, 139
  COVID-19 pandemic and, 89, 94, 95, 100
  culture of, 93–94
  customer data and, 91–92
  customer satisfaction as focus of, 91
  customer services and, 198
  data from other companies used by, 180,
    329n13
  Destinations, 199
  eBay and, 190, 191, 194–95, *195*
  Echo, 86
  Etsy and, 189
  in FAANG companies grouping, *see*
    FAANG companies
  financial services initiatives of, 198
  fixed costs of, 88, 89, 95
  Fresh, 97–98
  fulfillment and distribution infrastructure
    of, 88–89, 98, 99
  grocery business of, 96–98
  growth of, 95–103
  Handmade, 188–89
  health care initiatives of, 198–99, 332n4
  history of, 83–87
  Home Services, 198, 199
  in India, 101–3
  indomitability of, 177, 179–80
  international operations of, 100–103
  IPO of, 301n19
  Kindle, 86
  leadership principles of, 85
  Local, 333n7
  Luxury Stores, 186–87
  Marketplace, 84–85, 87, 180, 186,
    194, 311n2
  network effects and, 84, 87
  new businesses entered by, 86
  1-click ordering of, 90, 313n30
  percentage of e-commerce sales, 177
  Pharmacy, 332n4
  Prime, 85–86, 89–91, 101, 139, 140, 157,
    184, 193–95, 198, 313n35
  Prime Video, 91, 125, 129, 137,
    139–40, *151*
  product search and, 65, 161, 253, 262
  profitability benchmarking vs. S&P 500, *59*
  R&D spending of, 63, *64*, 88, 307n11

  sales taxes and, 51
  share price of, 94–95
  shipping costs and speed and, 85,
    86, 89, 90
  Sotheby's and, 183, 186
  third-party services and, 84
  Vehicles, 99
  Wallet, 198
  Web Services (AWS), 59, 63, 86–88, 94,
    103, 124, 169, 176, 198, 272, 301n19,
    307n11, 312n15, 312n18, 312n20
  Whole Foods acquired by, 97–98
Ambani, Mukesh, 103
American Airlines, 200, 201, 204
American Customer Satisfaction Index, 136
American Express, 4, 234
Anand, Bharat, 25–26
Ancestry.com, 30–31, 37, 271
Android, 114–17, 119, 120, 125, 126, 318n21,
    318n34
Angie's List, 198
Aniston, Jennifer, 149
antiques, 181–83, 186
antitrust law, 51, 77, 93, 160, 253–54, 313n41
  Amazon and, 91–92
  Facebook and, 77, 160
  Google and, 124, 160, 164, 169–70,
    327n13
  Microsoft and, 170
  privacy and, 255
AOL, 75–76
Apple, xv, xx, 14, 55, 56, 63, 86, 89, 106–28,
    272, 290, 317n9, 317n11, 318n27
  App Store, 113–17, *118*, 126, 318n34
  as brand, 107–8, 110, 120, 125–27
  car market and, 121–22
  competitive advantages of, *61*, 107–8, 110
  COVID-19 pandemic and, 122
  customer loyalty to, 119–20
  economics of, 110–20
  in FAANG companies grouping, *see*
    FAANG companies
  FaceTime, 114
  founding of, 106, 316n1
  Google and, 169
  iCloud, 122, 124, 126
  iMessage, 114
  iPad, 112–14, 120, 122
  iPhone, 106, 111–17, 119, *119*, 120, 122,
    125, 126, 316n3
  iPod, 111–14, 120, 125, 126, 317n14

iTunes, 111, 112, 122–23, 125–26,
    317nn14–15
  Jobs and, *see* Jobs, Steve
  Maps, 124
  Microsoft compatibility and, 111, 116,
    317n12, 318n23
  MobileMe, 123–24
  Music, 124–26
  network effects and, 113, 114, 120
  News Service, 42, *42*
  Ping, 124, 317n14
  profitability benchmarking vs. S&P 500, *59*
  R&D spending of, *64*
  refusal to license operating system, 112
  retail stores of, 112
  services of, 122–27
  TV+, 125, 129, 137, 140
Applied Data Finance, 271
art, 186, 330n31
artificial intelligence (AI), xiv, xxi, 35, 148,
    154, 253, 266–68, 270–73, 277, 280,
    283, 287–89, 294, 344n5
  Netflix and, 144
  specialization and, 281, 284
AT&T, xiii, 137, 169, 282, 322n35
Atari, 115
auction houses, 187, 188, 190
AuctionWeb, 191
automotive sector, 13, 98–99, 109,
    178–79, 273
  autonomous vehicles, 267
  brands in, 107–8
  dealerships, 277–78
  electric cars, 121–22
  parts, 190–96, 230
AutoZone, 192, 193
Azure cloud services, 169, 272, 312n20,
    344n19

Baidu, 64, 161
barriers to entry, 17–21, 58, 289
  see also competitive advantages
Bebo, *67*, 68
Benioff, Marc, 275, 276
Berkshire Hathaway, 49
Berlanti, Greg, 138
Best, 276
Best Buy, 89
Bewkes, Jeff, xiii, 131
Bezos, Jeff, xvi, 41, 83–84, 86, 87, 91–94,
    100, 102, 177

Biden administration, 51, 313n41
big data, *see* data
Bing, 35, 161, 165
Birdbox, 149, 325n82
BlackLine, 281–84, 289
Blockbuster, 153
Bloomberg, 221
Boeing, 282
Booking, xx, 180, 199, 208, 215,
    218–20, 224–25, 230–32, 239,
    241, 243, 247, 248, 270,
    289, 338n51
  Expedia vs., 226–30, *227*
books, 133–35, 152
book value, 58
Borders, xii
brands, 37, 233
  advertising and, 258, *259*, 262
  Apple, 107–8, 110, 120, 125–27
  automotive, 107–8
  building, compared with movie
    making, 108–9
  industry structure and, 108–10
  luxury, 108, 125, 126
  Trivago and, 233
break-even economics, xx, 28, *31*, 37
Brin, Sergei, 166
Bryer, Colin, and Carr, Bill, *Working
    Backwards*, 85, 91, 93–94, 312n18
BTIG, 179–81
Buffett, Warren, 49, 58, 199–200
Bullock, Sandra, 149
Business of Platforms, The (Cusumano,
    Gawker, and Yoffie), 14
business schools, 291–92
BusinessWeek, 115
Buuteeq, 219
BuzzFeed, 206

Cambridge Analytica, 79
Careerbuilder, 156
Carr, Bill, and Bryar, Colin, *Working
    Backwards*, 85, 91, 93–94, 312n18
Carr, David, 147
Casper, 8, 9
Cassidy, John, 168
Cats, 149
CBS All Access, 137, 146
CEOs, xvi
chat, 69
Chewy, 8–9, 93, 178, 301n17

China, 64, 65, 101–3, 161, 210, 239, 242,
302n27, 334n26
Christies, 190
Chrome, 254
Circuit City, xii
Civil Rights Act, 293
classified advertising, 98, 155–56, 181
employment, 155–56
cloud computing and storage services, 87, 264,
272, 276, 277, 281, 312n20
Amazon Web Services (AWS), 59, 63,
86–88, 94, 103, 124, 169, 176, 198,
272, 301n19, 307n11, 312n15, 312n18,
312n20
Google, 159, 168, 169
iCloud, 122, 124, 126
Microsoft Azure, 169, 272, 312n20, 344n19
Cognizant, 260
Comcast, 131, 132, 139
Peacock, 137, 139, 140, *151*
Comdex, 75
Commodore, 110–11
Compaq, 121
Competing in the Age of AI (Iansiti and
Lakhani), 267–68, 272–74
competitive advantages, 16, 58, 103, 294
adjacencies and, 167
of Amazon, *61*, 87–103
analog, sources of, *36*
of Apple, 107–8, 110
barriers to entry, 17–21, 58, 289
core categories of, 37
demand-side, *see* demand-side scale and
advantages
digital, sources of, 33–54, *36*, *38*
of FAANG companies, *61*
of Google, *61*, 160–61, 167
government as source of, 48–52
importance of understanding, 17–22
of Netflix, *61*, 142–51
supply-side, *see* supply-side scale and
advantages
template for assessing, *238*
of Turnitin, 279
complexity, 190, 220–22, 288
Comscore, 150
Concur, 234
content
aggregation and distribution of, 132–37,
151–52, 154–55
as king, 129–30, 132–34, 166

content creation, 139, 151–52, 154, 327n8
Amazon and, 91, 139
Apple and, 125, 126
Netflix and, xx, 131, 140–42, 147
rights and, 323n45
Content Trap, The (Anand), 26
Cook, Tim, 121, 122, 124
cookies, 254
Costco, 85, 89, 91, 312n9
COVID-19 pandemic, 8, 45, 57, 95, 248,
253, 257
Airbnb and, 238
Amazon and, 89, 94, 95, 100
Apple and, 122
auction houses and, 188
Etsy and, 182
food delivery and, 246
grocery shopping and, 97
Netflix and, 136, 150
ride-hailing activity and, 238, 245
travel industry and, 199, 200, 207,
226, 234
Craigslist, 13
Cramer, James, 55, 56
credit cards, 4–6, 212–13
Visa, 5, 212–13, 335n39
Credit Karma, 270
CRM (customer relationship management),
276, 279, 281
Curse of the Mogul, The (Knee, Greenwald,
and Seave), 95, 166
customer captivity, 34, 37, 89–90, 110, 144,
233, 278, 288, 294
Apple and, 120
in digital realm, 78
Etsy and, 185
in FAANG competitive advantages, *61*
Facebook and, 70–72
Google and, 161, 164–65
habit in, 34, 70, 78, 161
key risk to, 74
movies and television and, 133
Netflix and, 135, 150, 151
search costs in, 34, 70, 78, 161, 288
sharing economy and, 243–46
switching costs in, 34, 70, 78,
161, 288
travel agents and, 210
customer data, *see* data
customer relationship management (CRM),
276, 279, 281

Daily News, 40
data, xiv, 35–37, 74, 78, 165–66, 246, 258,
    266–68, 270, 271, 279, 287–89
    advertising and, 252–53
    Amazon and, 91–92
    Facebook and, 72–74, 254
    first-party, 254, 261
    Google and, 159–61, 163, 165–66, 254
    Netflix and, 144–46, 148–50, 154, 253, 258
    privacy and, 254–55
    third-party, 254, 261
dating applications, 29–30
Davis, Ernest, 266–67
dealer management systems (DMS), 277–78
Deloitte, 260
demand, 37
demand-side platforms (DSPs), 263, 343n35
demand-side scale and advantages, 25–28, *26*,
    30, 33, 35, 52–53, *53*
    in FAANG companies, *61*
    Facebook and, 72, 73
    Google and, 164–65
    linkage of supply-side advantages to, 165
    online travel agencies and, 206
    SaaS and, 277
Dentsu, 261
Deutsche Bank, 143
Diapers.com, 92, 178
dice.com, 156
Didi, 239, 242
Digital Commerce 360, 179
Diners Club, 4
Disney and Disney+, 126, 132, 137–42, *151*,
    157, 322n35, 326n91
diversification, 59–60
DMS (dealer management systems), 277–78
Dolittle, 149
dot-com boom, xvii–xviii, 8, 15, 16
DoubleClick, 160, 260, 343n35
DuckDuckGo, 161, 165
Dumb Pipe Paradox, 136

Early Warning, 30
eBay, 9, 13, 177, 182, 183, 187, 189, 194–95
    Amazon and, 190, 191, 194–95, *195*
    auto parts market and, 190, 191, 193, 194
EBITDA, 59, 269
ECNs (Electronic Communications
    Networks), 34, 50
e-commerce, xx, 7–9, 90, 103, 175, 177–97
    Amazon's percentage of, 177

auto parts, 190–96
    eBay, *see* eBay
    failures of, 301n9
    Etsy, xxi, 181–86, 189, 190, 288, 330n27
    1stDibs, 181–88, 190
    IPOs in, 8–9, *10*, 301n19
    penetration by sector, *178*
    scale and, 182–84
    see also Amazon
economic moats, 58
Economist, 169, 220
education, 50
    anti-plagiarism software, 279
efficiency, 19
Egencia, 234
Eisner, Michael, 141
Ellison, Larry, 106–7, 125, 276
employment classifieds, 155–56
entrepreneurs, 292–93
Epsilon, 261
ERP (enterprise resource planning), 281–83
    SAP, 280, 282–84
Etsy, xxi, 181–86, 189, 190, 288, 330n27
European Union, 49
Excel, 112, 282
Expedia, xx, 56, 180, 199, 204, 208, 218, 219,
    224–26, 231, 232, 234, 241, 242, 248,
    270, 338n51, 339n65, 340n9
    acquisitions of, 226, 228, 247
    Booking vs., 226–30, *227*

FAANG companies, xix–xx, xxi, 14, 15,
    55–65, *56*, 106, 129, 173–76, 293,
    294, 306n18
    acquisitions by, xx
    alternative formulations of, 56
    competitive advantages of, *61*
    diversification of, 59–60
    emails of top executives at, 62
    envy of, in Platform Delusion, 60–61
    profitability of, 58–59, *59*
    R&D spending of, 63–64, *64*, 73
    S&P index and, 56, *57*, *59*
    see also Amazon; Apple; Facebook; Google;
        Netflix
Facebook, xv, xix, xx, 7, 45, 49, 55, 56, 60,
    62–65, 66–82, 129, 144, 179, 289,
    320n1, 327n8
    acquisitions by, 51, 59, 65, 73,
        76–78, 290
    advertising and, 73, 176, 252–54

Facebook (*cont.*)
  antitrust law and, 77, 160
  Chat, 69
  competitive advantages of, *61*
  continuous improvement at, 74, 80
  culture of, 73, 74, 79
  customer data on, 72–74, 254
  deactivating and deleting accounts on, 72
  demand-side advantages of, 72, 73
  in FAANG companies grouping, *see*
        FAANG companies
  fake news and other subversive forces on,
        79, 80
  Farmville, 70
  focus as characteristic of, 73–74
  functionality additions to, *71*, 72–74
  Instagram, xx, 59, 65, 72, 76, 291, 310n35
  IPO of, 309n20
  launch date and peak usage of, *67*
  mission statement of, 308n2
  monthly active users on, *68*
  Netflix and, 144
  network effects and, 12, 60, 66, 72,
        73, 75–81
  operating efficiency of, 73, 74, 79
  profitability benchmarking vs. S&P 500, *59*
  R&D spending of, 63–64, *64*, 73
  scandals and loss of trust in, 79–80
  supply-side advantages of, 72–73
  third-party apps and, 70, 72
  timing of, 69, 70
  WhatsApp, xx, 59, 65, 72, 76–78, 290,
        291, 310n34
Farmville, 70
Federal Trade Commission (FTC), 52, 160,
        255, 313n41
FedEx, 193
Ferguson, Niall, 66
film industry, *see* movies
Financial Times, 40, 41, *42*, 236
Fincher, David, 147
1stDibs, 181–88, 190
first-mover advantage, 37, 69, 312n20
  of Netflix, 153
  scale and, 115–16, 153
Fitbit, 170, 255
"five forces" framework for assessing
        companies, 16–17
fixed costs, 24–28, *26*, *28*, 34, 35, 37, 75
  of Amazon, 88, 89, 95
  in FAANG competitive advantages, *61*

of Google, 161, 162
of movie production vs. aggregation, 133
music and, 134
R&D, *see* R&D spending
SaaS and, 279
specialization and, 64
flash sales, 8
Flipkart, 102
FlipKey, 242–43
focus, 73–74
Fogel, Glenn, 219
Food Lion, 97
Force.com, 281
Fortune, 123
Fox Broadcasting Company, 138, 322n35
FreshDirect, 97, 315n65
Freud, Sigmund, 61
Friendster, *67*, 68, 75
FTC (Federal Trade Commission), 52, 160,
        255, 313n41

Galileo, 201
Game of Thrones, 147
Gates, Bill, 129, 320n2
Gawande, Atul, 199
GDPR (General Data Protection Regulation),
        49–50
General Atlantic, 218
General Electric, 79
GetThere, 334n19
Gilt Groupe, 8
global distribution systems (GDS), 201–5,
        207–13, 220, 222–24, 231, 334n26,
        339n65
  Amadeus, 201, 207, *208*, 209, 211, 334n21
Goldman Sachs, xvii, 56, 269–70
Google, xv, 7, 8, 14, 45, 49, 55–57, 62–65, 68,
        80, 86, 87, 129, 159–71, 179, 217, 270,
        273, 289, 293, 343n40
  acquisitions by, 51, 52, 160, 170, 255
  advertising and, 159–61, 163–65, 176, 180,
        231, 252–54, 260, 327n12
  Alphabet parent company of, *see* Alphabet
  Android, 114–17, 119, 120, 125, 126,
        318n21, 318n34
  antitrust law and, 124, 160, 164, 169–70,
        327n13
  App Engine, 312n20
  Apple and, 169
  autocomplete feature of, 162–63
  Chrome, 254

Cloud, 159, 168, 169
competitive advantages of, *61*, 160–61, 167
customer captivity and, 161, 164–65
data and, 159–61, 163, 165–66, 254
data centers of, 162
demand-side advantages and, 164–65
DoubleClick, 160, 260, 343n35
in FAANG companies grouping, *see*
   FAANG companies
financial discipline of, 168–70
financial transparency of, 167, 168
fixed costs of, 161, 162
Google+, 67
"moon shot" projects of, 159, 168–70
mystique around business strategies of, 166
network effects and, 160–63, 170
online travel agencies and, 205–7
Orkut, *67*, 68, *68*
Play, 114, 115, 117, *118*
profitability benchmarking vs. S&P 500, *59*
R&D spending of, 63, *64*, 161–62, 166
restructuring of, 167–68
scale and, 161–63
search engine of, 35, 124, 159, 161–67,
   205–6, 231, 253, 326n4, 327n12
search engine marketing and optimization
   and, 256
70/20/10 rule at, 166–67, 327n17
Shopping, 196
supply-side advantages and, 161–62,
   165–71
travel sector and, 180, 231, 233, 270
YouTube, 65, 153, 159, 163, 164, 168,
   308n4, 320n1, 326n8
government as a source of competitive
   advantage, 48–52
government regulation, xviii, xx, 49–52, 77,
   78, 80, 81, 92, 102, 160, 164, 180,
   242, 254, 255, 282, 290
   see also antitrust law
Greenwald, Bruce, 120
groceries, 96–98, 103
Groupon, 8
growth, 20
   of Amazon, 95–103
   value and, 20, 95
Guardian, 232

habit, in customer captivity, 34, 70, 78, 161
Hart-Scott-Rodino (HSR) Antitrust
   Improvements Act, 52

Harvard Business Review, 226
Harvard Business School, 292
Hastings, Reed, xvi, 131, 135, 137, 142,
   144, 149
Haven Healthcare, 199
HBO, xiii, 131, 137, 140, 147, *151*
health care, 198–99, 267, 344n5
   Amazon and, 198–99, 332n4
Hedges & Company, 191
Herald Tribune, 40
Heroku, 281
Hewlett Packard, 110, 121
hi5, *67*, *68*
Hill, Harold, xvii
Hobbes, Thomas, 157
HomeAway, 226, 228, 241, 242, 247
Home Depot, 89
HomeGrocer, 96
Hotel Ninjas, 219
hotels, 222–23
   travel agents' reservations for, vs. airline seat
      sales, 220–26
Hotels.com, 218
Hotwire, 218
House of Cards, 131, 136, 147, 258, 323n45
Houseparty, 77, 93
Huawei, 119, *119*
HubSpot, 264
Huffington Post, 206
Hulu, 137, 139, 140, 148, *151*, 322n35

IAC Travel, 218
Iansiti, Marco, 267–68, 271–74,
   277, 280
IBM, xi, 63, 87, 110, 112, 114–15, 201, 260,
   317n9, 318n27
   Watson Health initiative of, 344n5
Icahn, Carl, 217
iCloud, 122, 124, 126
iMessage, 114
Indeed, 156
India, 101–3
Industrial Revolution, 267, 271–72
Infor, 282
Instacart, 97
Instagram, xx, 59, 65, 72, 76,
   291, 310n35
insurance companies, 30
Insurance Services Office (ISO), 30
Intel, 63, 111, 121
International Herald Tribune, 40

international operations, 99–101
    of Amazon, 100–103
    multi-local operations vs., 99
    of Walmart, 100–102
internet, xv–xvi, xx, 106, 200, 250
    Apple services for, 123
    customer captivity and, 78
    first boom in, xvii–xviii, 8, 15, 16
    scale and, 24–32
    search engines on, *see* search
    Telecommunications Act and, 51
Internet Retailer, 179
Internet Travel Network, 334n19
Interpublic, 261, 264
investment banks, xviii, 291, 292, 300n16
iPad, 112–14, 120, 122
iPhone, 106, 111–17, 119, *119*, 120, 122, 125,
    126, 316n3
iPod, 111–14, 120, 125, 126, 317n14
IPOs, 15–16
    e-commerce, 8–9, *10*, 301n19
Isaacson, Walter, 110, 114, 121
ITA Software, 206, 334n22
iTunes, 111, 112, 122–23, 125–26,
    317nn14–15
Ive, Jony, 121

Japan, 64, 65, 327n10
Jassy, Andy, 94
JD.com, 102
Jet.com, 314n47
Jio Platforms, 103
Jobs, Steve, xvi, 106–7, 110–11, 113, 116–17,
    120–21, 123–24, 316n1, 316n3,
    317nn12–13, 318n23
JP Morgan, 199
Jumia, 8
Justice Department, 51, 77, 124, 164, 169–70,
    213, 334n22
    see also antitrust law

Kalanick, Travis, 15
Kantar, 262
Kayak, 204, 219
Khan, Lina, 313n41
Khosrowshahi, Dara, 229
Kickstarter, 236
King, David, 225
Kozmo, 96
Kraft, Bryan, 143
Kroger, 97

Lakhani, Karim R., 267–68, 271–74, 277, 280
Lang, Bob, 55
Lashinsky, Adam, 123
law of large numbers, 75, 95
Left, Andrew, 131
Lending Club, 236, 269–71
Lending Tree, 270
LendUp, 271
Levin, Gerald, 320n2
LinkedIn, 56, 65, *67, 68*, 144, 156
LiveRamp, 264, 289, 343n40
Los Angeles Times, 305n10
Lotus, 112
Lowercase Ventures Fund I, 290–91
Lufthansa, 210–11
luxury marketplace, 186–88, 190
    on Amazon, 186–87
    antiques, 181–83, 186
    brands in, 108, 125, 126
    1stDibs, 181–88, 190
Lyft, 239, 242, 246

machine learning, 144, 165, 253, 266, 271,
    273, 281, 283, 284
    see also artificial intelligence
Mad Money, 55
Major League Baseball, xiii
malls, 5–8
Marco Polo, 147–48
Marcus, Gary, 266–67
marketing technology (martech), 256, 260,
    263–64, 342n19
marketplace businesses
    acquisitions by, 186
    Amazon Marketplace, 84–85, 87, 180, 186,
        194, 311n2
    eBay, *see* eBay
    Etsy, xxi, 181–86, 189, 190, 288, 330n27
    R&D of, 184, 186
    see also Amazon; e-commerce
Mastercard, 5, 212–13
MBA graduates, 291–92
media, 132–35, 151–52
    see also content; content creation; movies;
        music; newspapers; streaming media
        services; television
Meeker, Mary, 216
membership programs, 85–86
MercadoLibre, 101
mergers and acquisitions, *see* acquisitions
messaging services, 69, 114

metasearch, 204, 206, 207, 219, 220, 231–32, 270, 334n20, 338n57, 339n65
Mexico, 100, 101
Meyer, Erin, 149
Microsoft, xv, 14, 56, 63, 80, 87, 112, 114–16, *116*, 204, 276, 280, 282, 317n11
    antitrust law and, 170
    Apple compatibility and, 111, 116, 317n12, 318n23
    Azure cloud services of, 169, 272, 312n20, 344n19
    Bing, 35, 161, 165
    turnaround at, 272–74, 344n19
Mighty Little Bheem, 150
Moffett, Craig, 136
moguls, 134, 138, 167
Momondo, 219
Monster.com, 155–56
Moody's, 49
Morgan Stanley, xvii–xviii, 224
Motorola Mobility, 170
movies, 152, 325n83
    customer captivity and, 133
    Netflix and, 140–41
    producing, compared with brand building, 108–9
    producing, compared with television series, 140, 142
    scale and, 133
    streaming services and, *see* streaming media services
    studios, 130, 132, 133
    theaters, 5, 11, 130, 143
    see also streaming media services
Murder Mystery, 149, 325nn82–83
Murdoch, Rupert, xiii, 138, 223
Murphy, Ryan, 138
music, 133, 134, 152
    Apple iPod, 111–14, 120, 125, 126, 317n14
    Apple iTunes, 111, 112, 122–23, 125–26, 317nn14–15
    Apple Music, 124–26
    Apple Ping, 124, 317n14
    Spotify, 72, 124
MySpace, *67*, 68, *68*, 70

Nadella, Satya, 272–73
Nasdaq, xiii
Naver, 64, 327n10
NBCUniversal, 132, 139
Net-a-Porter, 188

Netflix, xii–xiii, 44, 55, 56, 59, 63, 91, 125, 129–58, 160, 175, 312n20, 342n9
Birdbox, 149, 325n82
    competitive advantages of, *61*, 142–51
    COVID-19 pandemic and, 136, 150
    customer captivity and, 135, 150, 151
    customer churn and, 145–46
    data and, 144–46, 148–50, 154, 253, 258
    DVD-by-mail service of, 131–32, 135, 144, 153
    in FAANG companies grouping, *see* FAANG companies
    film production and, 140–41
    first-mover advantage of, 153
    historic advantage of, 131–36
    House of Cards, 131, 136, 147, 258, 323n45
    life span of series on, 324n75
    Marco Polo, 147–48
    Mighty Little Bheem, 150
    Murder Mystery, 149, 325nn82–83
    network effects and, 143–44, 150
    number of subscribers of, vs. other providers, *151*
    original content developed by, xx, 131, 140–42, 147
    profitability benchmarking vs. S&P 500, *59*
    programming decisions at, 149–50
    R&D spending of, *64*
    recommendation algorithms of, 145
    scale and, 150
    social networking programs of, 144
Netscape, 15
network effects, xiv, xix, xx, 10–12, 23–32, 34–37, 144, 200, 246, 263, 267, 271, 287, 290, 294
    Amazon and, 84, 87
    Apple and, 113, 114, 120
    break-even economics and, xx, 28, *31*, 37
    and complexity of product or service, xx, 29, *31*
    in FAANG competitive advantages, *61*
    Facebook and, 12, 60, 66, 72, 73, 75–81
    Google and, 160–63, 170
    Netflix and, 143–44, 150
    SaaS and, 277, 279
    size and, 75, 309n21
    social platforms and, 81
    travel industry and, 175, 201–2, 207, 209, 220–21
    and users' ability to capture value or establish their own platform, 30, *31*

network effects (*cont.*)
  vulnerability of, 75–81
  winner-take-all models and, 12–15
neural networking, 148
News Corp, 139
newspapers, xvi, 26, 38–48, *41, 42,*
     154–55, 209
  advertising and classifieds in, 98, 155–56
  as aggregators and distributors, 154–55
New York *Daily News,* 40
New Yorker, 168
New York Post, 40
New York Times, 24, 38–48, *42, 46, 47,* 77,
     113–14, 117, 147, 155–57, 251, 304n6
NfX, 25
Nielsen ratings, 148, 150
Nokia, 115, 318n30
No Rules Rules (Hastings and Meyer), 149
NYSE, xiii

Obama administration, 50
O'Brien, Conan, 132
Ocado, 97
Oculus VR, 73
Omnicom, 261, 343n29
OpenTable, 220
Opodo, 205, 334n21
Oracle, 87, 106, 255, 264, 275,
     276, 279–83
Orbitz, 205, 226, 334n21
original content, *see* content creation
Orkut, *67,* 68, *68*
OTAs (online travel agencies), *see* travel
     agencies, online
Overstock.com, 86

Page, Larry, 166
Paramount Pictures, 130, 132, 141
Paramount+, 146
PayPal, 212–13, 260, 335n39
Peapod, 97
Pearl, Judea, 284
peer-to-peer (P2P) lenders, 246, 268–69
  Lending Club, 236, 269–71
PetroChina, 302n27
Pichai, Sundar, 168, 169
Pinkham, Chris, 87
Pinterest, 15, 65, 253
Pixar, 126
plagiarism, 279
Plaid, 213

platform(s), xi
  use of term, xiv, xv–xvi, 4, 6, *6*
platform businesses, xi, xvi
  ability of network users to establish their
     own, 30, *31*
  CEOs associated with, xvi
  pre-internet, 4–6
Platform Delusion, xvii, 200, 287, 294
  dual meaning of, xiv
  FAANG envy in, 60–61
  value destruction caused by, 287
  words and phrases in, xiv–xv
Platform Delusion, four pillars of, 3–22
  all platforms exhibit powerful network
     effects, 10–12
  digital platforms are structurally superior to
     analog platforms, 6–9
  network effects lead inexorably to
     winner-take-all models, 12–15
  platforms are a revolutionary new business
     model, 3–6, 37
Platform Revolution (Parker, Alstyne, and
     Choudary), 143
Porter, Michael, 17
Poshmark, 8, 9
Price Club, 312n9
Priceline, 213, 215–20, 225, 226, 336n12
Pricematch, 219
privacy, 254–55
product complexity, 190, 220–22, 288
product search, 65, 161, 253, 262
profitability, 19–20, 27–28, 58, 303n44
  of FAANG companies, 58–59, *59*
  profit margin, 58
Prosper Marketplace, 270
Publicis, 261, 262, 343n29
PWC, 260

Qualcomm, 35
Quibi, 137–38, 140
Quip, 281
Qzone, *67, 68*

radio, 49
RadioShack, 115
R&D spending, 153
  of Amazon, 63, *64,* 88, 307n11
  of Apple, *64*
  of FAANG companies, 63–64, *64,* 73
  of Facebook, 63–64, *64,* 73
  of Google, 63, *64,* 161–62, 166

of marketplace businesses, 184, 186
of Netflix, *64*
real estate, 98–99
  Zillow, 98, 180, 246, 271
Rebooting AI (Marcus and Davis), 266–67
Redstone, Sumner, 129–30, 320n2
regulation, *see* government regulation
Reliance Group, 102–3
restaurant reviews, 29
retail, 177
  see also e-commerce
Reuters, 140, 221
Revolve, 8
Rhimes, Shonda, 138
ride sharing, ride-hailing services, 29, 339n8,
    340n19
  COVID-19 pandemic and, 238, 245
  Lyft, 239, 242, 246
  Uber, xx, 15, 127–42, 245–48, 291, 339n8,
    340n9
Roberts, Brian, 131
Robinson-Patman Act, 92
RockAuto, 193, 194
RoomKey, 225
Russia, 64, 65, 79, 161, 334n26

SaaS (software as a service), 25, 274–84, 288,
    289, 293, 302n31
  Adobe, 256, 264, 276
  BlackLine, 281–84, 289
  growth of, *278*
  market capitalization of, *280*
  Salesforce, 255, 264, 275–76, 279, 281
  Turnitin, 279
Sabre, 201, 205, 333n14
Sacca, Chris, 290–91
Sage, 282
Salesforce, 255, 264, 275–76, 279, 281
sales taxes, 51
Samsung, 119, *119*
Sandler, Adam, 149
S&P 500, xxi, 63
  FAANG companies and, 56, *57, 59*
SAP, 280, 282–84
Sapient, 261
Sarandos, Ted, 142, 147
scale, 21–22, 23–24, 37, 70, 89, 110,
    233, 278, 294
  demand-side, *see* demand-side scale and
    advantages
  diminishing returns to, 75

in FAANG competitive advantages, *61*
first-mover advantage and, 115–16, 153
fixed costs and, 24–28, *26, 28*, 34,
    35, 37
Google and, 161–63
internet and, 24–32
marketplaces and, 182–84
movie production and, 133
Netflix and, 150
relative, 75, 89, 288
SaaS and, 277, 279, 280
sharing economy and, 239–43
specialization and, 64
streaming businesses and, 135
supply-side, *see* supply-side scale and
    advantages
Schmidt, Eric, 168, 258
search, 62, 65, 161, 164, 167, 326n4
  Bing, 35, 161, 165
  DuckDuckGo, 161, 165
  Google, 35, 124, 159, 161–67, 205–6, 231,
    253, 326n4, 327n12
  marketing and optimization tools, 256
  metasearch, 204, 206, 207, 219, 220,
    231–32, 270, 334n20, 338n57, 339n65
  product, 65, 161, 253, 262
search costs, in customer captivity, 34, 70, 78,
    161, 288
SEC (Securities and Exchange Commission),
    34, 145
Seinfeld, 141
Sequoia Capital, 290, 291
sharing economy, 175–76, 236–49
  Airbnb, xx, 199, 237–43, 245, 247–48,
    288, 340n9
  customer captivity and, 243–46
  scale and, 239–43
  see also ride sharing, ride-hailing services
Shatner, William, 215
shipping, 184
  free, 85, 90, 139, 157
  speed of, 85, 86, 89, 90, 139
Shopify, 189
ShopLink, 96
shopping malls, 5–8
Showtime, 146
Siebel, 276
Silver Lake Sumeru, 282
Sittercity, 236
SixDegrees, *67*, 68
Slack, 281

small- and medium-sized businesses (SMBs),
    274, 276, 282, 292, 293
  job creation and, 293
smartphones, 114, 116, 119
  Android, 114–17, 119, 120, 125, 126,
    318n21, 318n34
  iPhone, 106, 111–17, 119, *119*, 120, 122,
    125, 126, 316n3
  Nokia, 115, 318n30
  operating system market shares of, *116*
  vendor market shares of, *119*
smart software, *see* machine learning
SMBs, *see* small- and medium-sized businesses
Snap, 253
social media, 62, 66–70, 75, 76, 264, 289
  competition between, 77
  defining and calculating shares of,
    67, 308n4
  Facebook, *see* Facebook
  Instagram, xx, 59, 65, 72, 76, 291, 310n35
  launch dates and peak usage for, *67*
  misinformation on, 79, 80
  monthly active users on, *68*
  Netflix and, 144
  network effects and, 81
  trust and, 79, 80
  Twitter, 65, *67*, *58*, 291
software, smart, *see* machine learning
software as a service, *see* SaaS
Sorrell, Martin, 261
Sotheby's, 183, 186–88, 190, 331n40
South Korea, 64, 327n10
Spacey, Kevin, 147
specialization, 64, 288–89, 294
  AI and, 281, 284
Spotify, 72, 124
Sprout Social, 264
Square, 15
Square and the Tower, The (Ferguson), 66
SSA Global, 282
Stanford University, 292
start-ups, 287–94
Starz, 147
Stone, Brad, 93
Stop & Shop, 97
streaming media services, xiii, 91, 126, 135,
    137–40, 146, 150–51, 153
  advertising and, 148
  Amazon Prime Video, 91, 125, 129, 137,
    139–40, *151*
  Apple TV+, 125, 129, 137, 140

COVID-19 pandemic and, 150
  Dumb Pipe Paradox and, 136
  Hulu, 137, 139, 140, 148, *151*, 322n35
  Netflix, *see* Netflix
  original content and, *see* content creation
  scale and, 135
  total subscribers of, *151*
Sulzberger, Arthur, 24, 38, 39
supply, 37
supply-side scale and advantages, 25–28, *26*,
    30, 33, 37, 52–53, *53*
  in FAANG companies, *61*
  Facebook and, 72–73
  Google and, 161–62, 165–71
  linkage of demand-side advantages to, 165
  online travel agencies and, 206
  SaaS and, 277
SVOD (subscription video on demand),
    see streaming media services
Sweetgreen, 4
switching costs, 34, 70, 78, 161, 288
Synapse, 216

Tandy, 115
Target, 89, 189, 196
TaskRabbit, 236
Telecommunications Act, 51
television, 49, 132, 138, 148
  cable, 126, 152
  customer captivity and, 133
  movie production vs., 140, 142
  see also streaming media services
Tesco, 101
Tiffany & Co., 188
TikTok, xx, 65, 77, 93
Time Warner, xiii, 131, 139, 169, 322n35
Tirole, Jean, 5–6
Tilson, Whitney, 131
Time Inc., 216
toaster, curse of, 120
total addressable market (TAM), 28
Toys 'R' Us, xii
tragedy of the commons, 237
travel agencies, online (OTAs), 204–10, 213,
    220–21, 223–32, 234, 248, 339n65
  Booking, *see* Booking
  Expedia, *see* Expedia
  and hotel reservations vs. airline seat sales,
    220–26
  Priceline, 213, 215–20, 225, 226, 336n12
Traveljigsaw, 219

Travelocity, 205, 226, 334n21
Travelport, 201, 209–11
travel sector, xx, 9, 175, 198–214, 215–35
    airlines going direct to travel agents,
        210–13
    airlines going direct to travelers, 203–4
    birth of electronic platforms and, 201–3
    COVID-19 pandemic and, 199, 200, 207,
        226, 234
    global distribution systems in, *see* global
        distribution systems
    Google and, 180, 231, 233, 270
    metasearch and, 204, 206, 207, 219, 220,
        231–32, 270, 334n20, 338n57, 339n65
    network effects and, 175, 201–2, 207, 209,
        220–21
    travel management companies, 208, 234
TravelSky, 210
Travelweb, 217, 225
Trip, 199
TripActions, 199, 234
TripAdvisor, 199, 231–33, 243, 339n65
Trivago, 199, 233, 339n65
Trump administration, 45, 50
trust, 79, 80, 244–45, 288
TTD (The Trade Desk), 263, 289, 343n40
Tucker, Therese, 283
Turnitin, 279
21st Century Fox, xiii, 132
Twitter, 65, *67*, *58*, 291

Uber, xx, 15, 127–42, 245–48, 291,
        339n8, 340n9
Union Square Ventures, 255
United Health, 282
Universal Pictures, 132, 133
USA Today, 40–41

vacation rentals
    Airbnb, xx, 199, 237–43, 245, 247–48,
        288, 340n9
    HomeAway, 226, 228, 241, 242, 247
Valentine, Don, 290
value investing, 57–58
Varian, Hal, 159–60
Venere, 229
venture capitalists, 290–91
Verisk Analytics, 30
ViacomCBS, 129–30, 132, 146
video streaming services, *see* streaming media
    services

Visa, 5, 212–13, 335n39
VisiCalc, 112
Vrbo, 228, 241

WACC (weighted average cost of capital), 20
Walker, Jay, 215–17
Wall Street Journal, xv, 40–41, *42*, 43
Walmart, 89, 177, 196, 260, 314n47
    grocery business of, 97
    international operations of, 92, 100–102
Wanamaker, John, 258
WarnerMedia, 137
Washington Post, 40, 41, *42*, 305n10
Wasserman, Lew, 134–35
water cooler effect, 11, 143
Waters, Richard, 236
Watson Health, 344n5
Wayfair, xxi, 93, 178, 188, 289
Wayne, Ron, 316n1
Waze, 52
Webvan, 96
weighted average cost of capital (WACC), 20
Welch, Jack, 79
Wells, Frank, 141
West Elm, 189
WhatsApp, xx, 59, 65, 72, 76–78, 290, 291,
        310n34
Whole Foods, 97–98
Wilson, Fred, 21, 255
winner-take-all, winner-take-most, xiv, 26,
        36, 64, 289–90, 300n12
    network effects and, 12–15
Working Backwards (Bryar and Carr), 85, 91,
        93–94, 312n18
Worldspan, 201
Wozniak, Steve, 106, 316n1, 318n27
WPP, 50, 261–62, 343n29
Wu, Tim, 51, 77, 313n41

Yahoo, 64, 75–76, 327n10
Yandex, 64, 161
Yelp, 198
YouTube, 65, 153, 159, 163, 164, 168, 308n4,
        320n1, 326n8

Zappos, 178
Zillow, 98, 180, 246, 271
Zoom, 11–12
Zucker, Jeff, 250
Zuckerberg, Mark, 70, 73, 76–79, 81, 93, 144
    letter to investors from, 309n20